ITEMS SHOULD BE RETURNED ON OR BEFORE THE LAST DATE
SHOWN BELOW. ITEMS NOT ALREADY REQUESTED BY OTHER
READERS MAY BE RENEWED BY PERSONAL APPLICATION, BY
WRITING, OR BY TELEPHONE. TO RENEW, <u>GIVE THE DATE DUE
AND THE NUMBER ON THE BARCODE LABEL</u>.

FINES CHARGED FOR OVERDUE ITEMS WILL INCLUDE
POSTAGE INCURRED IN RECOVERY. DAMAGE TO, OR LOSS
OF ITEMS WILL BE CHARGED TO THE BORROWER.

**LEABHARLANNA POIBLÍ CHATHAIR BHAILE ÁTHA CLIATH
DUBLIN CITY PUBLIC LIBRARIES**

Dublin City
Baile Átha Cliath

PEARSE STREET BRANCH
BRAINSE SRÁID PIARSACH
TEL. 6744888

Date Due	Date Due	Date Due
	15. JUL	
	7·07	
11. NOV 03		
15. DEC		
02. APR 05		
31. JAN 06		

THE ILLUSTRATED HISTORY OF THE
NINETEENTH CENTURY

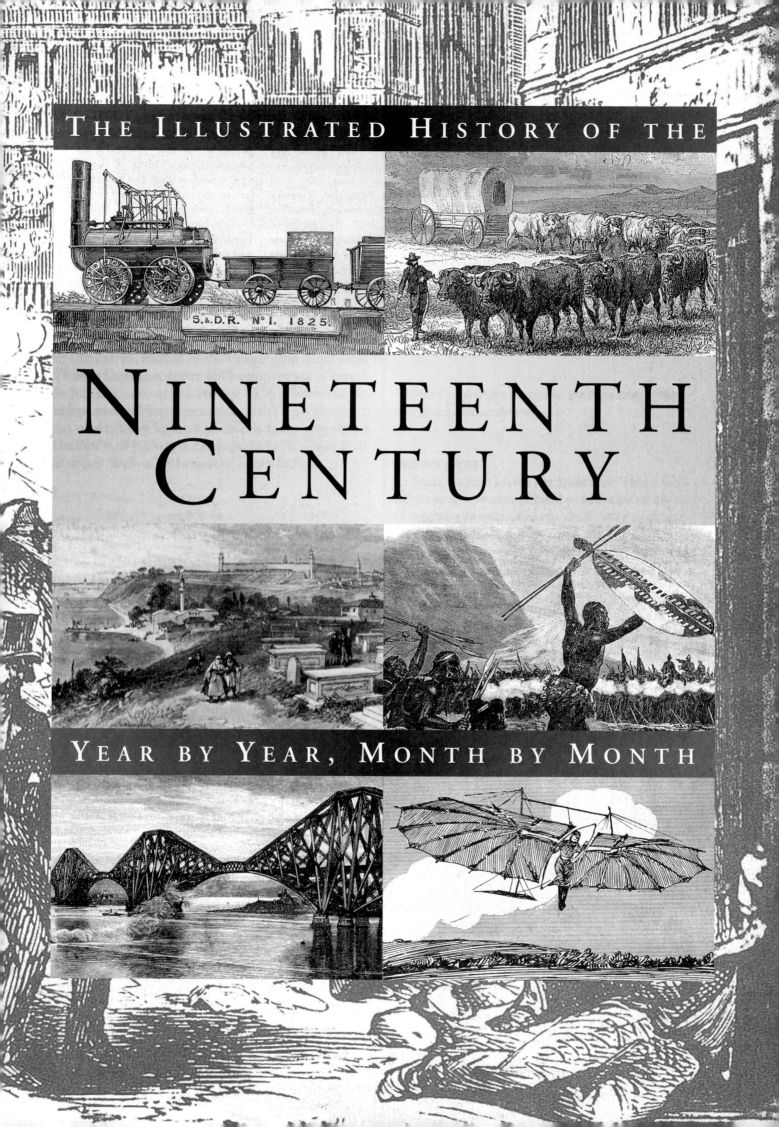

THE ILLUSTRATED HISTORY OF THE

NINETEENTH CENTURY

YEAR BY YEAR, MONTH BY MONTH

This edition is published in 2000 for Grange Books an imprint of Grange Book PLC. The Grange Kingsnorth Industrial Estate. Hoo. Nr. Rochester Kent Me3 9ND

First Published by Rebo International b.v, Lisse, The Netherlands

Edited, designed and produced by Book Creation Illustrated Ltd, 21 Carnaby Street, London W1V 1PH

Text: Simon Adams
      Margaret Crowther
      Will Fowler
      Ann Kramer
      Dan McCausland
      Theodore Rowland-Entwhistle
      Philip Wilkinson

Editorial: Cover (to) Cover a.t.e
Additional editorial assistance: Fiona Corbridge

Project co-ordinator: Tami Rex for Book Creation Illustrated Ltd

Design by Casebourne Rose Design Associates, UK
Typesetting by Casebourne Rose Design Associates, UK

Picture research by Vanessa Fletcher
Photography by Heritage Picture Collection, London, UK

ISBN No. 1 84013 375 9

10 9 8 7 6 5 4 3 2 1

CONTENTS

REVOLUTION, INDEPENDENCE AND NATIONALISM

GO BACK 100 YEARS from today, and the world at the end of the nineteenth century was recognizably similar to the world we live in today. Many of the same powerful nations existed then as now, although the maps of Eastern Europe, Africa and Asia were markedly different. Industrialization, new technology, urbanization, world trade and mass communications were making as strong an impact in 1900 as they do a century later.

Go back a further 100 years, to the start of the nineteenth century, and we are in a different world. No Germany or Italy, a newly independent and small United States, and a map of Africa showing little but the coastline and nothing of the interior. Industrialization was restricted to one country, and mass communications were unheard of.

The two events which transformed the political landscape over the course of this century both began in the closing years of the previous century. In 1789 the French rose in revolt against their Bourbon kings and started a revolution which engulfed Europe. At the same time, an Industrial Revolution gathered steam, literally, as Britain transformed itself into the powerhouse of the world. It is these dual revolutions, starting in two neighbouring states, that shaped the nineteenth century.

THE RISE OF NATIONALISM

The French Revolutionary cry of "liberty, equality and fraternity", itself based on earlier revolutionary sentiments expressed in the American War of Independence, introduced not just the dangerous ideas of freedom and democracy into a largely autocratic, in places despotic Europe, but also ushered in nationalism as a political concept. The concept of nation meant little to the vast majority of the population whose horizons were limited to the land on which they worked, and who often were born, worked and died in the same village or town, but it empowered a cultural intelligentsia both denied a place in the vast multi-lingual empires of the Hapsburgs, Romanovs and Ottoman Turks and frustrated by the petty territorial divisions of Germany and Italy.

The nationalism of the nineteenth century took two forms — a liberal nationalism based on constitutions and self-determination for subject peoples, and a right-wing patriotism that sought to build up a strong nation state. Both identified a nation by its common language and culture, but as linguistic borders are rarely clear-cut and culture can be manufactured as well as inherited, nationalism had a patchy record. Thus, the liberal nationalism that saw the independence of Latin America and Greece in the 1820s and the unification of Italy in 1861, among other successes, failed to achieve democracy or self-determination for subject peoples in the Austro-Hungarian, Russian and Ottoman Empires. Likewise, the right-wing patriotism that gave birth to a unified Germany in 1871 and led to European imperial expansion throughout the world saw both Russia and France tarnished by the stain of anti-Semitism at the end of the century.

By 1900 every major European country had sought its place in the sun, motivated by trade, the Bible and the flag, and backed up as necessary with the machine gun. Western European nations looked to Africa, Asia and the Pacific for their colonial gains, while Russia expanded south into central Asia and east into Manchuria. Outside Europe, the USA, having reached the Pacific coast with the acquisition of California in 1848, then acquired its own empire from Spain in the Caribbean and Pacific in 1898, while Japan began its expansion into east Asia with the acquisition of Taiwan in 1895.

There were exceptions to this imperial hegemony. Central and South America broke away from Spanish and Portuguese rule during the 1820s — although the Caribbean islands remained divided between Britain, France and The Netherlands — and Persia, the Himalayan states, Thailand and China remained free from outright European (and, in the case of China, Japanese) control, although all were subject to outside direction and influence. In Africa, only the free-slave state of Liberia and the ancient Christian kingdom of Ethiopia retained their independence. In the Pacific, Germany, Britain and France divided up the islands with the USA.

INDUSTRIALIZATION

If part of the impulse behind imperialism was national status and the flag, the main impulse was trade, for during the nineteenth century, the world's economy was transformed by industrialization. The Industrial Revolution which had begun in Britain during the second half of the eighteenth century transformed an already rich country into the world's first industrial state. The speed of this change is often exaggerated, as by 1801 no major British city apart from London had a population more than the 82 000 of Liverpool (and London remained under a million), and factories did not become the major industrial units until the 1830s. Indeed, as late as the 1840s, more than 75 per cent of British manufacturing took place in unmodernized industries little affected by steam power. But the development and application of new industrial processes and technologies — steam engines, spinning machines, iron foundries — and the construction of canals and then railways, gave birth to an industrial economy that then developed in Western Europe, in particular northern France, Belgium and the Ruhr in Germany, and in the second half of the century in the United States and Japan. If the first half of the century was

Above: George Stephenson and the "Rocket" in 1829. The railways would revolutionize industry.

dominated by a British industrial revolution based on manufacturing, textiles, coal and iron, the unification of Germany in 1871 ushered in a second industrial revolution based on the new steel, chemical and electrical industries.

The impact of this revolution was immense. Populations previously tied to the land now lived in large towns and cities and worked in factories and workshops rather than on the land. The growth of this mass working class caused great concern among the rulers of Europe as they saw power shifting away from land towards trade and commerce, and from the country to the city. Above all, both liberal reformers and old-style aristocrats were fearful of revolution and wary of social reform. Although the publication of the *Communist Manifesto* in 1848 had little immediate impact, socialist and communist ideas increasingly informed political debate in all industrialized countries.

The later nineteenth-century population was increasingly mobile. Railways replaced foot or

horsepower as the main form of transport, as well as playing an important part in national expansion — the two coasts of the USA were linked in 1869, and those of Canada in 1885, although the trans-Siberian railway did not finally cross Russia until 1916. The first steamship crossed the Atlantic in 1836 and with the development of propellers and iron hulls in the 1840s, international trade and travel were transformed. Raw materials such as cotton flowed into Europe, and manufactured goods flowed out, tying the economies of primary producer countries, such as Argentina and Australia, closely to industrialized Europe.

FORGING NEW NATIONS

In crude terms, the importance of nationalism and industrialization in international politics increased as the century progressed. The first fifteen years of the century were largely concerned with Europe's attempts to control and then reverse Napoleon's imperial expansion, the next 30 by European powers coming to terms with a Napoleonic legacy that not only inspired Greece and Latin America to pursue independence but also led to

Above: *Nationalist hero Giuseppe Garibaldi who, with his volunteer troops, fights to build a unified Italy.*

repression and reaction throughout Europe. In 1848 that order was threatened as the whole of Europe, with the notable exception of Britain, was convulsed in revolution, a curious mixture of liberal and nationalist revolt and agrarian discontent, which made the revolutions the last pre-industrial protests in Europe. As ever, revolution led to reaction, although the liberation of the serfs in Russia and the unification of Italy in 1861 ran counter to that trend, as did the opening up and democratization of Japan by 1868.

If 1848 marked one sort of landmark, the civil war which broke out in the United States in 1861 marked another, for it had all the hallmarks of a modern, industrial war. Thirteen largely rural southern states left the Union in defence of slavery, which still thrived on their cotton plantations, and were opposed by an increasingly industrialized north which would not accept secession. A large armaments industry and railway network ensured victory for the Union in 1865, but at a considerable price — more than 600 000 soldiers lost their lives, 21 per cent of all those under arms, a far higher percentage than in any First World War army. The slaves were freed, but so too was the ability of northern industrialists to expand throughout the Union and beyond.

With the unification of Germany in 1871 and the confirmation of Serbian and Romanian independence in 1878, the map of Europe was largely settled for the rest of the century. Four powerful and rival empires — France, Germany, Austro-Hungary and Russia — dominated the continent, with Britain keeping a wary neutrality in order to maintain a balance of power. Military and economic rivalry spilled over into imperial conquest, leading to the carve-up of Africa during the 1880s and increasing competition throughout the declining Ottoman Empire

and, above all, China. Those parts of the world not ruled by Europeans — notably Latin America — were nonetheless dominated by them economically.

If by this account, Europe appears to dominate to the almost total exclusion of every other continent, that is because the century was, to a large extent, a European, often British, century. Those parts of the world that resisted European domination, such as Japan, often remodelled and modernized themselves on European lines, while the United States, Canada, and such semi-independent dominions as South Africa, Australia and New Zealand, were all peopled by mass emigration from Europe. Only with the invasion of Taiwan by Japan in 1895 and the capture of Cuba and the Philippines by the USA in 1898, do we get some idea of the shape of the world to come in the next century.

Above: *The business of state carried on in the Senate of the government of France, in Paris.*

SCIENCE AND TECHNOLOGY

THE NINETENTH CENTURY constituted the latter half of a period in history often termed "the Industrial Revolution". Science and technology, and their relationship with industry, progressed very rapidly in many respects over this time. Indeed, it can be argued that the "modern" world was conceived as a result of the activity. Scientific discoveries and advances in our understanding of disciplines such as physics, chemistry, metallurgy and biology, opened the doors for new industrial processes and the application of new materials. This catalyzed an abundance of ideas for improving and inventing devices and tools for use in all areas of human life — from cooking to cleaning, locomotion to life-support, medicine to make-up. The production of textiles, metals and farm produce were the three primary areas to initially benefit from innovation. They quickly grew from being relatively local endeavours, designed to supply local demands, into mass-production industries geared for meeting the needs of national and even international markets.

Above: Industry and energy characterize the century. Some see it as progress, others as the "dark, satanic mills" of poet William Blake's imagination.

Above: *Casting metal ingots in the old-fashioned way. Mechanization soon takes over.*

NEW WAYS OF WORKING

By the start of the nineteenth century a new corporate working regime had been established, because advances in science and technology had provided the impetus for ever more efficient and ambitious manufacturing principles. Changes including the production line, interchangeable components, time-and-motion studies and shift-working had all seen such a remarkable reform in industry that the term "revolution" now seems more appropriate, in hindsight. At the same time, Europe and North America were witnessing a considerable demographic shift. Huge numbers of provincial people — put out of work by labour-saving farm machinery — migrated in their droves to live in the swelling towns, to find employment in the multitude of new factories. Populations in general expanded rapidly, only amplifying the demands made of industry. Higher urban populations, as well as providing larger marketplaces for commodities and consumables, also meant the

Above: *The flat-bed cylinder printing press makes newspaper production much easier.*

introduction of stresses and strains on the infrastructure of cultures relating to areas such as health and welfare, adequate accommodation and the supplying of goods.

Above: *The century sees the end of agriculture as the great employer, as workers leave the land for the factories.*

NEW FORMS OF ENERGY

For any industry to function at all it must be supplied with an adequate and reliable source of energy. Having managed with manpower, ox-power, horsepower, water and wind for many previous centuries, humanity made a crucial development by harnessing the power of combustible materials — coal in particular — in the form of steam, by heating water. Steam engines, or external combustion engines, became the driving force behind the Industrial Revolution, quite literally setting the wheels in motion. They drove belts, chains, pumps, cranks, cams, drive-wheels and drive-shafts — whatever was required to operate machinery, in mills, factories, mines and vehicles.

As well as providing a new source of energy for many established industries, steam engines made possible the rapid expansion of heavy industries to cater for ambitious engineering projects involving the production of large components made from iron and steel.

THE POWER OF ELECTRICITY

Steam power provided the brute force for the Industrial Revolution, but the nineteenth century saw an epochal event which, it can be argued, is the single most important development in scientific and technological history: the utilization of electricity. Received with some scepticism at first, because of its seemingly unpredictable and intangible nature — not to mention downright dangerousness — electricity would eventually become the "clean" source of energy for both industrial and domestic consumption and go on to become the most essential ingredient of cultural infrastructures across the world. It was soon discovered that electricity could be employed in all kinds of new inventions which would change culture forever. By the end of the century, these included: telephonics, telegraphy, wireless telegraphy and X-ray scanning. Telecommunications and communications also benefited from improvements in transportation. Steam-powered road vehicles, locomotives and ships made a

considerable impact for a good deal of the nineteenth century, but by the end they were being phased out by the introduction of electric vehicles and vehicles driven by internal combustion engines. The first internal combustion engines used gas as their fuel, but soon the fractional distillation of crude oil meant that petroleum and diesel oil became available as more convenient fuels, and all manner of vehicles had petrol or diesel engines fitted to them.

OIL AND PLASTIC

The components of crude oil also provided a range of new chemicals that would lead to the invention of new materials known as synthetics or plastics, which took the place of more traditional materials as well as finding unique applications as the result of their novel characteristics. An intimate understanding of the structure and chemical make-up of substances was another important scientific and technological development in the century. Medical disciplines such as pharmaceuticals, anaesthetics and surgery were all

Above: *Factory buildings and industrial canals dominate the landscape of the nineteenth century.*

improved by an enlightened culture which was beginning to understand how and why things work on a purely scientific basis. The expounding of Darwin's and Wallace's theory of evolution was just a part of this general enlightenment.

PROGRESS AND PERFECTABILITY

The combination of better communications and plenty of inspired devotees of science and technology meant a flux of ideas and innovations between nations, as a sense of collective responsibility for improving the world pervaded Europe and North America. Admittedly progress was also prompted by an awareness of economic competition between countries which would often be expressed by out-and-out warfare, but even combat provided an incentive for scientists and engineers to invent and develop technologies which made beneficial contributions to human life in one way or another despite the original aim.

Science and technology saw itself make headway in an exponential manner through the century. So much so that within the space of a hundred years, human life had changed beyond recognition in the Western world. And that is really the point. Progress in science and technology has always been motivated by a desire for people to improve their lifestyles, even though many developments have been born for warlike application or inadvertently found themselves being used in this vein. The nineteenth century was an incredible period in history because it marked a transition from the spiritual to a secular understanding of the world as the result of the onwards march of science and technology. It marked the advent of the "specialist" scientist and engineer, because the base of information had become so great

that it became necessary for people to concentrate on a particular field of activity to be able to keep the ball of progress still rolling. It even became possible to invent problems to solve, knowing that a solution could be found by a reasoned and calculated approach, as opposed to searching for solutions to problems almost arbitrarily, as had often been the case in the past. In short, humans realized that they had attained control over science and technology through an ever-accelerating accumulation of knowledge about the various fields of study. This new-found control marked a milestone in human history and instilled our collective culture with an air of confidence which has stayed with us ever since.

Below: *Purifying and refining copper, used in the wires and circuitry of the new power source, electricity.*

THE GREAT SHIFT IN SOCIETY

Above: *The elegant curve of John Nash's Regent Street, which makes London a fashionable place to be.*

IN 1800 THERE WERE JUST 22 cities in Europe with a population of more than 100 000, none in the Americas, and although census details are less precise, about fifteen in Asia. By 1913, there were 184 such cities in Europe, 61 in the Americas, and more than twenty in Asia. If one single image can be conjured up to describe the nineteenth century, it is the growth of the modern city.

INTO THE CITIES

Historically, cities had grown up around the monarch and seat of government, or on the junction of major trade routes or by a river. But the cities of the nineteenth century had other reasons for existing. Some, such as Newcastle in England or the cities of the Ruhr in Germany, were near coal or iron deposits; others, such as Chicago in the USA, because they were at the hub of extensive rail networks. These new cities were no longer the domain of the professional classes — lawyers, churchmen, government officials, bankers — but of manufacturers, tradesmen, skilled artisans, and unskilled labourers and factory workers.

The scale and speed of this growth was extraordinary. In little more than a century, London and Paris grew four times in size, Berlin nine times, and New

York 80 times. Although most countries, with the exception of Britain, remained overwhelmingly rural — Germany did not become predominantly urban until 1890 while only 40 per cent of the US population lived in cities in 1900 — the nineteenth century became an increasingly urban century.

The implications of this shift out of the countryside into the towns, were felt throughout society. Where once people were isolated on farms and small towns, now masses of the population lived, worked, and could be organized together. And the organization that had to take notice of that change more than any other was the government. Feudal-style *ancien régimes* based on land and aristocracy became rapidly irrelevant as an increasingly affluent middle class based in trade and commerce, and an increasingly vocal and unionized working class based in industry and the workplace, demanded a say in government.

REFORM OR REACTION?

In many European countries, this tension was largely unresolved, leading to the repression of all discontent and to the revolutions of 1848. In Britain, the conflict was played out over reform of the franchise. Under the existing system, power lay in the country shires and many of the great industrial cities, such as Birmingham and Manchester, had few if any representatives in Parliament. The Reform Act of 1832 redistributed parliamentary seats from the counties to the towns and doubled the electorate to 700 000, but with a total population of 19.9 million, few people in Britain were able to participate in government.

Where democratic reform did take place, the changes were limited. It was more a case, crudely, of the land-owning classes sharing some power with the middle classes rather than an attempt to enfranchise the population as a whole. For every country's ruling class, however defined, feared the power of the mob and its capacity to incite revolt or indeed revolution. What had engulfed France in 1789 could engulf another country again, even more so now that the population of cities was expanding so fast. Between reaction and complete reform, European governments steered a middle course designed to favour the middle class bourgeoisie in their pursuit of capital accumulation rather than placate a working class in pursuit of basic rights.

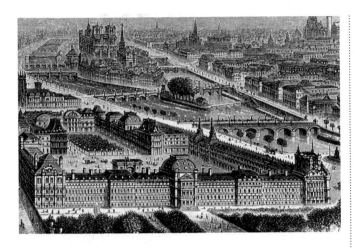

Above: *The wide boulevards of Paris were planned after 1848 to control any future revolutionary crowds.*

This policy, however, was not applied uniformly, for in dealing with mass populations in large cities, governments had to face up to the social consequences of urbanization. In cities without basic hygiene, running water, transport systems or often any basic amenities, public health became a matter of great concern. The scale of the problem was immense — in 1860, according to Georges Haussmann, who rebuilt Paris after 1853, more than a million out of the total population of 1.7 million lived in poverty or need, a figure replicated in most urban centres, making major cities uniquely vulnerable to epidemic and disease. Outbreaks of cholera, typhoid, malaria and smallpox were frequent. Across Europe and the USA, governments struggled with urban deprivation yet they were ill-equipped to deal with the complex issues that resulted, as direct intervention required taxes they were not prepared to levy and an interventionist role that went against the predominant *laissez-faire* attitudes of the day.

THE LOCAL STATE

Government at a city or urban level was therefore conducted through a combination of philanthropy, municipal authority and commerce. Although an era of diminishing faith, the century was still a religious age, albeit one increasingly attracted to scientific rationality, and many of the middle classes felt a moral obligation to help the deserving poor. Christian and Jewish friendly societies, charitable organizations, self-help and co-operative groups all thrived in the cities, providing everything from public baths and social housing to water troughs for horses and parks for public amusement. Progressive politicians, such as Haussmann in Paris and Joseph Chamberlain in Birmingham, used the structures of local government to create basic civic services, although the results were patchy: Haussmann

inherited 100km (62mi) of sewers in Paris and increased that to 560km (350mi) within twenty years, while Chamberlain promoted municipal provision of gas and water supplies. However, not every city was blessed with such vigour from its public servants. Most cities had to rely on commercial endeavour — the first steam-operated underground railway, which opened in London in 1836, was built and run as a commercial concern — and thus basic services remained mostly in the hands of private investors rather than under public ownership. However messy this patchwork of public, private and charitable endeavour might seem, the quality of life for all those who lived and worked in the cities improved as the century wore on. And that was as true in the European imperial cities of India, Australia and the Far East as it was in Europe and America.

Considerable civic pride was attached to these improvements, as scientific rationality brought with it a touching belief in "progress" and all the benefits that entailed. More progressive were the numerous regulations governing public health, working conditions, employment, education and, in Bismarck's Germany, invalidity and old-age pensions, which crept on to national statute books. By the end of the century, the realization that in order for a modern industrial state to survive and prosper it had to look after all its workforce, led to increasing government involvement in the welfare and education of all its citizens.

THE HIDDEN HALF

In this gradual shift towards active, interventionist government, there remained a clear demarcation

Below: *Revolutionaries seize the streets of Paris in 1848, one of the many periods of unrest that swept Europe.*

between the public and private spheres of life. The public sphere was men-only, and in a society that still aligned status with property, women were no more than the property of their fathers or husbands and thus restricted to the private sphere of house and home. The French Revolutionaries concerned themselves only with the "rights of man" and denied women the right of political organization. Even the Chartists, whose campaigns for democratic rights so galvanized Britain during the 1840s, demanded adult suffrage for men only.

Excluded from the public sphere of life, women had few rights. The first national women's meeting to address this issue was held in Seneca Falls, New York in 1848, but it was not until 1890 that major suffrage associations were formed in both Britain and the USA to lobby for the vote. Of those states that gave women the vote — Wyoming in 1869, Colorado (and New Zealand) in 1893, Idaho and Utah in 1896 — all were frontier territories where settlers had had to carve out a living for themselves; here, equal rights accompanied equal hardship. Elsewhere, women had to campaign vigorously just to get recognition for their basic rights to own property, let alone to get an education or participate in politics, and it was not until 1906 that the first European women gained the vote in Finland (a right granted, ironically, by the Russian czar who then ruled the country; in Russia itself, the czar was against anyone having the vote).

For women forced to remain in the home, the same benefits that made living in cities more bearable —

Above: *Settlers in the west of America.*

Right: *A new town on the plains of the Midwest. Thousands moved from Europe to the New World.*

running water, gaslight and, at the end of the century, electricity — made housework less of the massive burden it once had been. Labour-saving devices replaced some of the drudgery and, for those wealthy enough to afford them, an army of servants living below stairs replicated the class system beyond the front door, working long hours for little pay to run a vast household on behalf of wealthy employers.

CITY LIFE

Observing today the civic splendours of Victorian London and Haussmann's Paris, the grand planning of Vienna and the grid patterns of Melbourne or New York, is to see an urban structure and organization that evolved through painful negotiation between public and private spheres, between the needs of commerce and the demands of the workforce, and between the government's gradual assumption of control and regulation and the wish of the private citizen to protect his property and hold on to his wealth. As the shift from countryside to town continues to dominate this century, as it no doubt will the next, many of the issues that are now being confronted were first addressed, and solved, by those pioneer city-dwellers of the nineteenth century whose multiple legacies remain with us today.

PROGRESS AND INNOVATION

AS THE CENTURY OPENS, North America feels the full impact of the American Revolution. The newly-created United States establishes a new capital at Washington and doubles its size with the purchase of the vast Louisiana Territory. American explorers rapidly investigate the potential of the new lands. In Europe, Napoleon's expansionist policies dominate the decade. French armies sweep through Europe, defeating Austria, Russia and Prussia and invading Spain, Portugal and Italy. Although defeated at sea, France appears unstoppable on land. The Industrial Revolution, which began in the latter part of the eighteenth century, also gathers pace. Innovations in science and technology include the first steam-powered transport, the first passenger railway, gas lighting and the development of atomic theory.

1800–1809

KEY EVENTS
of the
DECADE

THE PEACE OF AMIENS

THE NAPOLEONIC WARS

CONFEDERATION OF THE RHINE

THE LOUISIANA PURCHASE

THE ACT OF UNION

HAITIAN INDEPENDENCE

SLAVE REBELLIONS

SLAVE TRADE OUTLAWED

INDIAN CONFEDERATION

LEWIS AND CLARK CROSS UNITED STATES

FLINDERS EXPLORES AUSTRALIA

HUMBOLDT MAPS SOUTH AMERICA

STEAM TRANSPORT DEVELOPED

BEAUFORT WIND SCALE DEVISED

TYPEWRITER INVENTED

AMINO ACIDS DISCOVERED

ATOMIC THEORY OUTLINED

BEETHOVEN'S "EROICA" SYMPHONY

GOETHE'S *FAUST*

WORLD POPULATION

978 MILLION

(ESTIMATE)

Horatio Nelson, then Vice Admiral, manoeuvring for victory at the Battle of Copenhagen, 1801.

Napoleon at Rossbach, Germany.

The rotary press made by William Bullock in 1865.

CONGRESS GOES TO WASHINGTON

*T*HE UNITED STATES MOVES ITS capital from Philadelphia to a new city, Washington, so-called after the country's first president. The US Congress meets in the new capital before the year is out. The Louisiana Territory is transferred from Spain to France. A 2000-strong slave rebellion is aborted in the USA. Alessandro Volta invents a practical means of storing electricity.

Above: *Alessandro Volta, inventor of the electric storage cell.*

✵ 1 8 0 0 ✵

JAN	17	Royalist rebellion in La Vendée, France, is crushed
MAR	28	The Irish parliament approves union with Great Britain
JUNE	14	Napoleon Bonaparte, France's first consul, defeats the Austrians at the Battle of Marengo
AUG	30	Black slave Gabriel Prosser plans revolt in the USA
SEP	5	Britain captures Malta from France
OCT	1	In a secret treaty, Spain agrees to sell Louisiana to France

NOV	4	Thomas Jefferson and Aaron Burr tie in US presidential election
	17	Congress meets in new US capital Washington, DC, for the first time
DEC	3	The French defeat the Austrians at the Battle of Hohenlinden
	24	Plot to kill Napoleon Bonaparte is uncovered in Paris

NEW US CAPITAL AND LIBRARY

In the United States, the departments of state begin to move from the original capital of Philadelphia to a new capital at Washington, which is named after George Washington, the first president of the USA. In November, the Congress holds its first meeting in Washington; the city has a mere 8144 inhabitants. The US Library of Congress is also established with $5000 to purchase 900 books and will be built in Washington.

ELECTION TIE

In the US presidential elections, the Federalists are defeated and the election ends in a tie between Republicans Thomas Jefferson, author of the Declaration of Independence, and Aaron Burr. Subsequently, the House of Representatives chooses Jefferson for president and Burr for vice-president.

LOUISIANA TRANSFER

King Charles IV of Spain (1784–1819) signs a secret treaty with the French leader Napoleon Bonaparte to transfer the vast Louisiana territory beyond the Mississippi back to France. Louisiana used to be French, but was given to Spain in 1763 after the French defeat in the Seven Years' War.

CHLORINATED WATER

Scotsman William Cruikshank devises a way to purify water supplies with the use of chlorine. This is the first time that water is chemically treated for the benefit of public hygiene.

ELECTRIC CELL

Italian physicist, Alessandro Volta (1745–1827) invents the first practicable means for storing electricity, and begins to market his new product. It is called the Voltaic pile, and consists of alternate layers of zinc and copper suspended in an acid solution.

IRON PRINTING PRESS

Robert Walker, of Vine Street, London, manufactures the first printing press made from iron components. It is installed at the premises of the Shakespeare Press, of St James's, London.

SCREW-FED LATHE

Thanks to his experience in designing locks, English engineer Henry Maudslay (1771–1831) is able to build the first screw-fed industrial lathe. This leads to the mass production of identical components, putting England at the forefront of industrial manufacturing.

Right: *Mining techniques in the pre-mechanized early years of the nineteenth century included working by descending levels, as practised in the mines of Saxony, Hungary and Prussia.*

Above: *The Old Forest Works at Swansea, Wales, 1800, at the beginning of the century of industrialization.*

Above: *Bottle kilns in Staffordshire, England, already the centre of the UK pottery and ceramic industry.*

SLAVE REBELLION
In January, freed black slaves petition the US Congress, opposing slavery. In August, a slave rebellion is planned by 2000 black slaves led by "General" Gabriel Prosser. Their plan to take over the Richmond arsenal, Virginia, is revealed by two of the slaves. Prosser and 34 others are convicted and hanged. Virginians respond by supporting plans for black emigration to Africa.

ON LITERATURE
The first well-known writing about literature by French-Swiss woman of letters Mme de Staël (1766–1817) introduces new ideas about writing and the *Zeitgeist*, that a work of literature will express the historical and moral climate of the place where it is written.

NEW LANARK
Welsh social reformer, Robert Owen (1771–1858), becomes manager of New Lanark, a model industrial town in Scotland. In New Lanark, which was founded in 1783 by Owen's father-in-law, 1300 workers are employed in cotton mills. Living and working conditions are exemplary and children receive daily education.

CATALOGUE OF LANGUAGES
Hervás y Panduro begins his *Catalogue for the Languages of the Nations*. It details the grammars of 40 languages and gives philological details of some 300 tongues. Panduro's work continues until 1805, laying important foundations for the scientific study of language.

PORTRAIT OF MME RECAMIER
This major portrait by French artist Jacques Louis David (1748–1825) is in his classical style, which was established during the Revolutionary period at the end of the previous century. It shows that the artist is still impressive and influential.

LES DEUX JOURNÉES (THE WATER-CARRIER)
This new opera by Maria Luigi Carlo Cherubini (1760–1842), one of a long series, is his masterpiece. It is fundamentally classical in style but its dramatic use of the orchestra and of ensembles will have impact on later, Romantic composers, particularly Beethoven.

CASTLE RACKRENT
Irish novelist Maria Edgeworth (1767–1849) establishes her reputation in this ground-breaking work, her first novel. It is an immediate success and begins the traditions of both the historical novel and the novel of regional life in the English language.

MARY STUART
Friedrich von Schiller's drama, *Maria Stuart*, begins the last phase of his career, in which he explores the theme of individual freedom versus responsibility.

INDIAN SURVEY
British surveyor William Lambton begins the Great Trigonometrical Survey of India, starting at the country's southernmost tip. The huge undertaking, made more difficult by jungle, tigers and malaria, will not be finished until 1870, and will cover 3200km (2000mi) to the north in the Himalayas. Lambton begins with base lines 11km (7mi) long and then uses sightings of the stars and a half-ton theodolite to establish the next fixed point. The new point then becames a sighting position and the survey progresses with painstaking care, creating a series of triangles up the sub-continent.

PUNCH AND JUDY
In the UK, Punch and Judy, who were taken to England from Italy in the eighteenth century, reappear as glove-puppets manipulated by puppeteers who travel the country. The popular puppet show also features a policeman and a crocodile.

Below: *Washington, custom built as the capital of the USA by Congress and named after the first president.*

Above: *The first presidential house, Washington.*

Right: *Thomas Jefferson.*

STEAM POWER BEGINS

*T*HE ACT OF UNION FORMALLY unites Great Britain and Ireland as the United Kingdom. Austria signs a peace treaty with France, and the 1000-year-old Holy Roman Empire comes to an end. Napoleon Bonaparte signs a concordat with the Pope. Czar Paul I of Russia is assassinated. The first self-propelled steam-powered road vehicle is built.

Above: *Cairo, recaptured by the British from the French who had invaded Egypt in 1798.*

✤ 1 8 0 1 ✤

JAN	1	Formal union of Great Britain and Ireland creates the United Kingdom
FEB	9	Peace of Lunéville between France and Austria
MAR	2	Spain declares war on Portugal
	4	US Congress chooses Thomas Jefferson as president
	14	William Pitt resigns as British prime minister; succeeded by Henry Addington
	21	Treaty of Aranjuez formally confirms transfer of Louisiana from Spain to France
	23	Czar Paul I of Russia assassinated
APR	2	Britain's Vice-Admiral Horatio Nelson wins the naval Battle of Copenhagen against the Danes
JUNE	6	Treaty of Badajoz ends Spanish-Portuguese War
	15	France and the papacy sign a concordat, giving the pope sovereignty over a limited territory
	27	The British capture Cairo from the French
SEP	12	Russia annexes Georgia
OCT	12	Turkey recovers Egypt from the French

Above: *Alexander hears the news of the assassination of his father, Czar Paul I.*

Above: A Chinese theatre; the Chinese city of Canton becomes the world's most crowded city this year.

ACT OF UNION

The Act of Union between England and Ireland comes into force, abolishing the Irish parliament in Dublin and giving Ireland a generous number of MPs in the British parliament in Westminster. The Irish parliament had been abolished because of British fears of Irish insurrection and the challenge by the United Irishmen intent on setting up an independent republic.

TREATY OF LUNEVILLE

Austria signs a peace treaty with France which gives France control of the left bank of the Rhine and rearranges the map of Italy, Switzerland and the Netherlands. The Austrian-dominated Holy Roman Empire collapses, 1000 years after its creation.

CONCORDAT

In Rome, Napoleon signs a concordat with the papacy under which the French government is allowed to control church appointments, subject to confirmation only by the pope. In return, the pope keeps control of the Papal States, central Italy, with the exception of Ferrara, Bologna and Romagna.

RUSSIAN CZAR ASSASSINATED

In Russia, Czar Paul I is assassinated by military officers after the failure of his policy towards France. First attacking and then fighting Napoleon, Paul managed to antagonize both the nobility and the army. He is succeeded by his son Alexander I (1777–1825).

STEAM ROAD VEHICLE

Having developed high-pressure steam engines for pumping flood water from mines, British engineer Richard Trevithick (1771–1833) builds the first self-propelled steam-powered road vehicle. He calls it his "steam carriage", and demonstrates it in London.

ELECTRIC NEEDLE TELEGRAPH

Frenchman Jean Alexandre demonstrates the use of his electric needle telegraph at Poitier in France. The movement of a needle indicates electrical pulses which can be decoded in sequence to extract the transmitted information.

PLATE-GLASS WINDOW

A tailor's shop at 16 Charing Cross Road, London, UK, becomes the first establishment to go to the extravagant lengths of installing a plate-glass window. The shop sets a precedent for displaying merchandise in a window, when its trade increases dramatically overnight.

SILK WEAVING

The Jacquard loom for weaving figured silk is developed by a French inventor, Joseph Marie Jacquard (1752–1834). Punched cards guide its movements.

FLINDERS EXPLORES AUSTRALIAN COAST

English explorer Matthew Flinders (1774–1814) sets sail around Australia, in the *Investigator*, given to him by the British Admiralty. His voyage lasts until 1803, during which he charts a large portion of the coast. In

Right: The ruins of the Parthenon, Athens, source of the Elgin marbles.

Above: *Nelson ignores orders and uses his own tactics to secure victory at the Battle of Copenhagen.*

Above: *A loom used for weaving silk brocade, a craft revolutionized by Joseph Jacquard this year.*

1803, having made his way along the south coast and round to Arnhem Land in the north, Flinders is forced to abandon his charting due to the poor condition of his ship. On an earlier voyage he had sailed to Tasmania with George Bass and confirmed that it was an island.

PESTALOZZI METHOD
How Gertrude Teaches Her Children (Wie Gertrud ihre Kinder Lehrt) by the Swiss educationalist Johann Heinrich Pestalozzi (1746–1827) shows that to educate a mother is to educate her family. His revolutionary system of education is based on love, understanding and the encouragement of every child's individuality.

WORLD'S LARGEST CITY
Canton, China, is the world's largest city with 1.5 million people. London is the largest city in the Western world with 864 000 inhabitants.

COALBROOKEDALE BY NIGHT
Philippe Jacques de Louthebourg (1740–1812) is a French painter working in Britain. He is one of the first artists to find the Romantic sublime in subject matter drawn from the Industrial Revolution. His picture of factories and mills, in front of skies lit by furnaces and fires, brings a new drama and awe to painting.

ELGIN MARBLES
British diplomat Thomas Bruce, Seventh Earl of Elgin (1766–1841), negotiates the removal of sculptures from the frieze and other parts of the Parthenon, Athens. The British Museum will eventually purchase the sculptures, nicknamed the "Elgin Marbles", where they remain, although the Greek people will later request their return.

CRITICAL JOURNAL OF PHILOSOPHY FOUNDED
German philosophers GWF Hegel (1770–1831) and FWJ Schelling (1775–1854) found the *Critical Journal of Philosophy*. The two are members of a group of German thinkers who reinstate idealism and metaphysics in the realm of philosophical thought.

FIRST CRACKERS
The first cold-water crackers made of rolled unleavened dough are produced by Josiah Bent of Milton, Massachusetts, USA, a retired ship's captain, to alleviate indigestion.

THE SEASONS
The Seasons by Franz Joseph Haydn (1732–1809) brings the style of religious oratorio to a secular subject, extending the range of large-scale choral music in a work that will remain a favourite with singers.

ATALA
Atala, the story of an Indian girl who converts to Christianity, wins Breton writer René de Chateaubriand instant fame and establishes his literary career, which had been previously interrupted by the Revolution.

FIRST CENSUS
The first accurate censuses are carried out in 1800 and 1801. They give population figures of:

Italy:	17.2 million	London:	864 000
Spain:	10.5 million	Paris:	547 756
Great Britain:	10.4 million	Vienna:	231 050
Ireland:	5.2 million	Berlin:	183 294
United States:	5.3 million	New York:	60 515

THE PEACE OF AMIENS

*T*HE TREATY OF AMIENS ENDS NINE YEARS of war between Britain and France. Napoleon Bonaparte, at the height of his power, becomes first consul for life. France annexes the Italian regions of Piedmont, Parma and Piacenza. In the UK, a Factory Act is passed limiting working hours for young people in textile mills. Westpoint Military Academy is founded in the USA.

Opposite: *Napoleon, soon to become first consul, asserts his authority over members of the Directory.*

✤ 1 8 0 2 ✤

JAN	26	Napoleon Bonaparte is proclaimed president of the Italian Republic (formerly the Cisalpine Republic)
MAR	27	Peace of Amiens ends war between Britain and France
MAY	19	First consul Napoleon Bonaparte creates the Legion of Honour
AUG	2	Napoleon Bonaparte is proclaimed first consul for life
	4	New French constitution effectively gives Napoleon more power
SEP	21	France annexes Italian region of Piedmont
OCT	23	France annexes the Italian duchies of Parma and Piacenza
DEC	31	The Peshwa (ruler) of Poona surrenders his land to the British East India Company

Above: *The manual threshing machine, this year superseded by a wheeled mobile version.*

Treaty of Amiens

Britain and France sign the Treaty of Amiens. This ends the war between them, which broke out in 1793. Britain agrees to restore all maritime conquests, except Trinidad and Ceylon, to France, Spain and Holland. France agrees to leave Naples, British and French troops evacuate Egypt, the independence of Portugal is recognized, and Malta is restored by Britain to the Knights of St John.

First Consul

In France, Napoleon Bonaparte becomes first consul for life, overturning the agreement made in December 1799 to limit his power to ten years. He also gains the right to appoint his successor. After his succession of brilliant military victories, Napoleon is now totally dominant in France, and across Europe.

Napoleon Sculpted

The Neoclassical style in sculpture reaches its peak in the work of the Italian Antonio Canova (1757–1822). His work is very popular, especially in England and France, where his statue of Napoleon brings him fame.

Wedgwood's First Photograph

Thomas Wedgwood, son of the British potter Josiah, works out how to create photographic images using the light-sensitivity of the chemical silver nitrate. He publishes the results of his work, but cannot find a way of fixing his images to make them permanent.

Above: *Conditions for factory workers, especially apprentices, are improved this year.*

Factory Act

Britain pioneers the first Factory Act — The Health and Morals of Apprentices Act — which limits the working hours for apprentices in textile mills to twelve a day. It also prohibits night work, and stipulates that apprentices be taught reading, writing and arithmetic by a suitable, remunerated teacher.

Travelling Waxworks

Swiss modeller Marie Grosholtz Tussaud (1761–1850) takes her remarkable collection of life-size waxworks to Britain where she tours with them. She exhibits a bust of Jean-Jacques Rousseau and other models made in Paris. During the years of the Terror in France, Madame Tussaud was forced to make death masks of members of the French royal family. In 1835, she will set up a permanent museum in London.

Wheeled Threshing Machine

Thomas Wigful, of King's Lynn in Norfolk, England, builds a mobile threshing machine. Like Jethro Tull's eighteenth-century seed drill, it has an immediate and significant effect on the productivity and efficiency of cereal farming.

Sugar Beet Manufacture

German scientist Franz Achard (1753–1821) establishes an industrial process for the extraction of sugar from beets; this follows the earlier discovery, by Andreas Marggraf (1709–82) of sugar in beet. As a result, refined sugar becomes available to the public for the first time.

Military Academies

Two military academies have been set up on either side of the Atlantic: the US Military Academy West Point, in the USA, and the Royal Military Academy Sandhurst in Britain. West Point is on the banks of the Hudson river, north of New York City and Sandhurst is in Berkshire to the southwest of London.

LOUISIANA PURCHASED

*T*HE USA BUYS THE VAST REGION OF LOUISIANA from France, more than doubling the size of the United States. After only one year of peace, war breaks out again between Britain and France. A Third Coalition is formed against France. Irish nationalists rise up against British rule. Morphine is discovered and the atomic theory of matter is expounded. Free-trial marketing is introduced in Connecticut, USA.

✷ 1 8 0 3 ✷

FEB	10	Napoleon Bonaparte restores independence to thirteen Swiss cantons and reduces the power of the central government
	25	At the Diet (conference) of Ratisbon the German States are put under the joint influence of Russia and France
MAR	1	Ohio becomes the seventeenth state of the USA
APR	30	The Louisiana Purchase: the USA buys a large area of North America from France
MAY	18	War between Britain and France breaks out again

JUNE	10	France occupies the German state of Hanover
JULY	23	Irish nationalist Robert Emmet leads an unsuccessful rebellion against British rule
OCT	19	Spain agrees to be neutral in Franco-British War

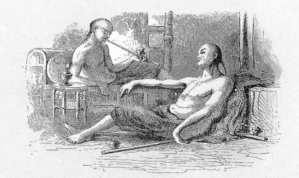

Above: *Opium smokers in China.*

FREE-TRIAL MARKETING

Clockmakers Eli Terry and Seth Thomas introduce free-trial marketing in Connecticut, USA. They offer their wooden clocks, which have interchangeable parts for mass production, to families on a no-money-down basis. At the end of the trial families pay rather than give up the clocks.

Above: *A handsome domestic clock, an example of the kind now available to all households.*

LOUISIANA PURCHASE

The former governor of Virginia, James Monroe (1758–1831), negotiates with Napoleon for the USA to buy Louisiana from France for 60 000 francs, with 20 000 francs to settle outstanding claims against the USA for damages. Louisiana stretches from Canada to the Gulf of Mexico; its acquisition more than doubles the size of the USA and gives it access to the Gulf through the port of New Orleans.

WAR RENEWED

War breaks out again between England and France, caused by French interference in Italy and Switzerland, and Britain's refusal to give up Malta immediately. A so-called Third Coalition — Britain, Austria, Russia, Sweden and Naples — forms to fight France and Spain.

COLONIAL POSSESSIONS

Britain acquires Tobago and St Lucia from France, extending its colonial empire in the Caribbean.

IRISH UPRISING

Irish nationalist Robert Emmet (1778–1803) leads an uprising in Ireland against British rule. As one of the leaders of the United Irishmen, who rose in revolt in 1798, Emmet planned to seize Dublin Castle and other strategic sites in the capital in the hope of the rest of the country taking up arms against the British. This fails to happen, however. The revolt is put down, and Emmet is executed.

MORPHINE AS PAINKILLER

Charles Derosne (1780–1846), a French chemist, discovers that the painkilling or analgesic drug, morphine, is contained within opium. Anaesthetics as a science begins to develop as a result.

ATOMIC THEORY OF MATTER

The idea that matter is made up from "indestructible" atoms is first expounded by English chemist John Dalton (1766–1844). His theory states that all atoms of the same element must be identical and that they differ from those of another element only by weight.

HARMONY SOCIETY

Harmonie, Pennsylvania, is founded as a celibate religious commune by the Harmony Society led by George Rapp, who has emigrated to the USA from Württemberg with a band of followers to escape persecution by the Lutheran Church.

CALEDONIAN CANAL BEGINS

Work begins on the Caledonian Canal to link east and west Scotland. In 1801, a canal across the Pennines was opened, linking east and west England, and completing the most advanced transport network in Europe.

LANDSCAPE ART

Studying colours from nature, and known for their fine brushwork and simple, elegant design, British artists Cotman and Crome found a new school of landscape art. Norwich becomes the first British provincial city with a society of artists holding regular exhibitions.

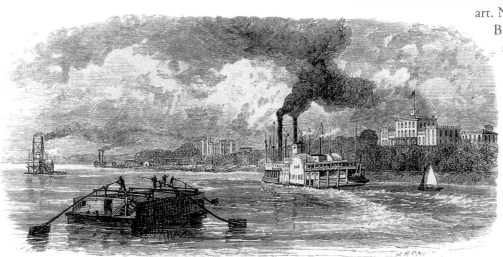

Left: *A view of Baton Rouge, Louisiana, the state bought this year from France by the USA.*

Left: *Battling by starlight on the plains of Argaum, India. General Wellesley (later the Duke of Wellington) successfully routs the French-trained Mahrattas under the Rajah of Berar.*

Below: *Britain and France extend their possessions in the Caribbean.*

GOVERNOR'S COURT, BANK OF ENGLAND
British architect John Soane (1753–1837) creates an individual style, based on Neoclassicism, but with elements drawn from his own imagination. His style will prove especially influential in the USA.

FIRST ABORTION BAN
The Ellenborough Act, passed by the British parliament, is the first law banning abortion in a Western country.

CHRIST HEALING THE SICK
American artist Benjamin West (1738–1820) uses a grand, theatrical style to portray events from history and the Bible. His religious works make a big impact.

Toussaint L'Ouverture
c. 1744/1746–1803

The Hispaniolan independence leader and anti-slavery fighter Toussaint L'Ouverture dies in prison in the French Jura. Originally named François Dominique Toussaint, the former colonial French army officer, a freed slave, was appointed governor of the French sector of the island (St Domingue) in the anti-slavery period following the French Revolution. He then played a leading part in the ten-year guerrilla struggle to liberate the whole island (the rest being a colony of Spain). Since 1797 he was effectively leader of the whole of Hispaniola, but was captured this year by an expedition sent by Napoleon to reinstate slavery. St Domingue will reclaim its freedom and be renamed Haiti in 1804.

DIE FAMILIE SCHROFFENSTEIN
German poet and dramatist Heinrich von Kleist (1777–1811) produces his first play, which, like his later works, demonstrates his ability to describe mental states and to show how people find it impossible to get at the truth. This and his other plays are influential on many schools of writers after Kleist's death.

COMPOUND STEAM ENGINE
British engineer, Arthur Woolf (1766–1837), constructs the first practicable compound steam-driven engine. It comprises pistons and cylinders of differing bore size to achieve a more efficient use of steam as it changes from high pressure to low.

NAPOLEON IN INDIA
Napoleon orders the military training of troops from the Mahratta people of western India. They attack the British in an attempt to crush British power in India.

SHELLS, STEAMBOATS AND SYMPHONIES

HAITI BECOMES THE FIRST INDEPENDENT CARIBBEAN nation. Napoleon is proclaimed emperor of France. Beethoven re-dedicates his "Eroica" symphony in protest. US President Thomas Jefferson is re-elected for a second term. The first exploding military shell is invented. Screw-propellers are fitted to a steamboat in the USA. Americans Lewis and Clark set off to explore the Louisiana territory.

✱ 1 8 0 4 ✱

JAN	1	Haiti proclaims its independence from France
FEB	12	German philosopher Immanuel Kant dies aged 80
	16	Plot led by Duc d'Enghien against Napoleon Bonaparte is uncovered
	21	Fulani tribe begins a holy war in Nigeria
MAR	20	Duc d'Enghien is executed
MAY	14	US soldiers Meriwether Lewis and William Clark begin their exploration of the West
	16	French senate proclaims Napoleon emperor of France

JULY	27	Twelfth Amendment to US Constitution establishes separate votes for president and vice-president
AUG	11	Holy Roman Emperor Francis II adopts the title of emperor of Austria
NOV	6	Thomas Jefferson re-elected president of the USA
DEC	12	Napoleon crowned emperor by Pope Pius VII
	12	Spain declares war on Britain

Holy War

During the year, the Fulani people begin a *jihad* or holy war in northern Nigeria. In 1808 they invade Bornu, near Lake Chad, and in 1820 establish the Hamdallahi caliphate in Mali.

Haiti Independent

A slave insurrection, led by Toussaint L'Ouverture since 1791 until his death in 1803, finally succeeds in overthrowing French rule. The island — the first independent nation in the Caribbean — becomes an empire under Jean Jacques Dessalines (1758–1806).

Emperor Napoleon

Napoleon is proclaimed emperor of France by the French senate. Pope Pius VII officiates at his coronation in Paris in December but Napoleon himself places the imperial crown on his own head.

Code Napoleon

The Code Napoléon, a radical new civil law, comes into force in France and the territories of the French Empire. It combines elements of Roman law with reforms introduced during the French Revolution, but considers accused persons guilty until proven innocent.

Jefferson Re-elected

US President Thomas Jefferson wins a second term after defeating his Federalist opponent, Charles Pinckney, by a large margin. George Clinton defeats Rufus King to become vice-president.

Humboldt Returns

German naturalist Baron von Humboldt (1769–1859) completes his exploration of South America and is hailed as a genius. Since 1799 he has travelled through

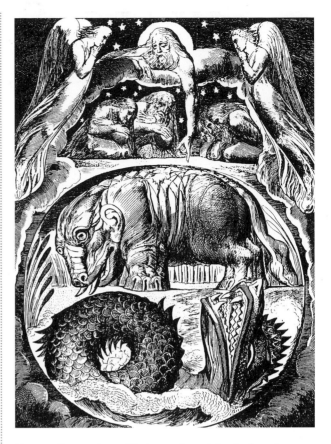

Above: *Engraving of Behemoth and Leviathan by poet William Blake, who writes "Jerusalem" this year.*

Venezuela, Cuba, Colombia, Ecuador and Peru, observing biology, geography and meteorology. He has also measured the cold current off the continent's western coast, named after him. After a perilous trip in flimsy boats, Humboldt and French botanist Aimé Bonpland (1773–1858), who travelled with him, have established that the Orinoco flows into the Amazon.

Left: *The delta of the Orinoco river, Venezuela, whose course has been charted by Baron von Humboldt. The Orinoco has an overall navigable length of 6920km (4300mi) and forms part of the border between Venezuela and Colombia.*

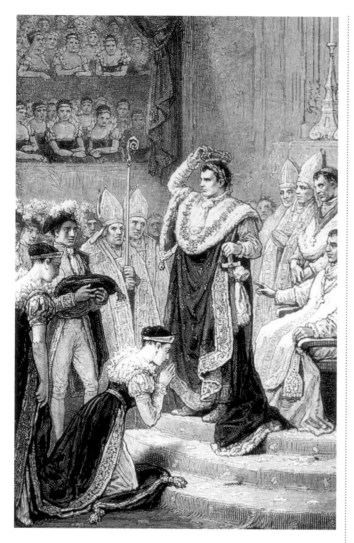

Above: *Napoleon seizes the imperial crown and places it on his own head at his coronation in Paris.*

LEWIS AND CLARK SET OFF
US President Jefferson's secretary Meriwether Lewis (1774–1809) and his colleague William Clark (1770–1838) set off at the head of an expedition to explore the newly-acquired territory of Louisiana and to find a route to the Pacific Ocean.

FREEDOM RAILROAD
An assisted escape route for runaway slaves begins when the mother of a freed slave, Stephen Smith, is led to freedom from the southern states of the USA to the north, where all states except New Jersey have banned slavery or introduced emancipation. The escape route will become known as the Underground Railroad.

VACUUM-BOTTLING
The world's first vacuum-bottling cannery is set up in Massey, near Paris, northern France, by a Parisian confectioner, Nicolas-François Appert (1750–1841), who devised his food-preservation technique in 1795 in response to an award offered by Napoleon Bonaparte.

STEAM RAILWAY LOCOMOTIVE
Having successfully demonstrated his steam-powered road vehicle, Richard Trevithick (1771–1833) now displays the first steam-powered vehicle to run on rails. The locomotive, which runs on Penydarren Railway in Wales, catalyses a transport revolution.

EXPLOSIVE SHELL
Henry Shrapnel (1761–1842), a British army officer, invents the first exploding military shell. The shells, which comprise a metal casing containing a mass of bullets, are first used in warfare against the Dutch, in Surinam.

ASTEROIDS DISCOVERED
Two minor planetary bodies or asteroids, orbiting the sun, are discovered by German astronomers, Heinrich Holbers and Carl Harding. They are the third and fourth to be observed and are given the names *Vesta* and *Juno*.

SYMPHONY NO 3 (OP 55), "EROICA"
German composer Ludwig van Beethoven (1770–1827) has composed a symphony on a scale unknown before. Known as "Eroica", it is longer and more emotionally expressive than any previous symphony, and greatly extends the scope of the form. Beethoven dedicates the work to Napoleon, but when he learns that his hero has accepted the Imperial crown, scratches Napoleon's name from the score.

Left: *Gioacchino Rossini, composer of the opera* Guillaume Tell *(1829) based on Schiller's play published this year.*

FLEGELJAHRE

This is the last of German novelist Jean Paul's series of great novels of court and upper-class life, dealing with problems of personality — the pitfalls caused by one-sidedness and the difficulties caused by idealism. Jean Paul (1763–1825), whose real name is Johann Paul Friedrich Richter, becomes the most popular novelist of his generation.

SCREW-PROPELLED STEAMBOAT

In New Jersey, USA, Col John Stevens (1749–1838) fits his steamboat *Little Juliana* with screw-propellers. She is the first ship to use them. The two four-bladed propellers allow the ship to maintain a speed of some 13km/h (8miph) hour or 7 knots.

JERUSALEM

British poet William Blake (1757–1827) begins work on what many consider his masterpiece, the epic "Jerusalem". In it, he develops his unique style of engraving both text and illustrations. His works are little known during his own lifetime, but are to have a lasting influence on later poets and artists.

WILHELM TELL

This, the last completed play of the German dramatist Johann Christoph Friedrich von Schiller (1759–1805) tells (and popularizes) the story of the legendary Swiss hero and marksman, Wilhelm Tell. The drama continues the writer's exploration of freedom and responsibility, in both the personal and political spheres.

SUSPENDERS OR BRACES

Galluses — suspenders or braces to hold up men's trousers — are patented by two inventors in the USA.

Above: *The Pacific Ocean, the goal for Lewis and Clark's expedition which sets off this year to find an overland route to the western seaboard of the USA.*

Immanuel Kant
1724–1804

The Prussian philosopher Immanuel Kant, originator of the School of Philosophical Idealism has died in Königsberg, where he spent his entire life, and where he was Professor of Logic and Metaphysics. He was the author of original works in the fields of natural sciences and astronomy, but his most influential work is found in his three treatises on philosophy: *Critique of Pure Reason* (1781), which argues that we are equipped with certain basic concepts and the ability to use them, through which we are able to structure and make sense of our empirical observations; *Critique of Practical Reason* (1788), describing a universal theory of ethics; and *Critique of Judgement* (1790) on the philosophical basis for making judgements in matters of aesthetics and that eighteenth-century concept, "Taste".

Joseph Priestley
1733–1804

The English dissident clergyman, former literary companion to Lord Shelburne, and one of the discoverers of oxygen, Joseph Priestley, has died in Pennsylvania. He had been better received in the United States than in his own country, where the internationally recognized pioneering chemist and author of *Letters to a Philosophical Unbeliever* (1774) and *Disquisition Relating to Matter and Spirit* (1777) was vilified as an atheist and pro-revolutionary thinker.

THE THIRD COALITION

WAR CONTINUES IN EUROPE as Britain and Russia form an alliance against France. Austria and Russia suffer defeats but Britain gains control of the seas after the Battle of Trafalgar. Napoleon crowns himself king of Italy. Weapons technology makes a major advance with the development of the percussion cap and self-propelled solid-fuel rockets.

✦ 1805 ✦

MAR	4	US President Thomas Jefferson begins his second term of office
APR	11	By the Treaty of St Petersburg Britain and Russia form an alliance against France
MAY	9	German poet Friedrich Schiller dies
	12	Albanian soldier Mehemet Ali becomes governor of Egypt
	26	Emperor Napoleon is crowned king of Italy in Milan
JUNE	4	France takes Genoa from Italy
AUG	9	Austria joins the Treaty of St Petersburg
OCT	20	The French defeat the Austrians at the Battle of Ulm
	21	British fleet defeats the French at Battle of Trafalgar
DEC	2	Napoleon routs Russian and Austrian armies at the Battle of Austerlitz

Above: *Nelson's monument in the crypt of St Paul's Cathedral, London.*

Above: *French troops on their way to the battlefield near Austerlitz, to fight for victory against Russia under Czar Alexander I and Austria under Emperor Francis II.*

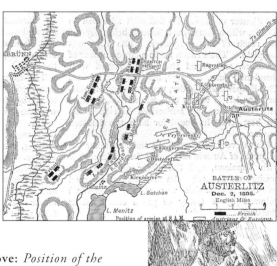

Above: *Position of the warring armies on the morning of the Battle of Austerlitz. French troops are shown as dark blocks, the Austrians and Russians as white.*

Right: *Battle-weary troops salute their victorious leader Napoleon after the Battle of Austerlitz.*

Above: *A sketch of the diabolically talented violin virtuoso Niccolò Paganini by Sir Edwin Landseer.*

Friedrich Schiller
1759–1805

That great figure of German literature Johann Christoph Friedrich von Schiller dies. Poet, dramatist, historian and critic, Schiller trained as a military surgeon but spent much time writing (coining the phrase "Sturm und Drang" for his verses) and reading. He was arrested for absenting himself from duty to watch the first performance of his first play *The Robbers* in 1782. He quickly completed two more plays and founded a theatrical journal. An Idealist, Schiller emphasized the aesthetic impulse as fundamental to human nature, and his poem on the freedom of the human spirit, the "Ode to Joy" was set to music by Beethoven in the Ninth Symphony; his work on the history of the revolt of the Netherlands led to his appointment as Honorary Professor of History at Jena. He formed a friendship with Goethe, and wrote the greatest historical drama in the German language, the trilogy *Wallenstein* (1796–99). Other works include *Maria Stuart* (1800), *The Maid of Orleans* (1801), and *William Tell* (1804), a manifesto for political freedom.

PEACE OF PRESSBURG

After the Austrian defeat at Austerlitz, Austria and Prussia make peace with France again. Prussia loses land in central Germany but is allowed to keep the British state of Hanover, while Austria gives up the Tyrol and all its lands in southern Germany, Italy and along the Adriatic. France now dominates Western Europe.

EGYPT INDEPENDENT

Mehemet Ali (c. 1769–1849), an Albanian soldier, becomes governor of Egypt, a province of the Ottoman Empire. Slowly, he builds up his power, gaining supreme authority in 1811 and establishing virtual Egyptian independence from Ottoman rule.

SOLID-FUEL ROCKETS

British military engineer, William Congreve (1772–1828) invents self-propelled missiles. His solid-fuel rockets are the first-ever battlefield rockets. Although inaccurate, and with a range of about 1365m (1517yd), they are to be used with some success in the naval bombardment of Boulogne in 1806 and at Waterloo in 1815.

SENSATIONAL VIOLINIST

The Italian violinist Niccolò Paganini (1782–1840) causes a sensation when he tours Europe. His virtuoso style, whether playing his own works or those of others, brings a new appreciation of violin playing — but leads some to suggest that his gift comes from the devil.

THIRD COALITION

Britain and Russia sign a treaty to form a Third Coalition against France. The two powers intend to liberate the northern German states from French rule, and are later joined by Austria and Sweden.

PERCUSSION CAP DETONATOR

An important development in warfare occurs when percussion caps for firearms projectiles are invented by Scotsman Alexander Forsyth (1768–1843). Although made for muzzle-loading guns, they forecast the beginning of modern weaponry.

ICE TRADE

An American businessman, Frederick Tudor, from Boston, Massachusetts, pioneers a trade in ice from New England as far south as South America and the Caribbean. He builds up a large business by experimenting with insulation and the design and building of ice-houses.

NIGER EXPLORATION

Scottish explorer Mungo Park (1771–1806) heads a 45-man expedition to explore the Niger river in West Africa. The expedition is a disaster and Park fails to navigate the length of the river and establish its mouth. Park dies at Bussa Rapids in 1806; it is unclear if he drowns or is killed by tribespeople.

THE PRELUDE

English poet William Wordsworth (1770–1850) completes his masterpiece, "The Prelude", a long autobiographical poem in blank verse. The work, which describes the poet's childhood and life as a young man, shows how his interest in the arts and his position in the Romantic movement were shaped by his early life.

Above: Romantic poet William Wordsworth, author of the long epic poem "The Prelude", in later years.

Below: A proud paterfamilias and his impressive brood. Thomas Malthus, cleric and scholar, is very much opposed to such an exuberant attitude to procreation.

DONA ISABEL COBOS DE PORCAL

In his portraits, the Spanish artist Francisco de Goya (1746–1828) reveals a broad technique which allows him to hint at the personalities of his sitters. Portraits of female sitters, such as this, often show the artist warming to his subject; other works, such as his royal portraits, are less flattering.

POPULATION WARNING

Thomas Malthus, a British cleric who in 1803 published a revised edition of his pamphlet *Essay on the Principle of Population*, is appointed Professor of Political Economy at Haileybury, a new public school for sons of employees of the East India Company. His essay, which questions the ability to raise food production to feed a rapidly increasing population, has caused a sensation.

MADOC

English Southey's narrative poem "Madoc" tells the story of the son of Owen Gwyneth, King of Wales, who sails to America and has a series of adventures with the "Aztecas". The poem is widely admired as one of a number of works which win Southey a government pension.

THE BATTLE OF TRAFALGAR

NELSON HAS BEEN chasing the French fleet for the past two years, following them to the West Indies and back. He finally catches them off Cape Trafalgar in Spain and completely destroys Napoleon's war fleet.

Above left: *Horatio Nelson, admiral of the fleet which wins the Battle of Trafalgar.*

Above: *A sample of Nelson's handwriting in a letter written just before the battle takes place.*

Left: *Gunners on board the* Royal Sovereign, *the ship commanded by Vice Admiral Collingwood.*

Opposite top: *Victory, the flagship of the British fleet at Trafalgar, at anchor off Portsmouth.*

Opposite top inset: *Tactics at Trafalgar; British ships are shown as white, French as black.*

Opposite below: *Nelson lies mortally wounded on the deck of his ship at the height of the battle.*

RHINE CONFEDERATION AND CONTINENTAL SYSTEM

NAPOLEON CONTINUES TO MARCH through Europe. He occupies Naples and Berlin and advances into Poland, putting his brothers on the thrones of Naples and Holland. He forms the Confederation of the Rhine and abolishes the Holy Roman Empire. Work begins on the Arc de Triomphe. American explorer Zebulon Pike sets out to investigate the American southwest, and Lewis and Clark return after successfully crossing the American continent.

❋ 1806 ❋

JAN	1	British take the Cape of Good Hope from the Dutch
FEB	15	The French occupy Naples
MAR	30	Napoleon makes his brother Joseph King of Naples
APR	1	Britain declares war on Prussia, which has seized Hanover
JUNE	5	Napoleon makes his brother Louis King of the Netherlands
JULY	12	France forms the Confederation of the Rhine from twelve German states
	15	US soldier Zebulon Pike is sent to explore the course of the Arkansas river
AUG	6	Napoleon abolishes the Holy Roman Empire
OCT	9	Prussia declares war on France
	14	The French rout the Prussians at the Battle of Iéna and Auerstadt
	16	Russia and Turkey go to war
	27	Napoleon occupies Berlin
NOV	21	Napoleon's "Continental System" closes European ports to British ships
DEC	15	Napoleon enters Warsaw, Poland

Above: *French statesman Charles Maurice de Talleyrand-Périgord, architect (with Napoleon) of the Confederation of the Rhine, a group of western German states.*

Above: *Marshal Joachim Murat, brother-in-law to Napoleon, leads the French charge at the Battle of Iéna against the Prussians in October this year.*

CAPE COLONY SEIZED

Britain seizes the Cape Colony from the Dutch, who are under French rule, in order to keep it from French control. The colony provides a useful port for ships sailing to and from British possessions in India.

CONFEDERATION OF THE RHINE

Germany, Bavaria, Württemberg, Mainz, Baden, and eight smaller principalities are reorganized and merged by France into the Confederation of the Rhine, which remains under French protection. In August, the Holy Roman Empire is finally abolished.

CONTINENTAL SYSTEM

Napoleon introduces the Continental System, which closes continental ports to British ships and blockades British ports. All French-ruled and neutral countries are forbidden to trade with Britain or its colonies; Britain retaliates in a similar way. The blockade causes considerable economic hardship for Britain and its allies, although it eventually does more damage to France.

Right: *British Army General Whitelocke at his court martial, the result of his bungling ineptitude and treachery during the invasion of Argentina by Britain this year.*

BONAPARTE KINGS

Napoleon makes one of his brothers, Joseph Bonaparte, King of Naples, and another, Louis Bonaparte, King of the Netherlands.

BRERA GALLERY

In Milan, Napoleon founds what is to become one of Italy's largest art galleries. Housed in a seventeenth-century palace which also contains the Brera Library, the Gallery has a notable collection of Venetian paintings.

ARC DE TRIOMPHE

Napoleon Bonaparte conceives the idea of a triumphal arch, the Arc de Triomphe in Paris, at the centre of a number of radiating avenues, in imitation of ancient Roman arches. Dedicated to the emperor's armies, it has since become a symbol of France as a whole. Jean François Chalgrin's design is not completed until 1836.

LEWIS AND CLARK RETURN

American explorers Meriwether Lewis (1774–1809) and William Clark (1770–1838) return after leading a government-backed expedition of 30 men west from St Louis and becoming the first Americans to cross their own continent. They set out in 1804 with the hope of moving up the Missouri river, which they believed might flow through the Rockies. A Native American woman helped the party through the Bitterroot Range to rivers that ran to the Pacific. The group, which only lost one member, carried their canoes for long distances and reached the ocean in 1805. They overwintered on the coast before returning to St Louis by land. In all they have covered 12 000km (75 000mi) and their expedition fires the imagination of Americans on the east coast.

BUENOS AIRES INVASION DEFEATED

Spanish Argentine colonial militia see off a British attack on Buenos Aires; they successfully fight off a second in 1807. The unsuccessful British attacks lay the seeds of a future Argentinian independence movement.

WIND FORCE SCALE

To aid meteorological forecasting, a scale for the relative strengths of winds is introduced. The Beaufort Scale, which ranges from 0 = calm to 12 = hurricane, is devised by Sir Francis Beaufort (1774–1857).

PIKE'S PEAK

American soldier Zebulon Pike sets off to the American southwest. He follows the Arkansas river into the Rockies in search of its source and then heads south into Spanish New Mexico. He observes what is later named Pike's Peak, in the Rockies, which he considers unclimbable after failing in his attempt. He then follows the Rio Grande valley and is imprisoned in Santa Fe by Spanish officials but is released and returns to St Louis in 1807. Pike's report and findings subsequently encourage Americans from east of the Mississippi to open up the southwest.

Left: *Napoleon at Rossbach, in the Confederation of the Rhine, overseeing the removal of a Prussian monument.*

Right: *Queen Louisa of Prussia reviews her troops before their battle with Napoleon at Iéna. The battle is fought to smash the Confederation of the Rhine, but Napoleon is victorious.*

THE SPIRIT OF THE AGE

The German historian and patriot Ernst Moritz Arndt (1769–1860) publishes the first part of *The Spirit of the Age*, in which he incites his people to shake off the yoke of French rule. The book begins a revival of German nationalism and launches Arndt's career of pressing for German nationalism and, later, reform.

COTTON THREAD

In Scotland, entrepreneur Patrick Clark produces a cotton thread that is as strong and smooth as silk. It is used to regenerate a textile industry disabled by the American blockade of supplies to Britain of French and Oriental silk.

BANK NOTE NUMBERS

Counterfeiting of bank notes prompts British engineer, Joseph Bramah (1748–1814), to devise a machine for automatically numbering each one. Automatic serial numbering proves to be very effective against fraudsters.

VILLAGE POLITICIANS

David Wilkie (1785–1841), recently moved to London from his native Scotland, becomes the most popular genre painter of his time with *Village Politicians* and similar canvases. His scenes of everyday and low life start a fashion for genre painting.

ROUNDARM BOWLING

English cricketer John Willes champions roundarm (later called overarm) bowling in favour of the legal underarm method.

CARBON PAPER

The days of laboriously rewriting documents to obtain copies are numbered with the introduction of "carbon" paper. Ralph Wedgwood, of London, saturates thin sheets of paper with ink and finds that they will leave a faithful duplicate impression when placed between two pieces of writing paper.

AMINO ACID

Biological sciences are brought into the modern age with the discovery of the first amino acid, asparagine, by French chemists Louis Vauquelin (1763–1829) and Pierre Robiquet (1780–1840).

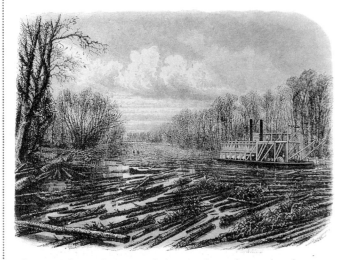

Above: *The Red river; while searching for its headwaters, Zebulon Pike crosses into New Mexico.*

TREATIES, BLOCKADES AND EMBARGOES

NAPOLEON REMAINS SUPREME in Europe and signs treaties with Russia and Prussia. The British blockade of French ports continues and the USA passes an Embargo Act to stop trade with warring countries. Britain outlaws the slave trade in its colonies. Gaslights appear on the streets of London and a Viennese physician argues that human personality can be interpreted from the shape of the head.

❧ 1 8 0 7 ❧

JAN	7	Britain blockades the coasts of France and its allies
APR	26	Russia and Prussia form an alliance to drive the French out of the German states
MAY	1	Britain makes the slave trade illegal in its colonies
JUNE	14	France defeats the Russians and Prussians at the Battle of Friedland
	27	Britain joins the Russo-Prussian alliance
JULY	7–9	France makes peace with Prussia and Russia
	8	Napoleon makes his brother Jérome King of Westphalia
SEP	2–5	British fleet bombards Copenhagen to prevent Denmark from helping Napoleon
OCT	27	France and Spain agree to conquer Portugal
NOV	29	Portuguese royal family flees to Brazil
DEC	22	US Embargo Act is designed to stop trade with warring European countries

Right: *The signing of the Treaty of Tilsit between France and Russia. A separate treaty is signed with Prussia. Continental Europe lines up against Britain.*

Royal Family Flees
The Portuguese royal family, led by Prince Regent John, flees from Portugal and establishes the Portuguese capital in Rio de Janeiro, Brazil. The Portuguese colony is now richer than its motherland, and becomes increasingly independent.

Britain Outlaws Slave Trade
The British parliament outlaws British involvement in the slave trade in all its colonies, although slavery remains in place for another 27 years. The campaign to abolish the trade has been led by members of the humanitarian Clapham Sect, notably William Wilberforce (1805–73). A squadron of Royal Navy ships is deployed to patrol the West African coast and seize slave ships.

Treaties of Tilsit
The victorious Napoleon signs the Treaties of Tilsit with Russia and Prussia against Britain. Both agree to join the Continental System against Britain, and to set up a Duchy of Warsaw under the King of Saxony. Prussia loses all its lands west of the Elbe and in Poland. In return, the Russian czar agrees to coerce Denmark, Sweden and Portugal in the war against Britain, and is given a free hand in Finland.

Stroll by Gaslight
Pall Mall, a famous avenue in London, becomes the first thoroughfare to be lit by gaslight. German-born Frederick Winsor installs thirteen lamp-posts, each with three jet-glass globes, supplied with gas from beneath the pavement. In 1813, Winsor will found the world's first gas company.

La Vestale
Gasparo Spontini (1774–1851) is one of the leading writers of French opera, and Napoleon's favourite composer. *La Vestale*, about a vestal virgin who betrays her work for love, is one of his most popular works, and a triumph which brings him fame all over Europe.

Passenger Railway
Although the steam locomotive is being developed, the first passenger railway service opens with horse-drawn carriages. It runs along a 12km (7.5mi) route from Swansea to Oystermouth in England.

Paper Machine
Paper is now available in continuous rolls, thanks to the invention of the industrial paper-making machine. The machine, which was designed and built by the English brothers Henry and Sealy Fourdrinier, with Bryan Donkin, uses wood pulp rather than flax obtained from old rags in the traditional way. The pulp is squeezed through the rolls and dried.

Percussion Ignition
Scottish inventor Alexander John Forsyth (1769–1843) patents a percussion cap, an improved detonating mechanism, which marks the first step towards the self-contained rifle and pistol cartridge.

Irish Melodies
Irish poet Thomas Moore (1779–1852) writes a long series of poems designed to be sung to traditional Irish tunes. The first volume appears this year. The delicate lyricism of his verses brings them popularity, and Moore is widely praised, notably by his friend Lord Byron.

Above: *A printing press designed to use a continuous web or roll of paper, available this year.*

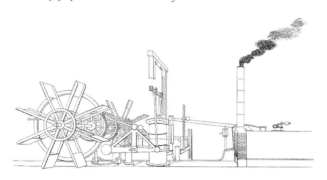

Above: *The internal workings of Robert Fulton's paddle steamer* Clermont, *which plies the Hudson this year.*

PHENOMENOLOGY OF THE SPIRIT

The German Idealist philosopher Georg Wilhelm Friedrich Hegel (1770–1831) is among the most important thinkers of his time. One of his most influential works, *Phenomenology of the Spirit*, is published just after he leaves his post at the University of Jena. It describes how the mind has progressed from mere consciousness through self-consciousness, reason, spirit and religion to absolute knowledge.

HISTORY OF THE ITALIAN REPUBLICS IN THE MIDDLE AGES

Swiss historian Jean Charles Léonard de Sismondi begins his greatest work. It will eventually run to sixteen volumes, describing in detail the power and greatness of Italy during the period of its independent city states. The work will become a bible for supporters of Italian nationalism.

READING BUMPS

Phrenology is brought to Paris by its founder, Viennese physician Franz Joseph Gall (1758–1828). He believes that bumps on the head are a guide to character, emotional traits and mental abilities.

Above: *The royal family of Portugal flee to Brazil, where they establish themselves in Rio de Janeiro.*

FOUNDATION OF THE GAELIC SOCIETY

The Gaelic Society meets for the first time in Dublin. Its foundation marks a renascence in Gaelic literature.

FIZZY WATER

Bottled carbonated water is produced and marketed by an American chemist, Benjamin Silliman, in New York.

ADOLPHE

Exiled French politician Benjamin Constant (1767–1830) begins writing his novel *Adolphe* when living in London. It will be published in 1816 and is noted for both its fine prose and its depiction of passion, the central character's love life recalling the author's own famous affair with the writer Mme de Staël. The work brings Constant his first great fame; later he will be well known as a Liberal politician in France.

Above: *The British fleet passing through the Dardanelles on the way to confront the French at Constantinople.*

Left: *Naval uniform worn by an able seaman in 1807.*

Above: *O'Connell Street, the heart of Dublin, home of the Gaelic Society.*

THE SLAVE TRADE ABOLISHED IN THE USA

THE USA JOINS BRITAIN in banning the trade in humans from Africa, but slavery continues within the United States. Napoleon advances into Spain, putting his brother on to the throne. This leads to the Peninsular War. Scandinavia becomes a new focus for tourism. Polarized light is discovered. The first temperance society is founded in the United States and Marc Isambard Brunel introduces the idea of mass production.

Above: *Slaves in the southern states of America. It is now illegal to import slaves from Africa.*

⚹ 1808 ⚹

JAN	1	The USA bans the importation of slaves from Africa British colony of Sierra Leone founded as home for freed slaves
FEB	2	The French occupy Rome
	16	A French army led by Marshal Joachim Murat invades Spain
MAR	2	Murat captures Madrid
	16	Czar Alexander I of Russia claims Finland as a province
MAY	2	Spaniards rise against the French occupation
	6	King Charles of Spain renounces the throne
JUNE	15	Napoleon makes his brother Joseph King of Spain; Murat later takes Joseph's place as King of Naples
AUG	1	A British army lands in Portugal. King Joseph flees from Madrid
	21	British troops under Arthur Wellesley defeat the French at Vimiero, near Lisbon

Above: *James Madison, who this year is elected as the fourth president of the USA. He will become known as the "Father of the Constitution".*

USA BANS IMPORTS OF SLAVES

The US government has prohibited the import of slaves from Africa, although the use of slaves remains in place. The importing of slaves from Africa into the USA is now illegal. Anyone knowingly purchasing an illegally imported slave can be fined $800, and equipping a slave ship incurs a fine of $20 000. However, the law, which was first introduced in March 1807 at the instigation of President Thomas Jefferson, who is critical of slavery, is largely ignored.

MADISON ELECTED PRESIDENT

Secretary of State James Madison (1751–1836) is elected as the fourth president of the USA, defeating the twice-unlucky Charles Pinckney. The incumbent George Clinton wins re-election as vice-president.

FRENCH INVADE SPAIN

French armies cross the Pyrenees and invade Spain, making Joseph Bonaparte King of Spain in place of Ferdinand VII. As a result, Britain sends troops to Portugal and Spain, starting the lengthy Peninsular War aimed at expelling the French.

PRUSSIAN EDUCATION REFORMED

Radical reform of Prussia's education system is introduced by Friedrich Wilhelm von Humboldt, Director of Public Instruction. He establishes a new, independent university in Berlin, replaces many grammar schools with *gymnasien* staffed by independent, professional teachers, and introduces a broad-based curriculum which includes German, mathematics and science.

Above: *The Battle of Vimeiro, Portugal, part of the Peninsular War, won by the British under Wellington.*

PARACHUTE JUMP
Jordaki Kurapento finally demonstrates that the parachute, first designed on paper by Leonardo da Vinci, does indeed work in practice. He has to bail out from his Montgolfier balloon when it catches fire over Warsaw, Poland.

FAUST, PART I
The great German writer Johann Wolfgang von Goethe (1749–1832) publishes the first part of *Faust*, perhaps the most influential of all works of this period. The Faust legend, which has been retold many times before by writers, becomes in Goethe's hands a symbol of the striving of the individual that is at the heart of the Romantic movement in literature and art.

MASS MANUFACTURE
French-born Marc Isambard Brunel (1769–1849), teams up with British engineer Henry Maudslay (1771–1831) to establish the first mass production process. Five machines, for executing the manufacture of ships' pulley blocks, can be operated by ten unskilled men, significantly increasing productivity, and laying the foundations for modern manufacturing techniques.

TYPEWRITER
A machine for writing by stamping characters and punctuation marks on to paper is devised by an Italian, Pellegrine Turri. He invents the typewriter for his blind friend, Countess Carolina Fantoni, so that she can correspond by letter.

POLARIZED LIGHT
Light whose transverse vibrational pattern is confined to a single plane, as opposed to normal light which vibrates in all directions, is discovered by French physicist Etienne Malus (1775–1812) by shining light through crystals. This will lead to the invention of polarizing sunglasses, which filter out reflected glare.

US TEMPERANCE
The first modern temperance society is founded in New York State, USA, by Dr Billy J Clark. Some 25 members vote to call it The Temperate Society and to discourage the drinking of alcohol.

THE CROSS ON THE MOUNTAINS
A master of Romantic landscape, the German painter Caspar David Friedrich (1774–1840) adds Christian symbolism to landscape in this work. The result, intended for use as an altarpiece, scandalizes many viewers, who believe that what is basically a landscape should not be used above a Christian altar.

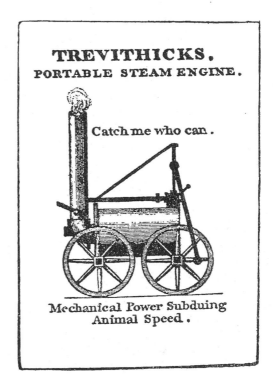

Left: *Arthur Wellesley, the Duke of Wellington, architect of the victorious British campaign in Spain.*

Below: *An advertisement for the portable steam engine, the first passenger locomotive.*

TOURISTS VISIT SCANDINAVIA
Scandinavia becomes a focus for tourism by English, German and Italian travellers after the closure of Western Europe by the Napoleonic Wars, resulting in a surge of interest in Nordic culture in Europe.

MILITARY ACADEMY
A French officers' academy is established at St Cyr.

STATE EDUCATION IN FRANCE
Napoleon completes his assumption of state control of education in France, merging all institutions of higher education in a new University of France, and gives its officials control of the national education system. Only graduates and members of the imperial university may open a school or teach publicly.

LA GRANDE BAIGNEUSE (VALPINCON BATHER)
One of Jean Auguste Ingres' first great paintings, this nude shows the ways in which Ingres will dominate French painting — the handling of line, the cool flesh tones, the assured painting of drapery. It is Neoclassicism personified.

MARMION
Scottish novelist Walter Scott (1771–1832) publishes his long poem *Marmion*. One of his greatest works of Scottish culture, it tells a story that has its climax at Flodden Field. It includes the famous song, "Lochinvar".

Below: *Joseph Bonaparte, King of Naples and Sicily and brother of Napoleon, who this year makes him King of Spain.*

THE NAPOLEONIC WARS

A SERIES OF WARS engulfs Europe as Napoleon I, ruler of France, aims to expand France's frontiers. The major powers, Britain, Austria, Russia and Prussia form coalitions but fail to halt Napoleon's rise.

✶ Key Dates ✶

WAR OF THE SECOND COALITION

Russia, Britain, Austria, Portugal, Naples, the Vatican and the Ottoman Empire ally against France.

- **MALTA June 12, 1798–September 5, 1800**
Valetta, captured by Napoleon in June 1798, is liberated by the British in September 1800.
- **GENOA April–June 1800**
The Austrians manoeuvre to block the French in the Black Mountains but are forced back. Both sides suffer 2000 battle casualties; 5000 Austrians are captured.
- **MONTEBELLO June 9, 1800**
Napoleon, attempting to relieve Genoa, is attacked by the Austrians. In a complex battle, the French suffer 500 killed; the Austrians lose 5000 prisoners.
- **MARENGO June 14, 1800**
A major French victory. A force of 31 000 Austrians attacks Napoleon who has a force of 23 000. Apparently defeated, Napoleon rallies his forces, and in an attack spearheaded by cavalry, drives the Austrians from the field. The French suffer 5900 killed, the Austrians 9400.
- **HOHENLINDER December 3, 1800**
The French under Moreau defeat a much larger Austrian force. The Austrians suffer 7000 killed or wounded, 12 000 prisoners and lose 87 guns.

WAR OF THE THIRD COALITION

Britain, Austria, Russia, Sweden, Naples form the Third Coalition against France and Spain. Austria is forced out in 1805; Prussia rejoins the coalition in 1809.

- **ULM October 7–20, 1805**
An Austrian army of 75 000 under Archduke Ferdinand is outmanoeuvred and trapped by Napoleon who is able to concentrate 150 000 men, subsequently reinforced by a further 50 000 men. The Austrians lose 50 000 of whom 20 000 are prisoners.

Left: *The young Napoleon Bonaparte.*

Above: *Napoleon seizes power from the Directory.*

- **ELCHINGEN October 14, 1805**
The French Marshal Ney (1769–1815) leads his corps across a repaired bridge to capture the village, driving out 20 000 Austrians and taking 3000 prisoners.
- **CALDIERO October 30, 1805**
Fought between 50 000 French under Massena and 80 000 Austrians under Archduke Charles. The Austrians withdraw but lose 3000 killed or wounded. French casualties are 4000 killed or wounded.
- **OBERHOLLABRUN November 16, 1805**
After capturing Vienna, Napoleon presses the Russian army of 40 000. Some 7000 men under Prince Bagratian successfully hold a roadblock at Oberhollabrun until dusk, then withdraw after suffering 50 per cent casualties.
- **AUSTERLITZ December 2, 1805**
Napoleon, with 75 000 men, meets and defeats a joint Austro-Russian force of 95 000 under Emperor Alexander and Emperor Francis II. The Austro-Russian army loses 12 000 killed and wounded and 30 000 including 20 generals, 186 cannon and 400 limbers. The French lose 6800 men.
- **CAPE TOWN January 8, 1806**
The Dutch colony under French control is captured by 6000 British troops under Sir David Baird.

- BUENOS AIRES **June 27, 1806**
General Beresford, assisted by Admiral Sir Home Popham, captures the city with 1700 men. The Spanish counter attack and he is forced to surrender, losing 250 killed or wounded.

- BUENOS AIRES **July 5, 1807**
During an attack and street fighting in the city a force of 9000 British troops under General Whitelocke suffers serious losses and is forced to surrender. The British then evacuate the Rio Plata region.

- MAIDA, CALABRIA **July 4, 1806**
A bayonet charge by 5000 British troops under Sir John Stuart breaks a French force of similar strength under General Reynier. The British are forced to re-embark when strong French reinforcements arrive.

- SAALFELD **October 10, 1806**
Prince Louis Frederick with 9000 Prussian-Saxon troops is trapped against the walls of Saalfeld by 6000 French troops under Marshal Lannes. The Prince is killed in a desperate cavalry charge and the Prussians lose 3000 men and all 20 guns. French losses are 200.

- IENA-AUERSTADT **October 14, 1806**
At Auerstadt the 66 000 men on the Prussian left flank are beaten after heavy fighting by a smaller force commanded by Davout. At Iéna, Napoleon, with 100 000 men, attacks a force of 70 000 Prussians. The defeated Prussians are harried by French cavalry. The French lose 11 000 killed or wounded, the Prussians 22 000 killed or wounded, 18 000 prisoners and 300 guns.

- LUBECK **November 6–7, 1806**
Marshals Soult and Bernadotte drive Blücher into Lübeck, which they storm and capture. Blücher escapes but is forced to surrender at Ratkow.

- PULTUSK **December 26, 1806**
Some 20 000 French troops are blocked by a force of 37 000 Russians. The Russians retire at last light, having suffered 3000 killed or wounded and 2000 prisoners.

- EYLAU **February 8, 1807**
Napoleon leads 46 000 French troops against 70 000 Russians under Bennigsen. A very tough but indecisive battle in which the Russians withdraw after suffering 12 000 dead to the French 20 000 dead and wounded.

- DANZIG **March 19–May 26, 1807**
The city, defended by Kalkreuth with 14 000 Prussians and 4000 Russians, is besieged by Marshal Lefebvre with 18 000 French. On May 15, 8000 Russians attempt to relieve the city but are defeated and Kalkreuth surrenders the city.

- HEILSBERG **June 5–10, 1807**
Bennigsen, with 90 000 Russian troops, attacks the French but falls back. Pressed by Napoleon he withdraws across the Alle river to a fortified camp at Heilsberg. Marshal Murat, commanding the French advanced guard, makes an over-hasty attack and suffers 8000 casualties. The Russians finally withdraw.

- FRIEDLAND **June 14, 1807**
Napoleon commits 80 000 French troops against 70 000 Russians commanded and poorly led by Bennigsen. The Russians suffer 15 000 killed or wounded with 10 000 prisoners, the French have about 9500 casualties. Following this French victory the Peace of Tilsit is signed.

- COPENHAGEN **September 1–5, 1807**
The Danes secretly agree to put their fleet of eighteen ships under French command. The Royal Navy bombards the city for four days, then lands 2000 troops under Lord Cathcart who quickly captures the port. The Danish fleet surrenders.

- SACILE **April 16, 1809**
A Franco-Italian army of 36 000 commanded by Eugène Beauharnais, Napoleon's step-son, fights a force of 46 000 Austrians under Archduke John. The Franco-Italian force withdraws after a tough battle; about 6000 men are killed.

- ABENSBERG **April 20, 1809**
Austria declares war on France. When battle is joined, the French have 90 000 men under Napoleon and the Austrians 80 000 under Archduke Charles. The Austrians suffer 2800 killed or wounded with 4000 prisoners; the French have 2000 casualties.

- LANDSHUT **April 21, 1809**
The Austrians under Archduke Charles Louis fall back after Abensberg. The Austrian General Hiller takes up positions near Landshut with 36 000 men. Marshal Lannes crushes this force and, crossing a burning bridge, storms the city of Landshut. Marshal Massena joins the battle with more forces and Hiller and the Austrians lose 9000 men and most of their guns.

- ECKMUHL **April 22, 1809**
The corps of Davout, Lannes and Lefebvre, 90 000 men under Napoleon, drive 76 000 Austrians under Archduke Charles from high ground.

- RATISBON **April 23, 1809**
Archduke Charles posts a strong rearguard at the walled town of Ratisbon as he withdraws. The French storm the town; Napoleon is slightly wounded. The Austrian garrison escape.

- ASPERN-ESSLING **May 21–22, 1809**
The French, with 48 000 infantry and 7000 cavalry, and the Austrians, with 90 000 men, fight one of the costliest battles in history. The village of Aspern is taken and retaken at least ten times. The French bridgehead over the Danube is pounded by 264 Austrian guns. The French Marshal Lannes and General St Hilaire are killed. The French lose 20 000 men; the Austrians suffer 23 000 casualties.

- RAAB **June 14, 1809**
Fighting through villages, the French push the Austrians back, inflicting 3000 casualties with 2500 prisoners.

- WAGRAM **July 5–7, 1809**
Crossing the Danube, Napoleon, with 190 000 men and 488 guns, attacks the Austrians, who number 139 000 men with 446 guns. A force of 8000 men under French General Macdonald breaks through the Austrian ranks.

THE NAPOLEONIC WARS

As well as fighting shifting combinations of Allies, Napoleon is also battling against the British alone, in various parts of the world, specifically where Britain has colonies or trading concerns to defend.

- **MOGILEV (Mohilev) July 23, 1812**
A Russian force of 60 000 attacks 28 000 French under Marshal Louis Davout in a strong position on the Dniepr river. The Russians lose 4000 men and are repulsed by the French.

- **MOGILEV (Mohilev) August 17, 1812**
A French force of 175 000 and a Russian force of 130 000 manoeuvre around the city. The French capture two suburbs but the Russians set fire to the town and withdraw. The Russians suffer 10 000 casualties, the French 9000.

- **VALUTINO August 19, 1812**
Napoleon, with 120 000 men, sets a trap for the Russians; however, the trap does not work and some 25 000 men on both sides are lost.

Above: *Napoleon on his Egyptian campaign. His dreams of a Middle Eastern empire are unfulfilled.*

- **BORODINO (Muscova) September 5–6, 1812**
The Russians halt Napoleon's drive on Moscow at Borodino. Under Kutuzov some 120 000 Russians hold the line. In a horribly sanguinary battle, the French lose 43 generals and 110 colonels among 30 000 dead and wounded. The Russians suffer 60 000 killed. Napoleon captures Moscow but is forced to withdraw in the winter. In the retreat from Moscow, French casualties are 400 000 men, 175 000 horses and 1000 cannon. The Russians suffer 250 000 casualties with an estimated 50 000 Cossack irregulars.

- **MALOYAOSLAVETS (Malo-Jaroslawetz) October 24, 1812**
As 15 000 French under Eugène de Beauharnais withdraw, they clash with 24 000 Russians under Kutuzov at the town of Malo-Jaroslawetz. The town is taken and re-taken several times. Despite heavy losses, the Russians force Napoleon to abandon the southern axis of withdrawal.

- **KRASNAOI (Krasnoye) November 17, 1812**
A costly holding action by the retreating French forces under Marshal Davout. In three days' fighting they lose 5000 killed or wounded and 8000 missing.

- **BEREZINA RIVER November 26–29, 1812**
Only 25 000 French troops reach the river but abandon more than 10 000 stragglers on the east bank when they burn the bridges. Most are killed by the Russians.

THE FRANCO-BRITISH WAR

- **ALEXANDRIA March 21, 1801**
The French, under Menou, are forced back against the walls of the city by General Ralph Abercromby. The French lose 3000 casualties, the British, 400, including their commander.

- **COPENHAGEN April 2, 1801**
Fought between eighteen British ships of the line, with 39 smaller craft and ten ships of the Danish fleet assisted by shore batteries. The British lose 1200 men killed and have six ships badly damaged. One Danish ship is sunk and nine damaged.

- **FINISTERRE July 22, 1805**
A combined Franco-Spanish fleet of twenty ships under Admiral Villeneuve, sailing from the West Indies, is attacked by Sir Robert Calder. The British capture two ships but fog and weak winds cheat them of a more complete victory. The British suffer 183 casualties, the French 476.

- **TRAFALGAR October 21, 1805**
A Franco-Spanish force of eighteen ships under Villeneuve encounters 27 ships of the British fleet under Horatio Nelson. Superior gunnery, signalling and ship handling give the British

Above: *Napoleon's troops cross the Alps to engage the Austrians at the Battle of Marengo.*

a complete victory. Eighteen French ships surrender, four others are later taken off Corunna.

WAR OF THE FOURTH COALITION

Britain, Russia, Prussia, Sweden, Spain and various German states combine to oppose France

• **LUTZEN May 2, 1813**
Napoleon holds five villages in front of Lutzen with 70 000 men against a Russo-Prussian force of 65 000 commanded by Wittgenstein and Blücher. After heavy fighting the king of Prussia and the emperor of Russia order withdrawal. The Allies suffer 20 000 casualties and the French 18 000.

• **BAUTZEN May 20–22, 1813**
A major battle between a Russo-Prussian force of 100 000 under Wittgenstein and Blücher and 150 000 French forces under Napoleon. The French force a crossing over the river Spree and take Bautzen, but lack of cavalry prevents them from exploiting their victory. The Allies suffer 15 000 casualties and the French 1300.

• **GROSSBEEREN August 23, 1813**
An Allied army of 80 000 commanded by the crown prince of Sweden covers the road to Berlin. Regnier's corps, part of Oudinot's French Army of the North, captures Grossbeeren but the Prussians under von Bulow re-take it. It is recaptured by the French, who suffer large losses and cannot exploit their success.

• **KATZBACH RIVER August 22–26, 1813**
Napoleon pits 130 000 veteran French troops against 100 000 Prussians under Blücher. Macdonald and his corps attempt to cross the river, but are counter attacked by the Prussians. French reinforcements arrive but are attacked. By close of day the French have 15 000 casualties and lose more than 100 guns.

• **DRESDEN August 27, 1813**
A combined Russian, Prussian and Austrian force of 200 000 fights a French force of 130 000 led by Napoleon. A flanking attack by Murat leads to the collapse of the Allied position.

• **KULM-PRIESTEN August 29–30, 1813**
The Austrians, Russians and Prussians under Schwartzemberg hold Kulm as they withdraw from Dresden. The French drive them out but are counter attacked, losing some 6000 killed and 7000 taken prisoner. Allied losses are 5000.

• **LEIPZIG (The Battle of the Nations) October 16–19, 1813**
Napoleon, holding Leipzig with 155 000 men, is faced by 100 000 Austrians and Prussians under Schwartzemberg and 60 000 Prussians under Blücher. In heavy fighting on the first day, the outnumbered French lose 27 000 men and the Allies 35 000. The French are beaten but make a costly but disciplined withdrawal. In three days fighting the French lose 60 000 men.

• **HANAU October 30–31, 1813**
The French, now reduced to 80 000 men withdrawing from Leipzig, meet 45 000 Austrians and Bavarians under Wrede. Napoleon smashes through the position and, Wrede having been seriously wounded, the Allies retreat after suffering 10 000 casualties to the French 6000.

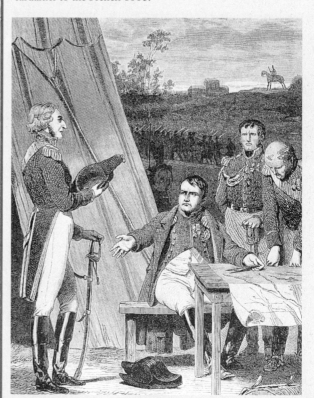

Above: *Napoleon and his staff plan their next move encamped near the battlefield.*

THE NAPOLEONIC WARS

While the wars with the various Allies continue all over France, Germany, Austria and Russia, Napoleon is also fighting the Peninsular Wars all over the Iberian Peninsula of Spain and Portugal.

- **BRIENNE January 29, 1814**

The chateau near Troyes is held by 30 000 Prussians and Russians under Blücher. Some 18 000 French troops under Napoleon drive them out and hold it against a night-time counter attack. The Allies suffer 4000 casualties and the French 3000.

- **CHAMPAUBERT-MONTMIRAIL February 10, 1814**

As the Prussians under Blücher advance on Paris, Napoleon launches three separate attacks that seriously delay the Prussians and Russians. At Montmirail 20 000 men under Sachen suffer 6000 casualties. At Château Thierry he attacks the 30 000 men under General York and takes 3000 prisoners. His final assault on Blücher costs the Prussians 3000 casualties and prisoners.

- **MONTEREAU February 18, 1814**

Russo-Prussian forces, commanded by Prince Eugene of Württemberg holding Montereau on the confluence of the Seine and Yonne rivers, are subject to an artillery bombardment and cavalry charge that breaks them. The French lose 2000, the Allies 2000 dead and 4000 prisoners.

- **CRAONNE March 7, 1814**

Despite being outnumbered and assaulting uphill, 37 000 French under Napoleon dislodge 90 000 Prussians in a daring bayonet attack. The French lose 5400 killed and the Prussians 5000.

- **REIMS March 13, 1814**

Napoleon concentrates 30 000 French troops against a force of 13 000 Russians and Prussians. For a loss of 1000 casualties the French inflict 6000 casualties and prisoners.

- **ARCIS-SUR-AUBE March 21, 1814**

A force of 60 000 Austrians under Karl Philipp Prince of Schwartzenberg attack 23 000 French troops. After inflicting between 2500 and 4000 casualties and losing 1700 men, the French withdraw.

- **LA FORE CHAMPENOISE March 25, 1814**

With the Allied army advancing on Paris, Marshals Mortier and Marmont concentrate their troops into a force of 30 000 men. In fierce fighting they lose 5000 men and many guns and are forced to retreat.

- **PARIS March 30, 1814**

Defended by only 20 000 regulars and the National Guard, Paris is assaulted by the Grand Army of the Allies. The Allies are victorious at a cost of 8000 men to the French 4000. Napoleon is forced to abdicate and Paris is occupied by the Allies.

Above: *A victorious Napoleon walks the field of battle contemplating his success.*

PENINSULAR WARS 1808–1814

Under the leadership of Arthur Wellesley, later Lord Wellington, the British, aided by Spanish guerrillas, fight a long campaign against French forces commanded by different marshals, generals and princes.

- **VIMEIRO August 21, 1808**

A British expeditionary force in Portugal commanded by Wellesley encounters 14 000 French troops under Junot. In the fighting the French lose 1800 men and 13 guns.

- **SARAGOSSA June–July 1818, Dec 20, 1808–Feb 20, 1809**

The population of Saragossa refuses to accept Napoleon's brother Joseph as King of Spain. The city is beseiged twice and ultimately stormed by the French.

- **CORUNNA January 16, 1809**

Marshal Soult's 20 000 French troops try to prevent the 14 000 strong British army from embarking at the port of Corunna. Under the leadership of Sir John Moore, the French are held off and lose 2000 men. The British lose 800, including Moore.

- **OPORTO May 12, 1809**

The French, under Soult, capture Oporto in Portugal. Returning to Portugal, Wellesley surprises Soult and captures the town. The French lose several thousand men in retreat.

- **TALAVERA July 28, 1809**
Wellesley, commanding a total force of 20 000 men with 20 000 Spaniards, fights 50 000 French under Marshal Victor. The Spanish break, leaving 16 000 British troops facing 30 000. In savage fighting, Victor loses 7300 men and 20 guns; British losses of 5400 leave them too weak to pursue the French.

- **BUSACO September 27, 1810**
A force of 25 000 British with 2000 Portuguese fights off 40 000 French under Massena. Corps led by Ney and Reynier assault the Allied force and suffer 4500 casualties; British casualties are 1500.

- **ALBUERA (Albuhera) May 16, 1811**
Fought by 46 000 British, Portuguese and Spanish under Marshal Beresford and 33 000 French under Marshal Soult. The core of the Allied force are 7000 British infantry. The French could have won the battle, but for the British steadiness under fire. By the close of the fighting only 1800 British are standing and the French lose more than 8000, including five of their generals.

- **TARRAGONA May–June 28, 1811**
Held by a Spanish garrison, the city is besieged by 45 000 French troops under General Louis Suchet. The French take a series of posts and finally assault the town suffering 6000 casualties. Spanish casualties are about 12 000 and 8000 prisoners.

- **FUENTES D'ONORO May 5, 1811**
Wellington with 34 000 men holds a position behind Fuentes d'Onoro and is attacked by a French force of similar strength under Marshal André Massena. Both sides lose about 1500 men; the French withdraw.

- **BADAJOZ March 17–April 6, 1812**
Garrisoned by 5000 French, Hessian and Spanish troops the city is besieged by the British who suffer the loss of 1500 men in the siege. On April 6 the British assault and capture the city; they lose 3500 men in the attack.

- **CIUDAD RODRIGO January 19, 1812**
Wellington besieges the town for twelve days, then assaults it. The 2000-strong garrison inflicts 1290 casualties on the British.

- **SALAMANCA July 22, 1812**
Manoeuvring for an advantage, the 40 000-strong army of Marshal Auguste Marmont clashes with the British under Wellington. The French suffer 12 000 casualties and the British 5000.

- **VITTORIA June 21, 1813**
Wellington, with an Allied army of 80 000 men, outmanoeuvres a force of 66 000 men under Marshal Jean-Baptiste Jourdan and in three assaults kills 8000 and captures 151 guns and 450 ammunition wagons. Allied casualties are 5000.

- **THE PYRENEES July 25–August 2, 1813**
Battles fought between Wellington's generals and Soult's army at Soravren, Roncesvalles, Maya, Satarem and Buenzas cost the French 14 000 casualties and the British 7300.

Above: *Napoleon aboard the British ship Bellerophon, on his way to exile on Elba.*

NAPOLEON'S HUNDRED DAYS 1815

Escaping from Elba in March 1815, Napoleon galvanizes France and is able to create a new army mainly because the French Royalist army has remained loyal to him in exile.

- **LIGNY June 16, 1815**
Battle between 84 000 Prussians under Blücher and 60 000 French under Napoleon. The Prussians are forced out of the position, losing 12 000 casualties to the French 8000. By prior agreement Blücher then withdraws towards the British position at Waterloo.

- **QUATRE BRAS June 16, 1815**
Marshal Ney with 25 000 French troops attacks the 36 000 Anglo-Dutch forces under Wellington at the cross roads at Quatre Bras. The battle is effectively a draw, with the French losing 4300 men and the Allies 4700. The Allies then withdraw to Waterloo.

- **WATERLOO June 18, 1815**
The defining battle of the Napoleonic Wars, this is fought between the British, Prussians and French. The Anglo-Dutch forces hold the field for the day until Prussian forces arrive clinching victory. In the one-day battle the British lose 15 000 dead and wounded, the Prussians 7000 and the French 25 000 plus 8000 prisoners and 220 guns. Napoleon abdicates and is exiled to the Atlantic island of St Helena.

- **WAVRE June 18–19, 1815**
A holding force of 15 000 Prussians under Thielmann delays the 33 000 French troops commanded by Grouchy, who had been ordered by Napoleon to keep the Prussians away from Waterloo. Grouchy finally forces the Prussians out of Wavre, twelve hours after the French defeat at Waterloo.

Papal States Annexed

NAPOLEON ANNEXES the Papal States and is excommunicated and the French are driven out of Portugal. Native Americans protest against the seizure of their land and form a confederation to end White expansion. An American engineer makes a seminal journey by steam paddleship and American humorist Washington Irving publishes a burlesque history of New York. Thomas Paine, hero of the American Revolution, dies.

✺ 1 8 0 9 ✺

JAN	16	Battle of Corunna in Spain: French defeat the British, killing British General, Sir John Moore
FEB	8	Austria declares war on France
MAR	1	US Nonintercourse Act replaces the Embargo Act, which has proved to harm the USA more than other countries
	4	James Madison is inaugurated as US president
APR	22	Arthur Wellesley is sent back to Portugal to replace Sir John Moore, killed at Corunna
MAY	12	Wellesley drives the French out of Portugal
	13	The French capture Vienna Napoleon annexes the Papal States
JULY	5	Napoleon defeats the Austrians at the Battle of Wagram
	6	Pope Pius VII excommunicates Napoleon following annexation of the Papal States
OCT	14	Austria makes peace with France and has to yield territory
DEC	16	Napoleon divorces his wife, Josephine de Beauharnais

Above: *Bayonets at the Battle of Talavera.*

METTERNICH BECOMES AUSTRIAN PREMIER

Austria and France go to war again, with the French army capturing Vienna in May and defeating the Austrian army at Wagram in July. As a result, the able and competent Prince Metternich (1775–1859) becomes chief minister of Austria in August and makes peace with France in October, losing land to France, Saxony, Prussia, Russia and Bavaria, and joining the Continental System against Britain.

NAPOLEON DIVORCES

Napoleon divorces his wife Josephine because of her failure to give him a son, and in February 1810 marries Marie-Louise of Austria, cementing the alliance between the two countries.

NATIVE AMERICAN FEDERATION

Tecumseh (c. 1768–1813), Chief of the Shawnee, and his brother The Prophet, declare that chiefs cannot surrender Native American lands without the consent of all tribe members. He demands that forest land between Ohio and the Great Lakes be reserved for Indians, and attempts to unite the forest tribes into an Indian Confederation to end White expansion into their lands.

Above: *Empress Marie-Louise of Austria, who is to be Napoleon's new wife.*

EDUCATIONAL METHODS

German educationalist Johann Friedrich Herbart (1776–1841) is appointed Professor of Philosophy and Pedagogy at Königsberg (Germany). Applying ideas on psychology to education, he emphasizes the importance of relating new concepts to the learner's experience, and of teaching moral education through experience. He believes in a broad educational basis, including mathematics and classical literature.

SEAGOING STEAMBOAT

The 95-ton *Phoenix* is taken on a voyage from New York to Philadelphia, by American engineer Col John Stevens (1749–1838). This seminal journey through open seas takes thirteen days and marks the beginning of self-propelled international shipping.

FABLES

The Russian poet Ivan Krylov (1768–1844) begins to publish his first volume of fables, short, witty narrative poems full of racy language, which bring him instant fame and popularity, and patronage by the imperial family. He is one of the first Russian writers to reach a wide audience.

LECTURES ON DRAMATIC ART AND LITERATURE

German poet, scholar, critic and linguist, August Schlegel (1767–1845), writes the lectures that become the key critical text of the European Romantic movement.

KNICKERBOCKER'S HISTORY OF NEW YORK

American man of letters, Washington Irving (1783–1859), consolidates his reputation as humorist with this burlesque history, supposedly written by Diedrich Knickerbocker, a descendant of New York's original Dutch settlers. The character becomes a byword for the worthy American-Dutch burgher.

Above: *American essayist and historian Washington Irving.*

ELECTIVE AFFINITIES

The conflict of attraction versus conventional marriage is dramatized in this novel, *Elective Affinities,* by Johann Wolfgang von Goethe (1749–1832). The resulting questioning of social convention becomes a hallmark of the Romantic movement, and of much later nineteenth-century literature.

QUARTERLY REVIEW FOUNDED

Publisher John Murray (1778–1843) founds the *Quarterly Review* which becomes the voice of the Tory point of view in England. It remains influential, in both literary and political circles, for about 100 years.

Above: *Vienna, captured by the French this year after a short but violent siege, during which bombs are dropped.*

MRS SPIERS

This sensitive portrait by Scottish artist Henry Raeburn (1756–1823) shows the development of his style to great effect. The portraitist is noted for his ability to paint straight on to the canvas without making drawings beforehand, a technique that looks forward to much later artists.

Above: *Marshal Jean Lannes, mortally wounded at the Battle of Aspern-Essling. He dies later in Vienna.*

Thomas Paine
1737–1809

Tom Paine, the Norfolk-born radical democrat has died in poverty. His revolutionary work, *The Rights of Man* (1792), in defence of the French Revolution, caused him to be indicted for treason in his native England, but he escaped to France where he was made a French citizen and a member of the National Convention but later imprisoned during the Terror. He had spent time in the United States and had supported the independence movement, and in 1802 he returned there but was ostracized for his free-thinking atheism, expressed in *The Age of Reason* (1794–96).

Above: *Tom Paine, the English-born revolutionary, more honoured in France than in his native land.*

WAR, PEACE AND NAPOLEON

*T*HE NAPOLEONIC WARS continue to dominate Europe until Napoleon's final defeat and exile in 1815. Following his overthrow, and the restoration of peace, the old European frontiers are restored as are the old monarchies, but the seeds of nationalism and revolution have been sown. In South America, Spanish colonies begin their long fight for independence, led by Simón Bolívar. In the United States too, nationalism grows, following the War of 1812 against Britain. The US-Canadian border is fixed along the 49th parallel. The world of science sees the development of steam-powered printing, the first use of plastic surgery, the discovery of chlorophyll, and the first blood transfusion. In Britain, the world's first industrial nation, the impact of industrial technology leads to bitter, but short-lived, protest.

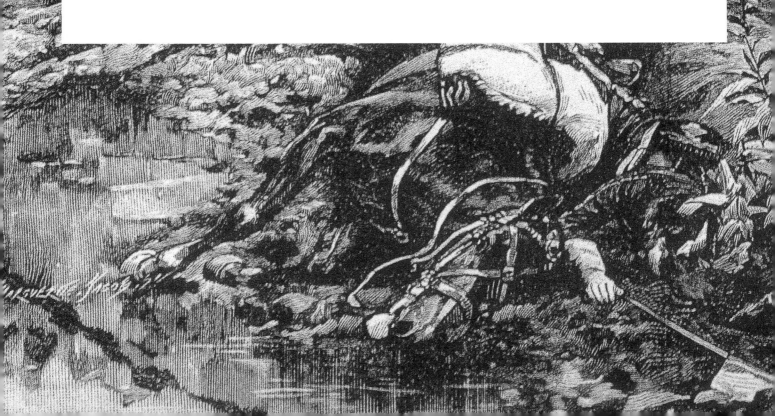

~ 1810–1819 ~

KEY EVENTS
of the
DECADE

REVOLTS IN VENEZUELA AND MEXICO

LUDDITE RIOTS

PENINSULAR WAR

BATTLE OF TIPPENCANOE

WAR OF 1812

PETRA RE-DISCOVERED

BATTLE OF LEIPZIG

NORWAY DECLARES INDEPENDENCE

HUNDRED DAYS

CONGRESS OF VIENNA

CARLSBAD DECREES

STEAM-POWERED PRINTING

HOMEOPATHY DEVELOPED

BREECH-LOADING RIFLE

CANNED FOODS PIONEERED

DINOSAUR FOSSIL DISCOVERED

STEAM WARSHIP LAUNCHED

JANE AUSTEN'S *PRIDE AND PREJUDICE*

MARY SHELLEY'S *FRANKENSTEIN*

WORLD POPULATION

1034 MILLION

(ESTIMATE)

~

Napoleon Bonaparte signs his abdication notice in Paris.

French guns captured at the Battle of Waterloo.

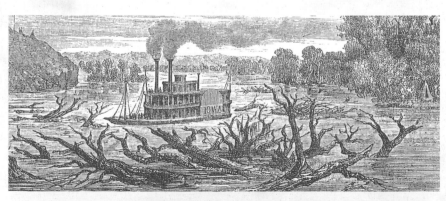

A paddle steamer on the Mississippi river.

REVOLTS IN SOUTH AMERICA

APOLEON ANNEXES THE NETHERLANDS and various north German states. Led by Simón Bolívar, Venezuela and other colonies in South America begin their long struggle towards independence. Steam-powered machinery begins to revolutionize printing. Homeopathy is pioneered by German physicist and doctor Samuel Hahnemann.

✵ 1810 ✵

JAN	6	Sweden joins Napoleon's Continental System against trade with Britain
MAR	23	Napoleon orders that all US ships seized by France are to be sold
APR	14	Simón Bolívar leads Venezuelan rebellion against French rule
MAY	1	USA resumes trade with Britain and France
	25	Spanish colonists in Rio de la Plata revolt against Bonapartist régime

JULY	1	Louis Bonaparte abdicates as King of Holland
	9	Napoleon makes Netherlands part of France
AUG	18	Sweden chooses French Marshal Jean Bernadotte as heir to the childless King Karl XIII
SEP	16	Revolt in Mexico against Spanish rule
	18	Revolt in Chile against Spain
DEC	10	Napoleon annexes several north German states

Above: *Walter Scott, prolific Scottish novelist and poet, publishes his poem "The Lady of the Lake" this year.*

Above: *Napoleon marries Marie-Louise of Austria, thereby cementing peace between France and Austria.*

SOUTH AMERICAN INDEPENDENCE MOVEMENT BEGINS

As news of the deposition of the Spanish King Ferdinand VII (1788–1833) and occupation of Spain by the French reaches South America, the future Argentina, Uruguay, Paraguay and Bolivia launch a bid for independence, forming the provinces of the Rio de la Plata. Under the influence of Simón Bolívar (1783–1830), a leading army officer, Venezuela refuses to recognize French rule of Spain and proclaims its allegiance to the deposed and imprisoned Ferdinand. In September, Mexico and Chile both revolt in favour of independence from Spain.

USA SENDS TROOPS TO WESTERN FLORIDA

The US government sends troops into Spanish-owned Western Florida following a revolt by settlers in Baton Rouge, who established their own republic. The move adds to US territory on the Gulf of Mexico.

DE L'ALLEMAGNE

French writer Mme de Staël (1766–1817) introduces contemporary German writers to a French audience for the first time, comparing her country with Germany to the detriment of the former. Controversy erupts and

Napoleon exiles her (not for the first time). Most copies of the original edition are destroyed. In 1813, the book is republished from England, and will prove influential.

THE LADY OF THE LAKE

This poem of love, adventure and dynastic struggle in Scotland by the Scottish novelist Walter Scott (1771–1832) extends his audience and makes still more popular his works on Scottish history and legend.

PRINZ FRIEDRICH VON HOMBURG

Heinrich von Kleist's devotion to Prussia inspires his drama *Prinz Friedrich von Homburg*. The play is notable for its positive view of the Elector of Prussia, and also for the realism of its depiction of its fallible hero.

STEAM-POWERED PRINTING

Hand-operated printing machines are replaced by machines driven by steam. It happens in Germany, the birthplace of printing, under the supervision of Franz Konig (1774–1833). The speed at which printing runs can be produced is increased enormously, marking a new era in publishing.

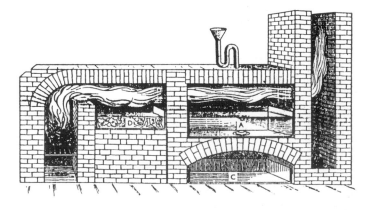

Above and right: *Soda manufacture using the process devised by Nicolas Leblanc (1742–1806). This method is superseded this year by Augustin Fresnel's new technique.*

SODA MANUFACTURE

French chemist Augustin Fresnel (1788–1827) develops a method of making sodium carbonate, or washing soda. Obtained from processing limestone and common salt, it is used in the manufacture of glass and for water softening.

GAY UNDERGROUND

The White Swan, a London gay bar, is attacked as part of a prolonged crackdown against "sodomites", revealing the existence of a male homosexual underground in Europe.

HOMEOPATHY

German physician Samuel Hahnemann (1755–1843) publishes *The Organon of Therapeutics (Organon der Rationellen Heilkunde)*. Pioneer of homeopathic medicine, Hahnemann argues that minute doses of a drug that produces symptoms in a healthy person can cure a sick patient exhibiting the symptoms.

PRUSSIA ABOLISHES SERFDOM

At the instigation of the Prussian statesman Friedrich von Stein (1757–1831), Prussia undergoes sweeping reforms, including the aboliton of serfdom. Former serfs may farm for themselves or sell the land they cultivated for their former lords.

Above: *Dr Samuel Hahnemann, the founder of the therapeutic system known as homeopathy.*

Right: *Agents from Britain and Sweden sign a treaty to join forces against Napoleon.*

Below: *The retreat from Coimbra, Portugal. This is one of Wellington's rare setbacks in the Peninsular War.*

RAGE AGAINST THE MACHINE

RITISH TEXTILE WORKERS protest against industrialism in a wave of machine-breaking. The Napoleonic Wars continue, with British victories against the French at the Battles of Fuentes d'Onoro and Albuera. In the USA, General William Harrison defeats the Indian Federation at the Battle of Tippencanoe. The breech-loading rifle is developed and gaslighting arrives in the home. A new novelist, Jane Austen, makes her name, and two brothers conquer the Jungfrau in Switzerland.

✤ 1811 ✤

JAN	22	Napoleon annexes the German Grand Duchy of Oldenburg
FEB	2	USA resumes trade ban on Britain
	5	Britain's King George III is declared insane; the Prince of Wales is appointed Prince Regent
	10	In the Russo-Turkish war, Russia captures Belgrade
MAY	5	British forces in Spain defeat French under Marshal Masséna at Fuentes d'Onoro
	14	Paraguay declares independence from Spain
	16	British army defeats the French under Marshal Soult at the Battle of Albuera
JULY	5	Venezuela declares independence from Spain
	14	Canadian explorer David Thompson reaches the mouth of the Columbia river
NOV	5	US President James Madison prepares for war with Britain over trade disputes
	11	Governor William Henry Harrison crushes a Native American revolt at the Battle of Tippencanoe

Above: *Fighting at the Battle of Albuera; British,
Spanish and Portuguese troops defeat the French.*

Above: Native American Indians from the northwest who are driven from their traditional lands by white settlers.

MACHINE-BREAKERS

In the UK, Nottinghamshire textile workers destroy machinery in the belief that the new machines are depriving them of their skills and livelihood. The men involved claim to be acting under the leadership of a fictitious King Ned Lud and become known as Luddites. By 1812 numerous outbreaks of machine-breaking are taking place in industrial England, although harsh punishments kill the movement off by 1816.

BATTLE OF TIPPENCANOE

The Indian Confederation is defeated in a battle at Tippencanoe, Indian Territory, USA, by a volunteer American army led by General William Henry Harrison, who has acquired — often in questionable circumstances — some 30 million acres of land on the northwest frontiers, which the Indians consider their birthright.

VENEZUELA DECLARES INDEPENDENCE

Venezuela declares its independence from Spain, as do the provinces of Paraguay and Buenos Aires. Throughout the South American continent, revolts grow in opposition to Spanish rule.

EARTHQUAKE

A severe earthquake in the Mississippi valley, USA, destroys the village of New Madrid, forming new lakes and draining old ones within the course of an hour.

BREECH-LOADING RIFLE

American gunsmith, John Hall (1778–1841), introduces the idea of a firearm that loads at the breech end of the barrel. Combined with percussion cartridges, the basic format for the modern gun is arrived at, changing the face of warfare altogether.

Below: *Life on an Orinoco paddleship in the newly independent country of Venezuela.*

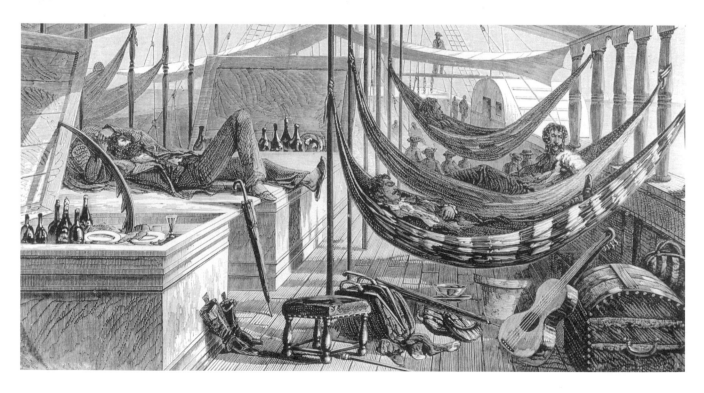

Above: *John Nash's elegant Neoclassical design for Regent Street and Piccadilly in London.*

Above: *Conscripts line up before the recruiting officer to join Napoleon's army in France.*

FIRST RUBBER GOODS

JN Reithoffer, of Vienna, Austria, develops a limited range of goods made from raw natural rubber, including the rubber or eraser from which the material derives its name. He uses turpentine as a solvent to render the latex, or rubber, pliable enough to shape his products.

DOCTOR QUALIFIES DISGUISED AS MAN

Disguised as a man, James Miranda Barry becomes the first woman to graduate as a doctor in the UK, where women are barred from training and qualifying as doctors. Barry continues to practise until her death, in 1865, when her true sex is finally discovered.

SENSE AND SENSIBILITY

With the first of her novels to be published, British novelist Jane Austen (1775–1817) establishes her reputation as a writer who can make everyday, middle-class life interesting; gradually the deep bite of her satire will also be recognized. Soon further novels will make her even more popular, and she gains praise from many leaders of taste, including Sir Walter Scott and the Prince Regent.

UNDINE

This story by German writer Friedrich Fouqué (1777–1843), of a water sprite who loves a mortal, appeals to Romantic sensibility. ETA Hoffmann (1776–1822) bases an opera on it.

REGENT STREET BEGINS

One of the most influential examples of city planning, British architect John Nash's Regent Street development transforms the centre of London. Its dramatic terraces influence other middle-class housing schemes in England and on the Continent.

MANHATTAN PLANS

Plans are approved to lay out the future streets of Manhattan Island, New York, on a grid pattern. New York, the largest city in the USA, with about 60 000 inhabitants, is expanding fast.

CHARTING THE COLUMBIA RIVER

Canadian explorer and fur trader David Thompson (1770–1857), reaches the Pacific at the mouth of the Columbia river. With his Native American wife, Thompson maps the length of the river during decades of work.

DOMESTIC GASLIGHT

Samuel Clegg installs gaslight equipment into the house of Joseph Ackerman in The Strand, London, which becomes the first home to be lit this way.

JUNGFRAU CLIMBED

Swiss brothers Johann Rudolph and Hieronymus Meyer become the first to climb the Jungfrau — 4158m (13 860ft) — in Switzerland.

Left: *English author Jane Austen, who this year publishes her first novel,* Sense and Sensibility, *begun in 1797.*

War between Britain and the USA

War breaks out between the United States and Britain following trade disputes and clashes between American frontiersmen and the British and their Native American allies. Fighting takes place on land and at sea. Napoleon invades Russia but is forced to retreat, the French army suffering terrible losses. The defeat marks a turning point in the war.

❊ 1812 ❊

Jan	19	In the Peninsular War, the Duke of Wellington captures Ciudad Rodrigo
Mar	20	In Britain, loom-breaking becomes a hanging offence, following Luddite riots
Apr	6	British capture Badajoz, Spain, after 20-day siege
	14	Louisiana becomes eighteenth state of the USA
June	18	USA declares war on Britain over trade disputes
	24	Napoleon invades Russia
July	8	Britain becomes an ally of Sweden and Russia

	22	Britain defeats the French at Salamanca, Spain
	31	Spanish troops recapture Venezuela
Aug	16	US General William Hull surrenders Detroit to the Canadians
Sep	7	Russians are defeated at Borodino and abandon Moscow
	15	Russians set Moscow ablaze
Oct	15	Defeated by the cruel Russian winter, Napoleon begins retreat
Dec	18	Napoleon, having abandoned his army, arrives in Paris
	29	US naval victory against British frigate

Louisiana Given Statehood
The state of Louisiana joins the Union as the eighteenth state. It becomes the first part of the vast Louisiana Purchase from France to be given statehood. Although slavery is still practised in Louisiana, the new state allows Black Americans to enlist in the militia.

Madison Wins Second Term
President Madison wins a second term as US president, defeating his Federalist opponent De Witt Clinton from New York. Elbridge Gerry, a Democrat-Republican from Massachusetts, wins the vice-presidential election.

Childe Harold's Pilgrimage
The first two cantos of this long poem by British poet Lord Byron (1788–1824) appear. A mixture of adventures, melancholy reflections and travel guide, the work is fantastically successful, establishing Byron's reputation, and causing the poet's famous remark, "I woke one morning and found myself famous".

Fairy Tales
Philologists, lawyers and mythographers, the German brothers Jacob (1785–1863) and Wilhelm Grimm (1786–1859) publish the first part of their collection of fairy tales. Widely translated, the stories are influential as entertainment and as inspiration for writers.

Above: *Napoleon and his troops retreat from Moscow in ignominy at the end of the disastrous Russian campaign.*

Above: *Lord Byron, who has fame thrust upon him by the publication of* Childe Harold's Pilgrimage.

SNOWSTORM: HANNIBAL CROSSING THE ALPS

This is one of the first of Joseph Mallord William Turner's canvases to show the drama and violence of the natural world. In *Snowstorm*, Turner (1775–1851) tries to keep a natural scale but uses the technique of the vortex to show the swirling wind and snow.

CANNED FOODS

A combined heat sterilization and canning process is pioneered by the British engineer Bryan Donkin (1768–1855). He develops the process and presents his first products to the British army, which recognizes an important contribution to the field ration supply.

RAILWAY BOGEY

The idea of having sets of wheels on bogeys is introduced by William Chapman. The advantage is that a variety of carriages and trucks can be placed on to the same bogeys, depending on the desired use for the railway.

CAMERA LUCIDA

A device called the *camera lucida* is built by British scientist William Wollaston (1766–1828). It enables scientists to make accurate drawings from images seen through microscopes.

BREECH-LOADER PATENTED

Swiss gunsmith Samuel Pauly, who is living in Paris, patents the first cartridge breech-loader and presents it to Napoleon. The breech-loader allows a solider to fire a rifle while lying prone on the ground, providing better protection to the soldier and ensuring greater accuracy.

ANCIENT CITY OF PETRA RE-DISCOVERED

Petra, an ancient rock-cut city in southwest Jordan, capital of the Nabataean Arabs until destroyed by the Romans in the AD100s, is rediscovered by Swiss archaeologist John Lewis Burckhardt. He goes on to become the first Christian to enter Medina in Saudi Arabia.

Below: *The Duke of Wellington in action at the Battle of Salamanca.*

SARAH SIDDONS' LAST APPEARANCE
British actress Sarah Siddons (1755–1831) has excelled in tragedy and serious drama, and Shakespearean heroines have been her special forte. This year she retires, on a high, after playing Lady Macbeth, her greatest role. A brief comeback in 1819 will not be successful.

Above: *The* Comet *is launched; it combines sail power with steam but has no side paddles.*

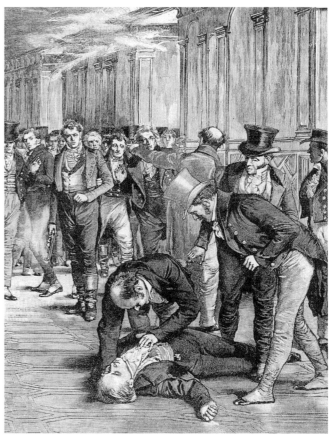

Above: *Spencer Percival, the British prime minister, assassinated by bankrupt broker John Bellingham.*

Left: *The engine that powers the* Comet *to drive it along when sailing is impossible.*

THE WAR OF 1812–14

FOLLOWING harassment of American shipping by British ships trying to enforce Britain's blockade against France, war breaks out between the USA and Britain. One of the major causes is the British practice of compelling British deserters and American sailors to serve on British ships. Tension has also been intensified by British support of Native Americans on the Canadian border. Following the Battle of Tippencanoe, Americans have demanded that Britain be expelled from Canada.

✷ Key Dates ✷
WAR ON LAND

● FORT DEARBORN
August 15, 1812
American General William Hull evacuates Fort Dearborn and orders the garrison to Fort Wayne. A Potawatomi war party assisting General Brock ambushes them, killing 24 soldiers and fourteen women and children, and capturing others.

● DETROIT
August 16, 1812
General Hull, with 2200 men, crosses the Detroit river and invades Canada on July 12. He withdraws to Detroit and on August 16 surrenders to General Brock's 2000 Canadians who have followed him south.

Right: *Soldiers plummet to their doom during the Battle of Queenstown Heights.*

● QUEENSTOWN HEIGHTS
October 13, 1812
About 4000 British under Brock are forced off Queenstown Heights by 5000 Americans commanded by Van Rensselaer. Brock is killed and the British rally, destroying the Americans who hold the Heights.

● FRENCHTOWN
January 22, 1813
A force of Kentuckians under General Winchester is defeated by a British-Canadian force under Proctor. About 500 Americans are captured and 400 killed in the fighting or massacred by Native Americans.

● STONY CREEK
May 9, 1813
An American force of 2500 jointly commanded by General Dearborn and naval Captain Chauncey, has been harassing the British and forces the 700 men in Fort George to withdraw. The British make a stand and, in a sharp action, inflict losses on the Americans, including the capture of two generals.

● SACKETS HARBOUR
May 28–29, 1813
The 600 men of the garrison of the American fort at Sackets Harbour beat off an attack commanded by the Governor General of Canada, Sir George Prevost.

● THAMES RIVER
October 5, 1813
A victory for 4500 Americans commanded by William Harrison over the British under Proctor and their Native American allies. Among the dead is the Shawnee Chief Tecumseh, who had criticized Proctor's tactics. The Native American alliance with Britain ends after this battle. The Americans suffer 45 casualties and the British and Native Americans 48 killed or wounded and 477 prisoners.

Above: *Native American Indians fight on the British side at the Battle of Thames River.*

• CHATEAUGAY RIVER

October 26, 1813

A force of about 3500 Canadian militia repulse attacks by 7000 Americans under General Hampton. The Americans suffer heavy losses.

• CHRYSLER'S FARM

November 11, 1813

Commanded by Colonel JW Morrison, 600 British troops defeat 3000 Americans under General Boyd. The British suffer 203 casualties, the Americans 249 with 100 prisoners.

• CHIPPEWA RIVER

July 6, 1814

General Riall, with 2400 British troops, attacks General Jacob Brown's 4000 Americans in strong positions and are repulsed with heavy losses.

• LUNDY'S LANE

July 25, 1814

Sir George Drummond with 3000 men is attacked by 5000 Americans under Winfield Scott. After losses on both sides of about 850, the Americans withdraw to Fort Erie.

• FORT ERIE

August 2–September 21, 1814

The American garrison of 2000 is besieged by a force of 3500 under Drummond. Two attacks are repulsed and, in a sortie on September 17, the Americans destroy British batteries and oblige Drummond to lift the siege. The Americans suffer 511 casualties; the British, 609.

• BLADENSBURG

August 24, 1814

Forcing the Americans under General Winder off the only bridge over the Potomac, General Ross pushes into Washington and destroys most of the capital. The British suffer 64 killed and 185 wounded, the Americans 26 killed and 51 wounded.

• FORT McHENRY, BALTIMORE

September 12–13, 1814

In an amphibious assault the British suffer 346 casualties. Out of a garrison of 1000 the Americans lose twenty killed, 90 wounded and 200 captured.

• NEW ORLEANS (after peace had been signed)

December 13, 1814–January 7, 1815

The city with a 12 000-strong American garrison under General Jackson is attacked by a British force of 6000 under General Keane. American ships are captured but when the British, now commanded by Edward Pakenham, make two attacks on January 1 and January 7, they are repulsed. The expedition withdraws, unaware that peace has been agreed.

✴ Key Dates ✴
WAR AT SEA

Above: *The short-lived engagement between the USS* Constitution *and HMS* Guerrière.

• USS CONSTITUTION V HMS JAVA

December 29, 1812

The 44-gun American warship fights a two-hour battle with the 38-gun British warship off Bahia, Brazil. Only when the *Java* is a flaming wreck does the crew surrender. The *Constitution* had earlier defeated HMS *Guerrière*.

• USS CHESAPEAKE V HMS SHANNON

May 29, 1813

In a 15-minute action HMS *Shannon* (Captain Philip Broke) with a crew of 330 and 38 guns, defeats the USS *Chesapeake* (Captain James Lawrence) with a crew of 379 and 38 guns. The Americans suffer 146 killed and the British 83. The *Chesapeake* is taken into Halifax as a prize.

• LAKE ERIE

September 10, 1813

An American squadron under Commodore Perry destroys the smaller British flotilla of six schooners. The British suffer 134 casualties and the Americans 123.

Above: *Fighting between HMS* Shannon *and USS* Chesapeake.

• LAKE CHAMPLAIN

September 11, 1814

Fought between fourteen ships under the American commander Captain Macdonough and sixteen British ships under Captain Downie. After a two-hour battle, four British ships are captured or destroyed.

Napoleon's Russian Disaster

Czar Alexander I, having rejected Napoleon's Continental System, the blockade of British goods which is damaging Russia's economy, Napoleon makes the disastrous decision to invade Russia and amasses the largest army Europe has ever seen. The 600 000-strong Grande Armée invades in June, battling with the czar's troops at Borodino, with great losses on both sides. Reaching Moscow in September, Napoleon finds the city in flames, sabotaged by its inhabitants. Short of supplies, his troops decimated, his winter quarters burned and the countryside deliberately devastated by the Russians, Napoleon orders a retreat. In the bitter winter, the retreat turns into a rout. Tens of thousands of French soldiers die from exhaustion, starvation and cold. Napoleon returns to Paris; only a few thousand of the Grande Armée reach the safety of Poland.

Above: *Napoleon enters Moscow.*

Right: *The city of Moscow. Most of the inhabitants abandon it before Napoleon arrives, and those left burn it to the ground rather than allow it to shelter Napoleon during the winter.*

Left: *A fast-riding Cossack volunteer challenges a band of French invaders.*

Left: *After the terrible defeat inflicted on him, Napoleon abandons his army and journeys back to Paris.*

Below: *Napoleon's inglorious retreat from Moscow into the bitter Russian winter.*

Below: *French soldiers leaving Russia; most of them will die of cold and starvation or be cut down by Cossacks.*

ALLIES BEGIN LIBERATION OF EUROPE

*F*OLLOWING NAPOLEON'S DISASTROUS DEFEAT in Russia, Europe goes on to the offensive. Prussia deserts France, and links up with Russia to fight Napoleon. Austria also declares war on France and plans are made for an Allied invasion. War also continues between the USA and Britain, with an American naval victory at Lake Champlain. The first complete dinosaur fossil is discovered in Britain.

Above: *English poet Percy Bysshe Shelley.*

Opposite: *King Joseph Bonaparte of Spain is forced to flee from Vittoria.*

❋ 1813 ❋

Mar	17	Prussia declares war on France
	27	Russians and Prussians occupy Dresden, Germany
June	21	Wellington defeats the French at Vittoria, Spain; King Joseph flees the country
Aug	26–7	Battle of Dresden, won by Napoleon
Sep	11	US ships defeat the British at the Battle of Plattsburg on Lake Champlain
	29	US troops recapture Detroit
Oct	16–9	Battle of Leipzig (Battle of Nations): Allies defeat Napoleon
	26	Austrians defeat the French in Italy
Nov	6	Mexico declares independence
	10	Wellington invades southern France

	15	Dutch rebel against France
	30	William of Orange returns to the Netherlands
Dec	29–31	British burn town of Buffalo, New York

Above: *Elizabeth Fry the Quaker reformer.*

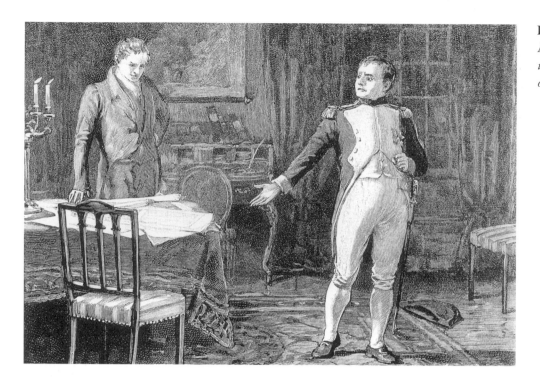

Left: *Napoleon and Prince Metternich of Austria fail to come to an agreement on an initial peace plan.*

LACE MACHINE
John Leavers, a British engineer, invents a machine for manufacturing "true" lace. Traditional hand-made lace was so expensive that it could be literally worth its weight in gold, so machine-manufactured lace has a ready market to supply.

QUEEN MAB
British poet Percy Bysshe Shelley (1792–1822) shows himself influenced by the revolutionary thinkers of Britain and France in "Queen Mab", one of his first poetic successes. The poem has a remarkable series of notes, which tackle controversial subjects such as atheism and "free love", making the work popular with radical thinkers.

TAXONOMY
Swiss botanist, Augustin de Candolle (1778–1841), introduces a new system for the classification of plants, based on shared characteristics. He also introduces the term "taxonomy" into scientific terminology as a way of differentiating between species and genera.

DINOSAUR
Lyme Regis, on the south coast of England, becomes the location of a palaeontological breakthrough. Leading palaeontologist Mary Anning (1799–1847) discovers and excavates the first complete dinosaur fossil. It is the fossilized skeleton of an ichthyosaur, some 150 million years old.

PHILHARMONIC SOCIETY
Concert-going, which had previously been a somewhat ad hoc affair, is put on a formal footing in London by the Philharmonic Society. The Society has been founded by members of the musical profession, initially to put on concerts in the Argyll Rooms, and later in the Hanover Square Rooms.

PRISON VISITOR
Quaker reformer Elizabeth Fry (1780–1845) visits Newgate prison in London where 300 women, together with their children, live in appalling conditions. She continues to devote herself to prison and asylum reform.

KEEP FIT
Swedish fencing master Per Henrik (1776–1839) founds the Gymnastic Institute in Stockholm and introduces Swedish Drill, a system of daily exercise which rapidly becomes popular worldwide.

ALLIES TO INVADE FRANCE
Prussia and Austria declare war on France. After a series of victories against France, the European Allies resolve to invade France after Napoleon fails to agree initial peace plans.

Left: *The Columbian press invented by George Clymer of Philadelphia, and available this year.*

Above: *The Highland Regiment at the Battle of Vittoria, which results in victory for the British under Wellington.*

Right: *Dresden, occupied by Russian and Prussian troops this year.*

DEFEAT AND EXILE

AFTER ELEVEN YEARS of near continuous warfare, the Napoleonic Wars come to an end as the Allies enter Paris. Napoleon abdicates and is exiled to Elba. The Allies meet at Vienna to discuss peace proposals and establish European boundaries. The Treaty of Ghent ends the War of 1812, although fighting continues briefly. The first steam-driven warship is launched in New York's harbour.

✦ 1814 ✦

MAR	12	Wellington captures Bordeaux
	30	Victorious Allies enter Paris
APR	11	Napoleon abdicates and is exiled to Elba
MAY	3	Louis XVIII enters Paris
	30	France recognizes the independence of The Netherlands
JUNE	4	Louis XVIII assumes the throne "by right", not by a vote
AUG	13	Cape of Good Hope becomes a British colony
	24	British troops enter Washington, DC, and set it on fire
NOV	4	Norway gets a new constitution
	11	Karl XIII is elected to the Norwegian throne
	21	Congress of Vienna, to sort out the future of Europe, begins
DEC	24	Treaty of Ghent officially ends the war between Britain and the USA

Above: *The Old Bailey, London's best-known law court, is completed this year.*

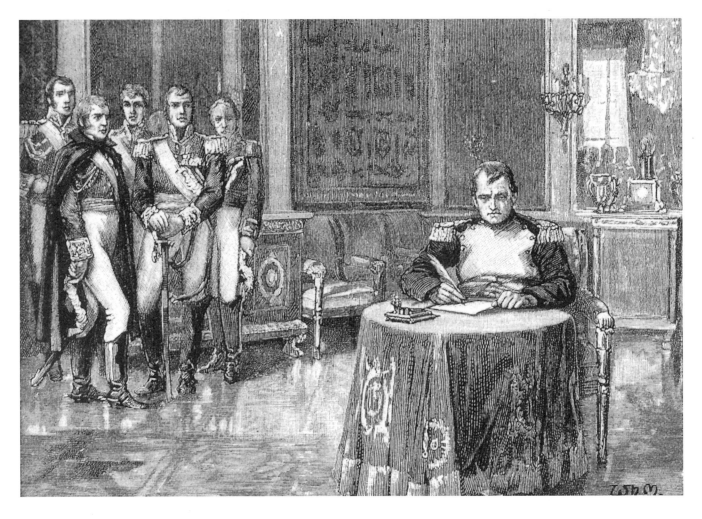

Above: *Napoleon signs his abdication notice in Paris.*

Above: *The island of Elba, where Napoleon is exiled until his escape in 1815.*

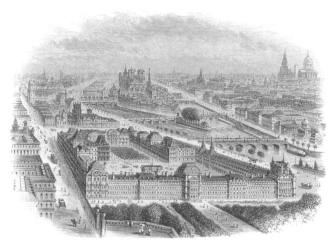

Above: *Paris, which is taken by the Allies this year. Napoleon is banished to Elba.*

ALLIES TAKE PARIS

The Allies arrive in Paris, Napoleon is banished to Elba and the Bourbon monarchy under Louis XVIII (1755–1824) is re-established. A peace treaty is signed in May, under which France agrees to recognize its 1792 frontiers and agrees to accept the independence of The Netherlands and the Italian and German states. In November, the Allies meet in the Austrian capital of Vienna and begin to make peace in Europe, rearranging the borders after the disruption caused by Napoleon.

HIGHLAND CLOSURES

The destruction of the homes of Scottish Highlanders and their expulsion from the estates of the landowners, which began earlier in the 1800s, gains momentum. Thousands of people are made homeless so the land can be turned over to sheep.

NEWSPAPER PRESS

The first newspaper to come off a power press is *The Times*. The Koening Press, of London, UK, are able to churn out 1100 sheets an hour, supplying a circulation of 4500 newspapers per day. The medium of journalism enters a new age.

TREATY OF GHENT

The British army captures the US capital of Washington and burns it down as war continues between the two countries. In December, the USA and Britain agree a peace treaty in Ghent, Belgium. The news of peace takes time to travel, and American troops rout the British army in New Orleans by the following January. Naval battles continue until March 1815.

PLASTIC SURGERY

Surgeon Joseph Constantine Carpue performs plastic surgery on a British army officer who is lacking a nose through mercury poisoning. A flap of skin is folded down from the patient's forehead and manipulated into the required shape.

STEAM WARSHIP

The US navy steamship *Demologos*, becomes the first steam-driven man-o-war. Designed by American engineer Robert Fulton (1765–1815), the vessel is launched in New York on October 29.

NORWAY CEDED TO SWEDEN

Norway declares independence from Denmark, which under the terms of a recent treaty had ceded Norway to Sweden. Sweden establishes full control of its new possession but in November a compromise is reached: Norway keeps its own parliament but Sweden and Norway share a monarch.

NOCTURNES

Irish composer and pianist John Field (1782–1837) devises the nocturne, a short, slow solo piano piece with a melody in the right hand accompanied by broken chords in the left. The form will be taken up most notably by Chopin.

THE SECOND OF MAY, 1808 AND THE THIRD OF MAY, 1808

This, the response of Spanish painter Francisco Goya (1746–1828) to the killing of Spanish insurgents by a French firing squad in 1808, becomes one of his most famous paintings. As well as being a deep expression of horror at human inhumanity, it is also influential in the painting world, inspiring later artists, with its drama, composition and use of light and dark tones.

Above: *French artist Jean Auguste Dominique Ingres.*

LA GRANDE ODALISQUE

The famous naked concubine by French artist Jean Auguste Dominique Ingres (1780–1867) scandalizes the critics — not because of its subject matter, but because the artist took liberties with the female form (elongating the back, for example) to improve the composition.

DEUTSCHE GEDICHTE

German poet Friedrich Rückert (1788–1866) has previously written under a pseudonym, but this is his first volume of poetry under his own name. Its political verses bring him much popularity in Germany, and he will follow up his success with love poems and translations.

Above: *These woodcuts by Robert Owen illustrate the effects of bad and good circumstances.*

HOLLAND ABANDONS SLAVE TRADE
Britain and the USA co-operate to suppress the slave trade, but with little effect. Sweden, however abandoned the trade in 1813 and Holland abandons it this year.

JEWISH RIGHTS
Denmark becomes one of the first European states to grant civil rights to Jewish people and to establish universal, state-subsidized elementary education.

PHILANTHROPIC CAMPAIGN
Pioneering British industrialist Robert Owen (1771–1858) joins Quaker philanthropist William Allen and the utilitarian philosopher Jeremy Bentham (1748–1832) in a campaign to introduce improved living conditions for all textile mill workers. In 1805 Owen kept workers at his New Lanark cotton mill on full pay after the USA blocked cotton exports to the UK. He runs shops for his workers that charge fair prices and sell only pure foods.

Below: *Cossacks attempt to capture Napoleon at Brienne; the Russians had marched on Paris by this time.*

Hundred Days and Congress of Vienna

NAPOLEON ESCAPES FROM ELBA and marches on Paris. A Quadruple Alliance is formed and, after a 100-day campaign, he is finally defeated at the Battle of Waterloo and banished to St Helena. The Congress of Vienna redraws the frontiers of Europe. A volcanic eruption in the East Indies causes climate change. Light refraction is explained and a new word, "biology", enters the language.

Above: *Marshal Gebhard Leberecht von Blücher.*

❋ 1815 ❋

JAN	8	Battle of New Orleans: Americans defeat the British, news of the peace not having reached them
MAR	1	Napoleon escapes from Elba, lands at Cannes; Marshal Ney, sent to oppose him, joins him
	13	Louis XVIII flees to Ghent, Belgium
	20	Napoleon enters Paris
	25	Quadruple Alliance to fight Napoleon: Britain, Prussia, Russia, Austria
APR	7	Volcano Tamboro explodes in Dutch East Indies: 92 000 people killed, world climate upset for a year
	12	Austria declares war on Joachim Murat, King of Naples
MAY	3	Austrians defeat Murat at Tolentino

JUNE	9	Congress of Vienna finishes sorting out European frontiers
	14	Napoleon leads an army into Belgium to confront the Allies
	16	Battle of Ligny: Napoleon drives Prussian army back
		Battle of Quatre Bras: Allies defeat French under Marshal Ney
	18	Battle of Waterloo: Duke of Wellington defeats Napoleon; Prussians led by Marshal Blücher pursue the French
	22	Napoleon abdicates again
JULY	7	Allies and Louis XVIII enter Paris
AUG	2	Napoleon is exiled to St Helena
DEC	7	Ney is shot after trial for treason

Below: *Marshal Michel Ney is tried for high treason and executed by firing squad.*

Hundred Days

Napoleon escapes from Elba and returns to France, starting a 100-day military campaign that ends in defeat at Waterloo in June. In August, he is finally banished to St Helena in the South Atlantic.

Congress of Vienna

The Allies agree the final peace treaty at the Congress of Vienna. Holland, Belgium and Luxembourg are united, Switzerland is guaranteed neutrality, Austria gains Venetia, and Prussia gains land in western Germany and northern Saxony. A German Confederation is set up under Austrian domination, and the Spanish and Portuguese royal houses are restored. Britain keeps all her imperial conquests. The emperors of Austria and Russia and the king of Prussia form a reactionary Holy Alliance, which other European powers are invited to join; France and most others accept the invitation, although Britain does not.

Light Refraction

The way light waves change direction by hitting reflective surfaces, known as refraction, is explained by French physicist Augustin Fresnel (1788–1827). It will give support to the transverse wave theory of light and will have a practical application in replacing mirrors with lenses in lighthouses.

Biology

Frenchman Jean Baptiste de Lamarck (1744–1829) distinguishes between vertebrate and invertebrate animals. While expounding this idea he also introduces the term "biology" into scientific language.

Safety Lamp

Englishmen Humphrey Davy (1778–1829) and George Stephenson (1781–1848) both invent miners' safety lamps. They are used for illuminating mine shafts where a naked flame might cause an explosion due to the presence of "firedamp" or methane gas.

The Three Graces

The Neoclassical style (smooth, perfect and white) of Venetian sculptor Antonio Canova (1757–1822) reaches its peak in this sculpture.

Right: *Delegates gather at the Congress of Vienna to establish the new shape of Europe after the final defeat of Napoleon.*

DIE ELIXIERE DES TEUFELS

German writer and composer Ernst Theodor Amadeus Hoffmann (1776–1822) is famous for a series of short stories and, most successful of all, this single novel. His work combines the dark and the bizarre in tales that grip the reader. Although his output is small, Hoffmann's grotesquerie earns him the role of Romantic prose writer *par excellence*.

ADMIRALTY, ST PETERSBURG

Russian architect Adrian Dmitrievitch Zakharov (1761–1811) rebuilds the St Petersburg Admiralty in a blend of styles — classical pillars, baroque dome and gothic spire — which is like nothing in Western Europe. It is a uniquely Russian synthesis.

YACHT CLUB

The Yacht Club is formed at Cowes on the Isle of Wight in Britain. The club is at the heart of the organization of yacht racing. It later becomes the Royal Yacht Club and is much imitated in other countries, including the United States where the New York Yacht Club is formed in 1844.

Left: *The uniforms, arms and armour worn by the cavalry of the French Royal Guard.*

VOLCANIC ERUPTION

An eruption of the volcano Tambora on Sumbawa island in the East Indies kills thousands, produces tidal waves, and causes a change in climatic conditions, bringing frost and heavy snows in June and July.

AMSTERDAM POPULATION DROPS

The population of Amsterdam, Holland, is found to have fallen from 221 000 in 1795 to 190 000 in 1815 as a result of the Agrarian Movement — the migration of the population to farming and the countryside.

BURCKHARDT IN MECCA

Swiss explorer Johann Ludwig Burckhardt (1784–1817) visits Mecca, the Muslim holy city, and stays for four months, making a detailed study. He is accepted as a true believer and a great Muslim scholar.

Robert Fulton
1765–1815

Pennsylvanian-born American engineer Robert Fulton dies, the first person to make a viable paddle steamer. He began his working life as a painter and studied in London. From 1797 he spent time in Paris, where he invented a submarine torpedo and experimented with ideas for steamboats. In 1806 his vessel the *Clermont* travelled 241.4km (150mi) along the Hudson river in only 32 hours. The year before his death, he launched the first steam warship.

Above: *A map of the deployment of Napoleon's and Wellington's armies at the Battle of Waterloo.*

Above: *The Battle of Waterloo in progress. Heavy rain early in the day prevents Napoleon's planned early attack.*

Above: *British troops capture French guns at Waterloo, despite the superiority of the French artillery.*

Above: *The Battle of New Orleans, last battle in the war between Britain and the USA.*

Above: *After defeat at Waterloo, Napoleon is unable to gather another army and is forced to abdicate once again. After failing to escape to the USA, he is exiled to the island of St Helena, off the west coast of Africa, where he will spend the remainder of his years.*

STETHOSCOPES, SCHUBERT AND SEVILLE

*I*N THE USA, James Monroe is elected president. Indiana becomes the nineteenth state of the USA. Florida becomes a refuge for freed slaves. Argentina declares independence from Spain. The German diet, or parliament, meets for the first time. The fire extinguisher and stethoscope are invented. Franz Schubert extends the range of the *Lied* and Rossini produces *The Barber of Seville*.

Left: *James Monroe, president-elect of the USA.*

✳ *1816* ✦

JAN	16	John, exiled Prince Regent of Portugal, is proclaimed emperor of Brazil	NOV	5	Prince Metternich opens the first diet (parliament) of the German Confederation
MAR	20	Maria, queen of Portugal, dies; she is succeeded by her son John, emperor of Brazil		5	James Monroe is elected fifth president of the USA
JULY	9	Under the leadership of General José de San Martín, the United Provinces of La Plata (Argentina) are declared independent from Spain	DEC	2	In Britain, Londoners riot over parliamentary reform
				11	Indiana becomes the nineteenth state of the USA

Above: *Gauchos on the Argentinian pampas; Argentina declares itself independent from Spain this year.*

MONROE ELECTED PRESIDENT
James Monroe (1758–1831), US Secretary of State, wins the presidential elections, easily defeating his Federalist opponent Rufus King. Daniel D Tompkins is elected vice-president. The following month Indiana becomes the nineteenth state of the Union.

EMPEROR OF BRAZIL
John, Prince Regent of Portugal, becomes emperor of Brazil, recognizing the wealth and semi-independence of the Portuguese colony. In March he becomes John VI of Portugal on the death of his mother, the insane Maria I.

INDEPENDENT ARGENTINA
At a congress at Tucuman, the United Provinces of La Plata, or Argentina, declare their independence from Spain.

GERMAN DIET
Under the leadership of Prince Metternich, chief minister of Austria, the first diet or parliament of the German Confederation opens. The Confederation includes 39 states, ranging from the vast and powerful Austria and Prussia to four small city states; some German states lie outside its borders, while some non-German states are included. Proceedings are dominated by Austria and Prussia, who impose restrictions on other states.

PERSIAN-AFGHAN WAR
Persian forces capture Herat, northwest Afghanistan, but are driven out by Afghans.

FIRE EXTINGUISHER
A 4.8-gallon (4 UK gallons) water-based fire extinguisher is invented by Capt George Manby in England. The mixture of water and pearl-ash (granula crystalline potassium carbonate), which he describes as "anti-phlogistic fluid", is forced from a copper cylinder using compressed air.

STETHOSCOPE
Medicine benefits from the invention of the stethoscope, which enables doctors to listen for irregularities in the heart and lungs of their patients. French physician René Laennec, its inventor, first employs the stethoscope in Necker Hospital, Paris, where he is chief physician.

Above: *Prince Clemens Lothar Wenzel Metternich, the Austrian statesman and ambassador to France.*

Above: *Mining with blast lamps, fired by bellows. These will soon be replaced with safety lamps.*

SEED PACKETS
The Shaker community of Union Village, Ohio, becomes the first to market vegetable seeds in packets. Horticulture will benefit significantly from this development by standardizing the quality of crops.

REFUGE FOR RUNAWAY SLAVES
In the United States, Florida, a free (non-slave) state, becomes a refuge for runaway slaves. American troops lay siege to Fort Apalachicola, abandoned by the British and used by slaves as a base to attack slave-holders, and 270 fugitives are killed in a powder explosion.

CELERIPEDE
The celeripede, a pedal-less bicycle, invented by the French physicist, Joseph Nicéphore Nièpce, is a primitive two-wheeled bicycle. It is moved by the action of feet on the ground.

ERLKONIG
With *Erlkönig* and hundreds of other songs, Viennese composer Franz Schubert (1797–1828) extends the drama, expressiveness and musical scope of the *Lied*. The musical response he sets to the words is both more subtle and more diverse than that of any previous composer, and Schubert's songs will influence virtually every future classical songwriter.

KUBLA KHAN
English Romantic poet Samuel Taylor Coleridge (1772–1834) wrote his masterpiece, "Kubla Khan", in 1797, the words and images allegedly coming to him in a dream after he had taken opium. This year he publishes the poem and it becomes a critical success because of its exotic imagery, in spite of the fact that the author says it is "a psychological curiosity".

ELGIN MARBLES
The marble frieze from the Parthenon, taken to London by Lord Elgin (1766–1841), a former British ambassador to the Ottoman Empire, has been bought by the British Museum for a nominal price. Elgin's claim to have had permission to remove the marbles from Athens is disputed. The Greek government will spend hundreds of years trying to get the marbles back.

Left: *Coffee farming in Brazil, which gets a new emperor this year.*

Above: *Samuel Taylor Coleridge publishes his poems "Christabel" and "Kubla Khan" this year.*

THE BARBER OF SEVILLE
One of the most famous and successful of all of his comic operas, Italian composer Gioacchino Rossini's (1792–1868) *The Barber of Seville* is a work of sparkling tunefulness and wit. A failure at its first performances, it soon convinces audiences, and becomes part of the repertoire.

ALLE PRESSAMENTE ALLE MORTE
Giacomo Leopardi (1798–1837), the sheltered son of an Italian nobleman, is becoming one of Italy's greatest lyric poets. This early work establishes him.

FIRST FIGHT
The fight between Tom Beasley and Jacob Hyer, "Father of the American Ring", in New York is considered the first in the United States to be fought under international rules and with paying spectators.

Above: *Franz Schubert, composer of "Erlkönig", the "Earl King".*

Left: *Shooting alligators on a plantation in the deep south of the USA.*

MISSISSIPPI, CHLOROPHYLL AND THE HOBBY HORSE

MISSISSIPPI BECOMES THE TWENTIETH state of the Union, creating an equal number of slave-owning and non-slave owning states. Simón Bolívar arrives in Venezuela to head up a rebel force. Chlorophyll, the green pigment in plants, is discovered, and an early precursor of the bicycle — the hobby horse — is invented. Parkinson's disease is identified. English novelist Jane Austen dies.

Above: *British inventor and engineer, James Watt.*

✤ 1817 ✤

FEB	10	Austria, Britain, Prussia and Russia agree to reduce the army of occupation in France
MAR	4	James Monroe is inaugurated as president of the United States
	4	Fearing revolution, the British government suspends Habeas Corpus (a law preventing a person from being held without trial)
APR	28	Britain and the USA agree to limit naval forces on the Great Lakes
JULY	6	Simón Bolívar declares all black slaves in Venezuela shall be free
	18	English novelist Jane Austen dies aged 41
SEP	23	Spain agrees to end the slave trade

OCT	18	German students meeting at Iéna make speeches about revolution
NOV	5	Mahrattas in India attack British in Indore, Nagour and Poona
DEC	10	Mississippi becomes the twentieth state of the USA

Above: *A new form of transport takes to the road.*

Left: *Waterloo Bridge, built across the Thames this year and named after the victory over the French.*

MISSISSIPPI
Mississippi becomes the twentieth state of the Union. As it is a slave-owning state, the Union is now divided equally between slave-owning and non-slave owning states; the new state only allows white male property owners to vote in elections.

OHIO TREATY
Native Americans in Ohio sign a treaty ceding their remaining four million acres of territory to the United States. In Georgia, backwoodsmen attack Indians close to the Florida border, starting the Seminole War.

VENEZUELAN LIBERATION
In 1816 Simón Bolívar unsuccessfully invaded Venezuela and was forced to retreat to Haiti. Now he returns to Venezuela to command rebel forces. He enlists the help of José Antonio Páez and seizes the lower Orinoco basin.

PUNISHMENT BY TREADMILL
The treadmill is introduced as a form of punishment in Brixton prison in London, UK. It was invented by William Cubitt of Ipswich.

CHLOROPHYLL
Chlorophyll, the green pigment in plants, responsible for photosynthesis, is discovered by two French chemists, Pierre Pelletier (1788–1842) and Joseph Caventou (1795–1877). An important botanical development, it will help scientists to understand the physiological workings of plants.

PARKINSON'S DISEASE
British surgeon James Parkinson (1755–1824) recognizes "shaking palsy" as a specific disease to which he contributes his name. It will later be termed Parkinsonism in recognition of its being a condition rather than a disease.

FLATFORD MILL
English artist John Constable's visual style is now mature, and he produces one of his most famous landscapes. Typically, it depicts the impact of humanity on the landscape, so that although he is painting nature with great vividness, it is a place which people have made, in marked contrast to the raw "sublime" of the Romantic poets.

CATTLE-REARING
Hereford cattle are imported for the first time into the USA and are raised in Virginia. They are to be bred for cattle-rearing on the Central Plains.

AMERICAN DESERT
American explorer Stephen Harriman Long (1784–1864) sets out to survey between the Platte and Canadian rivers, completing the survey in 1820. The report of his expedition erroneously labels the Great Plains region "The Great American Desert" due to the lack of trees.

MODERN ATHLETICS MEETING
The first modern athletics meet is held at Necton in England.

Left: *Steamboats on the Mississippi river. The state of Mississippi joins the Union this year.*

Right: *Mississippi is a slave state and depends on slave labour to harvest the cotton.*

Left: *Venezuela gains its independence this year and steamships ply the Orinoco river.*

Above: *Government spies and* agents provocateurs *foment unrest in the north of England.*

Above left: *The Seminole War is triggered by backwoodsmen in Georgia skirmishing with Indians.*

Above: *Political commentator William Cobbett leaves England for the USA this year.*

Jane Austen
1775–1817

The modest and retiring English novelist Jane Austen has died in Winchester of a mysterious wasting disease. One of the youngest of a country rector's seven sons and daughters, she drew her material from her happy but circumscribed life in Hampshire and Bath, and described herself as working on a small piece of ivory with a fine brush. Her closely observed stories of country drawing-room life show an understanding of morals and manners, a gift for dialogue, and a delicate sense of irony that will be increasingly well regarded by future generations. Her novels include *Sense and Sensibility* (1811), *Pride and Prejudice* (1813), and *Emma* (1816).

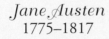

DIE AHNFRAU
The Viennese dramatist, Franz Grillparzer (1791–1872), establishes himself with the first performance of this early tragedy. It is influenced by the tragedy of fate (exemplified by Schiller), but shows how the characters are finally responsible for their actions.

HOBBY HORSE
German Baron von Drais patents the "Hobby Horse" or "Dandy Horse", a forerunner of the modern bicycle. It has no brakes or pedals. A rider sits on a beam between two wheels and propels the machine by pushing off with the feet.

The 49th Parallel

The US-Canadian border is fixed along the 49th parallel. Illinois becomes the 21st state of the Union. Chile declares independence from Spain following rebel victories against a Spanish army. The first ocean liner sets sail and the first recorded antenatal care takes place. In the literary world, Mary Shelley's complex novel *Frankenstein* creates an immediate sensation.

Above: *Mary Shelley writes her gothic masterpiece,* Frankenstein.

❧ 1818 ❧

Jan	6	In India, Indore comes under British rule	June	3	In India, Poona comes under British control
Feb	5	Death of King Karl XIII of Sweden; Jean Bernadotte succeeds him as Karl XIV	Oct	9	The Allies agree to end the occupation of France
	12	Chile declares itself independent of Spain		15	Austria, Britain, Prussia and Russia renew the Quadruple Alliance
	24	Spain agrees to sell Florida to the USA		20	The US-Canadian border is fixed at the 49th parallel
Apr	5	Bernardo O'Higgins and José de San Martín finally defeat a Spanish army in Chile	Dec	3	Illinois becomes the 21st state of the USA
May	26	Bavaria in Germany adopts a new constitution			
	28	Prussia abolishes internal customs duties			

CHILE INDEPENDENT

Independence from Spain is declared in the national capital of Santiago. The country safeguards its independence by defeating Spanish royalist forces in April.

49TH PARALLEL

The southern border of Canada from the prairies across to the Rockies is fixed between the USA and Britain at the 49th parallel. The Oregon territory on the Pacific remains under joint control. In December, Illinois becomes the 21st state of the Union; its total population is about 40 000, including the village of Chicago. Alabama becomes the 22nd state the following December.

OCEAN LINER

The 424-ton sailing-packet *James Monroe* is launched to become the first ocean liner. Owned by the Black Ball Line of America, her maiden voyage is from New York to Liverpool, carrying only eight passengers.

BLOOD TRANSFUSION

Guy's Hospital, of London, becomes the scene of the first transfusion of human blood. Dr Thomas Blundell uses the blood from several donors to supply his patient. It is not a success because little is known of blood groups, but it marks the beginning of important medical progress.

Above: *Elegance and fashion for both sexes characterizes the English Regency period.*

BITTERS

Angostura bitters are produced as a stomach tonic for people living in the tropics by a German physician, Johann Gottlieb Benjamin Siegert at Angostura (Ciudad Bolívar) in Venezuela. It is made from gentian root, rum and other ingredients.

CHUBB LOCKS

Jeremiah Chubb, a British ironmonger, invents a lock so secure that a professional lockpicker is unable to open it.

Left: *British poet John Keats publishes his poem "Endymion" this year.*

Above: *Canada's southern border is officially fixed along the 49th parallel.*

Left: *The Spanish make a last attempt to prevent Chilean rebellion, and there is a great battle at Maipo. Chile finally gains independence under Bernardo O'Higgins.*

Right: *A royalist cartoon caricatures freedom fighter Bernardo O'Higgins as a donkey being ridden by San Martín.*

NATIVE AMERICANS SELL LAND
Chicasaw Indians sell all their remaining lands north of southern Tennessee for $300 000, to be paid by the US government over 15 years.

PATTERN LATHE
American engineer, Thomas Blanchard (1788–1864), invents a lathe that uses a pattern to duplicate its movements. By copying a pattern, his lathe is put to work manufacturing gun stocks which are all exactly the same dimensions and therefore interchangeable.

DON JUAN
British poet Lord Byron's search for poetic mastery has been the search for the best verse-form. Finally he triumphs, with the use of the *ottava rima* (eight-line) stanza, which gives him scope for both narrative and wit. He publishes the first two cantos of *Don Juan*, a vast, sprawling mock-epic, which remains unfinished, many cantos later, at the poet's death. Critics hate the poem (it is coarse and "impious"); the public loves it.

ANTENATAL CARE
The first recorded act of antenatal care takes place when François Mayor, a Swiss surgeon, listens through a stethoscope to the heartbeat of a foetus in the womb and publicizes his findings. The technique becomes common obstetric practice in Europe.

FRANKENSTEIN
The gothic tale *Frankenstein, or the Modern Prometheus* by English writer Mary Shelley (1797–1851), causes an immediate sensation. It tells how the scientist's creation turns against its creator, becomes a murderer and destroys its maker in the end. Sometimes seen as the first work of science fiction, the novel's philosophical discussion of the power of the scientist as creator of life has a modern relevance.

THE WORLD AS WILL AND IDEA
German philosopher Artur Schopenhauer (1788–1860) describes a pessimistic philosophy which sees the Will as the only true reality. The world is created by the Will, but is evil, and it is mankind's duty to pursue a life of asceticism, so that the world will finally cease to exist. Both God and Free Will are illusions.

GOITRE TREATMENT
French physician Jean Dumas (1800–84) discovers that iodine can be used in the treatment of goitre. The swelling of the thyroid gland in the neck can be reduced by supplementing the diet with iodine, thereby improving the comfort of the sufferer.

BROOKS BROTHERS
Henry Sands Brooks imports woollen clothing and cloth from Britain. He opens a menswear shop in New York, which is to become the Brooks Brothers chain.

PACKING PORK
Salt pork becomes popular in Cincinnati, USA, where food merchants begin packing pork in brine-filled barrels.

NORTHWEST PASSAGE
Arctic navigator, Edward Parry (1790–1855), leads an expedition of HMS *Hecla* and HMS *Griper* to explore the Northwest Passage. The passage to the north of Canada had been sought for many years as a shortcut to the Far East. The ships winter in the area and disprove earlier reports of mountains blocking Lancaster Sound.

ENDYMION
The first major poem of English poet John Keats (1795–1821), *Endymion*, is panned by the critics. Its story of pastoral love is an allegory of the writer's search for perfection, told with lavish use of luxuriant imagery.

SINGAPORE AND SIMON BOLIVAR

THE CARLSBAD DECREES are introduced into the German Confederation to stamp out dissent and reduce revolutionary movements. South American liberator, Simón Bolívar, defeats the Spanish at the Battle of Boyaca. British troops fire on peaceful protesters in Manchester, UK. Singapore is founded. The paddle-steamer *Savannah* steams and sails across the Atlantic and mass-production of chocolate begins.

✵ 1819 ✵

FEB	6	British colonial administrator Stamford Raffles founds a settlement at Singapore
MAY	1	France introduces freedom of the press
AUG	7	Battle of Boyaca, Venezuela; royalist army surrenders to Bolívar
	16	Peterloo Massacre: in Manchester, England, troops charge a crowd listening to speeches about parliamentary reform, killing eleven people
SEP	20	In the German Confederation, the Carlsbad Decrees abolish the freedom of the press and bring universities under state control

DEC	7	Hanover in Germany adopts a new constitution
	14	Alabama becomes the 22nd state of the USA
	17	Simón Bolívar becomes president of the republic of Greater Colombia

Above: *The Rutt flat-bed cylinder, a hand-operated machine for printing books.*

Above: *Hussars cut down their fellow countrymen at the Peterloo Massacre in the north of England.*

111

Above: *Simón Bolívar, "the Liberator", becomes president of a new state, the republic of Greater Colombia.*

PETERLOO MASSACRE
The local militia fire on a 60 000-strong crowd gathered on St Peter's Fields, Manchester, UK, who are peacefully demanding parliamentary reform and an end to the Corn Laws, which are driving up the cost of bread. At least eleven people are killed and many hundreds injured. The shootings lead to a series of repressive measures against radicals.

BOLIVAR BECOMES PRESIDENT
Simón Bolívar, having established his capital at Angostura (now Ciudad Bolívar) attacks the Spanish viceroyalty of New Granada. Leading an army of some 2500 men, he crosses the Apure valley, climbs the bitterly cold Andean passes, and defeats surprised Spanish forces at the Battle of Boyaca. Three days later he enters Bogotá and in December is made president. A new state is created: the republic of Greater Colombia, consisting of present-day Venezuela, Colombia, Ecuador and Panama.

THE RAFT OF THE MEDUSA
With its rendering of a small subject on an heroic scale, French artist Théodore Géricault's picture is quickly seen as the Romantic painting *par excellence.* It portrays a group of survivors of a shipwreck on a raft; they are experiencing a moment of hope, as they see a ship in the distance, but the hope will be dashed.

FLORIDA
The USA and Spain sign a treaty granting the whole of Florida to the USA. The treaty ends 300 years of Spanish control over Florida, and allows the USA to end both the runaway slave colonies in the region and Native American incursions into the southern US states.

CHOCOLATE MANUFACTURE
The first eating chocolate to be manufactured in blocks and on an industrial scale, appears in Switzerland. François-Louis Cailler sets up his chocolate factory in Vevey, Switzerland, bringing the manufacturing of confectionery into a new age.

SINGAPORE
The East India Company under Stamford Raffles (1781–1826) establishes a British settlement on the island of Singapore in southeast Asia. The settlement is the first British colony east of India.

Above: *Chocolate is made available in blocks and quickly becomes very popular with the general public.*

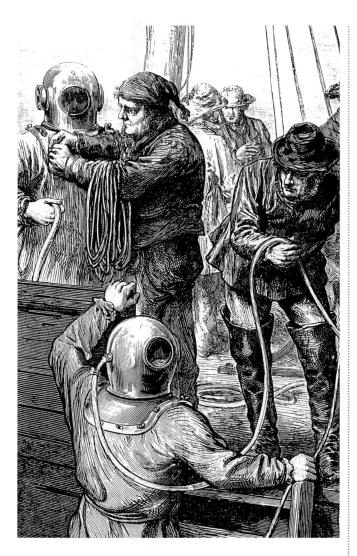

Above: *Augustus Siebe's pressurized diving suit allows divers to penetrate further into the ocean's depths.*

DIVING SUIT
The "modern" pressurized diving suit is invented by German engineer, Augustus Siebe (1788–1872). Although still supplied by an air-line, the diving suit enables divers to descend into deeper waters for purposes of exploration and marine engineering operations.

TROUT QUINTET
Franz Schubert's quintet, which includes a set of variations on his own song, "The Trout", hence its name, becomes one of the most popular of all chamber works. Its combination of humour and seriousness, drama and gentleness, make it typical of the composer.

TRANSATLANTIC STEAM CROSSING
The paddle-steamer *Savannah* becomes the first self-propelled vessel to cross from America to Europe. In fact she uses a combination of steam and sail, but nevertheless establishes steam power as the way forward for long-haul shipping.

NAPHTHALENE
The main constituent of moth-balls is discovered in coal tar by British chemist, John Kid (1775–1851). The white crystalline hydrocarbon also finds uses in the manufacture of dyes and explosives.

US PRIVATE SCHOOLS
The US Supreme Court distinguishes between public and private colleges and frees private institutions from state control, paving the way for the creation of hundreds of private schools.

CARLSBAD DECREES
Prince Metternich introduces the repressive Carlsbad Decrees throughout the German Confederation in order to stamp out dissent and check revolutionary and liberal movements. The following month, Prussia sets up a *Zollverein* or customs union with Schwarzburg-Sonderhausen in Northern Germany, the first step to establishing German unification.

GAS LIGHTS UP LONDON
In the UK, more than 50 000 London houses are lit by gas supplied by the Gas Light and Coke Co, which owns more than 450.6km (280mi) of gas mains. London's Oxford Street is a beautiful sight at night, with hundreds of small shopfronts lit by gas lamps.

EISTEDFODD REVIVED
The eistedfodd, the medieval Welsh gathering for literature, poetry and music, is revived at Carmarthen, Wales.

James Watt
1736–1819

The Scottish engineer and inventor James Watt, who devised the system of measuring power in terms of horsepower, has died. In 1763–4, when working as a mathematical instrument maker at the University of Glasgow he developed a means of vastly improving the steam engine by supplying a separate condenser and, with Matthew Boulton, began manufacturing the new engine for use in industry in 1774. He took out several patents during the 1780s, including one for a steam locomotive. His name will be given to the unit of power, the watt.

SLAVERY AND LIBERATION

*I*N THE UNITED STATES, slavery becomes a major issue as the country divides north and south between slave-owning and non-slave owning states. An uneasy compromise is reached with the Mason-Dixon line. Central and South American countries successfully achieve independence and with the Monroe Doctrine the United States prohibits European interference in American affairs and any attempt by European powers to re-colonize any part of the continent. Liberal revolts break out in Spain and Italy, and the Greeks successfully fight a bitter war of independence against Turkey.

Transport makes great strides as new canals and bridges are opened but the first step towards a transport revolution occurs when the world's first passenger railway service runs in Britain.

∽ 1820–1829 ∽

KEY EVENTS
of the
DECADE

MISSOURI COMPROMISE

SPANISH REVOLT

PERUVIAN WAR OF INDEPENDENCE

LIBERIA FOUNDED

GREEK WAR OF INDEPENDENCE

SANTA FE TRAIL ESTABLISHED

MONROE DOCTRINE

ANGLO-BURMESE WAR

JEDEDIAH SMITH CROSSES THE
MOJAVE DESERT

CHEROKEE NATION ESTABLISHED

BLAST FURNACE INVENTED

ELECTRIC MOTOR DESIGNED

BRAILLE INVENTED

SEWING MACHINE DEVELOPED

ELECTROMAGNETISM DEMONSTRATED

ERIE CANAL OPENS

CHOCOLATE MANUFACTURED

WORLD POPULATION

1090 MILLION

(ESTIMATE)

Charles X of France, the last of a long line of French kings.

The Battle of Navarino.

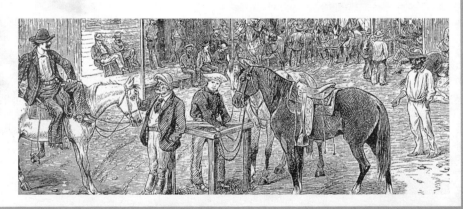

Cowboys in Texas.

COMPROMISE IN THE USA, REVOLUTION IN SPAIN

THE MISSOURI COMPROMISE divides the American states into slave-owning and non-slave owning states. John Monroe is re-elected president of the United States. Revolts break out in Spain, Naples and Portugal. South America continues to shake off Spanish domination as Peru makes the first moves towards liberation. The Venus de Milo is discovered, long trousers come into fashion, and Oersted demonstrates electromagnetism.

❧ 1820 ❧

JAN	1	Revolution breaks out in Spain
FEB	23	The Duc de Berry, heir to the French throne, is assassinated
MAR	3	Maine becomes 23rd state of the USA; it is a non-slave owning state
	6	Missouri Compromise: move to keep the numbers of slave-owning and non-slave owning states equal in the USA
	7	Ferdinand VII of Spain is forced to restore the constitution of 1812
	30	France renews censorship of the press
APR	4	US Land Law fixes the price of land at $1.25 an acre
JUNE	8	German Confederation is authorized to interfere in affairs of German states that cannot keep order

JULY	2	Revolt in Naples against the rule of Ferdinand I, King of the Two Sicilies
AUG	26	Revolution in Portugal

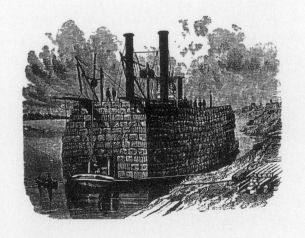

Above: *A cotton steamer on the Mississippi.*

MISSOURI COMPROMISE

In the USA, Congress agrees the Missouri Compromise under which Missouri is admitted to the Union as a slave state, Maine as a free state, and slavery is to be prohibited in the northern part of the Louisiana Purchase area, of which Missouri is a part. The Compromise is passed in an attempt to balance the growing divide between northern and southern US states. Slavery is prohibited north of the Mason-Dixon Line. However, the compromise pleases no-one, as the USA is now fiercely divided between those in favour of, and those opposed to, slavery.

PERUVIAN WAR OF INDEPENDENCE (1820–25)

After defeating the Spanish colonial rulers of Chile, José de San Martin, assisted by the Chilean fleet under Lord Thomas Cochrane, moves 4000 troops by sea to Peru. In July 1821, he enters Lima and declares Peruvian independence. He passes command to Simón Bolívar, the revolutionary leader, who defeats Spanish royalists at the Battles of Junin and Ayacucho in 1824. Upper Peru is named "Bolivia" in honour of Simón Bolívar.

JAMES MONROE RE-ELECTED

James Monroe is re-elected with a landslide majority against his Secretary of State, John Quincy Adams. Monroe gains 231 electoral college votes against just one for Adams. Vice-President Tompkins is also re-elected.

LONG TROUSERS

Long trousers finally supplant breeches as the gentleman's garb of choice. They were first introduced into the USA by sympathizers of the French Revolution. Knee breeches are now only worn by the older generation.

Above: Long trousers come into fashion and are worn with great enthusiasm by young blades about town.

Above: Fashions for women at the beginning of the decade emphasize the waist.

SPANISH REVOLT

In Spain, a revolt breaks out against Ferdinand VII's failure to adhere to the liberal constitution of 1812 and his decision to send troops to the South American colonies to crush the rebellions for independence which many in Spain support. The revolt is successful, and the liberal constitution is reinstated. In addition, the Spanish Inquisition, established in 1478 by Queen Isabel of Castile, is finally abolished.

REVOLT IN NAPLES

In Naples, a revolt against the dictatorial rule of Ferdinand IV (1751–1825), led by the Carbonari and other secret societies, results in Ferdinand promising to introduce a constitution similar to that of Spain. In February 1821 he appeals to Austria for help in suppressing the revolt, which results in its failure and the return of autocratic rule.

PROCESSED RUBBER

Thomas Hancock, of London, develops his "pickle", a machine which is used to process raw natural rubber or latex by masticating it into a workable consistency. The rubber can now be employed in the manufacture of various products, such as rubber sheets.

SUSPENSION BRIDGE

Sir Samuel Brown completes a suspended road bridge across the River Tweed in England. Called the Union Chain Bridge, it has a span of 108m (360ft).

PROTO-FOOTBALL

In the US, Princeton students are recorded playing Ballown, a precursor of American Football.

Right: *A printing press designed to print both sides of a sheet of paper at the same time. Such machines are introduced to newspaper printing at the beginning of the decade.*

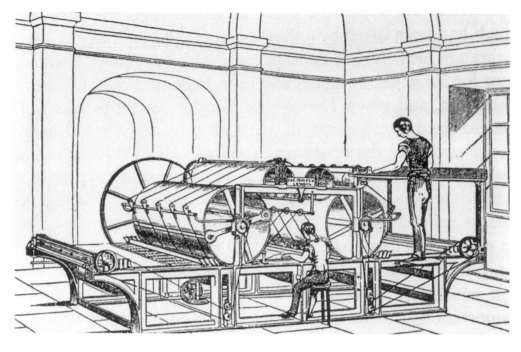

Above: *Actor Edmund Kean, who first trod the boards in London in January 1814, now plays America.*

KEAN PLAYS RICHARD III

British actor Edmund Kean (1789–1833) plays the lead role in *Richard III* in New York. Kean has established himself as the major Shakespearean actor of his time in his London debut as Shylock. His passionate and romantic style leads to two famous tours of the USA, of which this is the first.

THE EVE OF ST AGNES AND ODE TO A NIGHTINGALE

John Keats brings his style to fruition in works written in his last great year of creativity (roughly September 1818 to 1819) which are published in 1820. The imagery and passion of the "Eve", and the acceptance of mortality in the face of beauty in the "Ode" seem to sum up Keats' world.

FOOD SCARE

A food scare is caused by an English chemistry professor, Frederick Accum, who publishes *Adulteration of Foods and Culinary Poisons*, showing that food on sale in Britain is usually adulterated, some with poisons, and has to flee to Berlin to avoid prosecution.

VENUS DE MILO DISCOVERED

The Venus de Milo, a statue of the goddess of love, is found on the island of Melos. Based on an earlier classical Greek original, the Venus de Milo is one of the greatest works of Hellenistic art. It was carved by a sculptor from Antioch on the River Maeander in around 150 BC.

GEORGE III DIES

George III, king of Britain since 1760, dies at the age of 81. He had suffered from porphyria, a form of madness, since 1788. His son, Prince George, had acted as Prince Regent since 1810. George now succeeds to the throne in his own right as George IV (1762–1830).

ELECTROMAGNETISM

Danish physicist, Hans Oersted (1777–1851), links magnetism with electricity. He demonstrates the production of a magnetic field by flowing an electric current through a conductor and in doing so pre-empts the developments in electricity which follow.

SCHAUSPIELHAUS

German architect Karl Friedrich Schinkel (1781–1841), whose career is already established designing Neoclassical buildings in Berlin, extends his influence to Vienna, where he builds this new theatre.

IVANHOE

The first of Scottish author Walter Scott's novels to treat an English subject, *Ivanhoe*, a historical novel of knights and outlaws, Normans and Saxons, shows Scott extending his scope. The novel makes a big impact.

ARITHOMETER

Frenchman Charles de Colmar (1785–1870) mass-produces his calculating machine which he calls the "arithometer". Other calculating machines and early computers are soon being devised by scientists such as Charles Babbage (1791–1871).

SHIPS SIGHT GREATER ANTARCTICA

The ships of Russian Commander Fabian von Bellingshausen spot the edge of Greater Antarctica. Bellingshausen circles the continent, sailing within the Antarctic Circle for great distances.

REAL TENNIS

A Real Tennis court is built on the Champs Elysees, in Paris, France, as part of a revival of the medieval game.

Above: *French military uniforms of the decade.*

Above: *Malaga in southern Spain. A revolution in Spain this year reinstates the liberal constitution of 1812.*

THE DEATH OF AN EMPEROR

NAPOLEON BONAPARTE DIES on the island of St Helena. Anti-Turkish revolts break out in Greece. Peru declares independence from Spain, followed by Panama, Mexico and Guatemala. Faraday builds the first electric dynamo, heralding the start of the "electric age". New York streets are lit by natural gas. Pioneering American educationalist Emma Willard opens the first women's college in the USA.

✴ 1 8 2 1 ✴

JAN	26	Portuguese cortes (parliament) plans constitutional reform
MAR	5	James Monroe begins second term as US president
	13	Victor Emmanuel I of Sardinia (Italy) abdicates; succeeded by his brother Charles Felix
MAY	5	Napoleon I dies in exile in St Helena aged 52
	7	The British government takes over Gambia, the Gold Coast (now Ghana) and Sierra Leone from the Africa Company
JUNE	24	Simón Bolívar defeats the Spaniards at Carabobo, in Venezuela
JULY	28	Peru declares itself independent of Spain
AUG	10	Missouri, a slave region, is admitted as the 24th state of the USA
SEP	21	Guatemala declares independence from Spain
NOV	28	Panama declares independence from Spain
DEC	1	Santo Domingo (now part of the Dominican Republic) declares independence

PORTUGUESE CORTES

Following a revolt in Portugal in 1820 against the king's absence in Brazil and the regency at home, a *cortes* (parliament) is established. The following year, a new constitution is agreed. Portugal becomes a constitutional monarchy with a single chamber of parliament.

REVOLT AGAINST TURKS

In the Ottoman Empire, rebels led by Alexander Ypsilanti (1725–1805) cross into Moldavia and Wallachia and begin a revolt against Turkish rule. The Greeks support his invasion but it is only after his defeat in June that they too rise in revolt, beginning the lengthy Greek War of Independence.

BRITISH COLONIES IN WEST AFRICA

The Africa Company is dissolved and Britain takes over the direct control of Sierra Leone, then Gambia, and the Gold Coast. At the same time, Britain relaxes customs duties on timber imports, beginning a policy of free trade that is to dominate British politics for more than a century.

INDEPENDENCE IN SOUTH AMERICA

Mexico and Guatemala, followed by Panama and San Domingo, all declare their independence from Spain. Panama joins Colombia, while Guatemala joins Mexico. In Mexico, the new revolutionary government of Augustin de Iturbide (1783–1824) is supported by the USA.

Above: *Carl Maria von Weber, composer of the hit opera of the season,* Der Freischütz.

PERU DECLARES INDEPENDENCE

After the capture of Lima by Argentinian José de San Martin (1778–1850), Peru declares itself an independent republic from Spain. A new constitution is proclaimed in 1823 and Spanish troops are withdrawn after their defeat at Ayacucho in 1824.

FUNGI CLASSIFIED

A Swedish botanist named Elias Fries (1794–1878) devises a systematic way of classifying fungi. Similar developments are occurring with the classification of species across the entire spectrum of fauna and flora.

WEATHER CHART

German Heinrich Brandes introduces the diagrammatic representation of meteorological conditions by inventing the weather chart. It sets a precedent for weather forecasting by representing the weather in a tangible format, with obvious practical application.

DER FREISCHUTZ

The public respond enthusiastically to the first performance, in Berlin, of this opera by Carl Maria von Weber. With its blend of mystery, suspense and love, *Der Freischütz* establishes Romantic opera in Germany.

NATURAL GAS

The city of New York becomes the first to have a street lit by natural gas. Coal gas has been used for some time, but natural gas has proved difficult to contain for practical purposes, despite its abundant availability.

Above: *Dom Pedro, exiled king of Portugal, sees his country become a constitutional monarchy.*

Left: *Michael Faraday, the self-taught chemist and physicist.*

ELECTROMAGNETIC INDUCTION

Following Oersted's discoveries, English scientist Michael Faraday (1791–1867) uses the principle of electromagnetic induction to build a crude working model of an electric dynamo/motor. This proves to be a landmark event, signalling the start of the "electrical" age.

AMERICAN SCHOOLS

The English High School, the first free public school in the USA, opens in Boston, Massachusetts. Teaching is in English and its curriculum includes science, mathematics and history. The Troy Female Seminary is opened at Troy, New York, by Emma Hart Willard (1787–1870), pioneer of higher education for girls. Its radical new educational concept focuses on teaching subjects such as mathematics and philosophy.

GAMBLING

Since Louisiana legalized gambling in 1812, New Orleans has become a lucrative market for players of craps (derived from the French game, *hazard*) and other table games. *Poque*, a French card game, has evolved new rules and is now known as poker.

CONFESSIONS OF AN ENGLISH OPIUM EATER

British author Thomas de Quincey (1785–1859) makes his name with this autobiographical work. De Quincey is one of the first to write about addiction to opium and tells how the drug transforms his early experiences into symbolic dreams.

THE HAY WAIN

In what may be the most famous of all English landscape paintings, Constable brings to a climax years of studying and sketching in this favourite scene. He brings it to life, both by including important living elements (the man and the dog) and also by his technique, scattering highlights over the water. This technique mystifies the picture's first viewers.

ABOLITIONIST NEWSPAPER

In Ohio, Benjamin Lundy, a Quaker, publishes *Genius of Universal Emancipation*, an abolitionist newspaper.

Above: *Malaysian opium smokers. Thomas de Quincey describes opium addiction in his autobiographical novel.*

Left: *Gambling in Denison, Texas. Gambling has become legal in Louisiana, and soon spreads to many other US states.*

ADONAIS
This elegy to the dead poet John Keats is one of Percy Bysshe Shelley's most notable works, and a milestone in English Romanticism.

ROYAL PAVILION, BRIGHTON
The British Prince Regent employs John Nash to remodel his Brighton house in the "oriental" style. The result, a phantasmagoria of onion domes, fretwork and minarets, mixes different styles (Indian, Chinese) to create a building unlike any other.

CATHOLIC CATHEDRAL, BALTIMORE
This is the first major Catholic cathedral in the USA and the posthumous masterpiece of US architect Benjamin Latrobe (1764–1821).

Above: *A view of Baltimore, home to the first major Roman Catholic cathedral in the USA.*

Left and right: *Napoleon dies on St Helena and is buried there. In 1840 his body will be transferred to his tomb in L'Eglise du Dôme in Paris.*

Napoleon Bonaparte
(1769–1821)

Corsican-born Napoleon Bonaparte has died on the island of St Helena. His astonishing career began in the post-revolutionary period when, following his successes as commander of the army in Italy, in 1799 he was appointed first consul of France. In 1802, he was made consul for life. He introduced major social reforms, including the Code Napoléon, and in 1804 took the title of emperor. By 1807, a string of military successes had established him as head of a vast empire in Europe. However, his fortunes changed and he was defeated and forced to abdicate in 1814. He made a brief attempt to regain power but was finally overcome at the Battle of Waterloo in 1815 and banished to St Helena.

GREEKS FIGHT FOR INDEPENDENCE

*T*HE GREEKS PROCLAIM INDEPENDENCE from Turkey, ushering in a long and bitter conflict. Sympathy for the Greek revolt is widespread in Western Europe. In the United States, a major new trading route — the Santa Fe trail — is pioneered and an unsuccessful slave revolt is planned. Liberia is founded as a colony for freed Afro-American slaves. Caffeine is discovered and the Rosetta Stone is deciphered.

Above: *French artist Eugène Delacroix paints* Dante and Virgil Crossing the Styx *this year.*

⇒ 1822 ⇐

JAN	27	Greece proclaims its independence from Turkey; a long and bitter war follows
MAR	17	France introduces stricter control of the press
APR	22	Turkish forces occupy the Greek island of Chios, and massacre many inhabitants
MAY	19	General Augustus de Iturbide is elected emperor of Mexico
JUNE	24	Britain opens up trade between the West Indies and the USA
JULY	8	English poet Percy Bysshe Shelley dies aged 29
	15	Turks invade mainland Greece
SEP	23	Portugal adopts a new constitution
OCT	12	Brazil proclaims independence
	20	Congress of Verona: Austria, Britain, France, Prussia and Russia meet to discuss European problems
DEC	2	Orangemen riot in Dublin, Ireland
	4	Congress of Verona ends; France given power to intervene in Spain, where Ferdinand VII faces rebellion

Above: *George IV of England, who succeeded to the throne in 1820, at Holyrood Palace, Scotland.*

LIBERIA FOUNDED
The American Colonization Society purchases land in West Africa to set up a colony for freed slaves. Eighty-six freed Afro-American slaves travel to the colony, which, from 1824, is known as Liberia.

SLAVE REVOLT
Denmark Vesey (c. 1767–1822), a former slave who bought his freedom in 1800 for $600, which he won in a street lottery, plans and organizes an insurrection of some 9000 slaves in South Carolina, intending to take over Charleston. Betrayed by informers, Vesey is caught and hanged.

GREEK WAR OF INDEPENDENCE
Greeks fighting for their freedom from the Ottoman Empire, which controls southeast Europe, formally declare their independence from Turkish rule and draw up a liberal constitution. A cruel, repressive war follows in which the Turks massacre and enslave the Christian rebels. The Turkish army takes Janina and a Turkish fleet captures the island of Chios, slaughtering many inhabitants. The Greeks destroy the Turkish fleet. A Turkish army of 30 000 invades Greece, overrunning the whole peninsula north of the Gulf of Corinth. However, the Turks are unable to subdue the northern port of Missolonghi, which is defended by Greeks under Alexandros Mavrokordatos. By January 1823, the Turks have fallen back and the seige of Missolonghi has begun. In Western Europe, public sympathy is with the Greeks and volunteers arrive in Greece, including the poet Byron, who makes his way to Missolonghi in 1824.

BRAZIL DECLARES INDEPENDENCE
Brazil declares its formal independence from Portugal and proclaims Dom Pedro as emperor. A new constitution is adopted in March 1826, which allows for a hereditary monarchy and a general assembly of two chambers. Portugal recognizes Brazilian independence in August 1825, ending four centuries of Portuguese rule.

CRITICAL STATE
Charles Cagniard de la Tour (1777–1859), a Frenchman, discovers the phenomenon of the "critical state of liquids". It is the point at which vapour and liquid phases of a substance become indistinguishable during heating or cooling.

REVOLVER
The principal of having a firearm capable of firing more than one round by having a revolving section, is demonstrated for the first time in the five-shot flintlock made by Elisha Haydon Collier, an American living in London.

CAFFEINE
French chemist Joseph Caventou (1795–1877) discovers that alkaloid caffeine is the stimulant present in coffee. It is one of many discoveries which help scientists to understand the chemical make-up of the world around them.

MOH'S SCALE
German mineralogist, Friedrich Moh (1773–1839), proposes his method for expressing the relative hardness of a mineral. It begins with talc as the softest and runs through a series of minerals, gradually becoming harder until diamond is reached as the hardest.

SANTA FE TRAIL
William Becknell (?1796–1865), an Indian fighter and veteran of the War of 1812, leaves Missouri with a wagon train of traders for Santa Fe, Mexico, pioneering a new trading route. Last year, Becknell returned from the southern Rockies with the news that Mexico, now independent of Spanish rule, is free for trading. In the autumn, the first North Americans settle in Mexican Texas.

ROSETTA STONE DECIPHERED
The Rosetta Stone, inscribed in Greek and hieroglyphic and demotic Egyptian, and found near the Rosetta branch of the River Nile in Egypt in 1799, is deciphered by French Egyptologist Jean François Champollion. It will now be possible to read the papyri and tomb inscriptions of the Ancient Egyptians.

Above: *Former Foreign Secretary Lord Castlereagh, Marquis of Londonderry, dies this year by his own hand.*

DANTE AND VIRGIL CROSSING THE STYX
French artist Eugène Delacroix (1798–1863) exhibits this work at the Salon. The painting is bought for the French royal collection, and Delacroix is established as a leading artist.

DESTRUCTION OF HERCULANEUM
This is one of many highly dramatic paintings by John Martin (1789–1854) that become popular in France and the USA as well as in England. In Martin's work, people are overwhelmed by events and the landscape that surrounds them.

SYMPHONY NO. 8 (UNFINISHED)
Franz Schubert leaves his most famous symphony unfinished. The near-perfection of its two completed movements means that the work will be widely performed.

EUGENE ONEGIN
Russian novelist Alexander Pushkin (1799–1837) begins his masterpiece, a novel in verse which combines Romanticism and irony in a new way. It will influence many future artists, from Tchaikovsky, who bases an opera on it, to modern writers such as Vladimir Nabokov and Vikram Seth.

POEMS
Alfred De Vigny (1797–1853), sensitive and reserved French Romantic poet-philosopher, publishes his first volume of poems while still an army officer. His key themes of liberty, justice and human fate are already emerging.

ODES ET POÉSIES DIVERSES
French author Victor Hugo's first book of poems earns him acclaim; its royalist views lead to Hugo being granted a pension from Louis XVIII.

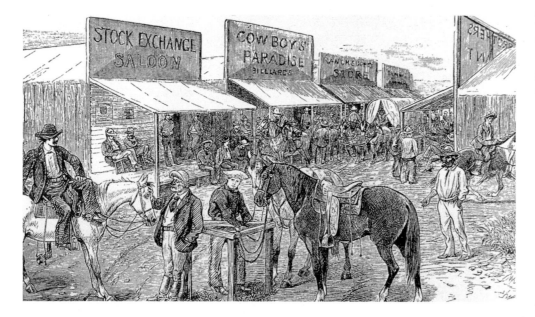

Left: *This year sees the beginning of settlement in Texas. Here cowboys gather in a small town on Sunday.*

Right: *Life on a frontier homestead in Texas.*

THE MONROE DOCTRINE

A SIGNIFICANT PLANK OF AMERICAN foreign policy is established when US President Monroe states that the US will no longer permit European colonization of the American continent or European intervention in American affairs. Bolívar becomes president of Peru. The Catholic Association is formed in Ireland to press for Catholic Emancipation. The first binoculars appear. Bourbon whisky is developed. The principle of refrigeration is discovered.

❧ *1823* ❧

MAR	18	Emperor Auguste Iturbide of Mexico is forced to abdicate
APR	6	French troops invade Spain to crush the rebellion
MAY	12	In Ireland, Daniel O'Connell forms the Catholic Association to campaign for more rights for Roman Catholics
JUNE	11	Ferdinand VII of Spain refuses to leave Madrid
	18	King John VI of Portugal annuls the constitution of 1822
JULY	1	Confederation of the United Provinces of Central America is formed by Costa Rica, Guatemala, Honduras, Nicaragua and San Salvador
AUG	31	In Spain, the French crush the revolutionaries at the Battle of Trocadero
SEP	10	Simón Bolívar is chosen as president of Peru
OCT	1	Ferdinand VII of Spain, restored, begins a reign of tyranny
NOV	13	Emperor Pedro dissolves Brazil's assembly (parliament) because of conspiracies
DEC	2	The Monroe Doctrine: US President James Monroe bans European countries from interfering in American affairs

Above: *The campaign in Ireland for Catholic rights is led by Daniel O'Connell. Moral force is preferred to violence.*

MONROE DOCTRINE

In his annual address to Congress, US President Monroe states that the USA will no longer permit European powers to intervene in the affairs of the American continent and proclaims that the era of European colonization of the Americas is over. The Monroe Doctrine is a response to threats by Russia, Prussia, Austria and France to support Spanish attempts to regain its colonies in Central and South America. British opposition to any expansion by these powers leads Britain to support the Doctrine, with naval force if necessary, thus linking British and American interests closely together.

CENTRAL AMERICA

During the year, the former Spanish Central American provinces, including Guatemala, declare their independence and form the United Provinces of Central America. Within the year, the last Spanish troops leave the mainland of Central and South America, ending more than 400 years of colonization.

SPANISH REVOLT CRUSHED

After French troops invade in June to suppress the liberal revolt underway since 1820, Ferdinand VII re-establishes full control in Spain and issues a decree for the execution of his enemies. A reign of terror breaks out in Spain.

Above: *James Fenimore Cooper, author of the "leather-stocking tales" based on his own experiences.*

Above: *Robert Stephenson, father of George, starts a foundry for the manufacture of steam locomotives.*

ITURBIDE RESIGNS

In Mexico, Augustin de Iturbide (1783–1824), self-styled emperor, is forced to resign, leading to the establishment of a republic in Mexico in 1824.

LOCOMOTIVE FOUNDRY

In Britain, father and son, George and Robert Stephenson, open the first foundry for designing and building steam locomotives, in Newcastle upon Tyne, England. Soon the age of steam transportation will reach its heyday.

SEASIDE PIER

Chain Pier, the first pier built for pleasure, opens in Brighton, on the southeast coast of England. It is constructed from an intricate framework of cast-iron components and is representative of the state-of-the-art in iron technology.

THE PIONEERS

American author James Fenimore Cooper (1789–1851) publishes *The Pioneers*, first in the series of works that will become known as the "leather-stocking tales" because of the leggings worn by the pioneer-scout central characters. In his books, Cooper perfectly evokes the atmosphere of the American wilderness, and the dangers of the pioneer life.

BOURBON WHISKY

The first sour-mash method of distilling whisky is pioneered in Kentucky by a Scot, Dr James Crow, who establishes the distinctive flavour of Bourbon whisky.

LIVING DOLL
German toy designer Johan Maelzel, of Germany, introduces his talking dolls in Paris. The dolls, which cost 10 francs each, are able to utter *"Maman"* and *"Papa"*.

BINOCULARS
The first known pair of binoculars appears in Paris. The devices are designed for three-dimensional magnified viewing of performances and are known as opera glasses. Probably first made by an instrument-maker, they soon catch on for military applications.

CATHOLIC ASSOCIATION FOUNDED
In Ireland, political leader Daniel O'Connell (1775–1847) forms the Catholic Association to press for Catholic Emancipation. Under British laws passed at the end of the seventeenth century, only Protestants are allowed to stand for the British parliament and hold other public offices, thereby excluding most Irish men, who are Catholic. The Catholic Association soon gains enormous support in Ireland.

US MILITARY DEFEAT BLACK HAWK
Black Hawk, the Sauk and Fox chief, forms an alliance with the Winnebago, Pottawotamie and Kickapoo to impede white settlement in Illinois, but is defeated by US military forces.

ASSAM TEA
Tea bushes found growing in Assam, India, are cultivated by Chinese workers smuggled into India by a British government agent, Charles Bruce.

Above: *George Stephenson begins to design and build locomotives for industrial and passenger use.*

WATERPROOF MACINTOSH
Charles Macintosh (1766–1843), a Scottish chemist, patents a cloth waterproofed by bonding rubber to it. The cloth is used for making raincoats, known as mac(k)intoshes.

REFRIGERATION
The principle of refrigeration is discovered by British chemist Michael Faraday. He finds that certain gases under constant pressure will condense until they cool.

RUGBY
In the UK, William Webb Ellis stakes his claim to be the originator of the game of rugby, by illegally picking up the ball and running with it during a game of football at Rugby School.

Edward Jenner
1749–1823

The English physician, Edward Jenner, who introduced safe vaccination against the deadly disease smallpox, has died. As a practising physician he observed the truth of the country tradition that people who had suffered from the harmless, non-infectious cowpox did not succumb to smallpox. An experiment on an eight-year-old boy proved that an injection of matter from cowpox sores prevented smallpox infection and Jenner published his results from this and further experiments in 1798. Within five years the practice of cowpox vaccination was established throughout Europe, and the Emperor Napoleon awarded Jenner a medal in recognition of his work towards the eradication of smallpox.

ALUMINIUM, PASTA AND CHOCOLATE

*T*HE FIRST ANGLO-BURMESE War begins. The US presidential election fails to result in a majority for any of the four candidates. Romantic poet Lord Byron dies fighting for the Greeks at Missolonghi. Spanish forces leave Peru. Danish and German chemists discover aluminium. Chocolate production begins in the UK. The first pasta factory is opened in Italy. French physicist Guy-Lussac invents the hydrometer.

Above: *Louis XVIII of France, sketched just a few minutes after his death.*

✦ 1824 ✦

FEB	14	First Anglo-Burmese War begins over seizure of Assam by Burma	AUG	6	In Peru, Simón Bolívar defeats a Spanish army at Junin
MAR	27	Brazil decides to hold elections for its parliamentary assembly	SEP	16	In France, Louis XVIII dies; succeeded by Charles X
				29	France suspends press censorship
APR	17	USA and Russia agree on boundary of Russian part of Alaska	NOV	2	US presidential elections: none of the four candidates gains a majority
	19	While supporting the Greek War of Independence, English poet Lord Byron dies from fever aged 36	DEC	1	Peruvians under General Antonio de Sucre defeat Spaniards at Ayachuco; Spaniards leave Peru
	30	Lisbon rebels against John VI of Portugal			
MAY	9	From the shelter of a British warship, John VI denounces Lisbon rebels			
	11	In Anglo-Burmese War, British capture Rangoon			

ANGLO-BURMESE WAR
The British governor-general of India declares war against Burma after the Burmese invade territory belonging to the East India Company. The British take the capital, Rangoon, and by 1826 they control much of the coastline, ushering in eventual British rule over the whole of Burma which will last for more than a century.

CADBURY'S CHOCOLATE
English Quaker businessman John Cadbury (1801–89) opens a tea and coffee shop in Birmingham, England, and begins experimenting with grinding cocoa beans and making chocolate.

Above: *Charles X succeeds his brother Louis XVIII to the French throne. He tries to revert to absolutism.*

BORDER DISPUTE SETTLED
The USA and Russia settle their border dispute in Alaska. In 1825 Britain agrees a similar treaty with Russia along its border with Canada.

SCOTCH MALT
Glenlivet malt whisky is produced by Scottish distiller George Smith in the first licensed Scotch whisky distillery.

Above: *John Quincy Adams is elected president of the USA after a close-run contest.*

Charles X Becomes King

In France, Charles X succeeds Louis XVIII as king and introduces a period of reactionary, conservative rule.

US Presidential Elections

In the USA, none of the four candidates — John Quincy Adams, Andrew Jackson, Henry Clay and WH Crawford — gains a majority in the presidential election. The House of Representatives meets in February 1825 and elects the Democrat-Republican John Quincy Adams (1767–1848) sixth president of the USA. The old Federalist Party of George Washington soon collapses, and the Democrat-Republican Party eventually splits in two, ushering in the two-party system which still dominates the US political system today.

Portland Cement

Joseph Aspdin (1779–1855), of Yorkshire, UK, invents Portland cement by burning a mixture of limestone and clay. The name is derived from its similarity in colour to Portland stone. It will prove to be a product of immeasurable importance for construction projects.

Iron Bridge

English railway engineer George Stephenson (1781–1848) designs and builds the Gaunless viaduct in County Durham, England. It is the first railway bridge constructed from components of cast iron and shows how versatile, as well as durable, cast iron can be.

Lifejacket

Charles Macintosh, pioneer of rubberized products, makes an inflatable lifejacket from rubber for a Captain John Franklyn. His design demonstrates just how useful inflatable rubber products can be, because they are so lightweight and compact.

Monorail

The idea of running vehicles on just one track — a monorail — instead of two, is put into practice by Henry Robinson Palmer at the Royal Victualling Yard in London. The idea behind the monorail is to save as much space as possible.

Above: *Heavy fighting in the Anglo-Burmese War, fought to defend land belonging to the East India Company from invasion by Burma. The British seize Rangoon.*

Lord Byron dies in Greece

Outpourings of public grief mark the death of the Romantic poet Lord Byron (1788–1824). Of English and Scottish parentage, he inherited his title from a great uncle, but lived his early childhood in some poverty. Despite being lame, he boxed and swam, lived and loved, and was in turn idolized and ostracized by society for his Romantic persona. After being abandoned by his heiress wife, who took with her their young baby, he travelled in 1816 to Switzerland (where he met Percy Bysshe Shelley), Venice (where Countess Guiccioli became his mistress) and Rome. Equally passionate in politics as in love, he supported the Italian revolutionaries in Italy, and the Greeks in their independence struggle against the Turks. Byron died of marsh fever, contracted at Missolonghi where he was fighting with the Greeks. His works include *Childe Harold's Pilgrimage* (1812), *Childe Harold* (1817) and *Don Juan* (1824).

Above: *George Gordon, Sixth Baron Byron of Rochdale, who dies this year after fighting in the Greek War.*

HYDROMETER
French physicist, Joseph Guy-Lussac (1778–1850), invents a hydrometer for measuring the percentage of alcohol in liquors. It works because water and alcohol have different specific gravities, so a mixture will measure somewhere between the two, depending on the ratio.

RUBBER BALLOONS
Michael Faraday (1791–1867) invents balloons made from natural rubber or "caoutchouc" as he calls it. The highly elastic material is ideal for containing gases, such as hydrogen and oxygen, in pure samples, for performing laboratory experiments.

PASTA FOR SALE
A commercial pasta factory begins production at Imperia on the Italian Riviera. It is opened by Italian entrepreneur Paolo B Agnese.

INDIAN KILLERS EXECUTED
Four white settlers in Indiana are convicted of killing nine Native Americans, including three women and four children, in an attack on a Native American village. They become the first white men ever to be executed in the USA for killing Native Americans.

RSPCA FOUNDED
The Royal Society for the Prevention of Cruelty to Animals (RSPCA), is founded in London, the first organization of its kind.

ALUMINIUM
Danish physicist, Hans Oersted (1771–1851), and German chemist, Friedrich Wöhler (1800–82), discover and isolate the metal aluminium — symbol Al. The new metal will eventually prove very valuable as a lightweight, lowly corrosive material.

SHAKER BARN
Shakers at the community in Hancock, New York State, build a round barn with a silo at its centre and stalls radiating outward. American dairy farmers copy this efficient innovation in animal husbandry, which spreads to the Midwest.

RHODE ISLAND REDS
The Rhode Island Red hen is bred for the first time at Little Compton, Rhode Island, USA. It is the result of an experiment in mating native poultry breeds with oriental fowl.

GOTHIC REVIVAL
The Gothic revival style of architecture is firmly established in London, UK, with St Luke's Church in Chelsea, designed by James Savage. Hundreds of churches will be built during the nineteenth century, in variations on this style.

THE DAWN OF THE RAILWAY AGE

JOHN QUINCY ADAMS becomes sixth president of the USA. The world's first steam-powered passenger railway opens in the UK. The Erie Canal is completed in the USA. The first wire suspension bridge is opened. Uruguay declares independence and Bolivia separates from Peru. Creek Indians lose their traditional tribal lands. Nicolas I becomes czar of Russia. Eli Whitney, creator of the cotton gin, dies.

❧ 1825 ❧

JAN	4	Ferdinand I of the Two Sicilies (formerly Ferdinand of Naples) dies; succeeded by son Francis I	JULY	6	In Britain, a new law allows workers to form trade unions but effectively bans strikes
FEB	24	Egyptian troops land in Greece to help Turks crush the independence movement	AUG	6	Bolivia separates from Peru, with Antonio de Sucre as head of state
	28	Britain and Russia agree Canadian frontier with Alaska		25	Uruguay separates from Brazil
MAR	4	US House of Representatives chooses John Quincy Adams as the sixth president	OCT	26	In the USA, the first boat to travel on the new Erie Canal leaves Buffalo on Lake Erie (arrives in New York City on November 4)
APR	27	Nobles who lost possessions in the French Revolution are compensated	DEC	1	Alexander I of Russia dies; succeeded by Nicolas I
JUNE	22	In Britain, a new law limits the working day for under-sixteen's to twelve hours		10	Brazil and Argentina go to war over Uruguay

Above: *France signs a treaty with Haiti, formerly the French colony of St Domingue, but now independent.*

Below: *A Bukharan wedding party. William Moorcroft is the first European ever to reach Bukhara.*

NEW HARMONY

The Scottish industrialist and philanthropist Robert Owen (1771–1858) establishes the utopian settlement of New Harmony in Indiana on 20 000 acres of land. The settlement is run on communal lines, with work and property shared equally among its inhabitants.

SOUTH AMERICA

In South America, the province of Upper Peru gains its independence from Peru as Bolivia. Uruguay gains its independence from Brazil. Once part of Argentina, Uruguay revolted in 1814 but was occupied by Brazil in 1820, leading to a struggle for control between the two rival powers. The two finally confirm Uruguayan independence in 1828.

NICOLAS I BECOMES CZAR

Following the death of Alexander I, his younger brother Nicolas I (1796–1855) becomes czar. Officers of the Russian army immediately stage the Decembrist Rising to demand a national assembly and constitutional reform, but the revolt is easily crushed.

ERIE CANAL COMPLETED

The 584km (363mi) Erie Canal is completed in the USA, linking Lake Erie with New York City via the Hudson river.

DRIVE BELT

Industrial drive belts made from rubber, reinforced with fabric, are manufactured by Thomas Hancock of London. The new material is favoured for its versatility, strength and flexibility.

CATERPILLAR TRACKS

English engineer, George Cayley (1773–1857), invents a prototype caterpillar track which he applies to a steam vehicle. The intention is to spread the load from the wheels of the heavy machine. Modified versions of his idea will be seen on tractors, excavators and military tanks.

FIRST PASSENGER RAILWAY

In the UK the Stockton and Darlington Railway opens, becoming the world's first public steam-powered railway passenger service. The 43.5km (27mi) journey is traversed using George Stephenson's Locomotive No.1, pulling an assortment of 28 wagons and coaches.

PORTABLE GAS

The Provincial Portable Gas Company of Manchester, England, begins supplying customers with bottled gas. The gas, which is compressed in iron cylinders, negates the need for pipeline supply and immediately proves a popular idea.

HUDSON RIVER SCHOOL OF PAINTING

The American painter Thomas Cole (1801–48) has founded the Hudson River School of Painting. This loose group of landscape painters mix the realistic and the ideal, giving American landscape a new grandeur, influenced by European Romanticism. For some 50 years, the group is the major force in American landscape painting.

RESPIRATOR

An inventor named John Roberts is awarded 50 guineas by the Society of Arts for his respirator machine. It is designed to supply the lungs with breathable air while the user is immersed in thick smoke or poisonous gases.

Alexander l of Russia
1777–1825

Alexander I, grandson of Catherine the Great, has died. He became czar in 1801 and put in motion various reforms in administration, education, science and the system of serfdom. He made peace with Napoleon at the Treaty of Tilsit in 1807, as a result of which Russia took over Sweden and, in 1809, Finland. When Napoleon broke this treaty and invaded in 1812, Alexander joined Prussia and Great Britain in the Alliance of the Fourth Coalition, which led to Napoleon's defeat and abdication in 1814. He also helped form the army that finally brought down Napoleon at Waterloo in 1815. In the post-Napoleonic era, Alexander, who developed religious mystic tendencies, founded the anti-revolutionary Holy Alliance with Austrian foreign minister Metternich.

Eli Whitney
1765–1825

The American inventor and firearms manufacturer Eli Whitney has died. After graduating from Yale he lived in Georgia, working as a teacher, but under the patronage of a general's widow he then studied law while living on her cotton plantation. There he invented the cotton gin, a machine for separating the fibre from the seeds, and for which he will be remembered. His machine was copied and he became impoverished as a result of taking out lawsuits to defend his rights. But his fortunes changed again when the government gave him a contract for manufacturing firearms; he died a wealthy man.

Above: *Czar Alexander I of Russia dies at Tagenrog and is succeeded by his brother Nicolas.*

Above: *Czar Nicolas I succeeds his brother as leader of Russia. He will take his country into the Crimean War.*

WIRE SUSPENSION
The first suspension bridge to use wire opens in Lyons, across the River Rhône. Cables comprising bundles of wire supply enormous strength, yet are flexible enough to cope with high winds, unlike cast-iron links, which are prone to stress-fracturing.

CREEKS LOSE LANDS
All remaining Creek land is ceded to the State of Georgia after substantial bribing of tribal chiefs and despite the withholding of consent by the majority of Creek people. Creek Indians flee to the woods and swamps after squatters and speculators move in.

SCANDINAVIAN QUAKERS ARRIVE IN NEW YORK
Emigration from Scandinavia to North America begins when a party of Quakers from Stavanger, Norway, fleeing hostility from the established Church, arrive in New York and establish a settlement in Upper New York State with the help of American Quakers.

DINING BEST-SELLER
The Physiology of Taste (*Physiologie du Gôut*) by Jean-Anthelme Brillat-Savarin (1755–1826), a refugee from Robespierre's Reign of Terror, is published in Paris. A witty treatise on dining, subtitled *Meditations on Transcendental Gastronomy*, it becomes a best-seller.

BRIDGER SIGHTS GREAT SALT LAKE
American fur trapper James Bridger (1804–81), one of the famous so-called mountain men, who are opening the Rocky Mountain region, has claimed to be the first white man to see the Great Salt Lake, Utah. Bridger claims that it is connected to the Pacific because of its saltiness, but many do not believe his tale.

I PROMESSI SPOSI
The masterpiece of Alessandro Manzoni (1785–1873), father of the Italian novel, *I Promessi Sposi* concerns two peasants, whose marriage plans are upset because a local lord is infatuated with the bride. The work is valued for its portrayal of character, and also for its essentially Italian themes — the oppression of Italy under foreign rule, and the life of the peasants.

SUSPICIOUS DEATH
A British spy, William Moorcroft, is said to have died in mysterious circumstances in Afghanistan. He had been travelling in Central Asia since 1819, becoming the first European to reach Bukhara. During his six-year wanderings he became involved in power politics in Tibet, passing himself off as a local horse trader.

BRITAIN AND RUSSIA, GREECE AND TURKEY

BRITAIN AND RUSSIA AGREE to guarantee Greek independence under Turkey. Brazil adopts a new constitution with an hereditary monarchy and general assembly. Cooking with gas becomes a reality with the development of the gas-fuelled stove. The University of Virginia is founded and Thomas Jefferson, former US president and author of the Declaration of Independence, dies.

Above: *Thomas Jefferson, who dies this year aged 83.*

❧ 1826 ❧

FEB	24	First Anglo-Burmese War ends
MAR	25	Brazil adopts a new constitution
APR	4	Britain and Russia agree that Greece should become self-governing under Turkey
	4	Former US President Thomas Jefferson dies on the 50th anniversary of the Declaration of Independence, which he drafted
	22	Pan-American Congress unsuccessfully tries to unite the American republics
SEP	28	Russia declares war on Persia over Transcaucasia
OCT	7	Russia gains control of Danube provinces and Serbia
DEC	19	In Germany, Prussia and Mecklenburg-Strelitz sign trade treaty

Above: *Gypsy life in the Caucasus.*

Above: *A bemused giraffe arrives in France to be exhibited in Paris.*

St Petersburg Protocol

Following the fall of Missolonghi last year, which only occurred after Egyptian forces had come to the assistance of the Turks, the Greeks put themselves under British protection and appeal for British assistance. By the St Petersburg Protocol, Britain and Russia agree to mediate between the Turks and Greeks on the basis of Greek autonomy under Turkish suzerainty.

University of Virginia

Former US President Thomas Jefferson helps to found the University of Virginia and designs the university as an "academic village". Its campus design, combining teaching and living accommodation (and accommodation for the students' slaves) influences many later American universities.

Telegraph Poles

Long Island in New York, USA, becomes the first place to display telegraph poles. They are erected at the Union race track to keep telegraph cables out of harm's way, and the idea soon catches on elsewhere.

Gas Cooking

Assistant manager of the Northampton Gas Co., England, James Sharp, builds the first practicable gas-fuelled stove. Two hotels purchase his invention and their remarks, about the consistency of heating and responsiveness of the flame, trigger a new trend in cooking.

Big Top

The Great North American Circus becomes the first to operate under canvas. The big top is an innovation in temporary shelter, enabling large shows to pack up and move on to a new location easily and efficiently, becoming a familiar feature of modern culture.

Courtyard Photograph

French scientist, Joseph Nicéphore Niépce (1765–1833), uses a camera obscura to take a permanent photographic image of his courtyard. It is a positive image taken with an eight-hour exposure on to a metal plate coated with bitumen of Judea.

String Quartet in B Flat, Op. 130

Beethoven transforms the string quartet form with this, the most daring of his quartets to date. The range of emotions it evokes and its musical scope are greater than in any previous quartet. Among its six movements (rather than the usual four) are a graceful Cavatina and the last movement, the notorious Grosse Fugue, which one critic declares is "as incomprehensible as Chinese". Beethoven later writes an alternative finale for the work, but the Fugue will survive.

Birds of America

The American ornithologist, John James Audubon (1785–1851), travels to Britain with his drawings of birds, which excite interest in Edinburgh and London. He arranges for his portfolios of Birds of America to be published in parts, beginning in 1827.

Harvard Adopts Gymnastics

Gymnastics is introduced to students at Harvard College, Massachusetts, USA, by Charles Follen, a radical German professor. The exercise system was formulated by a German, Frederick Ludwig Jahn who, in the early 1800s formed the *Turnverein*, an organization of "turners" or gymnasts.

Explorer Murdered

Scottish explorer Alexander Gordon Laing (1793–1826) crosses the Sahara from Tripoli to Timbuktu. He reaches Timbuktu safely but is caught up in anti-European feeling and is murdered. His pioneering maps of Timbuktu and the Niger are destroyed.

Crossing the Mojave

American fur trader and explorer Jedediah Smith (1799–1831) sets out across the Mojave and, in 1827, is the first to reach California overland. His journey blazes the way for wagon trains to follow.

Thomas Jefferson
1743–1826

The third president of the United States of America and independence leader Thomas Jefferson has died. Virginia-born and raised, Jefferson became governor of Virginia (1779–81) and was made a member of Congress in 1783. He was an official emissary to France with Benjamin Franklin in 1784 and was appointed Secretary of State by George Washington in 1789. Vice-president from 1797–1801, he became president in 1801, and soon had huge popular support with his Republican visions for the development of the United States as a network of independent farmers. Despite inheriting a slave plantation from his father, Jefferson was opposed to slavery and was responsible for the prohibition of the slave import trade (1808). In retirement (from 1809) he founded the University of Virginia. Trained as a lawyer, he also had a passion for building, and was responsible for the design of the Virginia State Capitol, Richmond, as well as being involved in the design of many of the university buildings.

Right: *A desert caravan of the kind seen by explorer Alexander Gordon Laing on his way to Timbuktu.*

MUSIC FOR A MIDSUMMER NIGHT'S DREAM
The young German composer Felix Mendelssohn (1809–47) is prodigiously gifted. He writes this overture to Shakespeare's comedy, which will later be followed by a whole collection of incidental music for the play. The lyricism of his music and its original ideas win it immediate success.

NATIONAL ACADEMY OF DESIGN
The US National Academy of Design is founded. An important institution, it will be a training ground for many of the most important American artists of the nineteenth and twentieth centuries. It will also put on regular exhibitions.

HORNIMAN'S TEA
John Horniman, an English Quaker, begins selling tea in sealed, lead-lined packages with a proprietary name, in response to Professor Frederick Accum's 1820 report that dried thorn leaves coloured with poisonous verdigris are being sold in Britain as China tea.

BIELA'S COMET
Austrian astronomer Wilhelm von Biela (1782–1856) observes a new comet. However, Biela's comet, as it is inevitably named, proves to be rather ephemeral. Splitting into two parts some twenty years later, it is recorded as a short-period comet.

THE LAST GREAT BATTLE OF THE SAILS

*F*RANCE JOINS BRITAIN and Russia in their policy of mediation over Greece. Their combined fleet defeats the Turkish-Egyptian fleet at the Battle of Navarino, the last great naval battle of the age of sail. The principle of the turbine is developed, and German physicist Ohm expounds his law of electricity. The Cherokee Nation is founded. The German composer, Ludwig van Beethoven, dies.

❋ 1827 ❋

JAN	26	Peru secedes from Colombia
APR	4	Britain, France and Russia tell the Turks to stop fighting the Greeks
JUNE	5	Turks capture Athens
	9	Turkey rejects call for truce
JULY	3	Pedro IV appoints his brother Miguel regent of Portugal
	6	Britain, France and Russia agree to force Turkey to make peace
AUG	16	Turkey again rejects truce

OCT	1	Russians defeat Persians in Armenia
	20	Battle of Navarino: Anglo-French fleet defeats Turkish-Egyptian fleet

Above: *The Royal Palace at Athens, captured by the Turks this year.*

Above: HMS Asia *at the Battle of Navarino, the last great sea battle to use wooden ships and sail power.*

GREEK WAR OF INDEPENDENCE

Russia, France and Britain agree to recognize the autonomy of Greece under Turkish suzerainty. The Turks refuse and in September, an Egyptian fleet arrives in Greece to support them. At the Battle of Navarino, the 24 modern ships of the Allied fleets of Britain, Russia and France destroy the Egyptian and Turkish fleet. Sixty vessels are sunk or driven ashore. Navarino is the last large-scale action fought between wooden sailing ships. Following the battle, the Greeks continue their fight for complete independence.

AFRO-AMERICAN NEWSPAPER

The Freeman's Journal, the first Afro-American newspaper, is published by John Russworm (1799–1851), who last year became the first black American college graduate, and Samuel Cornish, founder of the first black Presbyterian church. *The Journal* opposes slavery, which is abolished in New York state in July, and campaigns for the education of the 10 000 former slaves who gain their freedom, and all other black people.

Alessandro Volta
1745–1827

Count Alessandro Giuseppe Anastasio Volta, the Italian inventor and physicist, has died. His experiments and discoveries in the field of electricity have given his name to the unit of electrical potential difference, the volt. His best-known inventions are perhaps the first electric dynamo (the electrophorus), which will have many important and useful applications, and the electrochemical battery (1775–1800), harnessing the power of electricity, which he applied to the development of telegraphy.

Above: King Ahmadou presides over a royal "palaver" in Mali, one of the countries visited by René Caillié.

BROWNIAN MOTION
British botanist, Robert Brown (1773–1858), records a phenomenon to be called Brownian Motion. He notices the random motion of pollen grains under his microscope. It has important implications for physics because all microscopic particles are found to move randomly in a fluid medium.

DIE WINTERREISE
This great song cycle by Franz Schubert (1797–1828), probably his most important work of all, pushes to new limits emotional expressiveness, the power of word-setting, and the sheer effect of the linked group of classical songs. Schubert's skill in word-setting will influence most later composers who write for the voice.

LUCIFERS
English chemist John Walker (c. 1781–1859) begins marketing his invention, the matchstick. He invented matches by accident when he attempted to remove a blob of potash and antimony from the end of a stirring stick, which burst into flame. The matches are sold on the streets of British cities in packs of 100 and are called "Lucifers".

TURBINE
French engineer, Benoit Fourneyron (1802–67), invents the principle of the turbine. Powered by the force of falling water, it is installed and used successfully to power a tin-plate rolling mill at Pont-sur-Lognon, France. Turbines will become an essential feature of power stations world-wide.

CAILLIE SETS OUT FOR TIMBUKTU
French explorer René Caillié (1799–1838) takes an unusual route to the forbidden city of Timbuktu. He starts on the West African coast and travels disguised as an Egyptian Arab, moving freely around the city. After a 1600-km (1000-mi) trek north across the Sahara, he reaches Tangier in 1828, becoming the first European to see Timbuktu and return alive.

FARTHEST NORTH
Polar explorer and navigator Edward Parry (1790–1855) attempts to reach the North Pole by sledge from Spitzberg. His expedition is beaten by rough ice, which makes pulling sledges difficult, and by ice drifting away from his target. Even so, Parry's expedition reaches the farthest north so far.

Above: Edward Parry explores the far north but his expedition is thwarted by terrible weather conditions.

CHEROKEE NATION

The Cherokee of the southeastern USA, who adopted a republican form of government in 1820, establish themselves as the Cherokee Nation under a constitution with an elected chief, a senate, and a house of representatives. Their reorganization has been aided by an American-Cherokee scholar, Sequoyah (c. 1770–1843), who has developed an 85-character syllabary using symbols from the Roman alphabet, enabling records to be kept in the Cherokee language.

OHM'S LAW

A fundamental law for the behaviour of electricity is expounded by German physicist Georg Ohm (1789–1854). His law states that voltage across a conductor is equal to the combined product of the conductor's current and resistance.

THE SHEPHERD'S CALENDAR

Labourer and poet of rural life John Clare (1793–1864) publishes his most famous volume of poems. Part of a vogue for working-class country poets at this time, Clare rises above fashion to produce work of keen observation and emotional impact.

POEMS BY TWO BROTHERS

The future poet laureate of England, Alfred Tennyson, and his brother Charles, publish their first book of poems. It launches Alfred Tennyson (1809–92) on a career which will see him changing the role of poet from mere writer into sage and spokesperson for the nation.

Ludwig van Beethoven
1770–1827

The great German composer Ludwig van Beethoven has died in Vienna. The prodigy son of a drunken father, who, like his own father, was Court Singer to the Elector of Bonn, he was discovered by Haydn in 1792 and went with him to study in Vienna, where he remained for the rest of his life, and where he was at first fêted as a virtuoso improviser on the keyboard. His first opus was published in 1795 and he went on to produce a host of symphonies and chamber music, one opera (*Fidelio*, 1805), and the Missa Solemnis. Most of his music was mould-breaking, but perhaps none more widely accepted as so than the Ninth Symphony with its voice solos and choral finale, first performed — like the Missa Solemnis — in 1824. From then until his death he worked on what many consider to be the finest chamber work, the five "late" quartets. His life was bedevilled by his increasing deafness which was first recognized in 1798. He was granted the freedom of Vienna in 1815, and his death is the occasion of national mourning, one of the torch-bearers at his funeral being Franz Schubert.

DICTIONARIES AND DEMOCRATS

GENERAL ANDREW JACKSON, hero of the War of 1812, is elected US president at the head of the re-named Democratic Party. Russia declares war on Turkey. The blast furnace is developed. Noah Webster publishes his landmark *American Dictionary of the English Language*. Cocoa is the new fashionable drink. A French physician discovers human organs of balance buried in the ears.

Above: *Dom Miguel, proclaimed King of Portugal.*

✦ 1828 ✦

FEB	22	Persia cedes part of Armenia to Russia
MAY	9	In Britain, Roman Catholics and Nonconformists are allowed to hold public office
JULY	4	In Britain, Daniel O'Connell is elected MP for Clare, but is barred from taking his seat because he is a Catholic
AUG	6	Mehmet Ali, ruler of Egypt, agrees to evacuate Greece
	27	Argentina and Brazil agree that Uruguay is independent
OCT	11	Russians occupy Varna, Bulgaria, in the Turkish empire
NOV	4	General Andrew Jackson wins US presidential election

Above: *Dr Thomas Arnold of Rugby, reformer of the British public school system.*

Democrat Jackson Becomes President

Andrew Jackson (1767–1845) wins the US presidential election for the "new" Democratic Party. Jackson's radical party is a coalition of southern landowners and northern workers or city-dwellers. Originally known as the Democratic-Republican Party, it was founded around the time of Thomas Jefferson. Now the party drops the name Republican, to become the Democratic Party.

Webster's Dictionary

American English is at last given its due with the publication of *The American Dictionary of the English Language*, America's first scholarly dictionary. The dictionary is compiled by American lexicographer Noah Webster (1758–1843), author of the "Blue-Backed Speller" used to teach thousands of frontier children to read. In his dictionary, Webster defines 70 000 words and their American spelling and pronunciation.

Greek War of Independence

Russia declares war on Turkey and fights for total Greek independence. In July, the three allied powers agree in London to support the Greeks, as both France and Britain are fearful of Russian intentions in the region.

Blast Furnace

James Neilson (1792–1865) invents the blast furnace at his iron foundry in Scotland. "Blast" refers to the blasts of air used to superheat the contents of the furnace. Steel can now be produced at a faster rate.

Corrugated Iron

Englishman Richard Walker comes up with the idea for corrugated iron sheeting. The corrugations give thin sheets of iron structural strength but keep weight light.

Essay on Goethe

Scottish essayist Thomas Carlyle (1795–1881) publicizes his support for German Romantic literature by publishing his *Essay on Goethe*.

Fashionable Cocoa

Dutch chocolate-maker, Conrad J Van Houten, patents a new method of making chocolate using cocoa butter, the fat pressed from cacao beans. This discovery makes chocolate less expensive to manufacture. Van Houten also markets the drink cocoa, a mild stimulant, which becomes an enormous, and fashionable, success.

Organs of Balance

Jean Flourens (1794–1867), a French physician, discovers that the semicircular canals in the inner ear are organs of balance. The discovery is hailed as a significant contribution to our physiological understanding of the design of the human body.

Manly Sports

Educationalist Thomas Arnold (1795–1842) becomes headmaster of Rugby School, a boy's public school in England. A believer in "muscular Christianity", Arnold reforms the school system, introducing football and other team sports into the curriculum, and emphasizing formation of character.

The Spectator

In the UK a new radical periodical, *The Spectator*, is produced. A weekly periodical, it becomes known for its advocacy of parliamentary reform and will continue publication well into the twentieth century.

London Zoo Opens

London Zoo, founded in 1826 by the London Zoological Society with support from Sir Thomas Stamford Raffles (1781–1826) who established the first settlement at Singapore, opens in London. It will be a forum for zoological research into wildlife and its preservation in the wild and in captivity.

Shaka
c. 1787–1828

The first-ever Zulu leader has died, murdered by his half-brothers. In 1816, Shaka became clan leader and set up an army which conquered, subdued and exterminated other peoples, leading to the establishment of the powerful Zulu kingdom throughout most of southern Africa. A dictatorial leader, he is said to have become insane after his mother's death last year.

Franz Schubert
1797–1828

The young Austrian composer Franz Peter Schubert has died in his home city of Vienna, and is to be buried close to Beethoven. He composed more than 600 songs, many of which were written for his friend the opera singer Michael Vogl. Both Schubert and Vogl were well known for their recitals. Schubert also wrote many stage, chamber and orchestral works, operas, operettas and church music, although much of his work was never performed during his life, or was performed privately. His finest work includes the "Trout" quintet (1819), the quartet known as "Death and the Maiden" (1824), and his Unfinished Symphony.

THE CLARE ELECTION

CATHOLIC RIGHTS activist Daniel O'Connell is elected MP for Clare. As a Catholic, he cannot take his seat, but does so in 1830 after the Bill for Catholic Emancipation has been passed by Parliament.

Above left: *Daniel O'Connell, known as "the Liberator".*

Above: *The Marquis of Anglesey, Lord Lieutenant of Ireland, whose regime is hated by Irish Catholics.*

Left: *Catholics favour non-violent means to achieve their rights, but Protestants are ready to fight to prevent them.*

Opposite top: *The losing candidate concedes victory to O'Connell.*

Opposite below: *Tenant farmers queue to vote in favour of O'Connell.*

MOTORS AND LOCOMOTIVES

THE TREATY OF ADRIANOPLE ends the Russo-Turkish War. Turkey is defeated and recognizes Greek autonomy. US President Andrew Jackson is inaugurated. In the UK, George Stephenson's "Rocket" wins locomotive trials and the first practicable electric motor is designed by an American physicist. Braille, the first specialized writing for the blind, is successfully developed. Japanese artist Hokusai revives the art of the "floating world".

❋ 1829 ❋

MAR	4	Andrew Jackson inaugurated as seventh US president; John C Calhoun, who was Adams' vice-president, continues in that office	AUG	6	Charles X of France dismisses the prime minister, Vicomte de Martignac
				8	Prince de Polignac becomes French prime minister
APR	13	In Britain, the Roman Catholic Relief Bill allows Roman Catholics to sit in Parliament. The Earl of Surrey is elected (May 4) as Britain's first Roman Catholic MP	SEP	14	Treaty of Adrianople ends Russo-Turkish War; Turkey recognizes Greek autonomy
			OCT	8	In Britain, locomotive Rocket wins Rainhill trials for best engine
MAY	29	Sir Humphrey Davy, British chemist and inventor of the miners' safety lamp, dies aged 50			
JUNE	19	Sir Robert Peel, British Home Secretary, creates a new police force for London; its officers are nicknamed "Bobbies" or "Peelers" after him			

Above: *English settlers in New South Wales, Australia, mapped this year by Charles Sturt.*

TREATY OF ADRIANOPLE
The Treaty of Adrianople ends the Russo-Turkish War. The defeated Turks recognize the independence of Greece, Romania and Serbia. Russia gains land south of the Caucasus at Turkey's expense and Turkey also opens the Dardanelles to all commercial vessels.

CATHOLIC EMANCIPATION
Despite the opposition of King George IV, Catholic Emancipation is finally agreed by the British parliament, allowing Catholics to stand for parliament and hold other public offices.

EMBRYOLOGY
German biologist, Martin Rathke (1793–1860), makes the remarkable discovery that bird and mammal embryos have gill arches and slits. This is undeniable evidence that life-forms are evolved from a common primal origin.

SIAMESE TWINS ON SHOW
Chang and Eng, Siamese twins joined at the chest, set sail for England where they will be exhibited by American showman PT Barnum.

ELECTRIC MOTOR
The first electric motor for practicable application is designed by American physicist Joseph Henry (1797–1878). Faraday devised the concept, but various others evolved the motor into a form that will ultimately transform the world in many ways.

VENEZUELA MOVES TO INDEPENDENCE
The separatist movement in Venezuela, led by José Antonio Páez (1790–1873), which has been disrupting Bolívar's republic of Greater Colombia, almost since its formation, gains momentum. By the end of the year, Venezuela is seceding from the republic of Greater Colombia.

STANDARD LOCOMOTIVE
British engineer George Stephenson (1781–1848) wins the Liverpool steam locomotive race in the UK. His engine, Rocket, sets the standard for the layout of future locomotives, using a horizontal boiler and side-mounted drive pistons.

BRAILLE
Frenchman Louis Braille (1809–52) invents his specialized writing for the blind (including himself) and publishes his first braille book in Paris, France. Each letter of the alphabet is represented by an arrangement of raised dots and is the culmination of developments by others since 1819.

Left: *The Duke of Wellington duels with Lord Winchilsea who has accused the Duke, a Catholic, of plotting to introduce "Popery into every department of the State". Neither party is injured.*

WOMEN'S RIGHTS

The Free Enquirer newspaper is published in New York, USA, by Frances "Fanny" Wright (1795–1852), America's first woman lecturer, and Robert Dale Owen (1801–77), social reformer and son of Robert Owen. They use it to promote women's emancipation.

BRITISH BAN SUTTEE

Suttee, the practice common among Hindu families in India, when a widow burns to death on her husband's funeral pyre, is banned by the British in India.

CHOLERA SPREADS

A cholera outbreak which began in Sumatra in 1819 and killed thousands in China and the Philippines, is now spreading from Astrakhan through Russia and is becoming a pandemic, threatening Europe.

STURT MAPS MURRAY

Explorer Charles Sturt (1795–1869) sets out to cross New South Wales from Sydney to the mouth of the Murray river. During the course of his expedition, which ends in 1830, he maps Australia's two major

Right: *George Stephenson and his engine, Rocket, the fastest engine in its class. It reaches 48kph (30mph) in trials.*

Above: Mount Fuji, Japan, an inspiration to the artist Hokusai, who painted it 36 times.

rivers, the Murray and its tributaries, and the Darling. On one occasion he narrowly avoids an attack by 600 Aborigines as he travels down the Murray. The expedition also identifies large areas suitable for settlement by arriving Europeans.

RE-DESIGNING THE WHITE HOUSE
American architect James Hoban (?1762–1831) uses an English-influenced Palladianism to re-design the residence of the US president. Benjamin Henry Latrobe (1764–1820) contributed the design of the famous porticoes. The White House was begun in 1792, but it suffered damage during the War of 1812 and has been reconstructed and rebuilt since. The State Capitol, which was damaged badly in 1812, has also been remodelled.

LES CHOUANS
With this book, French novelist Honoré de Balzac (1799–1850) begins his vast series of interconnected novels and stories, *La Comédie Humaine*. It will occupy him for the rest of his life. By developing his fictional world over some 90 works, Balzac gives himself more scope than any previous writer. The device of allowing the characters in one book to know those in another expands his canvas — and keeps readers interested.

CONTES D'ESPANGE ET D'ITALIE
The first volume of poems by Alfred de Musset (1810–57) takes Romantic themes to new extremes, notably in their passion and their fantasy.

UKIYO-E
The art of Ukiyo-e, or the "floating world", in the shape of prints of people and landscapes, is being given new life by the Japanese artist Katsushika Hokusai (1760–1849), whose landmark *Thirty-six Views of Mount Fuji* is completed at around this time. As well as the mountain, it is famous for its portrayal of skies and water, notably in "The Wave".

SEWING MACHINE
The first sewing machine is developed by a French inventor, Barthlemy Thimmonier, who wins a contract to produce French army uniforms.

GOLF IN CALCUTTA
The Royal Calcutta Golf Club is founded; it is the oldest golf club outside Britain.

OXFORD AND CAMBRIDGE BOAT RACE
Oxford University beats Cambridge in the first Varsity Boat Race. The race, held on the Thames at Henley, UK, is the first intercollegiate sporting competition.

INDUSTRY AND EXPANSION

*T*HIS DECADE SEES the first settlers, in their covered wagons, moving westwards through the United States. As they advance, so Native Americans are increasingly pushed off their tribal lands, in an exodus that the Cherokee describe as the "Trail of Tears". American settlement in Mexico leads to rebellion in what will become the state of Texas. In Europe, the old reactionary political order begins to crumble. Liberal and nationalist revolts affect France, Spain, The Netherlands, Poland and the Italian and German states. In Britain, mass movements such as Chartism demand political change and voting rights are extended to middle-class males. Industrialism continues apace with major developments in transport and manufacturing. In the field of medicine, advances include anaesthetics and analgesics.

1830–1839

KEY EVENTS
of the
DECADE

REVOLUTION IN FRANCE

WESTWARDS SETTLEMENT

YOUNG ITALY SOCIETY FORMED

REVOLUTION IN ITALY

NAT TURNER'S SLAVE REVOLT

REFORM ACT, BRITAIN

THE US-MEXICAN WAR: SIEGE OF THE
ALAMO

GREAT TREK, SOUTH AFRICA

EGYPT GAINS INDEPENDENCE

SLAVERY ABOLISHED IN BRITISH EMPIRE

INDIAN WARS

AFGHAN WARS

GOTA CANAL OPENS

ELECTRIC TRANSFORMER BUILT

STEEL PLOUGH INVENTED

MECHANICAL REAPER INVENTED

ELECTROPLATING DEVELOPED

CHLOROFORM DISCOVERED

MORSE CODE DEVISED

CHOPIN'S ETUDES

WORLD POPULATION
1146 MILLION (ESTIMATE)

*Settlers make the long trek westwards across America
in search of new land and a new life.*

Heroic last stand at the Battle of the Alamo.

*McCormick's reaping machine
marks a further industrialization
of farming in the 1830s.*

Nationalism and Westwards Settlement

NATIONALIST REVOLTS BREAK OUT in France and the German states. Liberalism is victorious in France; new constitutions are agreed in the German principalities. Nationalism also appears in Belgium, which separates from The Netherlands. In the United States, the first wagonloads of settlers cross the Rocky Mountains to settle on the west coast. The Dutch introduce intensive cultivation techniques into Java. Proteins and paraffin are discovered.

✹ 1830 ✹

FEB	3	Greece is formally declared independent	AUG	2	Charles X abdicates; succeeded by son Louis XIX then by grandson Henri V
MAR	18	Ferdinand VII of Spain changes law to allow his daughter to succeed him		9	Henri V of France deposed; succeeded by Prince Louis-Philippe, the "bourgeois king"
	21	In Britain, Reform Bill to extend voting rights is rejected		25	Belgians rebel against Dutch rule
APR	27	Simón Bolívar abdicates as president of Colombia	SEP	11	Ecuador becomes a separate republic
				22	Venezuela separates from Colombia
JUNE	3	In England, riots led by "Captain Swing" break out, provoked by the introduction of theshing machines and subsequent rural unemployment	NOV	8	Francis I of the Two Sicilies dies; succeeded by his son Ferdinand II
	26	George IV of England dies; succeeded by his brother William IV		15	British prime minister, the Duke of Wellington resigns; succeeded by Lord Grey
JULY	5	French invade Algeria	DEC	17	Simón Bolívar dies at 47
	27	Revolution in Paris against Charles X		20	Austria, Britain, France, Prussia and Russia back Belgian independence

FRANCE INVADES ALGERIA

French forces invade Algeria in July and capture Algiers from the Ottoman Turks, marking the start of the French North African empire.

A NEW KING FOR FRANCE

Charles X attempts to restore the absolutism of the old French monarchy by issuing five ordinances for controlling the press, dissolving the parliament and changing the electoral system. As a result, Paris and other cities rise in revolt. In August, Charles abdicates and Louis-Philippe is elected king. A new, liberal constitution is adopted, ending, among other things, the recognition of Catholicism as the state religion.

REVOLT IN THE GERMAN STATES

In September, revolts also break out in Saxony, Hesse and Brunswick, where rulers are deposed and new constitutions agreed.

INDIAN LANDS TAKEN

The Indian Removal Act, passed in May, legalizes the removal of Native Americans to lands west of the Mississippi, while in the Treaty of Dancing Rabbit Creek, signed in September, Choctaw lands east of the Mississippi are ceded to the United States.

STEEL PLOUGH

American industrialist John Deere (1804–86) designs a combined ploughshare and mould board to be mass-produced in steel. His invention enables vast tracts of wild prairie and deforested land to be cultivated for growing crops.

PROTEINS DISCOVERED

The discovery of proteins is made in Germany by physiologist Johannes Müller. His findings make a significant contribution to the scientific understanding of the way life forms are fabricated and the essential dietary requirements for healthy growth.

POLLINATION IN PLANTS

Italian microscopist, Giovanni Amici (1784–1863), discovers the mechanism of pollination in plants. He shows that flora species reproduce in an essentially similar way to fauna species, and adds an important piece to the "jigsaw" of evolutionary thinking.

DUTCH POLICY IN THE EAST INDIES

The Netherlands Trading Company introduces a new cultivation system in Java based on the principle of *raubbau* (exploit and exhaust). Peasants are permitted to cultivate only coffee and other crops that are in demand in Europe, with devastating results to the native agriculture, economy and environment.

Above: *The royal procession at the coronation of William IV in London, who succeeds his brother George.*

SETTLERS IN THE WEST

During the autumn, the first wagons of settlers cross through the South Pass of the Rocky Mountains in the USA to settle on the west coast. The 800km (500mi) journey from the western Missouri river through Indian country takes about six weeks; the loaded wagons and even dairy cows make the journey with relative ease. The train is led by trader Jedediah Strong Smith and William Sublette of the Rocky Mountain Fur Co. The migrants are close to starving but have blazed a new route that avoids long distances, bandits in Panama and Mexico and the cost of sea travel around South America.

SOUTH AMERICA TAKES SHAPE

In September, the Republic of Colombia breaks up as Venezuela, Ecuador and Colombia all become separate, independent states. The countries of South America are now established with much the same borders as today.

BELGIUM AND THE NETHERLANDS SEPARATE

Nationalists revolt against Dutch rule and elect Leopold of Saxe-Coburg as King of Belgium. In November 1831 the European powers accept the separation of the two countries.

Above: *As white settlers encroach on their land, the traditional Native American way of life is threatened.*

Above: *In what will become Belgium, there is desperate fighting in the struggle for independence from the Dutch.*

A NEW CANAL

The Voornsche Kanaal is opened, connecting the Dutch port of Rotterdam to the sea.

THE AXE MAN

American Elisha King Root, sets up a mass production line for steel axes. The supply of his product in such prodigious quantity enables Americans to "tame" the forested wilderness and settle in areas previously deemed unsuitable for habitation.

HECTOR BERLIOZ, SYMPHONIE FANTASTIQUE

This programmatic symphony by French composer Hector Berlioz (1803–69) is the ultimate Romantic orchestral work. Berlioz uses the orchestra with great skill and originality, to evoke such episodes as "March to the Scaffold" and "Sabbath Night's Dream".

Simón Bolívar
1783–1830

The Creole revolutionary South American leader Simón Bolívar has died, after resigning this year. Bolívar was born of noble family in Caracas and studied law in Madrid. In 1817, he and José de San Martin took over the torch in the fight against Spanish colonialism from the defeated Francisco de Miranda, with Bolívar liberating the northwest part of South America from Spanish rule and establishing the republic of Gran Colombia in 1819. Venezuela and Ecuador seceded from this federation in 1828 when Bolívar made himself dictator, leaving him in control of Colombia and Panama. Bolivia is named in his honour.

CARICATURE AND THE KING

French artist Honoré Daumier (1808–79) has been publishing satirical caricatures in magazines since 1824, but he now becomes famous as the scourge of the French ruler Louis-Philippe.

PARAFFIN

The non-volatile fuel, paraffin or kerosene, is discovered by German scientist Baron Karl von Reichenbach (1788–1869). It will become a popular fuel for lighting and heating, before electricity and gas eventually become established as domestic forms of energy supply.

LE ROUGE ET LE NOIR

French novelist Stendhal (Marie Henri Beyle, 1783–1842) produces his own special blend of rationalism and Romanticism in his novels, of which this is perhaps the most famous. He is valued for his portrayals of heroes who are alienated from society.

FARMERS' AND MECHANICS' BANK, POTSVILLE

American architect John Haviland uses iron sheets, bent and moulded so that they resemble masonry, to face a brick building and produce probably the first cast-iron façade in America.

MAPPING THE NIGER

British explorer brothers John Lander (1807–39) and Richard Lemon Lander (1804–34) complete the exploration of the Niger in Africa, mapping the river from the Bussa Rapids, where Scottish explorer Mungo Park had come to grief in 1806, to the Gulf of Guinea.

Right: *Hayricks burn as the Swing Riots rage all over southern England.*

Above: *The tricolour crest of the Paris revolution.*

Below: *Fighting in the streets of Paris.*

Below: *Parisian revolutionaries seize the Hôtel de Ville during the riots against the dictates of Charles X.*

A NEW SOCIETY

A group of explorers forms the Royal Geographical Society. The society, based in London, springs from a discussion of the Raleigh Traveller's Club and quickly gains the patronage of William IV. Many expeditions are organized and funded by the Royal Geographical Society and it becomes the focus of discussion and argument as the world is explored and mapped.

REVOLUTIONS AND CHLOROFORM

Revolts break out in various Italian provinces as the move towards a unified Italy gathers steam. The first electric transformer is built. An adjustable dental chair is invented. Chemists working independently in France, the United States and Germany each discover chloroform, paving the way for pain-free surgery. Naturalist Charles Darwin sets out on his landmark voyage to South America.

☙ 1 8 3 1 ❧

JAN	25	Poles revolt against Russian rule
FEB	3	Austria's Italian provinces of Modena, Parma and the Papal States revolt
	3	Belgians choose Louis-Philippe's son as king, but Louis-Philippe vetoes it
	7	Belgians adopt a constitution
MAR	8	Hanover adopts a new constitution
APR	7	Emperor Pedro I of Brazil abdicates in favour of his son, Pedro II
MAY	26	Russians defeat Polish rebels
JUNE	1	British explorers John Ross and his nephew James Clark Ross reach the magnetic North Pole
	4	Belgians finally elect Prince Leopold of Saxe-Coburg, a naturalized Briton, as king
JULY	4	Former US President James Monroe dies at 73
AUG	2	A Dutch army invades Belgium
	20	French troops drive the Dutch out of Belgium
	21	Nat Turner leads black slave revolt in Southampton, Virginia
SEP	4	Saxony adopts a new constitution
	8	Polish revolt ends when Russians capture Warsaw
OCT	7	In Britain, second Reform Bill is thrown out by the House of Lords
NOV	17	Union of Colombia is formally dissolved
DEC	3	In Britain, third Reform Bill is introduced in the House of Commons

Mazzini and Young Italy

Patriot Giuseppe Mazzini (1805–72) founds the Young Italy society in Marseilles, dedicated to achieving *Risorgimento* (resurrection or rebirth) of a unified Italian republic.

Short-lived Independence

After the Polish diet (parliament) declares Poland independent in January, it dethrones Czar Nicholas and the Romanovs and becomes an independent kingdom in its own right. In a two-day battle in September, Russian forces retake Warsaw and the revolt collapses.

Revolution in Italy

In February revolts break out in Modena, Parma and the Papal States against reactionary rule. The rebels are influenced by the French Revolution of 1830 and strongly oppose the election of the reactionary Gregory XVI as pope. The revolts are later crushed by Austria and the status quo is restored.

Electric Transformer

Pioneering British scientist Michael Faraday (1791–1867) builds the first electric transformer. It enables the passage of electricity at different voltages for industrial and domestic usage, and makes a significant contribution to the safety of electricity.

Above: *Irish nationalist Daniel O'Connell is arrested this year for opposing the policies of the British government.*

Self-propelled Passenger Service

The route from Cheltenham to Gloucester in England becomes the first to witness the transportation of passengers with a self-propelled vehicle. Three Gurney steam drags are used for a regular service along the 14km (9mi) road.

Chloroform

Three chemists, from France (Eugène Soubeirain), America (Samuel Guthrie) and Germany (Justus von Liebig), each discover trichloromethane (chloroform) independently of one another. The chemical finds a significant use as an anaesthetic in all kinds of surgery, and survival chances are greatly increased.

Abolitionist Press

In the USA, *The Liberator* is founded by William Lloyd Garrison, a journalist and former co-publisher of the *Genius of Universal Emancipation*, which ended in his imprisonment. Garrison vows to continue publishing his outspoken abolitionist journal until slavery is abolished in the USA.

Left: *A Mormon baptism in America. Mormonism is established this year by Joseph Smith, who publishes his work,* The Book of Mormon, *and begins to gain converts.*

DENTAL CHAIR

The relative comfort of those unfortunate enough to need dental attention is increased by the invention of the adjustable chair by James Snell of London. The dental surgeon is the main beneficiary as he or she is better able to conduct operations.

SEWING MACHINE

French tailor, Bartélemy Thimmonier, has his sewing machine adopted by a Parisian clothing factory for the manufacture of military uniforms. However, angry mobs object to the automation of manufacture and halt the success of his invention.

MAGNETIC NORTH TRACKED DOWN

Scottish explorer John Ross (1777–1856) and his English nephew James Clarke Ross (1800–62) reach the magnetic North Pole, 1920km (1200mi) from the real pole, by sledge on June 1. John Ross also does a great deal of scientific work in high latitudes.

INDIANS CHEATED AGAIN

The Cherokee Indians sue for protection against gold prospectors intruding on their land, but while the Supreme Court upholds the nation's autonomy with inalienable rights to their territories, it rules that they are a domestic dependent nation unbound by the US Constitution and have no right to sue.

LA SONNAMBULA AND NORMA

Italian composer Vincenzo Bellini (1801–35) brings his lyrical, *bel canto* style to its highest peak of achievement in these two operas. *La Sonnambula* is especially successful, becoming a favourite with sopranos; *Norma*, with another great soprano lead role, will later be appreciated as Bellini's greatest opera.

ADULT EDUCATION IN THE USA

The National American Lyceum, an association for the instruction of adults based on local lectures, concerts and discussion groups, is inaugurated with talks by its founder, Josiah Holbrook, at a group in Millbury, Massachusetts. Some great names lecture to the Lyceum groups, which becomes a powerful force for promoting education and social change.

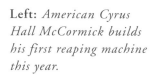

Left: *American Cyrus Hall McCormick builds his first reaping machine this year.*

Above: *Galapagos finches, whose beak-shapes inspire Charles Darwin to formulate his theory of evolution.*

DARWIN AND THE BEAGLE

HMS *Beagle* sets out on one of many surveying expeditions despatched by the British Admiralty. The voyage will last until 1836. What sets it apart is the presence on board of naturalist Charles Darwin. His observations in South America and on the Galapagos Islands in the Pacific lead to the development of his revolutionary theory of evolution.

ORIGINS OF MORMONISM

Visionary Joseph Smith leads 70 converts into Ohio, USA, where he establishes the headquarters of the Church of Jesus Christ of Latter Day Saints. He claims that his *Book of Mormon*, published in 1830, is a translation of a book of golden pages revealed to him by an angel.

Georg Wilhelm Friedrich Hegel
1770–1831

The influential German philosopher has died of cholera in Berlin, where he was professor at the university. His famous account of the dialectical process of reasoning, where thesis is contradicted by antithesis and a resolution found in synthesis (which becomes the thesis in a new process until the truth is reached), he believed describes progress in the world as well as in thought. This leads to dialectical materialism, the philosophy behind Marxism. The twenty volumes of his works include *The Phenomenology of Mind, Encyclopaedia of the Philosophical Sciences in Outline* (known as the *Grundrisse*) (1816–18) and *The Philosophy of Right* (1821).

THE ANNUAL CONVENTION OF PEOPLE OF COLOR

The first convention of free black people, the Annual Convention of People of Color, meets in June at the Wesleyan church on Lombard Street, Philadelphia, USA. The convention votes to study the conditions in which free Negroes [sic] are living in the USA, promote their education, and oppose Negro migration to Africa.

SLAVE REVOLT

Nat Turner (1800–31), a literate slave who believes himself chosen by God to lead black people to freedom, is hanged in November for having organized a slave revolt on August 21, when 60 white people were killed, and state and federal troops were called in.

BARBIZON SCHOOL EXHIBITION

The Barbizon school of French landscape painters hold their first exhibition in the Salon, Paris. They paint in the open air, finishing their work indoors, and specialize in twilight landscapes, influenced by Dutch and English art. Prominent members of the group are Théodore Rousseau (1812–67) and Charles François Daubigny (1817–78); Jean François Millet (1814–75) and Camille Corot (1796–1875) are also linked with the group.

Left: *Leopold Saxe-Coburg, a British subject, becomes the first king of the newly independent Belgians.*

Karl von Clausewitz
1780–1831

The Prussian general, who was Chief-of-Staff during the Waterloo campaign and director of the General War School in Berlin from 1818 until last year, has died. He had great influence on theories of military strategy, partly through his published works on the subject. His treatise *Vom Kriege* (*On War*), to be published in 1833, will be most influential of all.

SAILING SHIPS AND ELECTRIC DYNAMOS

MUSLIM LEADER Abd-el-Kader declares war on France. Great Britain introduces radical parliamentary reform, extending the vote to middle-class men. US president Andrew Jackson wins a second term. The US Senate rules that the government has exclusive rights over Native American tribal lands. The first fast sailing ships, or "clippers", are launched, in the USA. A Frenchman devises the first electric dynamo. Dress patterns make their first appearance.

Above: *Charles Grey, British prime minister and reformist.*

✻ 1832 ✻

JAN	19	Austrian troops quell riots in Italy's Papal States
FEB	26	Russia abolishes Poland's constitution
MAR	23	In Britain, House of Lords passes Reform Bill
APR	10	Turks declare war on Mehemet Ali of Egypt, who wants Syria as a reward for helping in a struggle over Greece
MAY	27	Turks capture Acre, Israel
JUNE	3	First "clipper" fast sailing ship is launched at Baltimore, USA
	7	Reform Act cleans up unfair voting system for parliamentary elections in England
	15	Egyptians take Damascus, Syria, from the Turks
JULY	9	Ex-Emperor Pedro of Brazil captures Oporto, Portugal, from King Miguel on behalf of his daughter
	17	In Britain, provisions of Reform Act are extended to Scotland
AUG	7	In Britain, provisions of Reform Act are extended to Ireland
	8	Greeks elect Prince Otto of Bavaria as their king
NOV	13	Andrew Jackson wins US presidential election
DEC	21	Egyptians rout main Turkish army at the Battle of Konieh
	24	French capture Antwerp and force the Dutch to recognize Belgian independence

Above: *Collecting tithes in Ireland is unpopular among the poor who are currently taxed but disenfranchised.*

A Second Term for Jackson
Democrat Andrew Jackson wins re-election in the US presidential election against opposition from Henry Clay. Martin Van Buren becomes the vice-president.

War between France and Algeria
Between 1832 and 1847, the charismatic Muslim leader and emir of Mascara, Abd-el-Kader, leads three campaigns against the French forces that are pushing into Algeria. The First War lasts from 1832 to 1834; the Second War from 1835 to 1837; and the Third War from 1840 to 1847. In the First and Second wars, el-Kader enjoys considerable success, signing a treaty that gives him control over the interior of Algeria. At Isly river on August 14, 1844 the French army, under Marshal Thomas R Bugeaud (1784–1849), decisively defeats the 45 000 strong army of Abd-el-Kader. Without the support of neighbouring Morocco, the Algerian leader surrenders to the French in 1847.

A King for Greece
The National Assembly elects Otto of Bavaria as King of Greece in August; he rules as Otto I until 1862.

Reform in Great Britain
After years of agitation and protest, the Great Reform Act is finally agreed by Parliament in June. The act transforms the British constitution, redistributing seats to the industrial cities and reforming the franchise, allowing the middle classes to vote for the first time.

Fast Ships
The first fast sailing ship, or "clipper", is launched on June 3. It has been constructed at the Kennard and Williamson's yard in Baltimore, Ohio, USA and designed for use in the China trade. The basic idea will lead to many and various new ships grouped as clippers.

Electric Dynamo
Frenchman Hypolite Pixii (1808–35) devises the electric generator or dynamo. It is of tremendous importance because it enables the conversion of kinetic energy from any source into electricity, and allows electricity to become a practicable energy supply.

The First Waterbed
Scottish surgeon Neil Arnott invents the waterbed. The reason for using water is to help with the distribution of weight and thereby prevent bed sores from developing in patients confined to their bed for long periods of time during convalescence.

Right: *Cholera sweeps through the cities of Europe this year, killing thousands. This scene shows fear and panic in the streets of Paris.*

BALTIC LINK
Sweden's Gota Canal opens, linking the Baltic at Arkösund to the North Sea at Gothenborg via a 386km (240mi) system of canals linking rivers and Sweden's Great Central Lakes.

PAINKILLERS
The analgesic or painkilling drug, codeine, is discovered by French chemist Pierre Robiquet (1780–1840). The white crystalline alkaloid is the active ingredient in morphine and is also useful as a sedative and a linctus.

CLAUSEWITZ ON WAR
Prussian General Karl von Clausewitz's seminal work *Vom Krieg* (*On War*) is published posthumously. It revolutionizes the theory of modern warfare.

INDIANS CEDE MORE LAND
The Chickasaw Indians follow the Creek, the Seminoles and the Sack and Fox in ceding their lands to the US after the Supreme Court rules that the government has exclusive authority over tribal Indian lands. The Sack cede lands east of the Mississippi after defeat under Chief Black Hawk at Bad Axe.

DRESS PATTERNS
The French fashion journal *L'Iris* (*The Iris*) issues paper dress patterns with its October issue. The idea catches on as the most obvious way for supplying duplicate instructions for clothing manufacture, both domestically and industrially.

JIM CROW
Jim Crow, a song-and-dance act by Thomas Dartmouth Rice, who staged the first blackface minstrel show in 1828, is a success in Louisville, Kentucky. "Daddy" Rice imitates the song and movements of a deformed slave, and the character comes to symbolize racial prejudice in America.

THE ROMANCE OF THE NORSE
Scandinavianism — the idea of a common Nordic past — is gaining currency in Nordic countries after a revival of interest in ancient history. The reprinting this year of *Northern Mythology*, published in 1808 by Nikolai Grundtvig, has given the movement impetus. This Danish cleric, who has agitated for constitutional reform, writes songs and poems retelling Nordic myths and history.

CHOPIN'S MAZURKAS

French-Polish pianist-composer Frédéric Chopin (1810–49) produces some of his earliest notable works, the mazurkas (stylized dances of Polish style, in 3/4 time). His works open up new avenues in piano music and influence composers such as Liszt and Wagner.

L'ELISIR D'AMORE

Having produced his first notable serious opera, *Anna Bolena*, in 1830, *bel canto* master Gaetano Donizetti (1797–1848) completes his first great comedy, *L'Elisir d'Amore* (*The Elixir of Love*). Like much of the rest of his huge list of works (around 70 operas, plus many other pieces), these operas are prized for their drama and vocal writing.

LITERARY SOCIETY

The Female Literary Society is founded by a group of literary women in Philadelphia, USA.

BOOK JACKETS

British publishers introduce paper jackets to protect their products, and soon discover that they offer a way of providing information about the books, and help to sell them.

INDIANA

The first of a series of novels by French writer George Sand (Amandine Aurore Lucie Dupin, 1804–76), *Indiana* champions the right of women to have their own lives, loves and independence. The heroine finally finds contentment on the island of Réunion.

Left: *George Sand, controversial French author, publishes her first novel* Indiana *this year.*

Georges Cuvier
1769–1832

The French so-called father of comparative anatomy and palaeontology, Léopold Chrétien Frédéric Dagobert, Baron Cuvier, has died. He used the name Georges Cuvier for his work. Having developed his interest in zoology as a young man in Normandy, he became Professor of Natural History at the College de France in 1789. He originated the natural system of animal classification, reconstructed extinct giant vertebrates from fossils, and opposed evolutionary theories positing instead the theory of catastrophism with the belief that extinctions were due to global floods which precipitated new forms of life. His many works include *Lessons of Comparative Anatomy* (1801–05), *The Fossilized Bones of Quadrupeds* (1812) and *The Natural History of Fish* (1828–49). He was made Minister of the Interior in the year of his death.

Jeremy Bentham
1748–1832

Jeremy Bentham, the English philosopher-radical has died. He founded utilitarianism, the philosophy of ethics which states that the best action will lead to the greatest happiness of the greatest number, a principle which can be used as a basis for social and legal policy. His key work is *Introduction to the Principles of Morals and Legislation* (1789). Bentham founded University College, London, where his embalmed body is kept for display.

Johann Goethe
1749–1832

Johann Wolfgang von Goethe, the great German writer, has died. Author of *Faust* (his life work, published 1808–32), he also wrote *The Sorrows of Young Werther* (1774), *Roman Elegies* (1795), *Wilhelm Meister's Apprenticeship* (1796), *Elected Affinities* (1809), *Wilhelm Meister's Travels* (1821–29), epic poetry and love poems. He was a trained lawyer and a court official to the Duke of Weimar, as well as a gifted student of anatomy and botany. Many of his poems were set to music by Schubert (often more than once), and he was revered by the German Romantics, even though he himself disapproved of their enthusiastic endorsement of the French Revolution, while much admiring the Emperor Napoleon. He also leaves an autobiography, *Poetry and Truth* (1811–14). Goethe is buried close to his great friend Schiller in Weimar and will continue to be a giant figure of German and European literature.

EGYPT ACHIEVES INDEPENDENCE

THE SLOWLY CRUMBLING Ottoman Empire grants Egypt independence, ceding Syria and Yemen to the new country. Prussia establishes a customs union in Germany. Creosote is produced and the first electric telegraph line is erected. Soda pop fountains appear in New York City. Russian dramatist Nikolai Gogol satirizes provincial bureaucrats in *The Government Inspector* and Polish-born composer Chopin publishes his Etudes.

✺ 1 8 3 3 ✺

JAN	1	Britain proclaims its ownership of the Falkland Islands
FEB	20	Russian fleet enters the Bosporus on the way to help Turkey against Egypt
MAR	1	US Congress gives the president power to collect certain high import duties, overruling objections by South Carolina
	4	US President Andrew Jackson begins his second term
	23	In Germany, Prussia sets up a customs union, the *Zollverein*
MAY	3	Turkey recognizes Egypt's independence, and cedes Syria to it
	21	The Netherlands agrees armistice with Belgium
JULY	24	In Portugal, Pedro's supporters capture Lisbon
AUG	2	Factory Act in Britain forbids children under nine working in factories
SEP	26	William IV of Britain gives Hanover (which he also rules) a new constitution
	29	King Ferdinand VII of Spain dies; succeeded by daughter Isabella II, aged three, with her mother, Maria Christina, as regent

Right: *The Grand Cascade in Yosemite valley. This year Trapper Joe Walker pioneers the westbound route to California which crosses this area.*

FALKLAND ISLANDS

Britain declares sovereignty over the remote and isolated islands known as Las Malvinas, off the coast of Argentina. They are renamed the Falkland Islands. The islands are a useful coaling station for ships rounding Cape Horn, but Argentina continues to claim them as its own territory.

ECONOMIC UNION IN GERMANY

By a series of treaties, Prussia establishes a *Zollverein* or customs union in Germany, which includes the southern states of Bavaria and Württemberg but excludes Austria. The economic union of Germany precedes its political union and continues the Prussian policy of excluding Austria from German affairs.

INDEPENDENCE FOR EGYPT

The Ottoman Empire grants independence to Egypt, under its ruler Mehemet Ali, and cedes Syria and Yemen to the new country. Following the independence of Greece, Serbia and Romania, and the French invasion of Algeria, the break-up of the Ottoman Empire is now well under way.

PROGRESS AGAINST SLAVERY IN THE USA

The American Anti-Slavery Society is founded at Philadelphia by Quaker businessman and abolitionist James Mott and his wife Lucretia Coffin Mott. Lucretia Mott (1793–1880) also founds the Philadelphia Female Anti-Slavery Society. Both societies support the work of William Lloyd Garrison.

CREOSOTE

German scientist and inventor of paraffin, Baron Karl von Reichenbach (1788–1869), distils the thick, dark liquid from wood and coal tar. It is found to be a very effective antiseptic and useful for preserving timber, since it kills off the organisms that cause rot or decay.

CHOPIN'S ETUDES

French-Polish composer Frédéric Chopin publishes his first notable collection of pieces in his non-dance vein. These studies will later be followed by preludes, ballades and nocturnes.

SCIENCE IN SCHOOL

Bruce Castle School of London becomes the first to have its own purpose-built science laboratory. It is indicative of the recognition that knowledge of science is of paramount importance to the economic and political success of the West at this time.

Left: *Andrew Jackson begins his second term of office as president of the United States.*

William Wilberforce
1759–1833

The Yorkshire-born English reformer, philanthropist and evangelical Christian William Wilberforce has died, just a month before the passing of the Slavery Abolition Act, which is to abolish slavery in the British Empire and for which he had worked with such commitment since 1788. He was a member of parliament from 1780 until his health forced him to retire in 1825. With the support of Thomas Clarkson and the Quaker movement, his campaigning led to the abolition of the West Indian slave trade in 1807, and as well as continuing to devote himself to the anti-slavery cause, he worked tirelessly for social welfare schemes at home.

POP COMES TO TOWN

The soda fountain is invented and marketed in New York by Anglo-American businessman John Matthews, a wholesaler of bottled carbonated water.

ABOLITIONISTS AND EDUCATION

Abolitionists in Boston, USA, David Lee and Lydia Maria Child, propose that blacks be educated; but a schoolmistress in Canterbury, Connecticut is imprisoned for admitting black girls to her school.

ELECTRIC TELEGRAPH

The first permanently employed electric telegraph line is erected in Germany. It sends astronomical information over 3km (2mi) from the observatory of WE Weber and JKF Gauss, to the Physical Cabinet in Göttingen.

CONCRETE STRUCTURE

The first major structure using Portland cement as a primary material is erected. The French engineer, M Poivel, uses concrete (a composite of cement and sand, reinforced with stones) to build the Algiers breakwater.

THE GOVERNMENT INSPECTOR

This play by Russian dramatist Nikolai Gogol (1809–52) is a satire on provincial worthies; it will be one of his most enduring works, and will translate into many different cultures and times.

CALIFORNIA HERE I COME

Trapper Joe Walker pioneers the California trail, crossing present-day Nevada and the Yosemite valley. The pass he finds through the Sierra Nevada on the return journey is named after him.

Richard Trevithick
1771–1833

The English mining engineer and inventor, who was born and raised in a tin-mining district of Cornwall, has died. As well as building improved stationary steam engines, Trevithick invented the ancestor of all passenger locomotives — a steam carriage which was so successful on its Camborne to Tuckingmill route that it was brought to London in 1803 and demonstrated, running from Leather Lane to Paddington, via Oxford Street. The locomotive engine had to be small in size and light in weight, yet powerful enough to pull wagons. A machine he built in 1804 weighed 5 tons and travelled 14km (9mi) at 8km/h (5mph), but the engine's weight tended to break the rails and in any case most people preferred the horse-drawn carriage. Partly because of lack of interest in his inventions, Trevithick spent the years from 1816 to 1827 in Peru, introducing steam engines to the silver mines there.

Left: *Agricultural labourers are leaving the land, driven off by new machinery and the lure of comparatively well-paid work in factories.*

Below: *Cotton mills in Manchester, England. The economy is about to change as manufacturing takes over from agriculture as the main industry.*

AN END TO SLAVERY IN THE EMPIRE

*T*HE SLAVE TRADE is abolished throughout the British Empire. France, Britain, Spain and Portugal form a liberal Quadruple Alliance. Civil war breaks out in Spain. Railway signals are introduced and the adhesive postage stamp is developed. In the United States, western expansion continues, a trading post is established at Fort Laramie and the first Native American reservations are set up.

❋ 1834 ❋

MAR	18	The Tolpuddle Martyrs: six labourers from Tolpuddle, Dorset, England, are sentenced to transportation for trade union activities
APR	9	Silk workers at Lyon, France, revolt in support of trade unions
	14	A rebellion in Paris is crushed
	22	Britain, France, Portugal and Spain form a Quadruple Alliance
MAY	26	Don Miguel gives up attempt to rule Portugal and goes into exile; Maria II da Gloria is restored
JULY	9	In Britain, Lord Grey resigns as prime minister; succeeded by Lord Melbourne

	10	Don Carlos, brother of the late King Ferdinand VII of Spain, claims the throne and begins a civil war
AUG	1	Slavery is abolished in the British Empire
	15	Britain passes an act to set up a colony in South Australia
SEP	24	Ex-Emperor Pedro of Brazil dies
OCT	16	Britain's Houses of Parliament destroyed by fire
NOV	15	Lord Melbourne resigns as Britain's prime minister. Sir Robert Peel takes over on December 9

Above: *The Houses of Parliament in London burn to the ground. Only Westminster Hall survives.*

ALLIANCE IN EUROPE

A Quadruple Alliance is formed between France, Britain, Spain and Portugal to support liberal constitutional government in Spain and Portugal. The liberal Quadruple Alliance forms a counterweight to the reactionary Holy Alliance of Russia, Prussia and Austria.

CIVIL WAR IN SPAIN

After the death of Ferdinand VII in 1833 and the succession of his daughter Isabella, civil war breaks out when his brother, Don Carlos, claims the throne. The war lasts until August 1839, when Don Carlos flees to France. Carlist claims to the throne continue into the next century.

SLAVERY ABOLISHED IN BRITAIN

Slavery is finally abolished throughout the British Empire and the slaves in the West Indian plantations are set free. Trade in slaves continues in the southern states of the USA, and also remains in place in Cuba, Brazil, and other American colonies and nations.

ROAD DEATHS

Scotland becomes the first country to witness the destructive potential of self-propelled vehicles. John Scott Russell's steam coach runs out of control in Paisley, killing five unfortunate bystanders, and prompting the introduction of road safety laws.

ELECTRIC MOTOR VEHICLE

American Thomas Davenport, demonstrates the locomotive possibilities of the electric motor by powering a vehicle around a short, circular track. His engine carries its own electric cell, making it heavy and inefficient, but it serves its purpose.

RAILWAY SIGNALS

The railway from Liverpool to Manchester, England, is the first to be fitted with signals for the instruction of engine drivers. With the use of single stretches of track for trains in both directions, the potential for disaster is averted.

WIRE ROPE

German Wilhelm Albert, and Englishman George Binks, invent the wire rope or cable. The cable comprises several steel wires which are arranged in a twist along the cable's length. The cable is immensely strong and tough, yet highly flexible.

Above: *Slavery is abolished throughout the British Empire. Barbadians celebrate emancipation in style.*

ADHESIVE POSTAGE STAMPS
Scotsman James Chalmers devises a postage stamp with an adhesive backing. Three years later his invention is assessed by Parliament, at the proposal for postal reform meeting, with Rowland Hill. The year 1840 will see the idea come into general use.

RESERVATIONS SET UP
Territory west of the Mississippi river, except in the states of Missouri and Louisiana and Arkansas Territory, is reserved by the newly established US Department of Indian Affairs for the permanent residence of Native Americans.

A SLAVE'S PATENT
Henry Blair becomes the first black US slave to be granted a patent — for a corn harvester he has invented.

A HISTORY OF THE UNITED STATES
The first volume of this classic early history by American historian and statesman George Bancroft (1800–91) is published. It covers events from the early settlers to the inauguration of Washington. Bancroft will continue work on the ten-volume work until 1874, later revising it.

GOING WEST
Expansion west of the Appalachians has its first stirrings in the US government sale of 28 million acres of public lands to settlers during this year. This year, the first trading post has been opened as far west as Fort Laramie in Wyoming by William Sublette and Robert Campbell.

LONDON CAB ESTABLISHED
Joseph Aloysius Hansom (1803–82) patents a design for a safety cab — the Hansom Cab — which he intends to introduce into London.

MERCHANTS' EXCHANGE, PHILADELPHIA
This notable Greek revival building is designed by American architect William Strickland. Especially admired is its cupola, based on the Choragic Monument to Lysicrates in Athens, which adorns the imposing rear elevation of the building.

HAROLD IN ITALY
Inspired by Byron's poem "Childe Harold's Pilgrimage", *Harold in Italy* by Hector Berlioz (1803–69) is noted for the unusual combination of viola and orchestra, though Berlioz saw it as more a symphony than a concerto. Its portrayal of Romantic themes makes it a classic of nineteenth-century music.

Above: *Edinburgh University, Scotland, begun by Robert Adam in 1789 and now finished by WH Playfair.*

Left: *Sheet mills for rolling tin plate. The tin-plate industry has been established since the beginning of the century.*

MECHANICAL REAPER

American inventor Cyrus Hall McCormick (1809–84) patents the mechanical reaper that he had built in 1831.

CARNAVAL

Robert Schumann (1810–56) writes "Carnaval", which will become his most popular solo piano work. A series of short pieces, which portray different aspects of the composer's personality together with other composers and figures from Schumann's own private mythology, the witty, tuneful work is effective without a knowledge of these inner meanings.

Above: *Composer Robert Schumann who this year publishes "Carnaval" and founds the bi-weekly journal* Neue Leipzige Zeitschrift für Musik.

General Lafayette
1757–1834

Marie Joseph Yves Roch Gilbert du Motier, Marquis de Lafayette, the French liberal general and statesman who fought for the Americans in the American War of Independence, has died. A hero of the American revolution, he was much admired by his friend George Washington. He formed part of the National Assembly in France after the Revolution of 1789 and drafted the Declaration of the Rights of Man, based on the American Declaration of Independence. During the post-revolutionary turmoils in France he was at one point forced to flee because of his moderation, but he returned in 1818 and held various government posts, and was commander of the National Guard during the July revolution of 1830 (which led to the abdication of King Charles X).

Thomas Malthus
1766–1834

The English clergyman and advocate of birth control, Thomas Robert Malthus, has died. In his work as a social theorist, Malthus systematically demonstrated that population growth would inevitably outstretch the availability of subsistence, and argued that it was necessary to take steps to cut the birth rate. His views (as expressed in *Essay on Populations*, 1798) were a grim rejoinder to the optimistic beliefs of enlightenment thinkers who held that there were infinite possibilities for human progress and perfection. His theories of politics, economics and society were further developed in *Principles of Political Economy* (1820), and his thinking influenced Darwin.

MORSE, COLTS AND COMPUTERS

*I*N SOUTHERN AFRICA, Dutch settlers begin a Great Trek to Natal. American soldiers are massacred by Seminole Indians. Samuel Morse develops an electric telegraph and Samuel Colt patents the revolver named after him. An "analytical engine" is designed. Using punched cards, it is the forerunner of the computer. Hans Andersen begins to publish his fairy tales and the *New York Herald* is founded.

Above: *Robert Peel, prime minister of Great Britain.*

✷ 1 8 3 5 ✷

MAR	1	General Juan de Rosas becomes dictator of Argentina
	7	Emperor Franz I of Austria dies; succeeded by his son Ferdinand I
	9	In Britain, Whigs and the Irish leader Daniel O'Connell plot to bring about the fall of Sir Robert Peel's government
APR	8	In Britain, Sir Robert Peel is defeated in the House of Commons and resigns. Lord Melbourne (Whig) forms a new ministry
MAY	12	German Grand Duchy of Baden joins the *Zollverein* (customs union)
JUNE	16	William Cobbett, English champion of the poor, dies at 72
	28	In France, an attempt to assassinate King Louis-Philippe fails
SEP	9	New local government system set up in Britain, with councillors elected by ratepayers
NOV	3	In Mexico, leaders of the Texans claim independence and set up a temporary government
DEC	11	Texans capture city of San Antonio

Above: *The Mansion House, London. The City of London has so far escaped the bracing wind of reform.*

SEPTEMBER SUPPRESSION
In France, the September Laws are passed, which repress the radical movement. The laws severely censor the press and restrict political opposition to the government.

REVOLUTION IN TEXAS
American settlers in Texas revolt against the rule of military dictator General Antonio López de Santa Anna, who had overturned the Mexican consitutional government in 1834. They declare their intention to fight for independence.

THE GREAT TREK
The Great Trek begins as Boers, the Dutch-speaking settlers in southern Africa, flee from the British administration in the Cape Colony of South Africa and trek northwards in ox-drawn covered wagons to Natal, to set up their own territory.

REVOLVER
Samuel Colt (1814–62), an inventor from Hartford, Connecticut, patents the revolver or six-shooter, the handgun that dominates the American West. Its effective range is 18–23m (25–30yd).

INDIAN WARS
The Second Seminole War, which began in November, is marked by the massacre of Major Francis L Dade and 108 soldiers by Seminole Indians under Chief Osceola, who is leading their resistance to being removed from their Florida territories to the West.

TRAVELS WITH DE TOCQUEVILLE
French aristocrat Alexis de Tocqueville (1805–59) publishes *La Democracie en Amerique* (*Democracy in America*) the record of his travels through eastern Canada and the United States to study the penitentiary system. He analyzes and praises the democratic system there.

STANDARDIZED TELEGRAPH
American inventor, Samuel Morse (1791–1872), designs an electric telegraph for practical use, which is adopted by the American railways. Devices at each end of the cable are used to transmit and receive long and short taps as signals.

ELECTRIC LAMP
A Scottish scientist James Bowman Lindsey (1799–1862) becomes the inventor of the incandescent electric lamp. The light is emitted from a glass tube containing a vacuum and is therefore perceived as a safe means of lighting factories using combustible materials.

TARMACADAM
John McAdam (1756–1836) invents the ubiquitous road surfacing material tarmacadam, named after him. It comprises stones bound together with tar or bitumen. Its success lies in its toughness and imperviousness to water, plus its thermoplastic workability.

GYNAECOLOGICAL WARD
Ireland becomes home to the first hospital ward set up in recognition of "women's problems". Evory Kennedy of the Rotunda Hospital, Dublin, establishes a requirement for the treatment of some female patients in isolation.

MECHANICAL COMPUTER
Charles Babbage (1791–1871), British mathematician, designs a machine, his "analytical engine", which carries out arithmetic calculations using data carried on punched cards; it is the forerunner to the modern electric computer.

DAS LEBEN JESU
German theologian David Friedrich Strauss (1808–74) publishes *Das Leben Jesu,* in which he presents the Gospels as a series of myths, under which lie basic

Above: *Farming in South Africa. Dutch Boers begin spreading northwards from the Cape towards Natal.*

historical truths that have nothing to do with the supernatural. It is translated into English by George Eliot. The book causes a storm, and Strauss is dismissed from his post at Tübingen University. His belief that Christianity as a religion is irrelevant, and that people need to create a new faith based on art and science, is ahead of its time.

DANISH FAIRY TALES
Danish writer Hans Christian Andersen (1805–75) begins to publish the series of pamphlets containing tales that constitute his greatest work. Many of the tales, from "The Emperor's New Clothes" to "The Ugly Duckling" remain favourites all over the world.

DANTON'S DEATH
This is the first of three great plays by Georg Büchner (1813–37) and depicts the fall (both worldly and spiritual) of the French revolutionary politician Georges Danton. This and Büchner's other plays are unknown during their author's short and tragic life (he dies in 1837 at the age of 24), but foreshadow nearly every later dramatic style, from naturalism to the theatre of the absurd.

Left: *An illustration from* The Ugly Duckling, *one of Hans Christian Andersen's popular fairy stories.*

Above: *Princess Marie-Amélie, daughter of Ferdinand I of the Two Sicilies and queen to Louis-Philippe.*

Above: *Louis-Philippe I, the "citizen king" elected to sovereignty by the French nation.*

MADEMOISELLE DE MAUPIN

Versatile French writer Théophile Gautier (1811–72) publishes *Mademoiselle de Maupin*, his first novel of note. It is prefaced with an essay which propounds the idea of art for art's sake. His work begins with the Romantic movement, but shows the progression towards the naturalism of the later nineteenth century.

NEW YORK HERALD FOUNDED

The 1-cent paper, the *New York Herald* is founded by the Scottish-born journalist James Gordon Bennett (1795–1872), a moment that is sometimes cited as the beginning of US journalism. The paper is popular, providing a mixture of information and sensation, which will be imitated the world over. But this mixture also causes some scandal at the beginning.

DRY ICE

Using a method established by Michael Faraday, the French chemist CSA Thilorier produces solid carbon dioxide, which can turn to gas without melting into liquid first. As it evaporates it cools the area around it. As it looks like ice but is never wet, it is called dry ice.

THE KALEVALA

The Kalevala, the Finnish national epic, contains one of the richest sources of mythology in any culture. It is a collection of folk poems collected and written down by the Finnish folklorist and writer Elias Lönnrot (1802–84). Coming at a time when Finland is still seeking its destiny as a nation, it helps to define the national identity, and deeply influences other Finnish nationalist artists and composers, such as Jean Sibelius (1865–1957).

TEXAS GOES FOR INDEPENDENCE

MEXICAN TROOPS ARRIVE in Texas to crush the Texan rebellion, resulting in the heroic and tragic defence of the Alamo fort at San Antonio. Ultimately, Texas gains independence. Arkansas becomes the 25th state of the Union. There is war in South America. The process of electroplating is patented and the gas ethyne, or acetylene, is discovered. A young British writer, Charles Dickens, introduces his fictional character, Pickwick, to an enthusiastic public.

❊ 1836 ❊

FEB	22	Statesman and rebel Adolphe Thiers becomes prime minister of France
	24	Mexican President Antonio de Santa Anna besieges Texan rebels in the Alamo fort in San Antonio
MAR	2	Texas formally declares independence from Mexico
	6	Santa Anna captures the Alamo and kills the remaining defenders
APR	21	Texans defeat Mexicans at the Battle of San Jacinto, thereby ensuring their independence
JUNE	10	French mathematician André Ampère dies at 61

	15	Arkansas becomes the 25th US state
	16	Chartist movement begins in Britain
SEP	2	Opposition to French Prime Minister Thiers' plan to invade Spain forces him to resign
OCT	28	Federation of Peru and Bolivia is formed
NOV	8	Democrat Martin Van Buren is elected US president
	11	Chile declares war on Federation of Peru and Bolivia

A New Colony in Australia

After the passing of an act of parliament in August 1834 allowing a colony to be established, Britain founds a new colony in South Australia.

Chartists in England

William Lovett forms the London Working Men's Association in London, starting the Chartist reform movement, which presses for constitutional reform. In May 1838 the movement publishes the People's Charter, which demands universal adult suffrage and secret ballots, among other changes. The Chartists' demands attract huge national support and, although the movement peters out in the 1850s, many demands are met.

New States for the Union

Arkansas joins the Union as the 25th state. Because the Arkansas constitution allows slavery, its admission was held up until Michigan, a free state, was ready to join; Michigan does so in January 1837.

A New President

Vice-President Martin Van Buren wins the US presidential election for the Democrats, becoming the eighth president of the country; his vice-president is Richard Johnson.

Baily's Beads

English amateur astronomer Francis Baily (1774–1844) discovers spots of light within the "corona" of the sun, visible around the rim of the moon during a total solar eclipse. This is one of the first optical studies of the sun, which is otherwise too dangerous to observe.

Electroplating of Metal

British engineers George Elkington (1801–65) and his brother Henry Elkington (1810–52), patent the process for electroplating. It

Left: Novelist Charles Dickens makes a speech to admirers of his new work.

Left: André-Marie Ampère, mathematician and physicist, dies this year.

finds various useful applications. As well as coating corrosive metals such as iron with relatively inert metals, it is possible to coat cheaper metals with thin layers of those that are more expensive.

Les Huguenots

This is the most popular opera of Giacomo Meyerbeer (1791–1864), one of the most successful composers of the time, and shows his ability to create grand effects both in music and in drama.

Stroboscope

Belgian physicist, Joseph Plateau (1801–83), invents the stroboscope, an instrument which produces regular flashes of light. It is used in photography for producing multiple exposures of moving objects, to reveal the nature of their motion.

Ethyne

Edmund Davy, a British chemist, discovers the gas ethyne, otherwise known as acetylene. It is burned with oxygen through an oxyacetylene torch and is used for the welding and cutting of metals due to very high flame temperature.

Ancient America

The ruins of the ancient pre-Columbian civilizations of Central America are described in books written by the American historian John Lloyd Stephens (1805–52), who visits the ruins of Chichen Itzà and other Mayan cities in the Yucatán.

A Life for the Czar

Having studied in Italy, Russian composer Mikhail Ivanovich Glinka (1803–57) returns to his native land and writes this opera, the first important opera with a Russian text and subject, by a Russian composer. It remains one of the most popular of all Russian works until the Revolution.

Sketches by Boz and The Pickwick Papers

The early *Sketches by Boz* by British writer Charles Dickens (1812–70) attract the attention of publishers Chapman and Hall, who encourage the development of the character Pickwick. With the appearance of *The Pickwick Papers*, first as a serial, then in volume form in 1837, Dickens' reputation as a popular novelist is made.

Left: *Martin Van Buren, the eighth president of the USA. He had been vice-president in 1832 and governor of New York before that.*

Above: *Burlington House, part of the University of London, created as an administrative entity this year.*

NATURE

American poet and essayist Ralph Waldo Emerson (1803–82) publishes this important essay, which develops the concept of Transcendentalism, a blending of mysticism and reverence for nature that embraces literary, social and economic thought. The ideas of Transcendentalism have a huge influence on American thought and writing, especially during the middle of the nineteenth century.

MISSION TO THE NORTHWEST

Marcus Whitman, a US Protestant missionary, travels west from Fort Laramie and founds a mission at Waiilatpu near Walla Walla, Washington. His wife, Narcissa, and Eliza Spalding are the first white women to travel overland to the northwest.

BLOOD SPORT BANNED

Massachusetts is the first state in America to ban cockfighting. Britain will outlaw the sport in 1849.

John McAdam
1756–1836

John Loudon McAdam, the Scottish road-maker, has died. From 1770 to 1783 he made his fortune in America and then spent most of it experimenting with road-building on his return to Scotland. His roads at first employed three layers of stones, and had a smooth paving surface which offered less resistance to carriage wheels. He invented tarmacadam, the road surface made of crushed stones bound with gravel. In 1827 he was made surveyor-general of metropolitan roads. The advance of the railway will mean that road-building comes to a halt in Great Britain from his death until the twentieth century.

Davy Crockett
1786–1836

Davy (David) Crockett, the colourful American frontiersman, has been killed defending the fort of the Alamo at San Antonio, Texas, in the battle to claim the territory from Mexico and make it part of the United States. He was a congressman for his native Tennessee from 1827–32 and 1833–35, and had only lived in Texas since his electoral defeat in 1835.

André Marie Ampère
1775–1836

The French mathematician and physicist André-Marie Ampère, whose name is given to the unit of electric current, the amp, has died. The son of a Lyons merchant, he was largely self-educated, using his father's extensive library, and went on to teach mathematics and experimental physics at the Ecole Polytechnique, the Imperial University and the College de France in Paris. His work (of the 1820s) in electrodynamics, which advanced discoveries in the field of electromagnetics made by Hans Christian Oersted, has applications in industry and telegraphy. He formulated Ampère's Law, which relates to the strength of a magnetic field induced by an electrical current flowing through a conductor, and devised the commutator, which alters or reverses the direction of an electric current.

Above: *The Alps, focus of mountaineering fever which
sweeps the leisured classes of Europe during this decade.*

REMEMBER THE ALAMO

TEXAS IS A MEXICAN PROVINCE, but has a population of 30 000 Americans. In 1832, it claimed its independence. Following the imposition of new restrictions by Mexico, the Texans rebelled and declared independence more forcefully on March 2, 1836. War breaks out between Mexico and Texas, and two major battles decide the outcome.

Above: *The Texans' last stand at the Alamo after superior Mexican forces have stormed the fortress.*

THE SIEGE OF THE ALAMO, FEBRUARY 23–MARCH 6

The Alamo is a Catholic mission building in San Antonio, the centre of the Texas Independence Movement. In February, Mexican General Antonio López de Santa Anna (1797–1867) descends on San Antonio with 5000 soldiers, vastly outnumbering the town garrison of around 150 men, including the frontiersmen Jim Bowie and Davy Crockett, under Lieutenant Colonel William Barrett Travis. They retreat to the Alamo to prepare for battle. A relief party of between 35 and 40 soldiers get through enemy lines to join them. There is to be no surrender. The siege begins on February 23. By March 5, the rebels have run out of ammunition and the next day the Mexicans storm the Alamo. All the men are killed, only women and children spared. The battle cry "Remember the Alamo!" commemorates this heroic stand.

THE BATTLE OF SAN JACINTO RIVER, APRIL 2

As the Mexicans besiege the Alamo, American General Samuel Houston (1793–1863) gathers forces. After their victory, the 1200-strong Mexican army pursues Houston, but is surprised and routed by his smaller force at the San Jacinto river. The survivors, including Santa Anna and his staff, are taken prisoner. In negotiations that follow they recognize Texan independence. In October 1836, the victor of San Jacinto, General Samuel Houston, is sworn in as the first president of Texas.

Left: *Mexican irregulars are as hostile as the regular army.*

Above: *Texan forces scout out the lie of the land before the Battle of San Jacinto.*

ENTER THE VICTORIAN AGE

Above: *Portrait of the young Queen Victoria.*

THE YOUNG PRINCESS Victoria becomes queen of England. Rebellion breaks out in Upper and Lower Canada. Britain seizes the port of Aden, in Arabia, ensuring control of the sea route to India. Thousands of Native Americans around the Missouri river die from smallpox. Higher education for women begins in the United States. The first kindergarten opens in Germany. The Boers complete their Great Trek in South Africa.

✳ 1837 ✳

JAN	26	Michigan becomes the 26th US state	NOV	22	Louis Joseph Papineau leads a rebellion in Lower Canada and wins the Battle of St Denis
MAR	4	Martin Van Buren is inaugurated as the eighth US president		24	Papineau loses the Battle of St Charles and escapes to France
JUNE	18	Spain adopts a new constitution			
	20	King William IV dies: he is succeeded in Britain by his niece Victoria, aged 18, and in Hanover by his brother the Duke of Cumberland, as King Ernst August	DEC	5	William Lyon Mackenzie leads a revolt in Upper Canada
				13	Mackenzie flees to Navy Island in the Niagara river
				29	Canadian forces burn the US steamer *Caroline*, which had been supplying Mackenzie
JULY	1	Ernst August of Hanover revokes the constitution agreed by William IV			

Above: *Supporters of the new Spanish constitution visit Queen Donna Maria of Portugal to enlist her help.*

A NEW QUEEN
The eighteen-year-old Princess Victoria succeeds her uncle, William IV, to the throne of Britain. Her accession breaks the link with Hanover which, because of its Salic Law forbidding women to sit on the throne, becomes an independent state ruled by Victoria's uncle, Ernst August, Duke of Cumberland.

ADEN SEIZED
Britain seizes the port of Aden from the local sultan, establishing British control over the mouth of the Red Sea and the sea routes to India.

REBELLION IN CANADA
Rebellion breaks out in Lower Canada (now Quebec), followed by Upper Canada (now Ontario), as rebels in the popularly elected assemblies clash with the governors and legislative councils. Tension between English and French settlers exacerbates the situation. The rebellion is crushed and in 1838 the Durham Report will recommend union of the two colonies, which will be achieved in 1840.

RECORDING TELEGRAPH
German Professor Carl Steinheil invents the recording single-wire telegraph, which works by punching messages onto paper tape. This method for permanently recording information proves a useful addition to telegraphic communications.

GALVANIZED IRON
Henry William Crauford of London patents the process of galvanizing iron. The process involves the coating of iron with zinc, thereby eliminating problems with rusting, to which iron is very prone.

PHONOGRAPHIC SHORTHAND
English schoolmaster Isaac Pitman (1813–97) devises his Stenographic Sound Hand, based on sounds rather than spelling, which enables speech to be written at over 50 words per minute. It is the first modern shorthand (there had been others in the sixteenth century), and transforms office and business practices.

SIOUX PUSHED WESTWARDS
Sioux Indians cede large areas of land east of the Mississippi, opening a path for a huge land rush. They move westwards to the mountains, to maintain their tribal life.

ELEGY ON THE DEATH OF PUSHKIN
Russian poet Mikhail Yurevich Lermontov (1814–41) produces his "Elegy", which attains notoriety because of its invective against certain factions in the Russian court. The poem is copied out by hand and is widely circulated. Lermontov is removed from his Guards regiment and sent to the Caucasus.

EDUCATION FOR WOMEN IN THE USA
Mount Holyoke Female Seminary, the first school for women in the USA, is funded and opened by American educator Mary Lyon. She teaches 80 young ladies of modest means whom, she believes, will become better wives, mothers and homemakers as a result of education.

CUNEIFORM DECODED
German archaeologist Georg Friedrich Grotefend (1775–1853) deciphers ancient Persian cuneiform inscriptions made c. 3000 BC, making possible detailed studies of ancient civilizations of the Middle East.

BIG SHOPPING
The Procter & Gamble store is founded in Cincinnati, USA, by William Procter, a soap-maker from England, and his brother-in-law James Gamble.

Above: *The arrival of the mail coach. At this time, mail coaches in England travel at an average speed of 14km/h (9mph) and need four horses to pull them.*

INFANT EDUCATION
The first kindergarten is established in Bad Blankenburg (Germany), its methods based on the ideas of German educationalist Friedrich Froebel (1782–1852), that children aged 3–6 should be educated in playgroups. Froebel's ideas are rapidly gaining popularity in Europe.

FAMINE IN JAPAN
A third year of famine in Japan results in countrywide riots and the burning of Osaka, after Shogun Ieyushi refuses to feed the starving people.

THE BOERS' NEW HOME
Boer trekkers cross the Drakensberg mountains and settle in Natal. They call the area, between British rule and Zulu control, the Free Province of New Holland.

EPIDEMIC DEATHS
In August, 15 000 Indians from the Mandan, Hidaksa, and Arikara tribes living around the Missouri river, die in a smallpox epidemic, thought to have been started by an American Fur Company steamboat passing through.

Left: *Niagara Falls, which stands at the gateway between USA and Canada. It straddles the border, which is decided this year.*

Below: *A Sioux village. The Sioux are gradually being pushed westwards by the expansionist activities of white settlers.*

Blood River and the Trail of Tears

BOERS DEFEAT ZULUS at Blood river, Natal, in southern Africa, establishing Boer control over the region. American troops drive the Cherokee from their traditional homelands. An American inventor develops the Morse Code. A mechanical excavator is invented, speeding the process of railway construction. The National Gallery, one of the world's greatest art galleries, is given a permanent site in London, UK.

❧ 1838 ❧

JAN	13	Canadian rebel William Mackenzie flees to New York City, where he is arrested and jailed
MAY	29	The Earl of Durham takes up a post as governor-general of all British territories in North America. He will last until October 9
JULY	31	Poor Law for Ireland sets up a scheme for relief based on workhouses
SEP	18	English economist Richard Cobden founds the Anti-Corn Law League
NOV	27	French occupy Vera Cruz, Mexico, to demand compensation for French citizens caught up in Mexican disturbances
	30	Mexico declares war on France
DEC	16	In South Africa, the Boers defeat the Zulus at Blood river
	24	The Sultan of Turkey curbs the powers of Prince Milos Obrenovich in Serbia

Above: *Rivalry on the seas between the old wooden sailing ships and new iron or steel steamboats.*

THE BATTLE OF BLOOD RIVER

In Natal, the Boers defeat a large Zulu army at Blood river, following the massacre of some 500 Boers by Zulus earlier in the year. More than 3000 Zulus are killed in the battle, which confirms Boer control over the region. The following year, the Boers establish the independent Republic of Natal.

MORSE CODE

American Alfred Vail (1807–59), a colleague of Samuel Morse, devises the code of dots and dashes representing letters of the alphabet, now known as the Morse Code, after the inventor of the telegraph. His method is welcomed as a standard format amidst various personal codes.

VAGINAL CAP

German doctor Friedrich Wilde invents the vaginal cap, a contraceptive device. It is the first use of rubber for surgical goods and provides one of the first conventional methods of birth control in the Western world.

PHOTOGRAPHIC PORTRAIT

A gardener employed by the Revd Joseph Bancroft Reade becomes the first person to be photographed on paper. He is depicted leaning against the greenhouse in the grounds of the vicarage in Buckinghamshire, England.

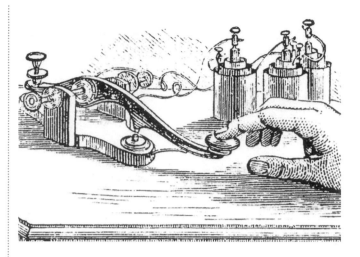

Above: *Morse code is devised by American Alfred Vail and becomes a standard form of communication.*

THE TRAIL OF TEARS

The Cherokees are driven from their Georgia homelands by Federal troops and state militia to Indian Territory west of the Mississippi, despite the Supreme Court ruling that Indians have sovereignty over their lands. More than 4000 of the 18 000 Cherokees die of exposure and poor nutrition en route. The survivors remember the exodus as the "Trail of Tears".

Above: *The Ganges flows across the northern plains of India past Delhi, between Lucknow and Cawnpore, the area under the domination of the British East India Company.*

Left: *The Irish Poor Law is passed; Irish paupers can now expect the same treatment as their English counterparts.*

National Gallery, London

One of the world's major art galleries, the National Gallery is given its permanent home in a Neoclassical building designed by William Wilkins (1778–1839). It was founded when the nation bought 38 paintings from the estate of John Julius Angerstein. It will become one of the few collections that has balanced, high-quality holdings of all classic art periods and schools.

Boxing Rules

Bare-knuckle boxing, popular in England since the mid-1700s, is made less brutal by the introduction of the London Prize Ring Rules. These are modifications of the unofficial rules drawn up by celebrated British pugilist Jack Broughton (1705–89) in 1743.

Times of India Founded

British domination of the Indian subcontinent extends to the press. The paper is first of all called *The Bombay Times and Journal of Commerce*, and is aimed at British residents of western India. It soon gains a reputation for the quality of its reporting. It will later grow from a twice-weekly to daily publication, and will gain wider circulation, until it becomes the *Times of India* in 1861.

Mechanical Excavator

The construction of the Western Railroad, in Massachusetts, is helped by the invention of the mechanical excavator by William Otis. Named the American Steam Shovel, it can do the equivalent work of dozens of labourers.

Distance of Stars

German astronomer and mathematician, Friedrich Bessel (1784–1846), makes the first calculation of the distance of a star, other than the Sun, from the Earth. He will later be shown to have made a measurement that is 50 per cent accurate.

College Education for Women

Oberlin College in Ohio, which opened in 1833 as Oberlin Collegiate Institute, a centre for training Congregationalists, which also admitted black men, becomes the first college of higher education in the USA to admit women on the same basis as men.

The Seraphim, and other Poems

This is the first work by English poet Elizabeth Barrett (1806–61) to gain recognition by critics and readers. It begins a steady increase in her reputation, which means that she is considered a far more important writer than Robert Browning, whom she will marry in 1846. Even so, her social ideas and her experiments in poetic form frighten many Victorian readers.

Left: *English poet Elizabeth Barrett publishes her first work this year.*

WARS FOR OPIUM AND AFGHANISTAN

*T*HE FIRST AFGHAN WAR breaks out between Britain and Afghanistan. Britain is also at war with China in the so-called Opium Wars. Englishman Fox Talbot develops positive photographic images from a negative, a major advance in the process of photography. American inventors develop vulcanizing and an experimental electrically-powered locomotive. English explorer Ross sets off in search of the Magnetic South Pole.

✴ 1839 ✴

JAN	20	At the Battle of Yungay, Chile defeats the Federation of Peru and Bolivia, which breaks up	JUNE	13	In Serbia, Prince Milos Obrenovich abdicates
				24	Egyptians defeat Turks at the Battle of Nezib
FEB	11	Lord Durham presents his report on Canada to the House of Lords	JULY	1	Sultan Mahmud of Turkey dies; succeeded by son Abdulmecid
	24	Uruguay declares war on Argentina			Turkish fleet surrenders at Alexandria, Egypt
MAR	9	Mexico agrees compensation for French victims of civil riots			
			OCT	1	Outbreak of First Anglo-Afghan War
APR	10	The Dutch agree frontier with an independent Belgium, and Luxembourg becomes an independent grand duchy	NOV	10	Opium War between Britain and China breaks out
	21	Turks invade Syria to confront Egyptians	DEC	3	Frederik VII of Denmark dies; succeeded by Christian VIII

Above: *This year, the Chartists present a petition of over a million signatures for political equality and social justice.*

Above: *Kennington Common, London, the site where the Chartists meet to discuss their political aims.*

Treaty of London

Five European powers, including Britain, sign the Treaty of London, which guarantees the neutrality of Belgium, confirms its independence from The Netherlands and establishes the independent Duchy of Luxembourg. The River Scheldt is opened to both Dutch and Belgian commerce.

The Beagle Diaries

Journal of Researches into the Geology and Natural History of the Various Countries Visited by HMS Beagle, the first major work of naturalist Charles Darwin (1809–92) is published. It is the fruit of his voyage as naturalist on board the HMS *Beagle* between 1831 and 1836. It shows some of the research that will eventually lead to his theory of evolution.

Modern Photograph

The technique of producing positive photographic images from a negative master copy is devised by Englishman, William Henry Fox Talbot (1800–77). It hails the beginning of modern photography by enabling the production of unlimited duplications.

Vulcanized Rubber

American inventor Charles Goodyear (1800–60) develops the process known as vulcanizing, by which rubber is permanently toughened by heating it under pressure with sulphur. Hard-wearing rubber goods are made possible, in particular vehicle tyres.

Electric Locomotive

An experimental electrically-powered locomotive is designed and built by American Charles Page. It is run on a standard-gauge track between Washington and Bladensburg by the Baltimore and Ohio Railroad Company.

Treadle Bike

The forerunner to the pedal bike is invented by Scottish blacksmith, Kirkpatrick Macmillan (1813–78). Rather than having pedals that revolve around a chain wheel, it features treadles which alternately drive the rear wheel by a cranking motion.

Microfilm

English photographer Benjamin John Dancer becomes the first to successfully reduce the size of a paper document by recording it on photographic film. In doing so he invents the concept of storing information on microfilm.

Artificial Fertilizer

The commercial production of superphosphate of lime makes a significant improvement in agricultural productivity in England. Agriculturalist John Bennet Lawes (1814–1900) first applies it to a turnip crop, with spectacular results.

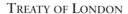

Left: *Edgar Allen Poe, troubled American writer, goes to Philadelphia to edit the* Burton's Gentleman's Magazine.

Right: The Fighting Téméraire, *perhaps the greatest, and certainly one of the most popular works of English artist Joseph Mallord William Turner (above).*

THE FIGHTING TEMERAIRE

Perhaps the greatest, and certainly one of the most popular works of English artist Joseph Mallord William Turner (1775–1851), *The Fighting Téméraire* portrays a beautiful ship of the line being towed by a black steam tug to be broken up. The painting's rich symbolism (the sunset, the blackness of the tug) seem to make the painting an elegy for a lost culture.

HOW AMERICANS EAT

Sylvester Graham publishes *Lectures on the Science of Life*, a study of American eating habits. He advocates eating fruit and vegetables, and bread made from whole wheat flour.

CAMERA OBSCURA

This collection of essays and short stories, published under the name Hildebrand, makes the reputation of Dutch writer Nicholas Beets. Its humorous portrayals of Dutch middle-class life make it legendary, and the book is printed many times and appears in revised editions.

VOICES OF THE NIGHT

The first major collection of poems by American poet Henry Wadsworth Longfellow (1807–82), *Voices of the Night*, is published. It contains didactic poems such as "A Psalm of Life" and establishes Longfellow as one of the major voices of the nineteenth century.

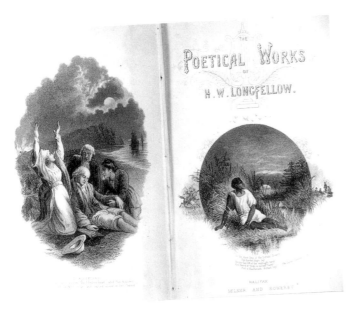

Above: Voices of the Night, *by Henry Wadsworth Longfellow (right), is published this year.*

Above: *Buckingham Palace, London. When Victoria moves in, it is still being renovated by Edward Blore.*

ABORTION LAW

The Offences Against the Person Act makes abortion illegal in the UK and the British Empire and punishable by three years' imprisonment. It is introduced at the insistence of the medical profession as a result of more enlightened attitudes in gynaecology and obstetrics.

GRAND NATIONAL

The first Grand National steeplechase horse race is held at Aintree racecourse in Liverpool, England. It is run over a 7¼km(4½mi) course with 30 jumps. The first race is won by a horse called *Lottery* and the event is so popular it is held every year in March or April.

BASEBALL INVENTED — OR NOT?

It is widely believed that Abner Doubleday devises and names the game of baseball in Cooperstown, New York. Research, however, shows that baseball is more likely to be an evolution of the English game of rounders and was being played in America decades before Doubleday.

SEEKING THE SOUTH POLE

English explorer James Clark Ross (1800–62) sets off with two ships in an attempt to reach the Magnetic South Pole. His maritime attempt is thwarted by the Antarctic coast. He explores a massive ice-shelf, which is later named after him, as is the Ross Sea between the Southern Ocean and Antarctica. Ross reaches further south than any man has yet travelled and returns in 1843. French and American expeditions also scout Antarctica in the same period.

JOLLY BOATING WEATHER

The first Royal regatta is held in July on the Thames at Henley in England. It soon becomes part of the annual sporting calendar.

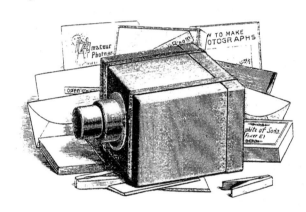

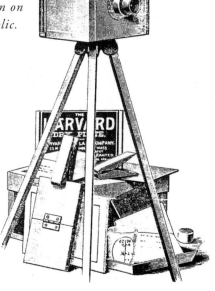

Left: *Louis Daguerre, who this year perfects his Daguerrotype process. Cameras (right) are soon on sale to the public.*

THE ANGLO-AFGHAN WARS

THE AFGHAN WARS are fought between Britain, as the colonial power in India, and Afghanistan. They are prompted by Britain's fear of Imperial Russian influence on the North West Frontier. There will be three wars in all. The first begins this year and will last until 1842. The Second War breaks out in 1878 and is resolved the following year to British advantage. It will not be until the twentieth century (1919) that Britain withdraws completely from Afghan affairs. The First War is notable for retreat from Kabul by British forces in the winter of January 1842. The troops are attacked by tribesmen and virtually annihilated. Peace comes in 1919 with the Treaty of Rawalpindi, which recognizes the complete independence of Afghanistan.

Above left: *British forces cross the Bolan Pass during the Second Afghan War on the way to battle with the Afghans under their leader Shere Ali.*

Above: *Candahar, the first capital of Afghanistan, occupied by the British after the Second Afghan War.*

Left: *Afghan soldiers cut down British troops and their followers on the disastrous retreat from Kabul at the end of the First Afghan War.*

Above: *British troops advance in the line of Afghan rifle fire during the first battle for Kabul.*

Right: *Colonel Cleland leads his lancers into the fray of the second battle for Kabul in 1879.*

Below: *The last stand at Maiwand, during the Second War, a disaster for the British, who lose over 1000 men.*

OPENING UP THE WEST

The decade sees the beginning of a new phase of expansion westwards from the settled area which extends to the Ohio river. Pioneers cross the Mississippi river, stopping short of the Great Plains. These are soon crossed and by the 1850s, there will be settlements on the western seaboard.

Above: *A "Prairie Schooner" emigrant wagon.*

Above: *Pioneers and adventurers sustain themselves by hunting and fishing along the trail.*

Below: *A family with all its worldly goods prepares to settle down to a new life in the northwest.*

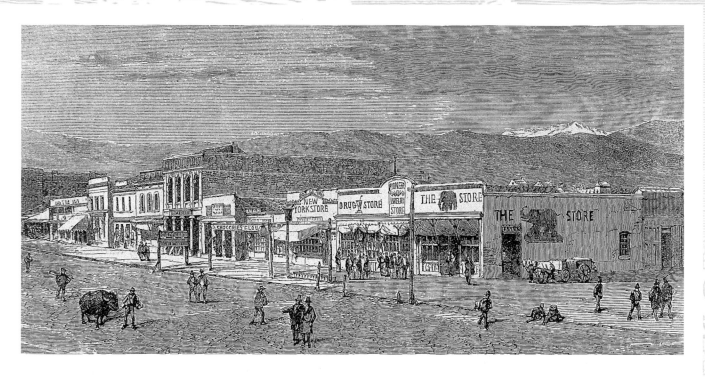

Above: *A street in Seattle, Washington. The township is established in 1851 by pioneers from Illinois.*

Below: *Rush hour in a township on the Plains. It has not taken long for towns to grow up in the new territories.*

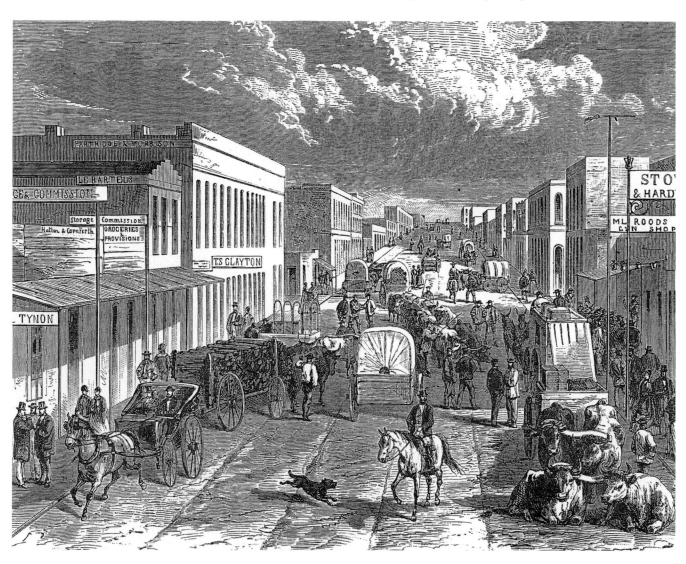

INSURRECTION AND REVOLUTION

REVOLUTION CHARACTERIZES the 1840s. In the United States, discrimination against women activists within the anti-slavery movement leads to the first-ever women's rights convention at Seneca Falls, in the USA. German philosopher Karl Marx writes *The Communist Manifesto*, a highly influential rallying call for the new industrial proletariat. Nationalism and liberalism continue to simmer until, in 1848, they finally erupt in simultaneous revolutions throughout Europe. Famine and hardship too are key causes, often generated by the harsh social effects of industrialization. Famine in Ireland, for instance, drives thousands to emigrate to the United States, which is increasingly seen as a place of wealth and hope.

1840–1849

KEY EVENTS
of the
DECADE

BOERS TREK TO TRANSVAAL

THE GREAT FAMINE

MEXICAN-US WAR

THE YEAR OF REVOLUTIONS

CALIFORNIAN GOLD RUSH

GARIBALDI AND ITALIAN INDEPENDENCE

FIRST PROPELLER-DRIVEN SHIP CROSSES
THE ATLANTIC

LEUKAEMIA IS IDENTIFIED

SMITHSONIAN INSTITUTE FOUNDED

THE PLANET NEPTUNE IS DISCOVERED

EDWARD EYRE CROSSES AUSTRALIA

EUROPEAN MISSIONARIES EXPLORE TIBET

FIRST PAPERBACK BOOK PUBLISHED

PRE-RAPHAELITE BROTHERHOOD
FOUNDED

WORLD POPULATION
1203 MILLION
(ESTIMATE)

*Revolution in France after the abdication of
King Louis-Philippe.*

The Austrians are victorious at the Battle of Novara.

*The Clifton Suspension
Bridge over the River Avon
is under construction
during this decade.*

DENTISTRY, SAXOPHONES AND PATHOGENS — OK?

*I*N NEW ZEALAND, MAORIS SURRENDER their land rights to the British. William Harrison is elected ninth president of the United States. The first college of dental surgery opens in Baltimore, USA. A new brass instrument — the saxophone — makes its appearance. A German pathologist suggests that pathogens, or parasitic organisms, are the cause of infection. And a new phrase — "OK" — enters the language.

Above: *The saxaphone is invented by Belgian Adolphe Sax.*

❋ 1840 ❋

FEB	5	By the Treaty of Waitingi, Maoris cede New Zealand to the British
	10	Queen Victoria of Britain marries her cousin, Prince Albert of Saxe-Coburg-Gotha
	26	In France, Adolphe Thiers forms his second government
MAY	6	Britain issues the world's first self-adhesive postage stamps, the Penny Black and Twopenny Blue
JUNE	6	Carlist wars in Spain end
	7	King Frederick William III of Prussia dies and is succeded by his son Frederick William IV
JULY	15	Austria, Britain, Prussia and Russia form a Quadruple Alliance in support of Turkey
	23	Britain passes an act uniting Upper and Lower Canada
AUG	6	Prince Louis-Napoleon Bonaparte, nephew of Napoleon, fails in a coup to overthrow the French government
	6	King Ernst August of Hanover seizes near dictatorial powers
OCT	7	King Willem I of the Netherlands abdicates to be succeded by his son Willem II
	28	In France, Alphonse Thiers resigns as prime minister
NOV	3	William Henry Harrison elected as US president
	5	Mehmet Ali of Egypt gives up Crete and northern Syria, but keeps southern Syria

New Zealand Becomes a Colony

By the Treaty of Waitangi, Maori chiefs surrender the sovereignty of their islands to Britain. In May 1841, New Zealand is formally proclaimed a British colony, and soon prospers as settlers move in to farm the land and raise sheep.

Harrison for President

William Harrison is elected the ninth president of the USA, defeating his old rival Martin Van Buren, thus reversing the result of the 1836 election when Van Buren beat Harrison. The new vice-president is John Tyler.

Dichterliebe (Poet's Love)

The setting of sixteen poems by Heinrich Heine by German composer Robert Schumann (1810–56) shows that he is able to develop the genre of the song cycle as established by Franz Schubert (1797–1828). It remains a favourite in the repertory.

Tales of the Grotesque and Arabesque

This collection of stories by American writer Edgar Allan Poe (1809–49) establishes him firmly as a major writer. It contains some of his best-known works, including "The Fall of the House of Usher".

Ocean Depths

A technique known as ocean sounding is carried out from HMS *Erebus*, off St Helena in the Atlantic. A depth of 4435m (2425 fathoms) is recorded by English explorer James Clark Ross and hails the beginning of ocean floor mapping.

Dental College

Baltimore College of Dental Surgery becomes the first institution solely established for the oral welfare of the public. Prior to this, dentistry had enjoyed a reputation for being a relatively insignificant area of medicine practised by unskilled "quacks".

Print Revolution

Independently, in America and England, labour-saving machines for distributing printing type are invented. The time saved by not having to perform the task by hand is considerable, so the machines are welcomed immediately.

Native Americans Forced to Move

Almost 100 000 Native Americans have now been forcibly removed to Indian Territory. Many woodland peoples find it impossible to adjust to the differences in terrain and climate, and their presence is resented by tribes such as the Comanches, traditionally resident in the area.

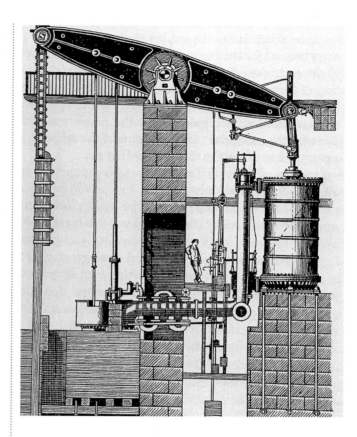

Above: *Taylor's Cornish pumping engine, an example of the stationary steam power now revolutionizing industry.*

A Modern Instrument

Belgian musical-instrument-maker Adolphe Sax, invents the instrument named after him. The saxophone is a keyed single-reed wind instrument of mellow tone and is recognized as the first modern sound.

The Cause of Infection

German pathologist Friedrich Henle (1809–85) proposes that infectious diseases are caused by parasitic organisms or pathogens. This will open the door to some very important advances in medicine.

Fixation of Nitrogen

French agricultural chemist, Jean-Baptiste Boussingault (1802–87), proves that plants obtain nitrogen from nitrates contained within the soil, as opposed to the atmosphere.

Electric Time

The electric clock is patented by a Scottish clockmaker, Alexander Bain, presenting the exciting prospect of internationally synchronized time becoming possible some time in the future.

A New Fruit

The Cox's Pippin, an apple developed by a Berkshire farmer, Richard Cox, bears fruit for the first time.

Above: *A portable steam engine used to drive a threshing machine. Steam power is taking over the world.*

ABOLITIONISTS IN CONFLICT

A World Anti-Slavery Convention is held in London, but Boston abolitionist William Lloyd Garrison (1805–79) does not attend in protest against the exclusion of women, which has caused a split in the movement.

NURSE TRAINING

Quaker reformer Elizabeth Fry (1780–1845) opens a nurses' training home in London called the Nursing Sisters, a non-sectarian institution. Women will work for a probationary period in one of the large teaching hospitals before being admitted as a sister. The service is free to the poor.

Above: *French thinker Pierre Joseph Proudhon, whose pro-anarchy argument is put forward this year.*

Niccolò Paganini
1782–1840

The legendary violinist, the Italian-born Paganini, has died in Nice after a long struggle against cancer of the larynx. From 1805 he was a star performer in Italy and during the years 1828–31 he was also acclaimed in Paris, Vienna and London, as well as in Germany. As a performer Paganini was a technical innovator and when still young he began to compose his own pieces to display his virtuosity. He also played and composed for the guitar. Many of this themes were used by other composers in homage to him.

A TONIC FOR THE NATION

Tonic water, a mixture of quinine, sugar and soda water drunk in the tropics to relieve the symptoms of malaria, is marketed as a social drink by the Schweppes company of London.

A NEW DRINK

James Pimm, a London restauranteur, creates a new alcoholic drink, known as Pimm's Number One.

PROPERTY IS THEFT

The French social theorist Pierre Joseph Proudhon (1809–65) publishes a pamphlet *What is Property?* in which he exposes the abuses of property and with the answer "property is theft", argues for anarchism.

TEA TIME

Afternoon tea is introduced by Anna, Duchess of Bedford, marking the beginning of a change in English social habits. Since 1839 black tea from Assam in India has been sold in London and is beginning to replace green China tea in popularity.

GOING TO AMERICA

The harsh provisions for the poor in Britain's new Poor Law, applied since 1834, which splits families up in sexually segregated workhouses, results in an increase in emigration from Britain and Ireland to the USA.

I'M OK, YOU'RE OK

The expression "OK" comes into vogue in American speech, although opinion is divided as to the origins of the phrase.

Above: *President William Henry Harrison, who begins the practice of flying the US flag over the White House.*

Below: *The young Queen Victoria marries Prince Albert, her first cousin.*

Above: *Afternoon tea becomes a cosy institution.*

COLONIES AND CHRISTMAS TREES

THE BRITISH EMPIRE continues to expand with the acquistion of a new colony, Hong Kong. Egypt finally gains independence from the Ottoman Empire. US President Harrison dies suddenly and is succeeded by John Tyler. Modern tourism begins when Thomas Cook opens a travel agency in London, UK. The first paperback is published in Germany. And Prince Albert introduces Christmas trees into Britain.

Above: *Vice-president John Tyler takes up the reins of power.*

✧ 1841 ✧

MAR	4	William Henry Harrison is inaugurated as ninth US president	AUG	28	British prime minister, Lord Melbourne, resigns
				30	Sir Robert Peel (Tory) forms a government in Britain
APR	4	President Harrison dies of pneumonia and is succeeded by his vice-president, John Tyler			
			NOV	2	Afghans massacre 16 000 British subjects during Afghan War
MAY	3	Britain proclaims New Zealand as a colony		29	Queen Victoria gives birth to a son, Edward, later known as the Prince of Wales
JULY	7	Explorer John Eyre completes first journey from South Australia to Western Australia			
	13	France joins Quadruple Alliance in support of Turkey			
	13	Allied powers agree the Convention of the Straits, barring shipping from the Dardanelles and Bosporus during peace time			

Above: *The British Navy battles with Chinese junks in the war that ends in August with the Treaty of Nanking.*

FRENCH EXPANSIONISM
During the year, France occupies Tahiti and the West African states of Gabon and Guinea as its colonial empire continues to grow in both the South Pacific and Africa.

INDEPENDENCE FOR EGYPT
The Sultan of Turkey finally accepts a treaty to recognize the independence of Egypt, providing Egypt gives up Crete and northern Syria; in return Mehemet Ali becomes hereditary ruler of Egypt. In July, the five major European powers — Russia, Prussia, Austria, France, and Britain — guarantee Ottoman independence and agree to close the Dardanelles Straits and the Bosporus to all warships in times of peace.

PRESIDENTIAL SURPRISE
John Tyler becomes the tenth US president after the sudden death of President Harrison, who caught a cold at his inauguration and died 30 days after taking office.

THOMAS COOK LEADS HIS FIRST EXCURSION
Englishman Thomas Cook (1808–92) begins his famous travel agency in London. His first expedition is by railway, from Leicester to Loughborough. Soon he will be bringing passengers to the Midland Counties Railway on a regular basis; by 1856 he will be organizing excursions to Europe.

HYPNOTISM
Scottish surgeon James Braid describes hypnotism and coins the term "hypnosis". It was formerly called "mesmerism" after Friedrich Anton Mesmer (1734–1815), a German physician who successfully used the technique to treat psychosomatic illness.

THE OLD RED SANDSTONE
Scottish geologist, poet and journalist Hugh Miller (1802–56) entrances readers with this book about his discoveries of fossils in sandstone quarries. The Victorians will value the work for its clarity, and it touches the mood of the times, leading to questions about evolutionary change.

ELECTRIC STREET LIGHTING
Paris becomes the first city to have a street illuminated by electric lighting. The Place de la Concorde has a number of arc-lamps installed by Messrs Deleuil et Archereau. The light is produced by an arc of electricity between two electrodes.

3D PHOTOGRAPHY
Englishman Henry Collen takes the first "three dimensional" photograph. It actually comprises a pair of two-dimensional photographs taken from slightly different angles, which are then viewed through a stereoscope to create the illusion of 3D.

Above: Victoria, Hong Kong, which is ceded to Great Britain this year, as seen from the Chinese mainland.

HONG KONG CEDED TO GREAT BRITAIN

British sovereignty is proclaimed over the island of Hong Kong off the southern coast of China. The war between the two countries is ended in August 1842, when the Chinese sign the Treaty of Nanking, in which they agree to open up Canton, Shanghai and three other ports to British and foreign commerce, give up their own monopoly on trade, accept British consuls, and pay a large indemnity to Britain for the damage caused during the war.

SOFT WATER

A method using lime for the softening of hard water is devised by British chemist, Thomas Clark (1801–67). It removes the problem of the build-up of calcium deposits or scale in pipes and vessels.

FIRST PAPERBACK

A volume containing a collection of works by British authors becomes the first paperback book. It is printed and published in Germany by Christian Bernhard Tauchnitz of Leipzig. It is marketed for English-speaking tourists travelling through Europe.

CROSSING AUSTRALIA

Edward John Eyre (1815–1901) survives a harrowing trek from Adelaide to Albany in the southwest corner of Australia. He began his crossing of the hostile Nullarbor Plain with a party of four. Only Eyre and one companion make it to Albany in the first land journey from east to west.

OH CHRISTMAS TREE

Prince Albert of Saxe-Coburg-Gotha, Consort of Queen Victoria, introduces the Christmas tree to Britain.

DARK STAR

Observing the movements of the dog star, Sirius, German astronomer Friedrich Bessel (1784–1846) theorizes that it must have a dark star companion. Ten years later, he is proved correct by American astronomer Alvan Clark (1804–87).

COFFEE BAR

The railway engineer and inventor Isambard Kingdom Brunel (1806–59) designs a circular bar on the platform of Swindon railway station, western England, for the sale of coffee to passengers.

SETTLERS REACH THE PACIFIC

The first wagon train to use the Oregon Trail reaches the Pacific in November. The pioneers endured terrible conditions in the Wyoming Basin before reaching the Colombia river.

UNIVERSAL SCREWS

The imperial system of standard screw threads, BSW (British Standard Whitworth), is invented by British engineer Joseph Whitworth (1803–87). It allows for the universal interchangeability of nuts and bolts throughout industry.

Above: Richard Cobden, supporter of free trade and Anti-Corn Law stalwart, becomes MP for Stockport.

Left: *Prince Albert introduces the Christmas tree into England from his native Germany.*

Below: *A blissful afternoon in Tahiti, which is colonized by France this year.*

CANADIAN BORDER ESTABLISHED

*T*HE US-CANADIAN FRONTIER is settled up to Oregon on the Pacific coast. The first Anglo-Afghan War ends with a British withdrawal. In the United States, John Fremont's expedition boosts western expansion. In Holland and Britain, temperance campaigners fight the "evils of drink". The New York Philharmonic Society is founded. French philosopher Auguste Compte develops a new science of society, termed "sociology".

❧ *1842* ❧

APR	12	Second National Convention of Chartists opens in London
	29	In Britain, Prime Minister Sir Robert Peel reintroduces income tax
AUG	9	The Ashburton-Webster Treaty settles frontier disputes between USA and Canada
	29	Treaty of Nanking between Britain and China gives Hong Kong to Britain
OCT	10	End of Second Anglo-Afghan War
DEC	19	The USA recognizes the independence of Hawaii

Above: *Telephone lines proliferate in major cities.*

BORDER SETTLED

The Ashburton-Webster Treaty, named after the diplomat Lord Ashburton of Britain and the US Secretary of State Daniel Webster, settles the disputed US-Canadian frontier in Maine to the west of the Great Lakes. The frontier between the two countries is now agreed up to Oregon on the Pacific coast.

END OF FIRST ANGLO-AFGHAN WAR

The first Afghan War with Britain ends with the British withdrawal from Kabul, the capital, after their failure to replace Dost Muhammad with a pro-British king, Shah Shuja al-Mulk.

NEW ANAESTHETIC

The first practical application of an anaesthetic during surgery comes with the administering of ether (ethoxyethane) to a student named James Venable. American doctor Crawford Williamson Long (1815–78) discovered the effect of ether by chance experimentation and used it to operate on a tumour.

Below: *British troops in Jelalabad; Britain withdraws from Afghanistan this year, ending the First Afghan War.*

SUBMARINE TELEGRAPH CABLE

The first telegraph cable to span a body of water is laid by Samuel Morse across New York Harbour. Many others will follow, eventually leading to a cable crossing the Atlantic ocean in 1866.

SKATING RINK

English inventor William Homer opens his iceless skating rink, the Glaciarium, in the Coliseum building at Regent's Park, London. The skating surface is made from a mixture of hog's lard and alum — a double sulphate of aluminium. Real ice is used in 1876.

STREET-CLEANING MACHINE

A significant contribution to the tidying of British city streets is made by engineer James Whitworth (1803–87), who develops a street-cleaning machine. Civic hygiene is a matter of importance, with better understanding of diseases.

DICKENS IN AMERICA

Charles Dickens, on his first tour of the USA, speaks well of the social climate, but denounces slavery and presses for the establishment of an international copyright law.

Above: *After a rather acrimonious tour of the USA, the English novelist Charles Dickens inserts his impressions of the new nation into his novel* Martin Chuzzlewit, *serialized between January 1843 and July 1844. Youthful American newspaper proprietor, Jefferson Brick, is seen here.*

Bernardo O'Higgins
1778–1842

The leader of the Chilean liberation struggle, the son (illegitimate) of Ambrosio O'Higgins, the Irish-born viceroy of Chile and (later) Peru, has died in exile. Through his parentage he was educated in England as well as Peru, and on his return to Spanish America he supported José de San Martin and Simón Bolívar in the anti-colonial struggle. After the overthrow of the Spanish in Chile by San Martin's Army of the Andes he was appointed leader of the revolutionary government (1817) and declared independence in 1818. Opposition of church, business and aristocracy succeeded in having him deposed in 1823.

DEAD SOULS

Russian writer Nikolai Gogol (1809–52) publishes *Dead Souls*, his masterpiece of satire, a comic epic, which he plans to extend with a second part, in which the negative characters of the first part are regenerated. But his true gift is satiric, and Gogol gives up on the more positive second part (he will later burn the manuscript of Part Two).

LAYS OF ANCIENT ROME

Historian and politician Thomas Babington Macaulay, First Baron Macaulay (1800–59) publishes his *Lays of Ancient Rome*, which re-create events in Roman history in regular rhythms and simple wording. The poems are instantly popular, with lays such as "Horatius", about the defence of a bridge leading to Rome, maintaining their popularity in British schools for a century or more.

PHILHARMONIC SOCIETY OF NEW YORK

The USA's oldest symphony orchestra (in continuous existence) is founded, with American conductor Ureli Corelli Hill in charge. It will lead the USA's musical life, attracting over the years such major conductors as Mahler, Toscanini, Mitropoulos and Bernstein.

THE MADELEINE

The ultimate Roman revival building, the Madeleine in Paris is designed as a copy of an octastyle peripteral Roman temple, complete with carved frieze and pediment, and slender Corinthian columns. The architect is Pierre-Alexandre Vignon (1763–1828).

AMERICAN FIZZ

Sparkling Catawba, the first American champagne, is produced in Ohio by vineyard pioneer Nicholas Longworth, using the native catawba grape.

COFFEE IN VIENNA

Viennese coffee houses have mushroomed since the first was opened in 1683 by a spy who obtained some coffee from the Turks. There are now reported to be some 15 000 in the city.

SOCIOLOGY INVENTED

French philosopher Auguste Comte (1798–1857) publishes the final volume of his *Cours de Philosophie,* in which he coins the term "sociology", and puts forward the idea of a science of society.

THE DEMON DRINK

The Netherlands Society for the Abolition of Strong Drink is founded to combat the social evil of indiscriminate gin-drinking. In Britain, temperance workers fight a rising tide of drunkenness — 35 000 new "pubs" and "gin palaces" have opened since the 1830 Beer Act allowed licensed ratepayers to brew and sell beer on their premises.

FREMONT GOES WEST

John Charles Fremont (1813–90) makes his first expedition to the Far West. Fremont follows in the footsteps of trappers and traders, but his travels west of the Rockies literally put many areas on the map. His 200-page report to the American Congress shows the West is a fertile area ready for exploitation. This overturns earlier beliefs of a wasteland and is greeted with an ovation. Fremont plays a huge role in encouraging America's rapid expansion westwards.

THE DUTCHMAN FLIES AND THE BOERS TREK

Boers are forced to continue their trek as Britain annexes Natal, southern Africa. The first tunnel under a navigable river is completed; it runs under London's River Thames. Underground sewers come into use in Hamburg in Germany. A major new music school opens in Leipzig. Composer Richard Wagner produces *The Flying Dutchman,* his first successful opera. Parisians make cigarette smoking a new, fashionable pastime.

❧ 1 8 4 3 ❧

JAN	27	In Britain, Queen Victoria opens the first tunnel under the Thames river	SEP	15	After a revolt in Greece, King Otto calls a national assembly
MAR	21	British poet Robert Southey dies aged 68	OCT	8	Britain and China sign commercial treaties
APR	11	Gambia becomes a separate colony from Sierra Leone	NOV	8	Queen Isabella II of Spain comes of age
				28	Britain and France recognize the independence of Hawaii
MAY	4	Britain seizes Natal, southern Africa, and makes it a separate colony	DEC	13	Basutoland (now Lesotho) comes under British protection
JUNE	17	Maoris in New Zealand rebel against British rule			
JULY	19	The *Great Britain,* the first screw-propelled ocean-going vessel is launched			

BOERS FORCED INLAND
Britain annexes the Boer Republic of Natal, forcing the Boers to continue their trek inland to Orange river country and across the Vaal river to the territory they name Transvaal. Later in the year, Britain formally annexes the Gambia, Basutoland and Sind, India.

THE FLYING DUTCHMAN
The Flying Dutchman, the first great opera of German composer Richard Wagner (1813–83) is produced in Dresden and, unlike previous works, is a success. As a result, Wagner becomes court music director at Dresden, where he will mount productions of operas by many past masters, and work on his own music.

THE LEIPZIG CONSERVATOIRE
German composer and teacher Felix Mendelssohn (1809–47) opens a new music school at Leipzig and ropes in notable musicians such as Schumann to help him. It becomes a model music school, well-known all over Europe.

BIGGER PICTURES
Two Americans working in London develop a machine for the enlargement of photographs. Alexander Wolcott and John Johnson install their enlarger into Beard's Portrait Studio at the Royal Polytechnic Institution.

Above: *The battle for Sind, on the Indus delta, which becomes part of British India this year.*

Above: *Irish statesman Daniel O'Connell at a political meeting. He is arrested for advocating a Free Ireland.*

Dr Samuel Hahnemann
1755–1843

Christian Friedrich Samuel Hahnemann has died in Paris, where he was administering his homeopathic remedies to a wide circle of grateful patients, often without charge, since 1835. After an orthodox medical training and ten years in practice, the German-born doctor developed the system of healing that he called homeopathy, in which infinitely small doses of various substances can be used to cure symptoms that the substance itself would normally cause. Despite the care with which he conducted his research and the success of his remedies, he was prevented from practising in one German town after another, although he lived for some ten years in Leipzig treating and teaching increasingly convinced patients and medical students. Finally he settled in Paris and was vindicated by the fact that homeopathy was beginning to be widely practised in both Europe and the United States by the time of his death.

Noah Webster
1758–1843

The American former teacher and lawyer, best known as a lexicographer and compiler of the *American Dictionary of the English Language* (1828), has died. Under the title *Webster's New International Dictionary of the English Language* this will remain a standard work into the twenty-first century. His American dictionary was inspired in part by his vision of the United States' new future as a distinct and independent English-speaking nation.

THE PRESENT STATE OF ECCLESIASTICAL ARCHITECTURE

Augustus Welby Pugin (1812–52), who has already published several books celebrating the Gothic style, confirms his position as main upholder of the Gothic in Britain. His work will inspire writers and designers from Ruskin to the Arts and Crafts Movement.

REFORM FOR THE MENTALLY ILL

Dorothea Dix (1802–87), a veteran campaigner for prison and asylum reform and instigator of fifteen state-supported hospitals, publishes a damning report into the treatment of the mentally ill in Massachusetts, USA. She claims inmates are chained naked and beaten with rods.

TUNNEL UNDER THE THAMES

The first tunnel beneath a navigable river is completed beneath the River Thames at Rotherhithe in London. It was designed by a French engineer, Marc Brunel (1769–1849), and his son Isambard Kingdom Brunel (1806–59). The tunnel is open to pedestrians only.

FIRST TELEGRAM

The Great Western Railway Company in England becomes the first to offer a telegraph service for public use. Telegrams — messages which are converted from writing into Morse Code and then back into writing at the other end — are immediately popular.

INSTANT SOAP POWDER

Babbitt of New York begin marketing their "Babbitt's Best Soap", the first powdered soap. It makes a convenient change from having to flake a block of soap for cleaning clothes. The high surface area of powder allows it to dissolve very quickly.

CIGARETTES

France becomes the country responsible for making smoking a chic pastime. The state-run, Manufacture Française des Tabacs makes its first batch of 20 000 gold-tipped cigarettes and sells them to the wealthy at a charity bazaar in Paris.

UNDERGROUND HYGIENE

Hamburg in Germany becomes the first city to benefit from the amenity of underground sewers. The improvement to civic hygiene is considerable despite the work involved, and the idea is soon adopted by other European and American cities.

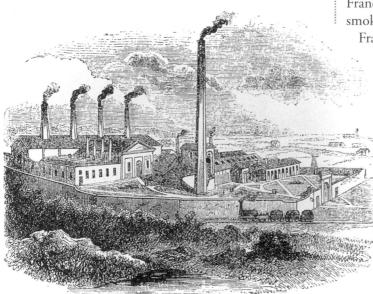

Left: *The Union Plate Glass Company. Plate glass is in demand for industrial and domestic building.*

ISAMBARD KINGDOM BRUNEL

Probably the greatest engineer of the century, Isambard Kingdom Brunel (1806–59) packs an enormous amount of activity into a short life. After studying in Paris, he works at first with his father Marc and later alone, planning and building tunnels, bridges, viaducts, boats, docks and railways. Dashing, charismatic and entrepreneurial, the deviser of many innovations and new methods, Brunel does not always play by the book and makes mistakes, and a few enemies, but his pioneering work still stands.

Above: *The pedestrian tunnel under the Thames at Rotherhithe, an early example of work by Brunel and his father.*

Right: *The Clifton Suspension Bridge over the River Avon, in Somerset, England. Planned by Brunel and begun in 1831, it will not be finished until after Brunel's death.*

Left: *The Great Eastern, built under Brunel's sole direction between 1853 and 1858. It is the largest vessel ever built at the time. Brunel pioneers iron-built boats. The Great Western (1838) is the first steamship to cross the Atlantic, and the Great Britain (1845) is the first ocean-going steamship to be driven by propeller.*

AIR-CONDITIONING AND PAIN-FREE DENTISTRY

DEMOCRAT JAMES K POLK is elected eleventh US president. Mormons fleeing from persecution make their way from Illinois to Salt Lake City. French missionaries make an epic journey to Tibet and Charles Sturt attempts the first north-south crossing of Australia. Nitrous oxide is used successfully to remove the pain of dental extraction. Air-conditioning is used for the first time to ventilate an American hospital.

❖ 1844 ❖

MAR	8	Carl Gustav of Sweden dies; he is succeeded by his son Otto I
	16	Greece adopts a two-chamber parliament
APR	16	US Secretary of State JC Calhoun signs the treaty to annexe Texas, but the Senate rejects it
JUNE	6	In Britain the Factory Act limits the working day to twelve hours for women and to six-and-a-half hours for children between eight and thirteen
	27	Mormon leader Joseph Smith shot dead by a mob
JULY	3	Treaty of Wanghsia allows US citizens in China to be tried by consular courts
AUG	6	France declares war on Morocco
SEP	10	Treaty of Tangier ends Franco-Moroccan War
NOV	8	James K Polk (Democrat) wins US presidency

POLK FOR PRESIDENT

The Democrat senator James K Polk is elected the eleventh president of the USA, defeating his Whig opponent, Senator Henry Clay. Polk campaigned on the slogan "54–40 or fight", a reference to the disputed Oregon border with Britain, which Polk wants at 54 degrees 40 minutes north, while Britain wants it much further south.

Above: *James Knox Polk becomes the eleventh president of the USA.*

CO-OPERATIVE BEGINNINGS

The first co-operative store is opened in Toad Road, Rochdale, Lancashire, UK, by 28 poor weavers, followers of the socialist Robert Owen (1771–1858). Goods are sold to members at market prices and profits on trading are divided between them. It establishes its own wholesale warehouse.

Above and below: *Salt Lake City, the vast Mormon community led by Brigham Young.*

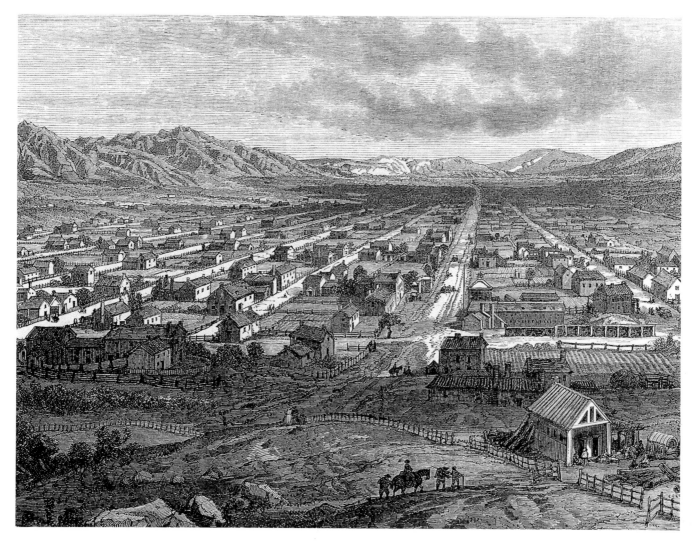

Left: *To many Europeans, Australia is a new world indeed. Explorer Charles Sturt attempts to cross the desert continent this year, but has to give up.*

MORMONS MIGRATE TO SALT LAKE CITY

Following the murder of Joseph Smith, Brigham Young leads a huge exodus of Mormons to find freedom from persecution. Wagon trains carry 4000 people, almost the whole Mormon community, from Illinois to the Great Salt Lake valley. Hopes for independence come to an end when the Salt Lake area becomes part of Utah in 1850.

LAUGHING AT PAIN

Nitrous oxide, or laughing gas, is administered as a pain-killer for the first anaesthetized dental extraction by American Dr John Riggs. His associate, and guinea pig, Dr Horace Wells, hails the event as marking "a new era in tooth-pulling" having experienced no pain whatsoever.

EUROPEANS IN TIBET

French missionaries Evariste Huc (1813–60) and Joseph Gabet make an epic journey to Tibet. Disguised as Buddhist monks they start off from north of Peking, cross China and Mongolia and enter Tibet from the north. They record the exotic sights of Lhasa before being forced to leave by the Chinese who fear Western intrusion. Huc and Gabet then head west to the Yangtze and follow the river to Macao on the coast.

THE WANDERING JEW

This novel is one of the most famous works of Eugène Sue (1804–57). The author is best-known for realistic depictions of low-life, and for the social concern expressed in his many novels. He has a profound influence on French writer Victor Hugo.

JOACHIM IN LONDON DEBUT

The young Hungarian violin virtuoso Joseph Joachim (1831–1907) makes a big splash with his London début playing Beethoven's violin concerto. From now on he will be in demand for concerto performances and for the work of his own string quartet. He will also inspire and premiére the concerto of his friend Brahms.

MUSKETEERS AND MONTE CRISTO

The amazingly prolific Alexandre Dumas (père) (1802–70) produces his two most famous works this year, *The Three Musketeers* and *The Count of Monte Cristo*. He is known for the adventure and epic sweep of his tales, and for his cavalier treatment of history, important as setting and background rather than for the accurate record of fact.

CROSSING AUSTRALIA

British explorer Charles Sturt (1795–1869), who has already crossed New South Wales, tries to make the first crossing of Australia from north to south. He sets out with cattle and sheep to provide supplies but is thwarted by the blazing heat. He makes it as far as the Simpson Desert but decides it would be folly to continue. During the return to Adelaide, Sturt almost dies in the Stony Desert.

DISTRICT NURSE

The districts of Bielefeld and Cleve in Germany are the first in the world to be served by district nurses. The Kaiserwerth sisters represent the beginning of a new approach to medicine which differentiates between the requirements of patients.

YMCA

The Young Men's Christian Association (YMCA) is founded in London, UK, by English social reformer George Williams (1821–1905) as a place where young men in business can find salubrious accommodation and spiritual and social support.

ELECTRIC RAILS

Henry Pinkus, an English engineer, patents the idea of actually using the iron tracks of a railway to carry the electrical current needed to power the locomotive. This development removes any need for carrying batteries of electric cells or using overhead wires.

FRESH AIR

The American Hospital for Tropical Fevers in Florida becomes the first building to be ventilated by an air-conditioning system. John Corrie installs the air-cooling device to improve the environment for both patients and medical staff.

Left: *Alexandre Dumas, père, one half of the prolific and popular father-and-son writing team.*

Right: *Alexandre Dumas, fils, author of many plays, essays, speeches and novels including* La Dame aux Camélias.

Joseph Smith
1805–1844

The American "prophet", whose call in 1820 led to the founding of the Mormon sect, has been murdered by a mob while held in Carthage jail under charges of conspiracy. After (he claimed) discovering, as a result of an angelic message, a new gospel known as the *Book of Mormon*, he founded the new Church of Jesus Christ of Latter Day Saints at Lafayette in New York State in 1830. It was received with great hostility in general, but his movement gained fervent converts too and in 1831 they went to build America's Zion in Missouri. After facing much violent local opposition they resettled in Illinois in 1840 and by the time of Smith's death they numbered 20 000 followers.

Manifest Destiny and Terrible Famine

A BELIEF IN "MANIFEST DESTINY" reflects the national mood of the United States, and Texas finally becomes the 28th state of the Union. Fighting breaks out between the British and Sikhs in India. Failure of the potato crop in Ireland marks the start of terrible famine. The SS *Great Britain* becomes the first propeller-driven ship to cross the Atlantic, and Henri Labrouste designs a revolutionary library for Paris. Pneumatic tyres are invented and self-raising flour comes into the kitchen.

✦ 1845 ✦

MAR	1	US Congress agrees the annexation of Texas
	3	Florida becomes the 27th US state
	4	James Polk inaugurated as president of the USA
	11	Further revolt by Maoris in New Zealand against British domination
MAY	23	Spain adopts a new constitution
DEC	6	British Prime Minister Sir Robert Peel resigns; he will be recalled on Dec 20
	11	Seven Roman Catholic cantons of Switzerland form the Sonderbund to protect their rights
	11	Anglo-Sikh War in India
	29	Texas becomes the 28th US state

SPREADING WESTWARDS

John O'Sullivan, editor of the *United States Magazine and Democratic Review*, argues that the USA has a "Manifest Destiny to overspread the continent allotted by Providence for the free development of our yearly multiplying millions". The article chimes in with the national mood to take over Texas and the Mexican-controlled California and other states, and to continue the westwards expansion.

FAMINE IN IRELAND

Potato blight begins to strike at the Irish potato harvest, leading to widespread crop failure and famine. Many people are evicted from their houses and farms as they fall behind with the rent.

TEXAS JOINS UP

The Republic of Texas becomes the 28th state of the Union after nine years as an independent state. Authority is formally transferred to the US government in February 1846.

LIBRARY OF S. GENEVIEVE, PARIS

This breakthrough building in Paris was designed in 1843 by French architect Henri Labrouste (1801–75) and building begins this year. It is the first French library to be designed as an independent building and it has a full iron frame which allows a broad roof span. It is one of the most notable structures of its time.

RESTORATION OF NOTRE DAME, PARIS
Work on this great cathedral spearheads the revival of the Gothic style in France. The project is carried out by major architect, theorist, and historian of architecture, Eugène-Emmanuel Viollet-le-Duc (1814–79), whose work will be followed closely by architects in Europe.

LES PRELUDES
One of the earliest symphonic poems composed by Hungarian composer Franz Liszt (1811–86), *Les Préludes* is based on a poem by the French writer Alphonse de Lamartine (1790–1869), but adopts a rather different programme. Liszt's suggestion is that life is a prelude to the unknown. It is one of the works that establishes him as an orchestral composer.

STRUWWELPETER
German doctor and writer Heinrich Hoffmann (1809–94) writes and illustrates *Struwwelpeter* for his children. A collection of fantastical cautionary tales, it will be translated into many languages and become a children's classic.

EARLY FEMINISM
American journalist, editor and Transcendentalist, Margaret Fuller (1810–50) reviews the history of women and urges women to become independent in a new book, *Woman in the Nineteenth Century*.

THE STARGAZING EARL
A 183cm (72in) telescope, thought to be the largest in the world at the time, is installed by amateur astronomer William Parsons, the Earl of Rosse, at Birr Castle in Ireland. The Birr Castle telescope is used to study nebulae and galaxies.

LOST EXPLORERS
HMS *Erebus* and HMS *Terror*, commanded by English explorer John Franklin (1786–1847), disappear while searching for the Northwest Passage. Forty search parties set out to rescue the crews but in 1859 Leopold McClintock finds Franklin's resting place and confirms there had been no survivors from the two ships' crews.

FREMONT ON THE TRAIL AGAIN
American explorer John Charles Fremont undertakes his second trip across the Rockies. He maps large areas of California. He is not able, however, to replicate the impact of his first journey of 1842.

PNEUMATIC TYRES
The principle of inflating rubber tyres with air is invented by RW Thompson of London. He calls them "silent wheels" and describes them as an "improvement in carriage wheels and other rolling bodies".

Above: *Famine in Ireland as the potato harvest fails. Thousands die and even more emigrate.*

HOTEL IN CAIRO
Shepheard's Hotel in Cairo, Egypt, opened on the bank of the Nile as the Hotel des Anglais by an English businessman, Samuel Shepheard, changes its name and becomes an international meeting place for business.

SELF-RAISING FLOUR
British baker Henry Jones comes up with the idea of self-raising flour. Rather than using yeast to produce the raising gases, he mixes in a quantity of a raising agent, which is a combination of baking soda and tartar.

ACROSS THE ATLANTIC BY PROPELLER
The SS *Great Britain*, designed and constructed by Isambard Kingdom Brunel (1806–59) in 1843, becomes the first propeller-driven ship to cross the Atlantic.

STICKING PLASTER
First aid benefits from the introduction of the sticking plaster, patented by Americans Dr William Shecut and Dr Horace Harvel Day. The plasters are marketed as "Allcock's Porous Plasters" for minor domestic injuries.

NEPTUNE, THE NEW PLANET
From the behaviour of other planetary bodies, the position of Neptune, the sixth planet, is calculated by British astronomer, John Couch Adams (1819–92). Neptune is finally discovered visually the following year by German astronomer Johann Galle (1812–1910).

PLAY HARDBALL
Hardball arrives with new rules for baseball drawn up by Alexander J Cartwright of New York City. Runners are tagged out rather than hit by a thrown ball. This allows a hard ball to be used, which transforms the sport. Some teams will not adopt a hard ball until 1860.

THE SIKH WARS

Fighting breaks out between the British East India Company and the Sikhs of Lahore as the Sikhs cross the Sutlej river into British India. Peace is restored the following year, when Britain takes control of the Sikh government in Lahore. A second war breaks out in 1848, as a result of which the entire Punjab is annexed by Britain in March 1849.

Above left: *Sikh forces and British troops clash at Maharjput during the First Sikh War.*

Above: *Officers' wives ride in style with Lady Gough, wife of Sir Hugh Gough, the victorious general at the Battle of Mukdi.*

Left: *Sir Charles Napier arrives to command the British in the Second Sikh War in 1849, but the war is already over.*

Opposite top: *Sikh leader Moolraj surrenders after the Siege of Mooltan in the Second Sikh War.*

Opposite below: *Sobraeon, the final battle for the Punjab. After fearful slaughter, the British defeat the Sikhs, many of whom perish in the waters of the Sutlej.*

MEXICO AND THE UNITED STATES AT WAR

*F*OLLOWING THE ANNEXATION of Texas by the USA, war breaks out between Mexico and the United States. Deaths from starvation rise in Ireland as the famine continues. Thousands leave Ireland to emigrate to the United States. Anaesthetic is used for the first time for a surgical operation. The dreadful living conditions of the industrial working class in England are exposed by socialist Friederich Engels and others.

Above: *John Greenleaf Whittier, abolitionist poet.*

✦ 1846 ✦

JAN	2	The French defeat rebels in Algeria		22	USA annex New Mexico
	21	In Britain, the *Daily News* is published with Charles Dickens as editor	SEP	23	German astronomer Johann Galle confirms the existence of the planet Neptune
MAR	9	First Anglo-Sikh War ends			
MAY	13	US declares war on Mexico over the refusal to sell New Mexico	NOV	28	Iowa becomes the 29th US state
	16	In Portugal, supporters of Dom Miguel force the country's rulers into exile			
	25	Prince Louis-Napoleon, imprisoned for treason in France, escapes to England			
	26	In Britain, the Corn Laws are repealed, allowing cheap corn to be imported			
JUNE	15	The 49th parallel is fixed as the US-Canadian boundary			
JULY	18	US troops capture Santa Fe, New Mexico			

Above: *Model of the proposed marine turbine engine devised by James Jamieson Cordes and Edward Locke.*

Left and below: *New processes for the extraction of metals are established towards the end of the decade. This year, James Napier patents a four-stage process involving saltcake and water. Below a furnace is shown in which the metal is mixed with iron oxide. It is being tapped to produce "pigs" (lumps of coarse metal). The copper pigs are refined in a second process and cast into moulds.*

IOWA JOINS THE UNION
The free state of Iowa joins the Union, a year after the slave state of Florida, keeping the fine balance intact between slave-owning and non-slave-owning states.

CORN LAWS REPEALED
The British Conservative government of Robert Peel falls apart after the Corn Laws are repealed, allowing cheap corn to come into Britain and thus lowering prices. The repeal of the laws is too late to help feed the hungry in Ireland, where the potato harvest fails for the second year running. Deaths from hunger are aggravated by a typhus epidemic, which will kill 350 000 people by 1847. It is estimated that by the time the famine ends in 1851, more than a million people will have died and another million have emigrated to the USA.

CANADIAN BORDER SETTLED
Britain settles the long-running Oregon dispute with the USA by agreeing to give up joint occupation and fixing the border along the 49th parallel with a dip to the south round Vancouver Island. The US-Canadian border is finally fixed.

PAOLO AND FRANCESCA
Painted after a trip to Italy, this subject from Dante confirms the English painter George Frederick Watts (1817–1904) as an artist of note. Watts will soon become famous for his allegorical and symbolist paintings, while he will make much of his money from portraits.

HISTORY OF GREECE
English politician and author George Grote (1794–1871) begins his enormous history of Ancient Greece up to the time of Alexander the Great. It remains the standard English work on the subject for many years, and is noted for its scholarship and depiction of life in Greece. The work is influenced by Grote's political liberalism.

VOICES OF FREEDOM
American poet John Greenleaf Whittier (1807–92), a keen abolitionist, produces this volume of poetry on the subject of slavery. Already a popular poet, Whittier helps the abolitionist cause with his writing, which also includes prose tracts on the subject.

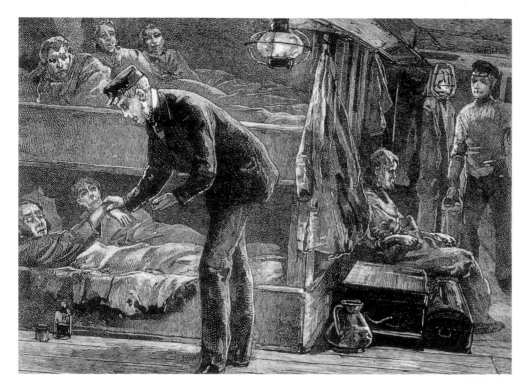

Left: *On board an emigrant ship at the time of the Irish famine. Many in Ireland have died of starvation and even more of famine fever. The lucky ones escape to new lives in the New World.*

BOOK OF NONSENSE

English artist and author Edward Lear (1812–88) writes an entertaining book for the grandchildren of the Earl of Derby. Lear's unclassifiable nonsense poems soon become favourites. His bizarre humour, skill with language and witty drawings are popular with readers. His use of the limerick verse form is influential.

TYPEE, A PEEP AT POLYNESIAN LIFE

This is the first novel by American author Herman Melville (1819–91). It establishes him as a writer of adventures of the sea and exotic locations. It becomes popular quickly (and remains his most popular work in his lifetime). The apparently simple tale asks deep questions about innocence — both of the cannibals that the hero stumbles on, and of the hero himself.

REFORM FOR THE POOR

The degrading living conditions of industrial workers are exposed in two reports: *The Condition of the Working Class in England in 1844* by Friedrich Engels (1820–95), a German socialist businessman established in Manchester; and a study of unhealthy slums in Liverpool, London, and Lancashire mill towns by Edwin Chadwick (1801–90) of the Poor Law Commission. Both propose sweeping reforms to reduce high disease levels among working people.

SAXOPHONE PATENTED

Belgian instrument-maker Adolphe Sax (1814–94) patents the saxophone, one of a family of instruments, which combines features of clarinet, oboe and brass instruments. Sax had shown the prototype in Paris in 1842. Composers such as Hector Berlioz begin to write for the instrument, but saxophones will come into their own with the advent of jazz in the twentieth century.

BREEZE BLOCKS

The idea of using a low-density filler, such as the ashes of coal, coke or charcoal, to mix with cement for making lightweight building blocks, is struck upon by Frenchman Jean-Aimé Balan. It also proves very useful during shortages of stone and clay.

Above: *Herman Melville; his first novel is published this year.*

SURGICAL ANAESTHESIA

University College Hospital in London is the scene of the first surgical operation under anaesthetic in England. Ether is administered with success, its effects having been first discovered by American physician John Crawford Long (1815–78) some four years earlier.

HOME-MADE ICE-CREAM

A portable, hand-operated ice-cream freezer for use at home is invented in New Jersey, USA, by Nancy Johnson.

Above: *Napoleon III escapes from imprisonment in France and flees to England, where he stays at Camden Palace, Chislehurst, Kent for two years.*

ALIVE IN KHAKI

The eminently sensible notion of dressing soldiers in camouflage uniforms, as opposed to bright colours, is adopted by the Queen's own corps of Guides at the Northwest Frontier between Afghanistan and India. Khaki becomes a popular colour with combatants!

A NEW MOON

Triton, the largest moon of Neptune, is discovered by British astronomer William Lassel (1799–1880). It is actually larger than the planet Pluto and later work will show it to be the coldest known place in the universe — covered in frozen nitrogen and methane.

KEROSENE LAMP

Canadian, Abraham Gesner of Charlotte Town develops the kerosene lamp. It provides a glow much brighter than the traditional oil lamp and becomes popular as a result, especially as kerosene or paraffin can be easily distilled from coal.

FAMINE AND IMMIGRATION

Immigration into the USA from Ireland and The Netherlands is increasing massively after the failure of Europe's potato crops causes famine from Scandinavia to Russia. More than 75 000 Irish emigrants are swelling the ghettoes of the eastern cities, while the Dutch join the thousands migrating to the Midwest.

THE FIRST PECAN

A slave on a Louisiana plantation succeeds in cultivating the pecan nut, the first known instance of its scientific cultivation in the world.

AN INSTITUTE FOR EDUCATION

The Smithsonian Institution, a museum in Washington, DC, is founded by the US Congress with a £100 000 bequest from the late James Smithson of London, who died in 1829 and left his entire fortune to the USA to create an educational establishment.

DECIPHERING THE PAST

The Journal of the Royal Asiatic Society publishes Henry Creswick Rawlinson's report of his studies of the Cuneiform Behistun Inscriptions of the ancient Persian King Darius I. His translation of the Persian part of the script opens the way to the decipherment of the Assyrian text, allowing Assyrian history to be studied in more detail.

RUGBY RULES

English public school, Rugby, publishes the rules of rugby football 23 years after schoolboy William Webb Ellis first picked up the ball and ran during a game of standard football.

A NURSING CAREER

The first career opportunities for women are offered by the Protestant Deaconesses at their Institution near Düsseldorf (Germany). They train women to nurse the sick. In 1844 they established a hospital for the poor in Utrecht (Netherlands) and founded the Dutch nursing movement; this year they accept a British society woman, Florence Nightingale, as a student.

Above: *A seed drill in use, one of the many agricultural improvements adopted in this decade.*

War between Mexico and the United States

THE CONFLICT FOLLOWS the US annexation of Texas in 1845 and the US assertion that the Rio Grande was its new southern border. After rising tension between the USA and Mexico, war finally breaks out after Mexican cavalry attacks US troops, although the US has been preparing for war for some time. In July 1846, US troops capture California and defeat the Mexicans in New Mexico in December. The war effectively ends in October 1847 with the capture of Mexico City, but a final treaty is not signed until February 1848. Zachary Taylor (1784–1850), one of the heroes on the US side, will later be elected president.

Left: *Mexican lancers charge the Illinois infantry at the Battle of Buena Vista.*

✵ Key Dates ✵

SIGNIFICANT BATTLES

● PALO ALTO

May 8, 1846

US troops under General Zachary Taylor rout the Mexican army of General Mariano Arista, inflicting 400 casualties.

● RESACA DE LA PALMA

May 9, 1846

General Taylor, with 1700 troops, is confronted by 5700 Mexicans blocking his route to Fort Texas. He attacks and the Mexicans flee. Casualties are 262 Mexicans killed and 355 wounded with 150 captured, Americans have 39 killed and 83 wounded. Winning these two battles allows Taylor to cross the Rio Grande.

● MONTERREY

September 23–25, 1846

General Taylor captures the city after tough street fighting in which the Americans lose 468 men and the Mexicans, under General de Ampdio, lose 367.

● SAN PASQUAL

December 6, 1846

The US "Army of the West" under Colonel Stephen Kearny defeats a Mexican-Californian force.

● SAN GABRIEL

January 9, 1847

Promoted to brigadier-general, Kearny, with a combined army-naval force defeats the Mexican force covering Los Angeles ending the Mexican-Californian resistance in the area.

● BUENA VISTA

February 22–23, 1847

General Taylor's force of 4500 Americans in a strong position dominating the Angostura Pass holds off the numerically superior Mexicans (18 000 men) under General Santa Anna. The Americans suffer 746 casualties, but 1500 Mexicans are killed.

● SACRAMENTO RIVER

February 28, 1847

Near Chihuahua, Colonel Alexander Doniphan and 900 Missouri-mounted riflemen confront a much larger Mexican force. Their accurate fire causes 600 casualties among the Mexicans, while only seven are lost in the Missouri force.

● VERA CRUZ

March 21–27, 1847

The well-built coastal fortress is held by 5000 Mexicans under General Morales. A US fleet lands 13 000 troops and bombards the fort for six days, forcing its surrender. Mexican casualties are 180 and those of the American 82.

● CERRO GORDO

April 17–18, 1847

Confronted by 12 000 Mexican regulars under the president, General Antonio Santa Anna, General Winfield Scott (1786–1866), with 8500 Americans, has a hard fight to break through the Cerro Gordo pass. The pass is near Jalapa, on the road between Vera Cruz and Mexico City. The fighting costs the Americans 63 killed and 337 wounded while the Mexicans have 700 casualties with 204 officers and 2837 soldiers taken prisoner. The victory leaves the road clear for the US forces to take Mexico City.

● CONTRERAS-CHURUBUSCO

August 20, 1847

In hard fighting only 10km (6mi) south of Mexico City, the Americans under Winfield Scott lose nearly 200 killed and 900 wounded from a force of 9000 and the Mexican force of 30 000 under Santa Anna lose more than a third. The Americans are once again victorious.

● MOLINO DEL REY

September 8, 1847

What is meant to be a diversionary attack by 3450 Americans under General Worth against Molino del Rey, prior to the main attack on the bastion of Chapultepec at Mexico City, becomes a major fight. The Mexicans suffer 2700 casualties, but the Americans have 135 killed and 653 wounded, and are forced to withdraw.

● CHAPULTEPEC

September 12–14, 1847

On September 12, General Scott and his men attack Chapultepec, a fortified hill at the gates of Mexico City in what becomes the last major battle of the war. The battle lasts for two days, until the Mexicans withdraw to the city and Scott's troops take the capital.

Left: *Mexican troops cut down in the Angostura Pass at the Battle of Buena Vista.*

THE EXPANSION OF THE RAILWAY

Railways had been developed in the eighteenth century to transport material from mines and in factories. It is not until 1825 that the first passenger railways open, first in Britain and then in the USA. After initial fears for people's safety, the idea takes off.

By 1835 there are more than 1600km (1000mi) of railway in the USA and by 1870, there are 21 700km (13 500mi) in Great Britain. Railway technology spreads throughout the colonies, especially India. The trains link major towns to the benefit of commerce.

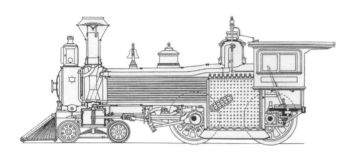

Above: *American engine built for the Old Colony Railroad in 1883. Its large grate can burn low-grade fuel.*

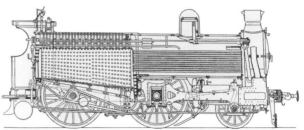

Above: *Belgian express locomotive built by Ml Bika in 1885. It also burns cheap low-grade fuel.*

Above: *Fast passenger tank engine built for the North British Railway in 1879 by Dugald Drummond.*

Right: *Crampton patent locomotive "Komet", built by the Karlsruhe Engine State Railway in 1854.*

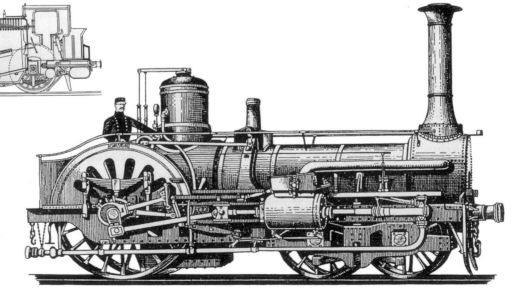

Right: *The engine known as the "Flying Dutchman" (on the right) achieves an impressive 96km/h (60mph). The confused system of rail gauges can be seen clearly, with the narrow on the left and the mixed on the right. By 1846, narrow gauge wins the day.*

Left: *The pioneer locomotive known as "Puffing Billy".*

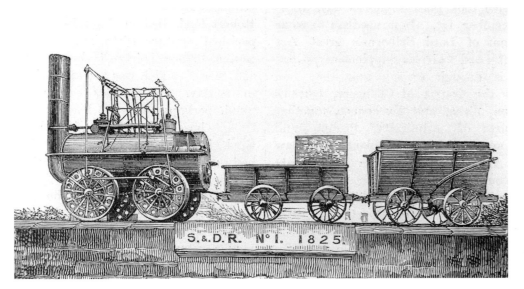

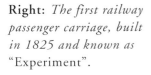

Right: *The first railway passenger carriage, built in 1825 and known as "Experiment".*

SHOPPING GOES UNDER COVER

LIBERIA BECOMES THE FIRST BLACK AFRICAN state to achieve independence. Escaped American slave, Frederick Douglass, publishes *The North Star*. Civil war breaks out in Switzerland. In the United States, Maria Mitchell becomes the first woman astronomer. Europe's first ever covered shopping arcade opens in Brussels. Leukaemia is identified by a German physician. Chloroform is used successfully to dull the pain of childbirth.

Above: *The philanthropic Earl of Shaftesbury, architect of the 1847 Factory Act in Britain.*

✤ 1847 ✤

MAR	4	In Hungary, Liberals dedicated to reform win election to the parliament
JUNE	8	Second Factory Act in Britain sets ten-hour working day for women and for 13–18-year olds
JULY	17	Austrian troops occupy Ferrara in Italy
	24	Civil war in Portugal ends
AUG	28	Liberia becomes a republic
SEP	3	Former Spanish regent Baldomero Espartero returns from exile
	14	US troops capture Mexico City
OCT	21	Roman Catholic Sonderbund cantons in Switzerland revolt and war breaks out. The cantons are defeated in December
NOV	4	German composer Felix Mendelssohn dies at 38

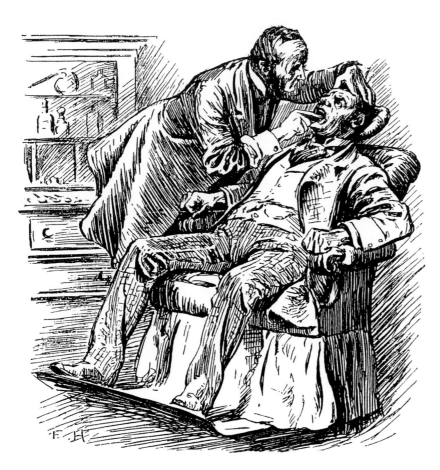

Left: *A new dentist's chair is devised this year but does not make dental operations any less painful.*

AMALGAM FILLING
Fillings for teeth using an amalgam of silver powder are introduced by Thomas Evans (1823–97). The simple process of removing decay and tamping the hole with amalgam, marks a milestone in dentistry.

A NEW COMET
Maria Mitchell (1818–89), American astronomer from Massachusetts, discovers a new comet. Mitchell is the first woman astronomer in America and establishes her own observatory in Massachusetts. She becomes Professor of Astronomy at Vassar College in 1865.

HOME DRESSMAKING
An American shirtmaker, Ebenezer Butterick, produces printed paper dressmaking patterns that can be made up using a sewing machine.

LIBERIA LIBERATED
Liberia becomes an independent republic under President Joseph Jenkins Roberts, the first black African state to govern itself since European colonization began.

DINING FOR REFORM
French statesman Adolphe Thiers (1797–1877) holds the first of his Reform Banquets in Paris to press King Louis-Philippe to reform his government. The banquets soon become very popular and demands grow for political reform.

UNREST IN THE CANTONS
Civil war breaks out after seven Catholic cantons, members of the Sonderbund, or separate league, refuse to give up cantonal sovereignty. The three-week war ends with the defeat and abolition of the Sonderbund, and the establishment in 1848 of a liberal constitution strengthening the state and limiting cantonal power.

EAST COMES TO WEST
New York's first Chinese immigrants arrive on a junk from Guangzhou. Chinese arrivals in San Francisco organize themselves into six societies, each representing a cultural region of China. The district they live in is called "Chinatown" by Americans who visit the restaurants opening there. Chinese are also beginning to settle in Hawaii.

SHOPPING IN THE SHADE
Europe's first covered shopping arcade, the glass-enclosed Royal Galeries Saint Hubert, opens in Brussels. Built by architect JP Cluysenaer, it is a revolutionary new shopping concept.

FREDERICK DOUGLASS
Frederick Douglass (1817–95), an escaped US slave who educated himself, publishes a weekly paper, *The North Star*, in Rochester, New York. He buys his freedom through earnings from his autobiography, swollen by publicity from a British tour in 1845, and becomes the Anti-Slavery Society's most articulate spokesman.

LESS PAIN IN LABOUR
Baby Wilhelmina Carstairs becomes the first child to be born with the aid of chloroform administered to the mother. Pain during childbirth is brought under control by Scotsman Dr James Young, and the rate of infant mortality during birth is reduced.

LEUKAEMIA DISCOVERED
Cancer of the blood — known as leukaemia — is recognized and described by German physician, Rudolf Verchow (1821–70). The proliferation of leucocytes or white blood cells is seen to suppress the apparatus for forming red blood cells.

Above: *Giuseppe Verdi, great Italian composer and hero of the Risorgimento writes his opera* Macbeth *this year.*

MACBETH

This early opera by Giuseppe Verdi (1813–1901) is not successful at first, but shows that the composer is already a dramatic master. He boils down Shakespeare's complex plot to its essentials, produces the required larger-than-life characters and even introduces a hint of the nationalism (Scotland's people cowed under the tyrant) that will make his works so popular in Italy.

SAFETY INSULATION

The need for electric cables to be held apart and out of harm's way is remedied by the introduction of insulating sheath. The Gutta Percha Company of London begins producing insulated cables and wires, thus improving electrical safety considerably.

THE BRONTES AND THE BELLS

Both Charlotte Brontë's *Jane Eyre* and Emily Brontë's *Wuthering Heights* appear this year, under the names Currer and Ellis Bell respectively. While Charlotte's book is successful, few readers understand the turbulent

Above: *The delicious scheming minx, Miss Becky Sharp, star of Thackeray's* Vanity Fair.

novel by Emily. But together, the works published by Currer, Ellis and Acton — as Anne Brontë is known — Bell cause much speculation in the literary world, and the sisters will make their identities known in 1848.

VANITY FAIR
English writer William Makepeace Thackeray (1811–63) sets his satire in the Napoleonic period, although he intends it to apply to his own time. Its vivid characters (especially Becky Sharp) attract readers, and this first important novel establishes Thackeray, a highly experienced journalist, as a major novelist.

BRITISH MUSEUM, LONDON
After many years of building, the new Central Hall of the British Museum complex, designed by Robert Smirke (1781–1867) is opened. The building will remain the exemplary headquarters of the national collection to the present.

MARTHA
The twenty operas of German composer Friedrich von Flotow (1812–83), little known today, are among the most popular of their time, for their rich melodies. *Martha*, adapted from an earlier ballet, is the most enduring.

ROMANS OF THE DECADENCE
French painter Thomas Couture (1815–79), a great teacher who included Manet among his pupils, exhibits his masterpiece, a portrayal of a Roman orgy against a meticulously researched architectural background. The moral idea behind the piece (loose living killed the Roman Empire) is typical of academic painting of the time.

THE CONQUEST OF PERU
Following his work on Mexico, American historian William Hickling Prescott (1796–1859) writes a history of the conquest of the Incas and so brings South American history before a wide audience for the first time. Prescott's vivid style makes his works attractive to a wide audience.

TOP GUN
The service revolver designed by Samuel Colt (1814–62) is issued to the US army. This, the first mass-produced firearm with a multi-chamber cylinder, changes the character of warfare. Rapid fire becomes the familiar pace of combat.

Above: *Colt revolver.*

Felix Mendelssohn
1809–1847

The German composer, conductor, pianist and organist Jacob Ludwig Felix Bartholdy-Mendelssohn has died from overwork and grief at the death of his sister Fanny. Like her he was a brilliant pianist, and he had been a child prodigy, giving his first public recital at the age of nine. He also began to compose as a child, and held public performances of his work from 1826. As a twelve-year-old he was introduced to Goethe (then 72), and a warm friendship developed. He was immensely appreciated in Britain, where he made ten visits to conduct and perform, the first in 1829 and the most recent in the year of his death. His most popular work includes the music for *A Midsummer Night's Dream* (1826–42), and "Fingal's Cave", the Hebridean overture of 1830–32; he composed piano and violin concertos, symphonies, songs, chamber and piano music, as well as choral and organ works. He was also partly responsible for the Bach revival, and in 1829 conducted the first performance of the *St Matthew Passion* since Bach's death.

REVOLUTION ALL OVER EUROPE

REVOLUTIONS SWEEP THROUGH EUROPE with uprisings in Sicily, Vienna, Paris, Milan, Rome, Prussia, Hungary and Parma. German philosopher Karl Marx publishes the *Communist Manifesto*. The first ever women's conference is held at Seneca Falls, New York state. General Zachary Taylor is elected twelfth US president. British painters form the influential Pre-Raphaelite Brotherhood. American poet Walt Whitman produces *Leaves of Grass.*

Above: *Walt Whitman, the founder of modern poetry in America.*

✦ 1848 ✦

JAN	12	Revolt in Sicily against the despotic King Ferdinand II
	22	Christian VIII of Denmark dies, to be succeeded by his son Frederik VII
FEB	2	End of the war between Mexico and the US
	24	Following a revolt in Paris, King Louis-Philippe abdicates and a republic is proclaimed
MAR	12	Revolt breaks out in Vienna, Austria
	13	Austrian statesman Prince Metternich resigns
	17	Revolt in Venice against Austrian rule
	18–22	Revolt in Milan
	19	Following a revolution in Berlin, King Friedrich Wilhelm IV grants concessions
APR	8	Czechs revolt against Austria and are suppressed
	29	Pope Pius IX declares the papacy neutral in the Italian troubles
	30	Revolt in Rome which lasts until July
JULY	19	A convention at Seneca Falls, NY, sees the start of the women's suffrage movement
	24	Battle of Custozza; the Austrian army under Marshal Johann Radetzky defeat Italians from Piedmont and Lombardy
NOV	7	Zachary Taylor elected US president
	24	Pope Pius IX flees from Rome
DEC	2	Emperor Ferdinand of Austria abdicates and is succeeded by his nephew Franz Josef I
	20	Prince Louis-Napoleon is elected president of France

CALIFORNIA DREAMING

Gold is found on the American river, not far from Sacramento in California, prompting a gold rush by eager prospectors who will hit the area in 1849.

SICILIAN REVOLUTION

In Sicily a revolt breaks out against the corruption of Bourbon rule under King Ferdinand II, the first of many liberal revolts that are to erupt throughout Europe this year.

MEXICO CEDES STATES

The Treaty of Guadalupe-Hidalgo ends the US-Mexican War, with the Mexicans ceding California, New Mexico, Texas and other southwestern states to the USA, which gains one-third more territory than it had at the start of the war.

UNREST IN PARIS

A revolt breaks out in Paris, France, caused by the economic depression and the failure of Louis-Philippe's government, which recently banned the Reform Banquets. Louis-Philippe abdicates in favour of his grandson, but a republic is established under the provisional government of Alphonse de Lamartine.

INSURRECTION ALL OVER EUROPE

Spurred on by events in Sicily and France, a revolt in Austria leads to the resignation of Prince Metternich (1773–1859), the conservative and repressive chancellor of state. Further revolts erupt in Venice, Prussia, Poland, Milan, Hungary and Parma against Austrian rule, as a revolutionary mood spreads throughout Europe. Pope Pius IX is forced to grant a constitution to the Papal States, but eventually has to flee Rome. During the year, the *Communist Manifesto* is published by Friedrich Engels and Karl Marx, urging workers of the world to unite and overthrow the capitalist system in favour of Communism.

SENECA FALLS

The world's first women's conference is held in Seneca Falls, New York state, to demand rights for women. Altering the Declaration of Independence into a Declaration of Sentiments, the women's conference, led by Elizabeth Cady Stanton (1815–1902) and Lucretia Coffin Mott (1793–1880), demands equality with men and an end to second-class citizenship. Also this year, a Married Women's Property Act permits divorced women to keep some of their possessions.

FINAL END TO THE FEUDAL SYSTEM

Serfdom is abolished by Vienna. Although it officially ended in 1781, feudal labour has continued in some provinces of the Austro-Hungarian empire.

Above: *Fighting in the streets of Paris, as France struggles after the abdication of Louis-Philippe.*

WAR HERO FOR PRESIDENT

General Zachary Taylor (1784–1850), hero of the US-Mexican War, is elected as twelfth president of the USA. Taylor, who claims never to have voted in his life and has gained a reputation as "Old Rough and Ready" for his homespun ways, fought as a Republican, defeating his Democratic opponent, Lewis Cass, governor of Michigan, by carrying fourteen of the 27 states. Millard Fillmore becomes vice-president.

Right: *General Zachary Taylor, the "rough and ready" president.*

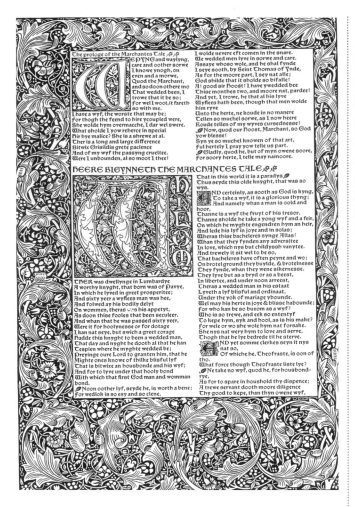

Above: *Chaucer's* Canterbury Tales *in an edition printed at William Morris' Kelmscott Press.*

Above: *William Morris, Utopian socialist, artist and craftsman, supports the Pre-Raphaelite manifesto.*

PRE-RAPHAELITE BROTHERHOOD

A group of English painters come together with common aims. Taking their name from the Italian painters before Raphael's time, they express serious ideas in a truthful way, based on a careful observation of nature. Their directness shocks their contemporaries and their vivid use of colour stands out. Members of the brotherhood include William Holman Hunt (1827–1910), John Everett Millais (1829–96), Dante Gabriel Rossetti (1828–82) and Ford Madox Brown (1821–93); Edward Burne-Jones (1833–98) and William Morris (1834–96) are also involved.

LEAVES OF GRASS

American editor and teacher Walt Whitman (1819–91) travels from New York to New Orleans. His journey inspires him to poetry and he begins the poems that will eventually make up *Leaves of Grass*, the first edition of which is published in 1855. He will carry on revising and bringing out new editions of the work for the rest of his life. Its sexual candour and loose, but lively, verse, mean that few contemporaries take notice, but these qualities will endear Whitman to future generations.

Above: *John Everett Millais, co-founder of the Pre-Raphaelite Brotherhood, in his later years.*

Above: *Europe begins to fear the ambitions of Russia when it takes advantage of the disarray on the continent.*

OPHELIA
Using a southern English riverbank as backdrop, and a model posed in a bath of water, John Everett Millais (1829–96) creates a vivid realism in his picture of the drowned Ophelia. It confirms his status as the finest artist of the Pre-Raphaelite Brotherhood.

THE WINNOWER
One of the great French painters of the mid-nineteenth century realist movement, Jean François Millet (1814–75) paints peasant life, but gives it a nobility derived from more heroic subjects. His work is taken up by socialist writers, although Millet himself rejects this interpretation of his work.

LA DAME AUX CAMELIAS
The younger Alexandre Dumas (1824–95) is established as a dramatic writer with this story of doomed passion. The tension between the heroine's life as a courtesan and the respectability of the family of the man she loves gives the novel mythic status. Dumas casts it into the form of a drama in 1852 and it inspires other works, such as Verdi's opera *La Traviata* (1853).

FURTHER EDUCATION FOR WOMEN
Queen's College, the world's first institution of higher education for women, opens in London. It is funded by the Governesses' Benevolent Association and Miss Murray, a maid-of-honour to Queen Victoria. The principal, John Maurice, trains women in classics, mathematics and sport.

Above: *Sir William Thomson, Lord Kelvin, devises a new scale to measure temperatures this year.*

George Stephenson
1781–1848

The inventor of the "Rocket" has died. Stephenson, the English railway engineer, was raised in a coal-mining area in the northeast of England and had little formal education. In 1815, having invented a safety lamp for use in the mines, he was awarded a prize of £1000, which enabled him to concentrate on his work in developing the first steam locomotive with coupled wheels. Stephenson, who worked with his brother Robert, was employed as engineer for the construction of the new Stockton to Darlington railway which opened in 1825 and for the Liverpool & Manchester Railway of 1830, as well as acting for other railway companies in England and advising in Belgium and Spain. In a competition in 1829, his engine the "Rocket" outperformed other engines in pulling power and speed, doing an incredible 48km/h (30mph).

MARY BARTON
Mrs Elizabeth Gaskell (1810–65) writes her first novel, *Mary Barton*, and it is praised by Charles Dickens. The realism of her regional novels, her understanding of ordinary people, and her humanitarianism win her a wide audience.

THORWALDSEN MUSEUM, COPENHAGEN
MGB Bindesbøll (1800–56) designs this Neoclassical museum to house works by Danish sculptor Bertel Thorwaldsen (1770–1844). He comes up with a Neoclassical design, but it is unlike any other European Neoclassicism, influenced in part by Ancient Egyptian architecture, in part by the interiors of buildings in Pompeii.

NAPOLEON FOR PRESIDENT
Louis-Napoleon, grandson of Napoleon Bonaparte, is elected president of France by a landslide majority after a new republican constitution is agreed. It sets up a single chamber, a strong presidency and direct election under universal male suffrage.

ENVIRONMENT AND DISEASE
Pathologist and surgeon John Simon (1816–1904), the first medical officer of health appointed in London, creates a model public health service. Other cities, such as Rotterdam — where there is no piped drinking water and a cholera epidemic rages — become interested in his methods. He demonstrates that environmental conditions influence the spread of contagious diseases, establishing the science of epidemiology.

GERMAN MIGRATION TO THE USA
The ending of the liberal movement in the German states sends a wave of immigrants to Wisconsin. New York, Boston, Cincinnati and Philadelphia receive many Jewish immigrants.

FLOODLIGHTING
The National Gallery of London becomes the first building to be floodlit. A set of electric arc lamps is installed by WR Staito and used with impressive effect. It marks the beginning of a trend for lighting important and prestigious city buildings.

STEAM FLIGHT
British engineer John Stringfellow successfully launches a self-propelled model aeroplane. The aircraft is powered by a steam engine with two propellers. The race is now on for the first-manned powered flight.

HUMANE TREATMENT IN SCANDINAVIA
Norway introduces the first-ever law enforcing humane treatment of mentally afflicted patients.

Above: *Venice, where there is also an uprising this year, although it will prove unsustainable.*

Left: *News of the Parisian revolt is brought to Louis-Philippe.*

OIL REFINING

The first factory for the refining of crude oil is established in Derby, England. The process, known more precisely as fractional distillation, breaks the raw material down into different chemicals or fractions, such as petroleum and diesel oil.

NEW BALLS

Robert Adam Paterson, a rector from St Andrews, Scotland, uses gutta percha, made of latex from South American plants, to make a new type of golf ball that is impervious to rain. Gutta-percha golf balls begin to replace the traditional featheries. The feathery — used for four centuries — is made up of a leather skin packed with down from geese and ducks.

ABSOLUTE TEMPERATURE

A new temperature scale is proposed by British physician William Thomson (Lord Kelvin, 1824–1907). The absolute or Kelvin scale is based on the same calibration as the centigrade scale, but begins at absolute zero — equivalent to minus 273.15°C.

THE ITALIAN STRUGGLE FOR INDEPENDENCE

NAPOLEON HAD PUT ITALY under French rule in 1796 but after his final defeat at the Battle of Waterloo, the Congress of Vienna returned Italy to its former masters. The Royal House of Savoy regained Sardinia and Piedmont; Naples and Sicily returned to French Bourbon rule; the Papal States, including Rome, reverted to the Pope; and the rest of the peninsula was governed by Austria. This state of affairs had already seen an attempted revolt in the early 1830s, led by Giuseppe Mazzini and put down by Austrian force. Now, in this year of almost universal revolutionary fervour, Italians try once again to throw off the yoke of foreign suppression. To begin with they are successful, with republics established in Rome, Milan, Venice and Tuscany. Sardinia and Naples are both granted constitutions by their kings.

Mazzini supports the Milan uprising and Giuseppe Garibaldi arrives from South America to lend his support to Rome. The republics are short-lived and are quickly and successfully put down by Austria. By 1849, this phase of insurrection will be over, but the quest for Italian independence and unity will continue into the next two decades.

Above: *Giuseppe Garibaldi, long-lived hero of the Italian Independence Movement, will play a great part in the struggle over the next twenty years.*

Above: *Pope Pius IX slips out of the Vatican in disguise when the Italian rebels threaten to invade Rome.*

Left: *Victor Emmanuel, who takes over the throne of Sardinia when his father, Charles Albert, abdicates.*

✷ Key Dates ✷

● BATTLE OF CUSTOZZA **July 24, 1848**
Led by Charles Albert (1798–1849), king of Sardinia, Italians from the Piedmont and Lombardy fight the Austrian army under Marshal Johann Joseph Radetsky (1766–1858). The Italians suffer about 7000 casualties and are driven out of Lombardy. Marshal Radetsky retakes Milan.

● BATTLE OF NOVARA **March 23, 1849**
Another battle for Lombardy. After seizing the fortress of Mortara, Radetsky's three Austrian army corps take on 50 000 poorly trained Piedmontese and defeat them utterly. After this rout, Charles Albert is forced to abdicate the Sardinian throne in favour of his son Victor Emmanuel.

● BATTLE OF ROME **April 30–July 2, 1849**
Garibaldi joins the revolutionary government of Rome which declares the city a republic. They successfully repel the French until April, when 7000 French troops attack, led by General Nicolas Oudinot (1791–1863). The Garibaldians defend the city effectively until July, when Garibaldi agrees to surrender and marches out with 5000 survivors. These men are hunted down by the Austrian army and are killed, captured or dispersed.

● SIEGE OF VENICE **July 20–August 28, 1849**
Venice under the leadership of statesman Daniele Manin (1804–57) rebels against the Austrians and declares itself the Republic of St Mark. A large army under Radetsky besieges the city. The Venetians hold out heroically, but an outbreak of cholera forces them to surrender. The siege of Venice is notable for the first aerial bombardment of a city: hot-air balloons carrying explosives are used, but they are not effective. After the surrender, Manin is not granted amnesty, but escapes to Paris where he lives until his death.

Above: *The victorious Austrian Marshal Radetsy after the Battle of Novara.*

GOLD FEVER AND CRUSHED HOPES

Above: *Henry David Thoreau, author of the influential* Walden.

AFTER INITIAL SUCCESSES, Italian, German and Hungarian revolutions are crushed. Hopes for independence fade as Austria reasserts control. A huge gold rush begins in California, transforming San Francisco from a tiny village into a booming city. Pernicious anaemia is identified. Elizabeth Blackwell becomes the first woman to qualify as a doctor in the USA. British explorer David Livingstone makes his first expedition to Africa.

❧ 1849 ❧

FEB	7	Rome declared a republic
	21	In India, British troops defeat the Sikhs
	22	Benjamin Disraeli becomes Conservative leader in Britain
MAR	4	Zachary Taylor inaugurated as twelfth US president
	4	Austria adopts a new constitution
	23	Following defeat by Austria, King Charles Albert of Sardinia abdicates; his son, Victor Emmanuel II, succeeds him
	28	German national assembly elects Prussian King Frederick William IV as German emperor: he declines

APR	14	Revolutionary Lajos Kossuth proclaims Hungary a republic
MAY	3–8	Prussia crushes a revolt in Dresden
JUNE	5	Denmark adopts a new constitution limiting the power of the monarchy
JULY	5	French troops enter Rome; the republic is doomed
AUG	2	Mehemet Ali, former viceroy of Egypt, dies at 79
	6	War between Austria and Sardinia ends
	13	Austrians defeat Hungarians and Kossuth flees
	28	Austrians recapture Venice

Above: *Napoleon III leads the army that defeats the Roman republic and restores Pope Pius XI to the Vatican.*

AUSTRIA TAKES ITALY

Following risings through Italy in 1848, which led to the expulsion of the Austrians and the departure of the Pope, Rome is declared a republic as a prelude to full Italian unification. During the year, however, Austria slowly wins back its territories and reasserts control over Italy, defeating Sardinia-Piedmont in March and making peace in August.

KING REJECTS IMPERIAL CROWN

After William IV of Prussia rejects the all-German imperial crown offered to him in May to unite the country, the German national assembly, set up in March 1848, collapses, marking the end of any attempt to unite Germany through parliamentary means.

THE STONEBREAKERS

Gustave Courbet (1819–77) is established as the leading French Realist artist with this painting and others like it. It depicts two workers at the back-breaking task of splitting stones, and conveys the misery of the work.

HUNGARY CRUSHED

The revolt of the Hungarians against Austrian rule, led by Lajos Kossuth (1802–94), who proclaimed Hungary a republic, is crushed by Russian and Austrian forces, ending any possibility of independence.

RUSHING FOR GOLD

The California gold rush begins as people from all backgrounds rush west with dreams of making their fortunes mining and panning for gold. Some make the journey overland from the east coast, but most either sail round Cape Horn or cross the Isthmus of Panama and sail up the Pacific coast. More than 10 000 Australians cross the Pacific. San Francisco is transformed from a tiny village to a city of 25 000 in a matter of months.

RELIGIOUS FREEDOM IN SCANDINAVIA

The new Danish constitution is the first Scandinavian law to enshrine the principle of religious liberty — which Norway introduced in practice in 1844. It establishes freedom of the press, relieves *cottars* (agricultural labourers) from compulsory service and abolishes corporal punishment for adult workers on the land. All men over 30 "with their own cloth and table" can vote.

Above: *There is insurrection against France in Algeria as revolutionaries take advantage of the troubles in Europe.*

Above: *Sikh leader Maharajah Dhuleep Singh meets the British as the Punjab is annexed after the Sikh wars.*

Mehemet Ali
c. 1769–1849

The first great national leader of Egypt has died. Mehemet Ali was in fact an Albanian who came to Egypt in 1801 as commander of the Turkish (Ottoman) army which supported the country against the French. In 1805 he became viceroy of Egypt, and in 1841 founded a hereditary dynasty which will remain unbroken until 1952. Despite his background he was a pro-Western modernizer, seeking to remain independent of the Ottoman sultan, and introducing European systems and ways. He gained the support of the French in 1830 when he attempted to claim Syria in settlement after helping the sultan defeat the Greek revolution, and under his rule Alexandria became a great cosmopolitan city with a large French community. His reign was a significant step in the decline of the Ottoman Empire.

MEMOIRES D'OUTRE-TOMBE
Childhood in a sombre chateau, the drama of the Revolution and the world of the Empire are all captured in the posthumous autobiography of French politician and writer René de Chateaubriand (1768–1848). It is probably his greatest work.

PROTOTYPE TELEPHONE
An obscure Cuban, named Antonio Meucci, builds the very first telephone. Although it is impracticable for clear communication, Meucci is the legitimate inventor of the phone some 28 years before Alexander Graham Bell perfects his more practical version.

DRY CLEANING
Parisian, M Jolli-Bellin, makes the accidental discovery that a mixture of turpentine and oil — which he dubs "camphene" — is useful for dry cleaning clothing, as opposed to wet cleaning with water. Certain textiles are given a new lease of life as a result.

WOMAN DOCTOR
Elizabeth Blackwell, an emigrant from England who was brought up in New York city and in Cincinnati, becomes the first woman to qualify as a physician in the USA after graduating from Geneva College, New York.

Katsushika Hokusai
1760–1849

The Japanese artist of venerable age has died. His Expressionist woodcuts in the style known as *ukiyo-e* (the Floating World) have become well-known in the West and greatly influence contemporary French artists. Among his works are the 15-volume *Managwa (Random Sketches)* and *Thirty-six Views of Mount Fuji.*

THE SEVEN LAMPS OF ARCHITECTURE
English critic John Ruskin (1819–1900) publishes his great work on architecture in the interval between volumes of his influential *Modern Painters* (in which he champions Turner and other British artists). Ruskin's insistence on the moral values of architecture will be especially influential during the nineteenth century.

IS THERE ANYBODY THERE?
Spiritualism originates in New York state, where two young sisters, Margaret and Katherine Fox, claim to hear rapping sounds which they interpret as communications from spirits. They hold séances and arouse interest in the afterlife. Many well-known writers and artists become interested in the phenomenon.

WHERE DID YOU GET THAT HAT?
The bowler hat (derby) is produced by London felt-hat makers Thomas Bowler Ltd for an English aristocrat, William Coke of Holkham in Norfolk.

Above: *Spiritualism is in vogue and séances become a popular pastime.*

Below: *The bowler hat is introduced into the gentleman's wardrobe.*

Left: *Queen Victoria and Prince Albert visit Kilmainham hospital in Ireland. The visit to Ireland is a triumph of public relations; the queen is welcomed with uniform enthusiasm from Cork in the south to Carrickfergus in the north.*

Above: *The Battle of Sobraon, the last conflict in the Second Sikh War. The British are victorious.*

Fryderyk (Frédéric) Chopin
1810–1849

The Franco-Polish composer and pianist has died of consumption in Paris. By the age of eight he was the darling of aristocratic salons, and he began to study composition at the age of twelve. As a young student at the Warsaw Conservatory he already had work published. He moved to Paris after the Russian invasion of Poland in 1831 and there, already in the first stages of tuberculosis, he was introduced by his friend Franz Liszt to the writer George Sand. The two lived together for ten years but separated in 1847. Shortly before his death Chopin had been giving a series of memorable concerts in Glasgow, Edinburgh, Manchester and London and he returned to Paris knowing death was near. He will be remembered for his many ballades, nocturnes, mazurkas and polonaises.

PERNICIOUS ANAEMIA

A vitamin deficiency, called pernicious anaemia, is identified by British physician, Thomas Addison (1793–1860). Inadequate absorption of vitamin B_{12} (cyanocobalamin) is characterized by spinal nerve deterioration and a sore tongue.

FREE EDUCATION

The College of the City of New York (CCNY) opens. It offers higher education without tuition fees, enabling thousands of poor immigrants to become educated.

LIVINGSTONE'S FIRST EXPEDITION

David Livingstone (1813–73), who will come to epitomize the European explorer, makes his first expedition accompanied by his wife and children and some friends. He had been sent to Cape Colony in 1840 by the Missionary Society of London. He travels as far north as the Upper Zambezi, making detailed maps and notes. Livingstone believes that by combining exploration with missionary work he can open up areas to trade, thereby "civilizing" Africans.

Left: *A "forty-niner" pans for gold in California at the height of the gold rush. Few make their fortune.*

Above: *Using "long toms"; water is mixed with the dirt and sand to wash out the gold dust.*

Edgar Allan Poe
1809–1849

The influential American poet and writer Edgar Allan Poe is found dying in Baltimore in delirium possibly related to the alcohol addiction which he had sought to overcome earlier this year. Orphaned as a small child he was adopted by a wealthy Virginia merchant and educated partly in England where the family lived for five years. After various temperamental difficulties he worked as a journalist while writing poetry. In 1836, though some twenty years her senior, he married his thirteen-year old cousin, and after she died in 1847 attempted suicide. Just before his death he had become engaged again. Notable works are his poems "Israfel" (1831), "The Raven" (1845) and "Annabel Lee" (1848), the horror story "The Fall of the House of Usher" (1839), and the detective story (a genre of his devising) "The Murders of the Rue Morgue" (1841–42). His decadent interest in the unwholesome as well as his creative talent will profoundly influence other artists, particularly in France, and his work will be translated by Charles Baudelaire (1821–67) the French Symbolist poet.

Above: *Fighting in the streets of Budapest as Austria and Russia crush the bid for independence in Hungary.*

Above: *David Livingstone, the missionary and explorer, sets out on his first journey to Africa this year.*

EXHIBITIONS AND EXCURSIONS

A DECADE OF WORLD FAIRS AND WORLD EXPLORATION. Great Britain leads the way with the Great Exhibition of 1851, swiftly followed by the New York World's Fair and the *Exposition Universelle* in Paris. The USA now runs coast-to-coast as California becomes the 31st state and the Gadsden Purchase of land from Mexico assures a permanent overland route. France gets a second empire, Italy gets independence and unification, and Russia is stopped in her expansionist tracks as France and Great Britain ally with Turkey to fight in the Crimea. The rest of the world gets a glimpse of Japanese culture after a 200-year silence. In Africa, David Livingstone follows the Zambezi, Heinrich Barth crosses the Sahara and Burton and Speke search for the source of the Nile. In the south of the African continent, Dutch Boers consolidate their settlements. Australia and New Zealand begin to govern themselves. Gold fever still rages and there is a new mania, mountaineering.

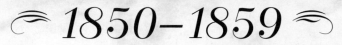

1850–1859

KEY EVENTS *of the* DECADE

SELF-GOVERNMENT FOR AUSTRALIA

REVOLT IN CHINA

JEANS INVENTED

THE GREAT EXHIBITION

SEWING MACHINE PATENTED

NEW YORK TIMES FOUNDED

THE FIRST AMERICA'S CUP

THE TRANSVAAL ESTABLISHED

COUP D'ETAT IN FRANCE

PASSENGER LIFTS

THE GADSDEN PURCHASE

THE CRIMEAN WAR

HAUSSMANN'S PARIS

BLOOMERS FOR WOMEN

JAPAN OPENS UP

FALSE TEETH

BESSEMER STEEL PROCESS

SEPOY REBELLION

NEANDERTHAL MAN DISCOVERED

THEORY OF EVOLUTION

ITALIAN INDEPENDENCE

WORLD POPULATION

1260 MILLION (ESTIMATE)

The Crystal Palace, built to house the world's first trade exhibition.

Fear and loathing at Eureka.

HMS Warrior, *Britain's first iron-hulled warship.*

THE POPE RESTORED AND CAVOUR IN PIEDMONT

ORDER IS RESTORED IN EUROPE after the revolutions of the late 1840s. Three Australian colonies are granted self-government, and there is insurrection in China. California gold miners queue up to buy hardwearing jeans "just like Levi's", two German explorers record their journey south of the Sahara and a Swedish Nightingale tours America to great acclaim.

Left: *Pope Pius IX, who is restored to the Vatican this year by the French after fleeing from Garibaldi in 1849.*

✵ 1850 ✵

JAN	29	In the USA, Senator Henry Clay introduces a compromise plan for slave states
MAR	30	Frederick William IV of Prussia summons a German parliament
APR	12	The French restore Pope Pius IX to the Vatican
MAY	1	France abolishes universal suffrage
JULY	9	American President Zachary Taylor dies; succeeded by Vice-President Millard Fillmore
AUG	5	Australian colonies of South Australia, Tasmania and Victoria are granted self-government
	9	Texas gives up a claim to New Mexico
SEP	9	California becomes the 31st US state, and is free of slavery
	18	US Congress passes Fugitive Slave Law, whereby escaped slaves must be returned to their owners
	20	US Congress accepts the Clay Compromise; slavery banned in the District of Columbia
OCT	11	Count Camillo Cavour becomes a minister in Piedmont, Italy
NOV	29	Prussia is forced to abandon a plan for a united Germany without Austria
DEC	23	Dresden Conference of German states begins

Above: *Coleman's patent expanding lever harrow, developed during this decade for faster harrowing.*

Above: *Garrett's cup-feed drill, one of many mechanisms now being developed to adjust sowing rates.*

SUDDEN DEATH IN THE WHITE HOUSE
President Zachary Taylor dies in the White House of a coronary thrombosis and is succeeded by Vice-President Millard Fillmore.

REBELLION IN CHINA
The Taiping Revolt breaks out against Manchu rule in China. The rebels, inspired by a mixture of Christianity and radical, egalitarian social policies, capture Nanking in 1853 but fail to take the capital, Beijing. At its height, the rebels control much of central China; more than twenty million people lose their lives before the revolt is crushed in 1864.

ADVANCE AUSTRALIA
Britain grants self-government to three Australian colonies — South Australia, Tasmania and Victoria. New South Wales and Queensland will gain self-government in July 1855.

A NEW STATE
California is admitted to the USA as the 31st State of the Union.

POPE RESTORED
French forces restore Pope Pius IX to Rome and garrison the city. The pope annuls the liberal constitution and restores his control over the Papal States.

POWER IN PIEDMONT
Count Camillo Benso di Cavour (1810–61) becomes minister in Piedmont, part of the Kingdom of Sardinia. In November 1852 he becomes prime minister and begins to work towards Italian unification under Piedmontese leadership.

SONNETS FROM THE PORTUGUESE
This volume of poetry is the best-known work of English poet Elizabeth Barrett Browning (1806–61). It describes the development of her relationship with Robert Browning, but disguises this by passing off the poems as translations.

Left: *Traders from the deserts of West Africa bringing skins to market. This year German explorers Barth and Overweg will be among the few Europeans to visit this area of Africa.*

Above: *Norwegian dramatist Hendrik Ibsen, who writes his first play,* Catalina, *this year.*

A SCHOOL FOR LADIES

The North London Collegiate School for Ladies is founded in Britain by pioneering educationalist Frances Mary Buss (1827–94), the first woman to call herself a headmistress. She raises controversy by introducing gymnastics classes, for which she designs loose-fitting clothing, as the laced corsets worn by women at the time are unsuitable for exercise.

Honoré de Balzac
1799–1850

The French novelist Honoré de Balzac has died, having written 85 novels in the past twenty years, yet still in poverty, and not well-known outside his own country. His works of social realism include the series *La Comédie Humaine* (*Human Comedy*) published from 1842 until after his death. Three months before he died he married Eveline Hanska, a Polish woman with whom he had conducted a long correspondence.

THE NIGHTINGALE ON TOUR

Swedish soprano Jenny Lind (1820–87) is one of the most famous singers of the nineteenth century. Her success in her native country leads to engagements all over the world and to her famous nickname, "the Swedish nightingale". Her greatest success comes in America, where she tours under the aegis of the great showman PT Barnum. She begins to make vast sums of money, much of which she gives to charity.

EDUCATION IN AUSTRALIA

The University of Sydney in New South Wales is the first institution of higher education to be founded in Australia. It is to be followed by a university in Melbourne, capital of Victoria, which is to become a separate British colony in 1851.

IN MEMORIAM

As a response to the death of his friend Arthur Hallam, Alfred, Lord Tennyson (1809–92) had begun, in 1833, to write a vast elegy. It is published anonymously this year. It consists of a collection of sections which meditate on Hallam's life and death, and pose questions about life, faith and doubt, which are central to Victorian concerns. As a result, the poem is a great success. Today it is valued as much for its descriptions of doubt as for its affirmations of faith.

LEVI JEANS

A Bavarian immigrant to the USA designs hard-wearing work trousers made from cloth intended for tents and wagon awnings, with riveted seams for extra strength. Levi Strauss begins by selling his product to prospectors during the gold rush before marketing them more widely.

REFRIGERATION PLANT

Although not the inventor of compression cooling, American, Alexander Catlin Twining, becomes the first to operate a refrigeration plant. Using ethyl ether as his coolant in cast-iron cisterns, he is able to produce some 900kg (2000lb) of ice per day.

BABY TRANSPORT FOR ALL

Previously built as a bespoke, one-off vehicle, the perambulator, or pram, goes into mass production. John Allen of London is motivated by a desire to see all and sundry with prams that retail at a reasonable cost.

HYPODERMIC SYRINGE

British physician Alfred Higginson (1808–84) invents a syringe for the withdrawal of blood samples. The hypodermis is the region of skin beneath the outer layer, or epidermis, which is how the device gets its name.

Above: *Nathaniel Hawthorne publishes* The Scarlet Letter, *his first successful work.*

Above: *Robinson and Russell's steam sugar cane crushing mill. It is designed to be easily transportable.*

MORE RIGHTS FOR WOMEN

The first National Convention for Women's Rights is held in Worcester, Massachusetts, USA, called by the feminist reformer Lucy Blackwell Stone (1818–93) and attended by 1000 people from eleven states. This year, women are employed as shopkeepers for the first time in the USA.

NINEVEH AND BABYLON

The British archaeologist Austin Henry Layard (1817–94) completes his excavations of the palaces of the Assyrian kings of Nineveh and the city of Babylon in the Middle East, which he began in 1845. He has sent magnificent antiquities to the British Museum in London.

MISSION TO AFRICA

German traveller Heinrich Barth (1821–65), accompanied by geologist Adolf Overweg, sets out from Tripoli on a journey backed by the British government and the Anti-Slavery Society. Those opposed to the trade in humans feel that knowledge of the area south of the Sahara would aid in the destruction of the slave trade. Barth and Overweg cover 16 000km (10 000mi) of West Africa in five years, and Barth records his observations in five volumes.

SQUASH

The game of squash is well-established at Harrow School in England by this year. The game takes its name from the squashy ball used by schoolboys as they wait to play the game of rackets, which uses a hard ball on a court three times the size of a squash court. It is played around the world under English or American rules — the main difference being a thinner, longer court used in America. Squash is now far better known than rackets.

THE SCARLET LETTER

This is perhaps the greatest of the novels of American writer Nathaniel Hawthorne (1804–64). The book is set in Puritan New England and analyses ideas such as those of sin and the Puritan outlook, which are fundamental to Hawthorne's ancestry and to the North American psyche as a whole.

TEN-PIN FUN

Bowling becomes a popular pastime in the USA. It developed from the game of Dutch Pins brought to America by Dutch settlers in the seventeenth century.

LIGHTER SKATES

EW Bushnell of Philadelphia constructs the first all-steel ice skate. The new skate is lighter and stronger than earlier types.

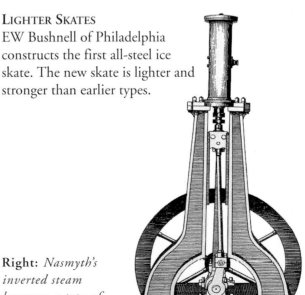

Right: *Nasmyth's inverted steam hammer, a type of stationary engine in use in this decade.*

A Crystal Palace and Australian Gold

$\mathscr{P}$RINCE ALBERT DISPLAYS AN INTUITIVE GRASP of marketing by organizing the Great Exhibition, a showcase for British goods set out for all the world to see. Prince Louis Napoleon of France seizes imperial power and is then backed by a unanimous vote from the people. The first edition of *The New York Times* hits the news-stands of the USA and gold is found in Australia. Isaac Singer brings the sewing machine into the home, the first of many labour-saving appliances that this century will see.

❋ 1851 ❋

Mar	16	Spain adopts Roman Catholicism as its only religion
Apr	7	Gold is discovered at Summerhill Creek, New South Wales, Australia
May	1	In London, England, Queen Victoria opens the Great Exhibition
June	2	Erie railroad is the first to reach the Great Lakes of North America
July	1	Victoria, Australia, becomes a separate colony
Sep	14	US author James Fenimore Cooper dies at 61
	25	Chinese rebels proclaim the *T'ai P'ing T'ien-kuo* (Kingdom of Heavenly Peace)
Nov	18	King Ernest Augustus of Hanover dies; succeeded by his son, George V
Dec	2	In a coup d'état, President Louis Napoleon of France changes the constitution
	19	Britain's foreign secretary, Lord Palmerston, supports the new French constitution; Queen Victoria forces him to resign
	21	By a plebiscite, the French people approve the new constitution
	31	Austria abolishes its constitution

Gold in the Antipodes

Gold is discovered at Summerhill Creek, in the Blue Mountains, north of Bathurst, prompting a gold rush, with prospectors pouring in from Britain, the USA and elsewhere. By 1861, Australia's population will have tripled.

First World Fair

Queen Victoria opens the world's first international fair — the Great Exhibition — in London's Hyde Park. The Great Exhibition of the Works of Industry of all Nations attracts some six million visitors. It is housed in the Crystal Palace, a building in which Joseph Paxton (1801–65) shows the potential of producing metal and glass prefabricated structures that are quick to build.

Napoleonic Coup d'Etat

Louis Napoleon seizes power in a coup d'etat and reforms the constitution, allowing him to gain more power. Risings against his coup are easily suppressed.

Rigoletto

Perhaps Giuseppe Verdi's most popular opera, a tragedy, *Rigoletto* is composed (in 40 days), and receives its first production in Venice. It will remain popular for its tunefulness, strong plot (based on a play by Victor Hugo) and vivid characters (especially the hunchback Rigoletto himself).

Yale Lock

American inventor, Linus Yale (1821–68), invents the barrel or cylinder locking mechanism. It is made possible because of an ability to produce precision parts, and means that locks can be made much smaller and easier to fit into doors.

Above: *Prince Albert, the royal innovator and architect of the Great Exhibition held in London this year.*

New York Times

Henry J Raymond founds the newspaper, *The New York Times*, which soon becomes known as the most authoritative in the USA. It will attract some of the USA's most distinguished editors and journalists.

Scientific Meeting

Paris plays host to the first international scientific congress. Titled the "International Sanitary Congress", the meeting establishes and legitimizes the importance of sharing scientific discovery and invention on the world stage for the benefit of humanity.

Left: *The magnificent Crystal Palace, designed by the engineer Sir Joseph Paxton for quick assembly. With fitting symbolism, each exhibition unit is 2.5m (8ft) wide and 51 units make up the width of the palace. In total it is 563m (1848ft) long.*

Below: *A multi-spindle drilling machine, a step towards the mechanization which is to transform industry.*

Right: *Printing drum from the power loom for weaving tapestry carpet, developed this year.*

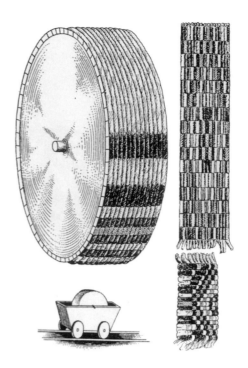

SOLAR ECLIPSE

Italian astronomer Angelo Secchi (1818–78) records a photographic image of a solar eclipse. It is fairly dangerous to achieve since it involves a lens looking at the sun, but is a useful record of a relatively infrequent event.

BIG GUNS

The first successful breech-loading cannon is built by the German firm Krupp. It fires 6lb shells. Breech-loading allows gun crews to fire faster.

Hans Oersted
1777–1851

The Danish physicist who discovered electromagnetism in 1820, Hans Christian Oersted, has died. The discovery came about when he noticed that a nearby electric current caused a compass needle to deflect. In 1825, using electromagnetism, he became the first to extract the metal aluminium from aluminates. Electromagnetism has many practical applications: Samuel Morse used it to develop the electric telegraph (1837), activating an electromagnet in the receiver by means of an electric current. It is used in extracting a metal from its ore, in the metal-plating process and in pumps for liquid metal. Electromagnetic devices will form the basis of electrical engineering, to be used in starter motors, cathode ray tubes, radar, switches, alarms *et al.* Oersted's name is given to the unit of magnetic field strength.

PRACTICAL SEWING MACHINE

The age of labour-saving devices in the home begins with the manufacture of domestic sewing machines. Although the prototype has already been established in France, American inventor and manufacturer Isaac Merritt Singer (1811–75) develops the first hand-operated practicable machine and starts production in Boston.

SLAVE REVOLT

Free Negroes storm a jail in Boston, USA and release a slave named Shadrach. Under the 1850 Fugitive Slave Bill, runaway slaves may be captured in any state and returned to their southern owners. Bounty hunting is rife, with a $10 reward for each slave.

Right: *Isaac Singer's prototype sewing machine. Although rather crude, every feature is in place.*

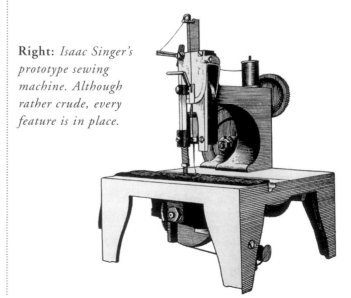

Above: *Whalers approach a "right" whale. Whales inspire Herman Melville to write his novel* Moby Dick.

Mary Wollstonecraft Shelley
1797–1851

The novelist and (second) wife of the poet Percy Bysshe Shelley, and creator of the monster *Frankenstein*, has died. She was the daughter of the feminist Mary Wollstonecraft and the writer William Godwin, but her mother died during her infancy. She eloped with Shelley at the age of sixteen, in 1814 (accompanied by her half-sister) and married him in 1816. They lived in Europe, where their adored son William died in Rome. Shelley himself was drowned in a sudden squall near Livorno (1822) while on his way back from a visit to the poet Byron, and after his death his wife returned to England with their other child and lived partly on an allowance from her husband's father and partly by her writing. As well as the classic horror story *Frankenstein, or the Modern Prometheus* (1818), she wrote *The Last Man* (1826), *Rambles in Germany and Italy* (1844) and other works.

MOBY DICK

This story of obsession and the sea is the masterpiece of the American novelist Herman Melville (1819–91). It advances the capabilities of the novel, opening it up into a kind of encyclopedia, in which anything relevant to the central subject (here, the whale) can be accommodated. It is a landmark book, though little appreciated at the time.

THE FIRST AMERICA'S CUP

The yacht *America*, which had crossed the Atlantic, beats the best of the British yachting fleet off the Isle of Wight. The win is allowed to stand despite fierce protests from British sailors who believed the Americans had contravened the rules. The cup won by the owners of *America* becomes known as the America's Cup and on July 8, 1857, is given to the New York Yacht Club as the prize for a competition which will bear its name for the next two centuries.

TIFFANY SILVER

The jeweller Charles Lewis Tiffany, who opened a stationery and oriental goods store in New York in 1837, has become famous for the silverware he began making in 1848. Last year he opened a branch of his store in Paris and this year he has introduced the English sterling silver standard as a guarantee of quality.

Left: *All over France there are riots and uprisings against the coup d'état staged by Louis Napoleon in December. They have little effect.*

PRIZE MONEY

Robert McClure and the crew of HMS *Investigator* win an award of £10 000 for being the first to sail from Asia to Europe via the Northwest Passage. They lose their ship in 1853 and return to Britain on another vessel, reaching home in 1854.

PYRIDINE

A Scottish chemist, Thomas Anderson (1819–74), discovers the chemical pyridine. It is a heterocyclic compound which finds uses as an important solvent for the manufacture of other chemicals. It is also used in producing drugs that combat infections.

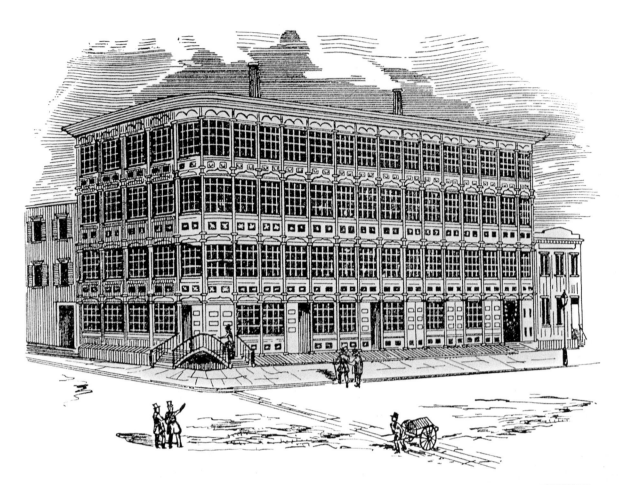

Above: *Cast-iron façade in New York. Strong yet cheap, cast iron is rapidly becoming the building material of choice for many architects.*

Right: *A steam plough is demonstrated on a German farm. Agriculture is becoming industrialized.*

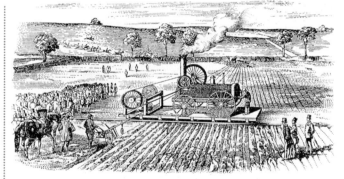

Below: *A cross-section of Garrett's improved threshing machine, showing how the wheat is separated.*

John James Audubon
1785–1851

The American ornithologist and illustrator has died. The somewhat flamboyant son of a French sea captain and a Creole woman, he was raised in France by his father. Sent by him to Philadelphia, he began his study of birds, which he would trap or shoot and wire into lifelike poses to serve as his models. He rose from bankruptcy to being the owner of a comfortable country house and grounds on the Hudson river through publishing his *Birds of America* in England (1827–38), the miniature edition of which (1840–44) became a best-seller.

THE GREAT EXHIBITION

PRINCE ALBERT HAD LAUNCHED the idea of an exhibition in 1849 and invited public subscriptions to pay for the building to house it. James Paxton's Crystal Palace goes from drawing board to completion in eighteen months and the Exhibition opens in May, displaying 13 000 exhibits, most of them British. Income from the exhibition is used to fund the Albert Hall and the museums at South Kensington.

Above: *The Crystal Palace at the original exhibition site, Hyde Park. Next year it will be moved to Sydenham.*

Above: *Queen Victoria formally declares the Great Exhibition open. Over six million people will visit it.*

Above: *An urn made by Josiah Wedgwood.*

Above: *A Dutch casket in the Renaissance style.*

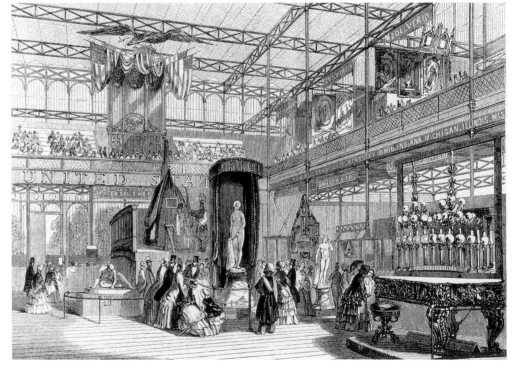

Above: *The exhibition space devoted to the arts, crafts and manufacturing skills of the United States.*

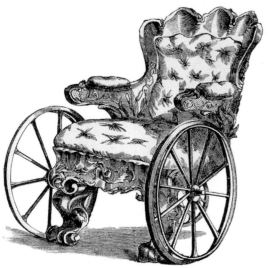

Above: *An invalid chair designed by James Heath of Bath. The sitter can move it about a room unaided. It becomes known as a Bath chair.*

Right: *A damask hanging by Ackroyd & Son of Halifax. Its design is based on those found in the Moorish Alhambra Palace in Spain.*

Above: *Fish knife, fork and slice by Rodgers & Son of Sheffield. Note the kingfisher on the slice blade.*

Above: *A Louis-Quatorze-style console table made and exhibited by M Jeanselme of Paris.*

ENTER THE SECOND EMPIRE

Above: *Russian writer Ivan Turgenev produces his first work this year.*

NEW ZEALAND FOLLOWS AUSTRALIA towards self-government. Louis Napoleon becomes Emperor Napoleon III and sets about expanding French colonies. The skies are crowded with manned gliders and hot-air balloons. In the southern hemisphere, the Transvaal is established in southern Africa. Flushable public lavatories are introduced in England along with a whole infrastructure of sewers and reservoirs, which can only be good for the health of the nation.

✻ 1852 ✻

JAN	14	France's new constitution gives the president supreme power
	17	The South African Republic (the Transvaal) is established
FEB	3	Argentine dictator General Juan Manuel de Rosas is overthrown
	17	France re-introduces press censorship
APR	1	Second Anglo-Burmese War breaks out
MAY	8	By a treaty, Austria, Britain, France, Prussia, Russia and Sweden guarantee Denmark's independence
JUNE	30	Britain grants New Zealand representative government
SEP	14	Henri Giffard makes the first flight in a steam-powered airship
NOV	2	Franklin Pierce (Democrat) is chosen as America's president
	4	Count Cavour becomes Piedmont's prime minister
DEC	2	The Second Empire is founded in France: Louis Napoleon becomes Emperor Napoleon III
	20	In Britain, Lord Derby resigns as prime minister; Lord Aberdeen forms a coalition government

Above: *Arthur Wellesley, Duke of Wellington, dies this year and is buried with great pomp and ceremony.*

Above: *Inside a cannery. Although screw-top jars are invented this year, food in cans is still in great demand.*

Left and above: *Author and abolitionist Harriet Beecher Stowe and her house at Mandarin, Florida.*

HOME RULE FOR NEW ZEALAND

Britain grants New Zealand representative self-government, giving the islands considerable autonomy in their government.

PIERCE FOR PRESIDENT

Franklin Pierce (1804–69) a Democrat from New York, wins the presidential election by a landslide against his Whig opponent, General Winfield Scott. He becomes the fourteenth president of his country.

THE EMPIRE STRIKES BACK

The Second Empire is declared as Louis Napoleon (1808–73) is proclaimed Emperor Napoleon III, ushering in a time of stable imperial rule and a massive extension of colonial rule in the South Pacific (New Caledonia is taken over in 1853) and North Africa.

WORK

Influenced by the Pre-Raphaelites and by the outdoor painting of the French Barbizon School, Ford Madox Brown (1821–93) begins to paint *Work*, which is inspired by the artist's view of the moral centrality of the arts and the need for social reform.

UNCLE TOM'S CABIN

Having been published in serial form in 1851–52, the anti-slavery novel by Harriet Beecher Stowe (1811–96) appears in book form. The novel is highly successful, and valued for its depiction of the suffering caused by slavery, although its ending (the black characters become missionaries in Africa) is later criticized.

Louis Braille
1809–1852

The French educationist Louis Braille has died. Braille, who was blind from the age of three, devised a system of raised writing that can be read by the hands, and which can also be written, changing the life of blind people. He was educated at the Institution de Jeunes Aveugles in Paris and went on to become professor there.

EMAUX ET CAMEES

The finely wrought lyrics of this book by French writer Théophile Gautier (1811–72) are widely influential, both for their beautiful construction and for the view that art is the supreme value. It is considered by many to be his best work.

A SPORTSMAN'S SKETCHES

These prose sketches of Russian peasant life are the first writings to bring fame to Russian writer Ivan Turgenev (1818–83). He will use similar country settings and atmospheric descriptions in his later novels.

KING'S CROSS STATION, LONDON

This railway station, with its massive twin iron-and-glass barrel-vaulted train sheds, is the biggest station in England when it is completed. The architect is Lewis Cubitt (b. 1799).

SCREW TOP

A Frenchman is the first to patent a screw-top fitting for bottles. François-Joseph Beltzung sees a need for conveniently resealable vessels that will be more reliable and consistent than corks and stoppers with wire clips.

FIRE ALARM

Boston, Massachusetts becomes the first city to feature an electrically operated fire alarm system. Some 50 signal boxes are fitted around the city so that anyone in need of assistance can run to their nearest box and make a telegraph call to the fire-fighting department.

VICTORIA FALLS

Scottish missionary and explorer David Livingstone (1813–73) is the first European to cross Africa from west to east. His journey lasts from 1852 to 1856. Travelling along the Zambezi, he comes across a massive waterfall and names it Victoria Falls after Queen Victoria of Great Britain.

SINGER'S SEWING MACHINES,

Above: *An advertisement for Isaac Singer's sewing machine, now patented and ready for domestic use.*

FIRST AIRSHIP

French engineer Henri Giffard builds and flies the first airship. It is cigar-shaped, 43m (144ft) long and driven forward by a 3 horse-power motor and propeller at a stately rate of 8km/h (5mph). It flies for 27km (17mi) over Paris, but does not have the power to turn round.

Above: *The personification of Empire; this year, the French elect Louis Napoleon to be their new emperor.*

GOING DOWN UNDER

Famine in Europe has resulted in mass emigration to the Antipodes. Otago on South Island, New Zealand, is popular for Scots with sheep-farming, mining and engineering skills, while the Irish settle in South Australia, founded in 1834 by Edward Gibbon Wakefield (1796–1862), a British colonial theorist. Victoria is settled for the first time by West Australian ranger Edward Henty.

BRAND NEW BAGS

Brown paper bags strong enough to hold shopping are invented by Luther C Crowell of Massachusetts, USA, and a machine to fold and seal them is patented by Frances Wolle.

HEALTH AND HYGIENE

The first flushable public convenience is opened in London, built to a revolutionary new design first displayed at the 1851 Great Exhibition by engineer George Jennings. A network of public conveniences is planned across London, together with an extensive new sewerage system, public washing and laundry facilities in all poor areas, and several new reservoirs to supply fresh water.

THERE'S A WORD FOR IT

Roget's *Thesaurus of English Words and Phrases* — the first English language thesaurus — is published by English physician Peter Mark Roget (1779–1869), one of the founders of London University.

Above: *Prince Louis-Napoleon, before he takes on his imperial role.*

Right: *The coronation of Emperor Napoleon III takes place in the Cathedral of Notre Dame on January 1.*

Nikolai Gogol
1809–1852

The brilliant Russian writer Nikolai Vasilevich Gogol-Yanovski has died during Lent, weakened by self-imposed rigorous fasting and shortly after burning the manuscript of what should have been the sequel to his greatest novel *Dead Souls*. He is to become known as "the father of Russian realism" because his writing deals with the commonplace in terms of people and surroundings, but he uses these ingredients in an eccentric and highly creative way. His study of the history of Russia in the Middle Ages earned him a chair in history at the University of St Petersburg, which he kept until 1835. His satirically witty and controversial play *The Government Inspector* was performed in 1836 and after this he exiled himself to Germany, Switzerland, Paris and Rome. He returned to Russia in 1848 after a visit to the Holy Land. His output consisted mainly of short stories, including the two-volume collection *Evenings on a Farm near Dikanka*, published in 1831 and 1832. Despite the success of this and other work, he always felt that he was the object of violent hostility.

POETRY FROM PARNASSUS
The Parnassian school of poetry is founded in France with the publication of *Poèmes Antiques* by Charles Marie Leconte de Lisle (1818–94). He and his colleagues favour a classical, precise, objective poetical style, in reaction against the excesses of the Romantics.

EXPRESS MAIL
Wells, Fargo & Co. begins as an express delivery service between Buffalo, NY and Detroit, USA. Its owners are Henry Wells, who last year set up an express service between New York city and Buffalo, and William George Fargo.

PASSENGER LIFT
American inventor Elisha Otis (1811–61) installs the first safety passenger lift or elevator. It is mechanically operated, but electric motors will soon be used, allowing city development to move upwards as opposed to outwards.

MANNED GLIDER
True manned flight is witnessed in England. Sir George Cayley (1773–1857) persuades his coachman to pilot his "controllable" glider. The aircraft glides some 500m (560yd) without killing its reluctant passenger.

Below: Louis Napoleon stages his coup d'état and evicts the judges from their chambers.

RUSSIA AND TURKEY GO TO WAR

RUSSIA ENCROACHES ON TURKEY, "the sick man of Europe", but this move prompts traditional enemies France and Great Britain to ally and come to Turkey's aid. This will end in the Crimean War. On a lighter note, William Steinway begins making quality pianos in New York, Mrs Amelia Bloomer introduces the female trouser and the potato crisp is born. It is no longer acceptable to send convicts to serve their time in Australia, and Baron Haussmann is redesigning the boulevards of Paris.

❋ 1853 ❋

JAN	29	Emperor Napoleon III of France marries Spanish Countess Eugénie de Montijo
FEB	19	Prussia and Russia sign a trade treaty
MAR	4	Franklin Pierce inaugurated as the fourteenth US president
	19	Russia claims a protectorate over Turkey's Christian subjects
MAY	21	The Turks reject Russia's claim
	31	Czar Nicolas I of Russia orders the occupation of Turkey's Danubian Principalities, now Romania
JUNE	20	Anglo-Burmese War ends
JULY	2	Russia invades the Danubian Principalities
SEP	24	In the Pacific, France annexes New Caledonia
OCT	4	Turkey declares war on Russia
NOV	15	Queen Maria II da Gloria of Portugal dies; succeeded by son Pedro V
DEC	30	The Gadsden Purchase: the USA buys a strip of land south of the Gila river from Mexico

THE SICK MAN OF EUROPE

Czar Nicolas I tells the British ambassador to Russia that he wants closer Anglo-Russian relations over the Ottoman Empire, where "we have a sick man on our hands". The British distrust Russian moves in the area, especially after Russia suggests a partition of the empire and claims a protectorate over its Christian subjects. War between Turkey and Russia breaks out in May as Russia invades the Danubian Principalities and in December destroys the Turkish fleet.

THE GADSDEN PURCHASE

The US government agrees the Gadsden Purchase with Mexico under which, for $10 million, it gains vast tracts of land in the southwest, including the strategic overland route to California and the proposed route of the southern transcontinental railroad.

MINIÉ POWER

The Minié rifle, invented by Claude Etienne Minié (1804–79) sees extensive service in the Crimea, especially at Balaclava, where it is deployed with devastating effect by the 93rd Highlander Regiment. The rifle fires the Minié bullet, developed in 1849. The combination of rifling and bullet shape gives increased range, accuracy and penetrative power over musket balls.

Above: *The Palace of Fontainebleau. The Fontainebleau forest is to be the first nature reserve in the world.*

HAUSSMANN'S PARIS

Paris begins to take its modern shape, with the great boulevards of Georges Haussmann (1809–91) transforming the plan of the city. The aim is to provide a great capital for the Second Empire — and one which can easily be policed, since memories of 1848 are still vivid.

STEINWAYS IN NEW YORK

German piano-maker Heinrich Engelhard Steinweg (1797–1871) emigrates to America, bringing his pianos with him. He changes his name to Steinway. The company will develop piano design until its products become the keyboards of choice for many composers and concert pianists.

BLOOMERS INVENTED

Mrs Amelia Bloomer, delivering a Fourth of July Address to the Massachusetts Constitution Convention to advocate womens' rights, creates a stir by dressing in loose-fitting Turkish style pantaloons under a bodice and short skirt.

Above: *Pope Pius IX establishes a Catholic bishopric in The Netherlands this year, causing a great deal of controversy.*

POTATO CRISPS
Native American George Crum invents the potato crisp. He is attempting to produce thinner French-fried potatoes and begins an eating trend that will eventually cross the Atlantic to become popular in Europe.

PRINTING ON TIN
Charles Adams of London perfects his lithographic process for printing on tinned iron sheeting. The tin surface is chemically primed to make it ink-receptive before printing can be done. Boxes, canisters and toys all benefit from his invention.

EQUAL EDUCATIONAL OPPORTUNITIES
Antioch College opens in Yellow Springs, Ohio, USA, the first college claiming to offer equal opportunities to men and women. It is founded by a Board of Education official, Horace Mann.

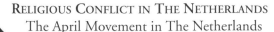

RELIGIOUS CONFLICT IN THE NETHERLANDS
The April Movement in The Netherlands follows the revocation of anti-Catholic laws by Willem II, permitting monasteries to be set up. Pius IX unilaterally establishes a bishopric in Utrecht, a traditional Calvinist stronghold, provoking religious revolts.

NATURE RESERVE
The French forest of Fontainebleau becomes the first officially designated nature reserve.

CORRIDOR COACH
Railway coaches for the comfort and convenience of passengers on long-distance journeys are introduced by Messrs Eaton and Gilbert for the Hudson river Railroad. The 14m (45ft) carriages feature compartments, a side corridor and washroom.

FREE READING IN SCOTLAND
A pioneering scheme to build up a network of public libraries funded by local taxes, established in England and Wales in 1851, is extended to Scotland.

Above: *Building a house on the South Pacific island of New Caledonia, which becomes a French colony this year.*

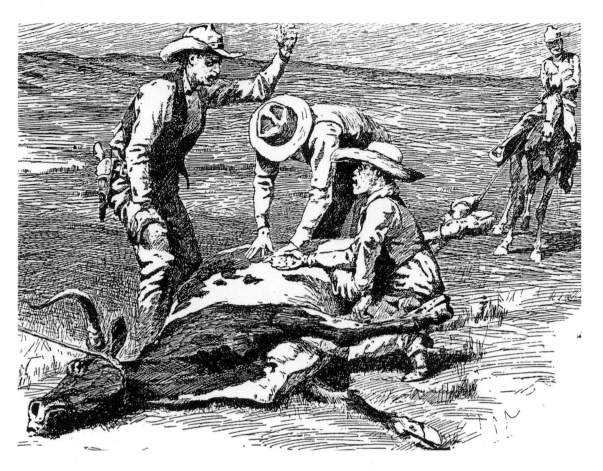

NEW YORK WORLD'S FAIR

The first US World's Fair opens in New York, exhibiting American agricultural and industrial products. It is modelled on the 1851 Great Exhibition in London, complete with a Crystal Palace.

THE SCHOLAR GIPSY

Matthew Arnold's most famous poem is published. Telling the story of the Oxford scholar who joins the gypsies and haunts the countryside, the poem pits the faith of the hero against the "divided aims" of modern times. It sums up the feeling of change detected by many intellectuals in the mid-century.

RETIRING MAVERICK

Rancher Samuel A Maverick rounds up his cattle from the Matagorda peninsula, Mississippi, where he turned them loose unbranded, and sells them prior to retiring from ranching. His name becomes a term used for unbranded cattle and people who stray from the accepted way of doing things.

NO MORE CONVICTS

The transportation of criminals from Britain to Australia and New Zealand is to stop following the refusal of Australian settlements to accept any more convicts. The British government is to introduce alternative forms of punishment in a new Penal Servitude Act.

Above: *Cowboys at the round-up. Most cattle-owners brand their animals; unbranded cattle are nicknamed "mavericks", after unconventional rancher Sam Maverick.*

Right: *President Franklin Pierce tries to avert the US Civil War and backs the treaty with Japan.*

THE CRIMEAN WAR

THE WAR, known as the "Russian War" to those who fight it, is waged between Russia and Turkey with most of the action taking place on the Crimean peninsula on the Black Sea. Britain and France enter the war as Turkey's allies in 1854, Sardinia joins in 1855. This war sees the first use of steam-driven cross-country vehicles and the concept of armoured fighting vehicles. The first use is made of chloroform as an anaesthetic during surgery on soldiers. Peace terms are agreed in Paris in 1856.

✴ Key Dates ✴

• **OLTENITZA November 4, 1853**
The Turks under Omar Pasha overwhelm the Russian army in Wallachia. This is the first Turkish victory over Russia in a century of conflict.

• **SIEGE OF SILISTRIA March 20–June 22, 1854**
The Turkish garrison of the fortress, besieged by the Russians, is assisted by two British officers Captain Buller and Lieutenant Nasmyth. The Russians are forced to raise the siege after losing over 12 000 men.

• **ALMA September 20, 1854**
A force of 40 000 Russians under Alexander Sergeievich Menshikov (1789–1869) holds the heights near the Alma river. A combined Franco-British force of 26 000 under Lord Raglan (1788–1855) and Marshal Jacques Saint-Arnaud (1796–1854) cross the river and take the heights at bayonet point. The Russians suffer 1200 killed and 4700 wounded and captured, the British 3000 casualties and the French 1000.

• **SIEGE OF SEVASTOPOL (Sebastopol)**
October 17, 1854–September 11, 1855
The failure of the Allies to follow up the victory at the Alma allows the Russians time to retreat to the fortress and naval base of Sevastopol. The French capture of the Malakoff redoubt on September 8 makes Sevastopol untenable and the capture of the base marks the end of the war. Russian losses are about 75 000, British 11 000 and French 12 000. In the first "modern" use of

Above: *Although superior in number, the Russians are driven back at the Battle of Kars.*

Right: *Omar Pasha, or Michael Latas (1806–71), is Croatian by birth and served in Austria's army before fleeing to Muslim Bosnia and finding favour with the Ottoman ruler Abdul-Medjid.*

chemical weapons, sulphur fumes, are suggested as a way to choke the Russian defenders.

• **BALACLAVA October 25, 1854**
Fought between 30 000 Russians under Menshikov and the British forces under Lord Raglan. A three-phase battle includes the stand by the 93rd Highlander (the "thin red line"), the successful charge of the Heavy Brigade and the disastrous charge of the Light Brigade. Of the 700 men in the Light Brigade who charge, only 195 return. Nevertheless, victory goes to the Allies.

• **INKERMAN November 5, 1854**
An attack by 50 000 Russians under Menshikov against the 8000 British troops holding positions at Inkerman, degenerates in dense fog into a "soldier's battle"— effectively hand-to-hand fighting. At Sandbag Battery the Russians lose 1200 killed. By the close of the day Russian casualties are 12 000, British 2500 and French 1000.

• **TCHERNAYA August 16, 1855**
The Russians, under Prince Michael Gorchakov (1795–1861), attack positions held by three French and one Sardinian division. After severe fighting they are repulsed, suffering 5000 casualties to the Allies' 1200.

Left and below: *The Highlanders hold the line at the Battle of the Alma; high command fails to make the best of victory.*

Below: *The Charge of the Heavy Brigade at the Battle of Balaclava, a victory for the Allies, but at great cost.*

Above: *Lord Raglan, commander of the British troops at the Battle of Balaclava.*

Left: *The Battle of Inkerman, where the fight is won by desperate hand-to-hand combat.*

Left: *Carnage on the bridge at Sevastopol as men and horses struggle at close quarters.*

Above: *The view of Sevastopol from the Allied attack point to the right of the naval base.*

Above: *Alexander II, who has just become czar, reviews his army at Sevastopol.*

Below: *Captain Lyons and his Flying Squadron sabotage the Russian fleet at Taganrog to cut enemy supply lines.*

Above: *General Franz Todleben, architect of the defensive earthworks at Sevastopol, the Redan and the Malakoff.*

JAPAN OPENS THE DOOR TO THE WEST

*T*HE WAR IN THE CRIMEA ESCALATES. The world's first war correspondent, Willy Russell of *The Times*, brings home the sordid realities of the battlefield, inspiring Florence Nightingale to set up her hospital in Scutari. In South Africa, the Boers set up an independent state, and US naval Commander Matthew Perry makes history by bringing Japan into the nineteenth century. False teeth are made from porcelain, rather than wood, and Alfred Wallace begins to think about evolution.

✳ 1854 ✳

MAR	12	Britain and France form an alliance to counteract Russian expansion in the Balkans
	26–27	Britain and France declare war on Russia (the Crimean War)
	31	The Treaty of Kanagawa opens Japan up to trade with the USA
MAY	30	US Congress passes Kansas-Nebraska Act, allowing those territories to decide whether to allow slavery or not
JUNE	3	The Elgin Treaty regularizes trade between Canada and the USA
	29	US Senate ratifies the Gadsden Purchase
JULY	6	Republican Party formed in the USA to oppose the Kansas-Nebraska Act
	13	Khedive [viceroy] Abbas Hilmi of Egypt murdered; succeeded by his cousin Sa'id
AUG	3	A revolution puts Bartolomeo Espartero back as regent of Spain
	22	Russian troops quit the Danubian Principalities; Austrian soldiers take over
SEP	11	Allied British and French troops land in the Crimea (now in Ukraine)
	20	Battle of the Alma
OCT	17	Siege of Sevastopol begins
	25	Battle of Balaclava
NOV	4	British nursing pioneer Florence Nightingale lands at Scutari, near Constantinople
	5	Battle of Inkerman

Left: *Peers and commoners present a patriotic address to Queen Victoria on the eve of the Crimean war.*

Below: *Constantinople, the centre of the Ottoman Empire, under threat from Russian expansionism.*

ORANGE FREE STATE
By the Convention of Bloemfontein, Britain agrees to leave the territory north of the Orange river and allow the Boers to set up an independent Orange Free State.

TREATY OF KANAGAWA
Commander Matthew Calbraith Perry (1794–1858) of the US Navy signs the Treaty of Kanagawa, opening up two ports to US trade. For more than two centuries, the only Japanese contact with the outside world has been through a small Dutch trading post at Nagasaki. Henceforth, Japan begins to look westwards and modernize its constitution and economy.

FRANCE AND BRITAIN ALLY AGAINST RUSSIA
France and Britain declare war on Russia as a result of its anti-Turkish policies begun in 1853. In August, Britain and France join Austria in stating the Vienna Four Points to end the war: Russia's abandonment of its claim to protect Christians in the Ottoman Empire, a revision of the Straits Settlement governing shipping in the Dardanelles in favour of European powers, free passage in the mouth of the Danube, and a Russian guarantee on the integrity of the Danubian provinces and Serbia. During the year, the British Baltic Fleet attacks the Russians; in September Anglo-French forces land in the Crimea.

KANSAS-NEBRASKA ACT
The US Congress passes the Kansas-Nebraska Act, allowing citizens in the newly created territories to choose whether to allow slavery. The act repeals the Missouri Compromise of 1820, which prohibited

slavery in the northern part of the Louisiana Purchase area, in effect allowing the spread of slavery into the midwest. The act increases tension between pro- and anti-slavery forces across the USA. Anti-slavery Whigs and other liberals form the Republican Party in opposition to the pro-slavery Democratic Party.

WALLACE'S THEORY OF EVOLUTION
British naturalist, Alfred Russel Wallace (1823–1913) travels to the Malaysian Archipelago, where he observes the animals of the region over the next eight years. He develops his own theory of evolution from his discoveries.

ALPINE FEVER
Sir Alfred Wills reaches the top of the Wetterhorn and sparks the beginning of the "Golden Age" of climbing in the Alps. Over the next ten years almost all the major alpine peaks are conquered.

WALDEN, OR LIFE IN THE WOODS

This masterpiece by American writer Henry David Thoreau (1817–62) is ignored at the time, but proves to have a huge influence. The book describes Thoreau's experiment in self-sufficiency in a cabin at the edge of Walden pond. His closeness to the world of nature, to the Native American past — and to the contrasting world around him (railways, materialism) — is evoked.

PERFORATIONS FOR STAMPS

Previously divided by cutting with scissors, the Penny Red becomes the first stamp to be manufactured with perforations. Slits between stamps have been experimented with, but lines of punched holes or perforations are found to be the best solution.

FALSE TEETH

American dentist, Mahlon Loomis (1826–86), creates a revolution in dentistry by introducing dentures or artificial teeth made from fired China clay or kaolin. The addition of glazes will establish porcelain as the state-of-the-art material for false teeth.

Above: *Florence Nightingale, the lady with the lamp, at work among the wounded in her hospital at Scutari.*

Below: *The hospital and cemetery at Scutari, established to help the casualties of the Crimean War.*

Above: *Elisha Otis demonstrates the safety and capabilities of his original safety elevator.*

Above: *William Russell, correspondent in the Crimea for* The Times. *His graphic reports cause outrage in England.*

PLASTER OF PARIS
Gypsum cement, otherwise known as Plaster of Paris, is applied by Dutch physician Anthonius Mathijsen (1805–78) to the dressing of broken limbs to immobilize them while they heal. The fast-setting plaster cast is a vast improvement on the use of splints and braces.

PNEUMATIC TUBE
A British engineer Josiah Clark (1822–98) invents the pneumatic message tube. Installed into factories and shops, it provides a convenient means for sending documents and money by means of a canister which is drawn along a tube by compressed air.

MEASURING PLANES
Swiss mathematician, Jakob Amsler (1823–1912), designs the planimeter, an analogue instrument for calculating the surface area of uneven surfaces or planes. It works by using a needle which follows the surface irregularities and translates them into a simple reading.

EDUCATION OPPORTUNITY
America's first college for black students, Ashmun Institute (which becomes Lincoln University), is chartered in Chester, Pennsylvania.

Below: *Antelope hunting in South Africa. This year, the Dutch Boers set up the independent Orange Free State.*

THE EUREKA INCIDENT

At the Eureka Stockade in the Ballarat goldfield in New South Wales, 23 diggers protesting against suspected corruption and the lack of political representation are shot dead by troops and police. The government subsequently sets up a royal commission to enquire into the problems, leading to substantial reform of the government in the colony.

Above: *The Eureka diggings, with Ballarat in the background.*

Above: *Panning for gold at the Eureka diggings.*

Below: *Government poster.*

V.   R.
Colonial Secretary's Office,
Melbourne, 8th December, 1854

£400
REWARD.

Whereas Two Persons of the Names of

LAWLOR AND BLACK,
LATE OF BALLAARAT,

Did on or about the 13th day of November last, at that place, use certain

TREASONABLE AND SEDITIOUS LANGUAGE,

And incite Men to take up Arms, with a view to make war against Our Sovereign Lady the Queen:

NOTICE IS HEREBY GIVEN

That a Reward of £200 will be paid to any person or persons giving such information as may lead to the Apprehension of either of the abovenamed parties.

DESCRIPTIONS.

LAWLOR.—Height 6ft. 11 in., age 35 hair dark brown, whiskers dark brown and shav'd under the side, no moustache, long face, rather good looking and is a well-made man.
BLACK.—Height over 6 feet, straight figure, slight build, bright red hair worn in general rather long and brushed backwards, red and large whiskers meeting under the chin, blue eyes, large thin nose, ruddy complexion, and rather small mouth.

By His Excellency's Command,

WILLIAM C. HAINES.

Right: *Troops storm the stockade behind which the diggers are entrenched, and kill 23 of them.*

THE OPENING UP OF JAPAN

On March 31 this year, American Commander Perry signs the Treaty of Kanagawa, establishing a new relationship between Japan and the Western world. Europe and the US are fascinated, and greatly influenced, by the different art and culture that are revealed.

Right: *Mount Fuji, the sacred mountain of Japan. There is an extinct volcano at the summit.*

Above left: *Actors and dancers at the court of the Mikado.*

Above right: *Japanese grooms employed by the emperor.*

Right: *The Buddhist temple at Nagasaki.*

Above: *A Japanese street-scene, complete with fortune-teller.*

Left: *The interior of a pagoda. Japanese pagodas are usually made of wood.*

Opposite above: *The ceremonial combat of Yoshi-Tsuné and Benki.*

Opposite below: *Lessons in a Japanese school. The pupils' behaviour does not appear very different from that of European children.*

BESSEMER, BUNSEN AND BABBAGE

*I*NGENIOUS HENRY BESSEMER devises a simple way to make better-quality steel for less money. Pioneer work on computers by Charles Babbage comes to fruition in George Scheutz's mechanical, programmable computer. Czar Nicolas, instigator of the Crimean War, dies and passes the baton on to his son Alexander II. In America, Henry Wadsworth Longfellow introduces the hypnotic rhythm of his long poem "Hiawatha".

Above: *Sir Henry Bessemer, inventor of a revolutionary steel-making process.*

✦ 1855 ✦

JAN	26	Piedmont in Italy joins the Allies against Russia	MAY	5	Britain's muddled conduct of the Crimean War leads to the formation of an Administrative Reform Society
FEB	6	In England, Viscount Palmerston becomes prime minister	AUG	11	In the Crimean War, the Allies enter Sevastopol
MAR	2	Czar Nicolas I of Russia dies; succeeded by his son Alexander II		18	Austria gives its clergy control of matrimonial law, education and censorship
	30	Britain and Afghanistan form an alliance against Persia (Iran)			
	31	English novelist Charlotte Brontë dies	NOV	21	Sweden joins the Allies against Russia

Above: *Czar Alexander II, who ascends the Russian throne on March 2 this year, after his father's death.*

PAVILLION DU REALISME

At the Paris World Fair, French artist Gustave Courbet (1819–77) creates an independent Realist pavilion, in which he exhibits 40 of his own works, including the vast — 6m- (19ft-) wide — *Artist's Studio*. Realism is seen as a movement of consequence in French art.

THE SONG OF HIAWATHA

The most popular work of Henry Wadsworth Longfellow (1807–82) retells Native American stories. Its unusual (trochaic) rhythm makes it popular, as does its subject matter, which is very unusual for "white" American literature of this time.

Above: *Czar Nicolas I, instigator of the Crimean War, dies during the conflict.*

LA REVE ET LA VIE

This posthumous collection by French poet Gérard de Nerval (1808–55) includes poems whose meaning is often unclear, but whose words, images and rhythms are strangely haunting. Nerval said that attempts to explain them were best not made, and this view was taken by the Symbolist writers, whose work they will influence.

THE WARDEN
This is the fourth novel by English writer Anthony Trollope (1815–82), but the first in which he gets into his stride and on to his home turf, the fictional "Barsetshire". More Barsetshire novels will follow, earning Trollope success.

THE BESSEMER PROCESS
A simple process for reducing the amount of carbon in pig iron to produce steel is invented by British engineer, Henry Bessemer (1813–98). Oxygen blown through the molten iron burns off the carbon as carbon dioxide and produces even more heat to boot.

Above: *Lord Palmerston becomes prime minister of England and directs the British policy towards Russia.*

CHINESE RIOTS IN THE USA
Anti-Chinese riots in Washington State, which came to a head when mayor, sheriff and deputies threw Chinese citizens out of town, are quelled by troops. In San Francisco, where over 18 000 Chinese had arrived by 1852, resentment is also rising at their refusal to adopt American ways, and for the formation of the Tong secret society promoting vice and prostitution in the city.

Above: *Marshal Aimable Jean-Jacques Pellisier, who takes Sevastopol this year.*

PROGRAMMABLE COMPUTER

Inspired by the theoretical work of Charles Babbage, Swedish scientist George Scheutz designs and builds the first mechanical programmable computer. It can calculate to four orders of difference and provide printouts accurate to eight decimal places.

MEASURING THE EARTH'S MOVEMENT

Italian meteorologist, Luigi Palmieri (1807–96), invents the seismograph. Made for measuring the intensity of earthquakes and tremors, it traces a line on a revolving drum using a nib mounted on a very sensitively adjusted needle mechanism.

DEGREES FOR WOMEN

Elmira Female College, New York, becomes the first American educational institution to grant academic degrees to women.

TENSION OVER SLAVERY

John Mercer Langston, a clerk in Brownhelm County, Ohio, becomes the first black person elected to public office in the USA, and addresses the American Anti-Slavery Society. Meanwhile, violent clashes occur in the new Kansas territory over the slavery issue.

HOME COOKING

A domestic gas oven is marketed in Britain by Smith and Philips, twenty years after the first commercial gas stove, designed by gas company employee James Sharp in 1826, was installed in his kitchen.

STRONG MEDICINE

Kerosene is made from raw petroleum by Dr Abraham Gesner, a New York physician, who promotes it as a patent medicine.

Charlotte Brontë
1816–1855

The English novelist, the only one remaining of seven Brontë children, has died in pregnancy. Under the name Currer Bell she published *Jane Eyre* in 1847 and was the author of three other novels. She worked as a pupil-teacher in Brussels for a short while but spent most of her life in her father's rectory at Haworth in a remote part of Yorkshire, living with her writer sisters Anne (Acton Bell, author of *Agnes Grey*, d. 1849) and Emily (Ellis Bell, author of *Wuthering Heights*, d. 1848) and their opium-taking brother Branwell (who also died in 1848). She had married her father's curate in the year before her death.

Søren Kierkegaard
1813–1855

The Danish philosopher and founder of Existentialism has died. Trained in the Hegelian school, he rejected this as ignoring the partial, subjective and limited nature of human judgement. From the fact that there can be no objectivity in human judgement it follows that there can also be no external authority. Our actions spring from the free exercise of the Will, and this freedom of choice also emphasizes our moral responsibility, an aspect of his thinking that may later lose its emphasis. His works include *Either/Or: A Fragment of Life* (1843), and *The Sickness Unto Death* (1849).

Above: *Slaves working on the cotton presses in Galveston, Texas. Despite protests, slavery is still legal in southern states.*

Right: *A Native American in war costume. The poet Longfellow introduces white Americans to the Native American culture.*

EARLY PLASTIC

The first synthetic material, or plastic, is patented by British chemist Alexander Parkes (1813–90). Celluloid — then known as xylonite — is a hard, resin-like substance which finds various uses, such as photographic film, although it is highly flammable.

BURTON IN ARABIA

Richard Francis Burton (1829–90), English orientalist and explorer, publishes the first volume of *Personal Narrative of a Pilgrimage to El-Medinah and Meccah*, his account of a trip he made in 1853 to the Muslim holy cities of Mecca and Medina (Saudi Arabia) disguised as a Pathan.

PRINCIPLES OF PSYCHOLOGY

The English philosopher Herbert Spencer (1820–1903) publishes *Principles of Psychology*, in which he applies the doctrine of evolution to sociology.

L'Exposition Universelle

Not to be outdone by Great Britain, France stages its own Great Exhibition, *L'Exposition Universelle*, the Universal Exhibition, in Paris. It is opened by Emperor Napoleon III and boasts over 20 000 displays from all around the world, with the emphasis on France and her colonies. The exhibition halls and galleries occupy more space than did the Crystal Palace in London and are made from glass, cast iron and stone. Over five million people visit. The event is such a success that it becomes a regular feature of Parisian life, with an Exposition held every ten years or so from now until 1900.

Right: *The Agricultural Concourse at the exhibition dominated by a display from the Society of Horticulture.*

Left: *In the machine hall of the exhibition, with train engines from all over the world.*

Below: *The section of the exhibition devoted to the products of the French colonies in Africa, Southeast Asia, the South Pacific, the Middle East and the Caribbean.*

Medals, Mauvine and Mountains

$\mathcal{P}$RO-ACTIVE ABOLITIONIST JOHN BROWN helps to massacre five men, for which he will be hanged. The Crimean War comes to an end, and Queen Victoria introduces a medal to recognize the bravery of her soldiers. A new species of ancient humanity, *Homo neanderthalis,* is discovered in Germany, hire purchase is introduced in America, and a team of British surveyors measures the Himalayas. Gustave Flaubert writes *Madame Bovary,* condensed milk brings nutrition to urban communites and William Perkin gives the world purple dye.

✦ 1856 ✦

JAN	29	Queen Victoria institutes the Victoria Cross "for valour"	SEP	15	The Constitution of 1845 is restored in Spain
FEB	13	The British annex Oudh in India	OCT	8	Chinese board a British ship, starting an Anglo-Chinese War
	18	Turkey reforms its prisons, ends torture and promises religious freedom			
			NOV	1	Short-lived war breaks out between Britain and Persia (Iran)
MAR	16	Birth of an heir to Napoleon III: the Prince Imperial		4	James Buchanan (Democrat) is elected US president
	30	Treaty of Paris ends the Crimean War			
APR	15	Austria, Britain and France guarantee Turkey's independence			
MAY	24	In the USA, abolitionist John Brown leads the "Pottawasatomie Massacre" of five pro-slavery men			

Left: *Queen Victoria presents the first Victoria Cross,
a medal for valour on the battlefield.*

WAR WITH CHINA

Chinese officials board a British ship in Canton and imprison the crew for suspected piracy. War breaks out between the two countries when Britain bombards Canton. The war ends in June 1858 when Britain gains Kowloon and other territory in Hong Kong; China however refuses to recognize the treaty, but in October 1860, after an Anglo-French force invades the country and advances on Beijing, agrees to further commercial concessions, including the legalization of the opium trade, and opens up eleven more ports to European commerce.

THE HIGHEST MOUNTAIN

The Himalayan peaks are measured. Sir George Everest (1790–1866) takes over the Great Trigonometrical Survey of India, begun in 1800, when William Lambton dies. He oversees a series of observations on the border with Nepal which allow the survey team to measure the Himalayan peaks. Peak XV is the highest and it is named after Everest.

BUCHANAN FOR PRESIDENT

Democratic candidate James Buchanan (1791–1868) is elected US president on the fourth attempt.

Above: *Chinese officers haul down the British flag on the* Arrow *during conflict between Britain and China.*

NEANDERTHAL MAN

A human skull is discovered in the Neanderthal valley in the German Rhinelands by Johann C Fuhrott and identified by French surgeon Paul Broca (1824–80) as belonging to a branch of the human species that predates modern humans and is named *Homo neanderthalis*.

HENRY IRVING'S DEBUT

English thespian Henry Irving (1838–1905) begins his career at the Sunderland Theatre. He will be famous for his Shakespearean roles, especially such problematical characters as Shylock and Malvolio, in which he brings a new subtlety to his portrayals.

SUBMARINE PHOTOGRAPHY

Seaweed becomes the subject of the very first photographic image to be obtained beneath the waves. Englishman, W Thompson, succeeds in taking an exposure with his 5 x 4 inch plate camera at a depth of some 6m (18ft), on the Weymouth coast.

Amadeo Avogadro
1776–1856

The Italian mathematical physicist and chemist Amadeo Carlo Avogadro, formulator of Avogadro's Law has died. The importance (and validity) of his hypothesis that equal volumes of all gases contain the same numbers of molecules when at the same temperature and pressure is not widely recognized among scientists until several decades after his death, when his contribution to atomic and molecular science will be more fully appreciated.

LACROSSE IN CANADA

The Montreal Lacrosse Club is created. The club is the first of its kind for the sport which developed from a game played by Native Americans.

KINETIC ENERGY

The concept of momentum is defined as kinetic energy by British physicist William Thomson, Lord Kelvin (1824–1907). Kinetic energy is the energy or effort of motion in a body which would have to be matched to bring it to rest instantaneously.

EASY TERMS

Trade-in allowances and instalment purchase are offered for the first time by Isaac Merrit Singer, the American inventor who improved the design of the sewing machine. He offers an allowance of $50 on old machines and pioneers a purchase plan that allows $5 monthly rental fees to accumulate towards the sale price.

PEACE IN THE CRIMEA

The Treaty of Paris ends the Crimean War; Russia respects the integrity of Turkey and the Danubian Principalities of Moldavia and Wallachia, cedes Bessarabia to Turkey and guarantees the neutrality of the Black Sea. A later treaty between France, Britain and Austria guarantees Turkey's independence and integrity.

NEW DICTIONARY

Nouveau Dictionnaire de la Langue Française is published by French lexicographer Pierre Larousse (1817–75).

Right: *The apparatus devised by Sir William Henry Perkin for making aniline dye. The reactants are heated with superheated steam and stirred by means of a steam engine.*

Above: *The Bessemer steel-making process in action. It makes steel more economical to produce.*

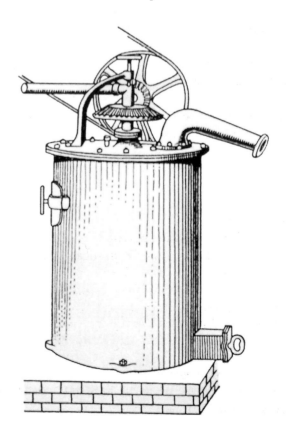

Above: *In the USA, abolitionist John Brown, who led the "Pottawasatomie Massacre" of five pro-slavery men is captured at Harper's Ferry.*

Condensed Milk

An American food technologist Gail Borden (1801–74) develops condensed milk. It is reduced by evaporation to a thick concentration which is preserved by the addition of sugar. Before the practice of pasteurizing milk is introduced, it is a nutritious substitute for fresh milk in urban areas.

Madame Bovary

This first novel by French writer Gustave Flaubert (1821–80) begins life as a serial. It takes the French literary world by storm. His account of Emma Bovary's dreams, of which she seeks fulfilment in extra-marital affairs, leads to both Flaubert and his editor being tried for offences against public morals; they are acquitted. The novel's frankness and its literary style make it a classic.

Synthetic Colour

Mauvine, the first synthetic aniline dye, is discovered by British chemist William Perkin (1848–1907). It is hailed as an important breakthrough for the textile industry, which traditionally uses very expensive natural dyestuffs.

Domestic Gas Fire

Robert Bunsen (1811–99) uses the principle developed in his Bunsen burner to invent a safe domestic gas fire. The introduction of gas heating in the home as the result is a seminal moment in the evolution of home comfort and convenience.

Above: *Gustave Flaubert, whose controversial novel,* Madame Bovary, *is published this year.*

Above: *The Himalayas in Nepal, surveyed this year by Sir George Everest. The highest peak is named after him.*

MUTINY AND MASSACRE IN BRITISH INDIA

*T*HE DRED SCOTT CASE RESULTS IN THE denial of US citizenship to any black person, free or slave. The Civil War takes a step closer. In India, sepoys, Indian soldiers working for the British East India Company, mutiny at being given cartridges greased with animal fat. Terrible slaughter occurs before the rebellion is put down, but it is the beginning of the end for the British in India. In France, Charles Baudelaire writes *Les Fleurs du Mal* and invents modern poetry; in Africa, Burton and Speke squabble about the source of the Nile.

❖ 1857 ❖

MAR	4	James Buchanan (Democrat) is inaugurated as the fifteenth US president
	4	Anglo-Persian War ends
	4–5	In Ireland, a Fenian (revolutionary) rising is quickly put down
	7	Dred Scott Case: US Supreme Court rules that no blacks, free or slave, can be a US citizen
MAY	10	In India, sepoys (Indian soldiers) revolt against the British, and seize Delhi
JUNE	1	British navy sinks a Chinese fleet
	4	France and Russia sign a trade treaty
	8	British troops begin siege of Delhi
	26	Rebels capture Cawnpore and butcher the European garrison, women and children

SEP	20	Delhi falls to the British
NOV	17	British troops under Colin Campbell relieve the residency at Lucknow
DEC	6	British recapture Cawnpore
	29	In China, British troops take Canton

Above: *Elizabeth Blackwell qualifies as the first woman doctor this year.*

Left: *James Buchanan, the fifteenth president of the USA.*

Above: *The palace at Delhi during the time of the British rule in India.*

MUTINY IN INDIA

A mutiny among Indians serving in the British East India Company army soon spreads throughout British-ruled India. The mutineers seize Delhi and other major cities and restore the former Mughal emperor to the throne, but are eventually defeated by superior British arms.

THE GLEANERS

The realistic style of French artist Jean François Millet (1814–75) reaches maturity in paintings such as *The Gleaners*. His peasants have a nobility not previously accorded to them in art.

A FAUST SYMPHONY

This musical interpretation by Hungarian composer Franz Liszt (1811–86) of the Faust legend consists of three musical portraits or "character pictures": Faust, Gretchen and Mephistopheles. Daring in its harmonies, and in its mixture of the poetic and the vulgar, it stretches Romanticism in music.

EQUAL RIGHTS IN DENMARK

Danish women are granted equal rights of inheritance and access to all forms of employment after the popularity all over Scandinavia of *The County Governor's Daughter* by Norwegian feminist writer Camilla Collett (1813–95). It describes the miseries of looking for a husband and raises public consciousness of the need for women's rights.

SCENES FROM CLERICAL LIFE

The first fictional writings of George Eliot (aka Mary Ann or Marian Evans, 1819–80) attract immediate attention. There is much fascination about the identity of the author, whom people believe must be a clergyman, such is the realism of the tales.

STEEL RAILS

Cast-iron railway tracks, prone to fracturing, are replaced by tracks made from the far stronger and less brittle steel. Derby station in England is the first stretch of track to consist of steel runners.

Above: *Henry Havelock, who played a commanding role in the Sepoy Rebellion.*

STEAM PLOUGH

A British engineer, John Fowler (1826–64), applies steam power to the task of ploughing fields. The process of tilling the land, which traditionally uses vast amounts of horse- and manpower, is suddenly made much easier and less time-consuming.

Auguste Comte
1798–1857

The French thinker and founder of the school of so-called positive philosophy, Auguste Comte, has died. The former mathematics teacher, who was befriended by the English philosopher and reformer John Stuart Mill and George Grote the historian and politician, was the author of the six-volume work *Cours de Philosophie Positive* (1830–42) and the four-volume *Système de Politique Positive* (1851–54), and will be credited with laying the foundations of sociology.

Above: *Sepoys refuse to use cartridges they think are contaminated with animal fat. This triggers rebellion.*

CAMPAIGN FOR IRISH INDEPENDENCE

John O'Mahony sets up the Fenian Brotherhood in New York to campaign for an independent Irish republic; the following year the Irish Republican Brotherhood is established in Dublin by James Stephens. Both work closely together in campaigns against British rule in Ireland.

TOILET PAPER

New Yorker Joseph Gayetty, produces the first paper specifically designed for ablutionary application. Sold in 500-sheet packs, it is marketed as a remedy for the pain "suffered by those afflicted by haemorrhoids or piles, during toiletry procedures".

GLYCOGEN

French physiologist, Claude Bernard (1813–78), discovers that the mammalian body is able to store reserves of energy as glycogen in the liver and muscles. Glycogen can be quickly broken down to produce glucose when urgently required.

Above: *Brittania uncovers the source of the Nile in a cartoon linking the discovery to the legend that the Nile springs from a hidden pitcher.*

Below: *Usui tribesman bring provisions to the Nile seekers Speke and Grant, seen plotting their route in a grass hut.*

PROGRESS AGAINST SLAVERY

Dred Scott, a Missouri slave, sues for freedom under the terms of the Missouri Compromise, but it is denied him by a ruling of the Supreme Court. *The Impending Crisis of the South, and How to Meet It* is published this year by a North Carolina farmer, Hinton Rowan Helper, who believes that slavery is unprofitable because it is more costly than free labour and injurious to small farmers.

GOING UP

The first passenger elevator is installed in New York's Haughwout Departmental Store by Elisha Graves Otis (1811–61), who first demonstrated his safety lift at a New York industrial fair in 1854.

MEDICINE FOR WOMEN

The New York Infirmary for Women and Children is opened in New York by Elizabeth Blackwell (1821–1910), the first woman in the USA to qualify as a doctor, and is run entirely by women.

ALIMONY ARRIVES

Britain's Matrimonial Causes Act rules that a husband's responsibility as a provider continues after a marriage has ended and orders the world's first alimony payments.

ANTI-PORN LAWS

The British parliament passes the Obscene Publications Act, the first modern legislation to control the trade in pornography. The authorities may now enter premises and seize material thought to be obscene.

GARIBALDI RETURNS

Giuseppe Garibaldi sets up the Italian National Association to campaign for a united Italy under the leadership of Piedmont.

UNBIASED EDUCATION

The Primary Education Act is passed in The Netherlands guaranteeing primary schools freedom from Calvinist or Roman Catholic bias.

BURTON AND SPEKE SEARCH FOR THE NILE

The Royal Geographical Society sponsors English explorers Richard Burton (1829–90) and John Hanning Speke (1827–64) to discover the source of the Nile, which has become the Holy Grail of African exploration. Journeying together from Zanzibar, Burton and Speke are the first Europeans to reach Lake Tanganyika but do not discover whether the river to the north fills or empties the lake.

LES FLEURS DU MAL

French poet Charles Baudelaire (1821–67) is revealed as a major poet in this volume, which brings new subjects, and a new forthrightness, into poetry. Its concerns range from the idealism of love to its corruption, and many of the poems evoke despair and death. Some of the poems are condemned as obscene, and Baudelaire is ordered to remove them from the book.

MILE-HIGH CLUB

Climbers form the Alpine Club in London, a sign of the sport's growing popularity. British adventurers lead the conquest of the Alps but supported by European guides.

Left: Hosseinabad Gardens and the Tomb of Zana Ali at Lucknow, scene of a five-month-long siege during the Sepoy Rebellion.

Above: *A Chinese shadow show. British troops take
Canton this year and Chinese culture spreads to Europe.*

The Sepoy Rebellion

THE MUTINY begins among the sepoys or Indian soldiers in the East India Company Army at Meerut, near Delhi, who believe that the paper cartridges they have been issued with are waterproofed using animal fat. Since the cartridges are normally torn open with the firer's teeth this would constitute eating pig or cow — a breach of religious practices of the sepoys, who belong to Hindu or Muslim faiths. Although initially successful, quarrels among the rebels means that they are subdued by the British after bitter fighting and several sieges. However, the consequences of the rebellion are significant. The British Government relieves the British East India Company of their power in India and the rift between Britain and India promotes nationalism and eventual independence.

✱ Key Dates ✱

● **CAWNPORE June 6–24, 1857**
The tiny British garrison commanded by General Sir Hugh Massy Wheeler (1789–1857) is besieged by mutineers under Nana Sahib. When they surrender on the promise of safe passage, soldiers and civilians are murdered.

● **DELHI June 8–September 20, 1857**
Delhi is defended by 30 000 mutineers and initially only partially besieged by 3500 British troops under General Henry William Barnard (1799–1857). The British are reinforced and on September 14 the city is attacked. The palace holds out until September 20. British casualties are 4000.

● **LUCKNOW July 1, 1857–March 21, 1858**
The small garrison and British families defend the Residency until relieved on November 19, 1857. The relief column from Cawnpore defeats 12 000 mutineers at Alumbagh and capture the Secunderbagh before they reach the Residency. The garrison loses 483 killed and the relief column 535. Lucknow is then attacked by the British between March 1 and 21. Sir Colin Campbell (1792–1863) routs the 25 000 mutineers and the British cavalry pursues them 22km (14mi); British losses are 99.

● **FUTTEYPUR (Fatehpur) July 12, 1857**
General Henry Havelock (1795–1857) defeats a large force of rebels as his troops advance to relieve Lucknow.

● **ARRAH July 25–August 3, 1857**
Mr Boyle, sixteen Englishmen and 60 Sikh police hold a house against repeated attacks by three regiments of rebellious sepoys under Kur Singh; they are relieved by a force led by Major Vincent Eyre (1811–81).

● **ONAO July 28, 1857**
British troops under General Havelock make a successful frontal attack on a strong position killing 300 mutineers and taking fifteen guns.

● **GORARIA November 23–24, 1857**
A strong position, held by 5000 mutineers, which takes the 3000 British troops under Brigadier Stuart two days to dislodge.

● **JHANSI March–April 2, 1858**
The mutineers had captured the town and fort in June 1857. Sir Hugh Rose (1801–85) besieges it in March 1858 and on April 2 his forces storm and capture it.

● **KALPI May 19–23, 1858**
Rose besieges the town and though the garrison makes two sorties, they are ineffective and it falls on May 23.

● **GAULAULI May 22, 1858**
The column under Rose catches up with 20 000 mutineers under Tantia Topi and routs them in a bayonet charge.

● **GWALIOR June 17–19, 1858**
A large force of mutineers, under the Ranee of Jhansi, is driven out of the military area of the town by forces under Rose on June 17. For two more days British forces drive them from the town, inflicting heavy losses.

Above: *The Highlanders under Sir Colin Campbell capturing the guns at Cawnpore.*

Above: *The slaughter at Cawnpore. Rebels massacre the garrison, women and children.*

Right: *Captain Hodson, known as "Great in Battle" by his Indian regiment, surveys the scene before entering Delhi.*

Left: *The rebel sepoys storm into Delhi. For political reasons, there is no garrison stationed there and so the British civilians are sitting targets.*

The Sepoy Rebellion

Left: *British troops blow up the Cashmere Gate at Delhi. The rebels are under siege inside the city.*

Below: *The rebellion spreads to Lucknow. General Hearsey remonstrates with the rebels.*

Above: *Sir Colin Campbell, Commander-in-Chief of the British army.*

Right: *Lieutenant Havelock and the Madras fusiliers hold the Chabargh bridge across the canal to Lucknow.*

Below: *Insubordination in the ranks; in fact, few sepoys in the Lucknow garrison turn against their British employers.*

Above: *Captain Hodson, who had been the hero of Delhi, is killed at Lucknow.*

Above: *The relief of Lucknow by Sir Colin Campbell's troops after five months of siege.*

Fingerprints, Telegrams and Photography

NAPOLEON III ESCAPES WITH HIS LIFE after the failure of an assassination attempt. France goes to war in Indo-China. Gaspard Tournachon, friend and mentor to the outrageous Impressionists, takes the first aerial photograph from a hot-air balloon over Paris. In southern France, a young girl believes she has met the Virgin Mary, and Lourdes becomes a focus for pilgrims. Central Park is shaping up in New York, the tin-opener is invented and Britain forces the Chinese to buy opium. The first transatlantic telegram is sent.

✷ 1858 ✷

JAN	14	Italian revolutionary Felice Orsini tries to assassinate Napoleon III in Paris; he fails, but ten people are killed	JUNE	26	Anglo-Chinese War ends
			JULY	8	British proclaim peace in India
FEB	19	British prime minister, Lord Palmerston, resigns		20	Napoleon III and Count Cavour plan unification of Italy
	26	Lord Derby (Tory) forms new British administration	AUG	2	British government takes over the rule of India from the East India Company
MAR	21	In India, British finally recapture Lucknow	OCT	7	King Frederick William IV of Prussia is declared insane; his son Wilhelm becomes regent
MAY	11	Minnesota becomes the 32nd US state	DEC	23	Alexander I of Serbia is deposed; succeeded by Milos Obrenovic I

NEW STATES
Minnesota joins the USA as the 32nd state of the Union, followed by Oregon in February 1859; both are free states.

ITALIAN UNITY ON THE HORIZON
Napoleon III and Count Cavour sign an agreement at Plombières to work towards Italian unification, giving Sardinia-Piedmont a powerful ally against Austrian control of northern Italy.

A VICEROY FOR INDIA
Shaken by the experience of the Indian Mutiny, the British wind up the East India Company, which surrenders its power to the crown. The governor-general is replaced by a viceroy.

FRENCH CONQUEST IN INDOCHINA
French missionaries sent to Indochina have been successful in converting many Vietnamese to Catholicism, to the discomfort of their rulers. After some missionaries are murdered, Napoleon III sends troops and France begins to make inroads. Over the next two decades, French protectorates are set up in Tonkin (northern Vietnam) and Annam (central Vietnam). Cochin China (south Vietnam) becomes a French colony. Another protectorate is set up in Cambodia and by 1893 the French also control Luang Prabang in Laos.

DERBY DAY
This huge panoramic painting by English artist William Powell Frith (1819–1909) is one of the most popular of its time. It is famous for the artist's use of photographs for reference. It is so successful that the copyright for the engraving is bought before the work is finished.

COVENT GARDEN OPERA HOUSE
After a fire, the Opera House is rebuilt to designs by Edward Middleton Barry (1830–80). It will establish itself as the country's premier opera house (especially after the burning down of Her Majesty's Theatre in 1867), and many important operas will have their first British performances here.

ORPHEUS IN THE UNDERWORLD
The first successful comic opera by German composer Jacques Offenbach (1819–90), a satire on the Orpheus myth, is produced in Paris and is well received — audiences are amused by its wit, even if they affect to be shocked by its cavalier parody of serious operatic styles. It contains the famous can-can, which is received with the same ambivalence.

Above: *Napoleon III, who survives an assassination attempt against him this year.*

THE AUTOCRAT AT THE BREAKFAST TABLE
Oliver Wendell Holmes (1809–94), Harvard professor, brings out his best-known work. Its form constitutes a new take on the prose essay — the pieces consist of discourses by the writer, with other characters occasionally butting in. The essays are admired for their wit and learning.

STEEL-HULLED SHIP
The *Ma Robert* is the first ship to be constructed with an entirely steel hull. Built at John Laird's shipyard in Liverpool, it is the very vessel that carries David Livingstone up the Zambezi river during an expedition to the African continent.

FINGERPRINTING
India is the country that first witnesses fingerprinting, but not initially for forensic purposes. Civil servant, William Herchel, begins taking hand prints of illiterate workers for identification, before using fingerprints, as a magistrate, to prevent fraud.

TRANSATLANTIC TELEGRAM

"Go to Chicago" is the first telegram sent via the newly laid transatlantic telegraph cable. Englishman John Cash is the sender, initiating the start of international telecommunications, which will transform global cultures.

AERIAL PHOTOGRAPH

The first "bird's-eye view" photographic image is taken from a balloon at an altitude of 79m (262 ft). The image is of the outskirts of Paris and is taken by French portrait photographer Gasparo-Félix Tournachon (1820–1910). Tournachon uses the adopted name "Nadar" and is an enthusiastic supporter of the Impressionists.

THE RINGSTRASSE, VIENNA

Emperor Franz Joseph I (1830–1916) transforms Vienna with a great circular street around the route of the old city walls. The Ringstrasse is punctuated with major public buildings (Rathaus, Parliament, Army Museum) in various styles. The whole scheme is a vast national status symbol.

SUN SIGNALS

The heliograph, a system using sunlight reflected off a tripod-mounted mirror, is developed for long-range signalling. On a clear day, the signals can be seen as far away as 50km (31mi).

Above left and right: *The empress and emperor of China. This year sees Britain imposing a legal opium trade in China after some years of war.*

SAFETY CAN OPENER

American inventor Ezra Warner devises a hand-operated device for opening tin cans. The US army, who are fighting the Civil War, especially appreciate the idea, since their rations are in tins which they previously have had to open with chisels.

FIRST POSTCODES

London has now grown so large that postmen sorting the mail can no longer treat it as a single town. Rowland Hill (1795–1879), the post office official already responsible for such innovations as the adhesive stamp and the pre-paid penny post, has divided the city into eight districts based on the points of the compass: N = Northern District and WC = West Central. These are the world's first postcodes.

A SHRINE IS BORN

Bernadette Soubirous, a fourteen-year-old girl from Lourdes in France, begins having visions of conversations with a woman who is widely believed to be Mary, mother of Jesus Christ. The town of Lourdes will become a place of Catholic pilgrimage, with a reputation for the healing of the sick.

Above: *Covent Garden Opera House, London, is rebuilt this year after a disastrous fire guts the old one.*

A PARK FOR NEW YORK

New York's Central Park, landscaped by Frederick L Olmsted and Calvert Vaux, opens, although it is not yet complete. It is situated in Manhattan, to the north of most of New York's population, and covers 340 hectares (840 acres).

BIG BEN CHIMES IN

The clock in St Stephen's Tower — 96m (320ft) and overlooking the Houses of Parliament in London — begins operating, and its great bell, popularly known as "Big Ben", sounds across London. The first stroke of each hour is confirmed twice a day at the Royal Observatory, Greenwich, as accurate to within one second, making it the world's most accurate clock, and astonishing horologists.

ROTHSCHILD IN PARLIAMENT

Lionel de Rothschild (1808–79), a member of the famous banking family, becomes the first Jewish member of the British parliament in the House of Commons. Although elected several times since 1847, he could not take his seat until a new oath for non-Christian members was introduced.

THE OPIUM TRADE IN CHINA

Britain imposes a legal trade in opium, in China in the face of opposition from the Chinese government. Draconian laws controlled opium-smoking until the 1830s, when British traders planted opium in India and began selling it cheaply and illegally in China through corrupt merchants. Since China has been forced to grant concessions to Western traders during the Opium Wars, millions of Chinese have become addicted.

Above: *Oliver Wendell Holmes publishes his witty* Autocrat at the Breakfast Table *this year.*

HAUTE COUTURE

English dressmaker Charles Frederick Worth (1825–95) opens a shop in the Rue de la Paix, Paris, where he sells his own designs, creating the first house of *haute couture*. Empress Eugénie is a valued customer.

GRAPES IN CALIFORNIA

The first varietal grapevines are planted at Buena Vista in the Valley of the Moon, California, by Agoston Haraszthy de Moksa, who introduces Tokay, Zinfandel and Shiraz varieties from his native Hungary.

PRESERVATION

The Mason jar is patented by New York metalworker John Landis Mason. A glass container with a screw top lid and a rubber gasket, it is reusable and can be used for storing and preserving fruit, vegetables and other foods.

NILE CONTROVERSY

After arguments with his colleague Richard Burton, John Speke ventures alone to a lake to the northeast of Lake Tanganyika. He names it Lake Victoria. Speke champions this body of water as the Nile's source (he was right but had no proof) while Burton backs Lake Tanganyika. Their disagreement lasts many years.

Above: *What the chic Parisienne and her children are wearing this year, when* haute couture *officially begins.*

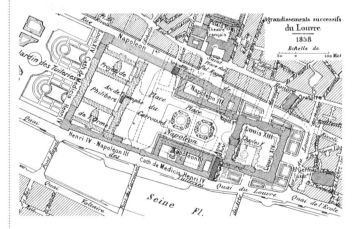

Above: *Map showing the proposed enlargement of the Louvre Museum in Paris.*

EXPRESS TRAVEL

A stagecoach of the Overland Mail Company reaches Los Angeles twenty days after leaving St Louis. It has travelled non-stop for 4160km (2600 mi), except for changes of horses, and heralds faster travel across the American continent.

Left: *The first transatlantic telegram is sent this year from England to Chicago. It is the beginning of the communications explosion.*

Left: *One of Calvert Vaux's bridges for Central Park, the Playmates Arch, located below the 65th Street Transverse Road that links Sixth and Seventh Avenues.*

Right: *Glen Span, another Central Park Bridge, located at Seventh and 102nd Streets. Vaux's designs reflect his preference for natural materials.*

EVOLUTION AND UNIFICATION

The slaughter at the Battle of Solferino is so appalling it prompts a Swiss doctor to set up the Red Cross and paves the way for the Geneva Convention, which tries to bring a modicum of humanity into war. Italian patriots have rather more success on their second attempt to gain independence and by the end of the decade, most of Italy will be unified under one king. Diffident botanist Charles Darwin at last publishes a theory he has been working on for twenty years. An ill-advised landowner introduces rabbits into Australia.

✦ 1859 ✦

JAN	19	France signs a treaty with Sardinia-Piedmont
FEB	14	Oregon becomes the 33rd US state
APR	29	Austria sends troops into Sardinia-Piedmont
MAY	3	France declares war on Austria
	22	Ferdinand II of the Two Sicilies dies; succeeded by son Francis II
JUNE	4	French defeat the Austrians at the Battle of Magenta
	10	Lord Palmerston forms Liberal/Whig administration
	24	French and Sardinians defeat the Austrians at Solferino

JULY	8	Swedish king Oscar I dies; succeeded by his son Charles XV
	11	France and Austria make peace
OCT	16	US abolitionist John Brown seizes a federal arsenal at Harpers Ferry, West Virginia
DEC	2	John Brown is hanged for treason
	10	Queensland becomes a separate Australian colony

Right: *Persian musicians and poets; the translation of Persian love poetry by Edward Fitzgerald has made the romance of the East very popular in the West.*

WAR AND DIPLOMACY IN ITALY

After Austria threatens Sardinia-Piedmont, her army is defeated by a joint French and Sardinian force at Solferino. The following month, by the Treaty of Villafranca, Austria agrees to cede Parma and Lombardy to France for subsequent cession to Sardinia, but keeps Tuscany, Modena and Venice. Count Cavour resigns in disgust at French duplicity. In November, it is agreed that Piedmont can take over Lombardy in return for France gaining Savoy and Nice.

JOHN BROWN HANGED

Anti-slavery campaigner John Brown (1800–59) is hanged for treason after leading a pro-slave rebellion. He attempted to seize the arsenal at Harpers Ferry, West Virginia and turn the town into a base for an uprising by slaves, but is seized by US marines under the command of Robert E Lee. Two of Brown's sons are killed in the Harpers Ferry incident.

DOMESTIC ELECTRIC LIGHTING

An incandescent platinum filament lamp is the first to be used for domestic electric lighting. The lamp, powered by a battery of galvanic cells in the cellar, is used to illuminate the parlour of Professor Moses G Farmer's home in Salem, USA.

GOING FOR GOLD

American George Hearst becomes a millionaire overnight after buying a half-share in one mine and a one-sixth share in another, which proves the richest in the newly discovered Comstock Lode in Nevada.

OIL RIG

Edwin Drake (1819–80), an American engineer, builds the first drilling rig for obtaining subterranean oil in America. His apparatus becomes the standard practicable means for extracting the valuable new source of fuels and chemicals.

HELP YOURSELF

The doctrine of self-help is expounded in a book published in London called *Self-Help* and written by Scottish essayist and social reformer Samuel Smiles (1812–1904). It supports a doctrine of non-interference by the state in the economic and social lives of its citizens, known as *laissez-faire*.

THEORY OF EVOLUTION

English biologist Charles Robert Darwin (1809–82) expounds his theory of evolution by natural selection, by publishing *On the Origin of Species by Means of Natural Selection*. Darwin has been working on the theory for some twenty years but he is prompted to publish by a letter he receives from Alfred Russel Wallace (1823–1913) explaining the same idea. The theory causes a great deal of controversy and debate.

FAUST

The Faust legend finds its most enduring place in opera, and this version of the story makes Charles François Gounod (1818–93) the most famous composer currently working in France. Its delicate melodies, fine orchestration and voice writing set the style for French grand opera of the late-nineteenth century.

Left: *Earl Russell, foreign secretary of the British government this year.*

Right: *Kicking down an exploratory oil well by the spring-pole drilling method.*

STORAGE BATTERY

French physicist Gaston Planté (1834–89) develops a practicable means for storing electricity. His storage battery is a collection of lead acid cells based on the voltaic pile, which are able to convert chemical energy into a direct electrical current as required.

PLAY SPACE

The world's first children's playgrounds open in Manchester, England, where areas with climbing bars and swings have opened in two public parks.

THE FIRST OF THE IRONCLADS

La Gloire, a 5617 tonne steam-powered, ironclad timber-built ship armed with 36 163mm guns is launched by the French navy. She has a top speed of 13 knots. In England, the *Warrior* is built, the first real iron-hulled, iron-clad man-of-war.

Isambard Kingdom Brunel
1806–1859

One of the pioneers of metal construction, the English inventor, railway engineer and shipbuilder has died, over-worked and disheartened by lack of interest in his work. Among Brunel's many works are the elegant Clifton Suspension Bridge, Bristol (designed 1828 and finally to be completed after his death in 1864), Hungerford Bridge, Charing Cross, London (1841–45), which is to be largely dismantled in 1860 to make room for the railway, and the lofty rail shed at Paddington Station, London (1852–54). His father was the French Sir Marc Isambard Brunel and the son took up his father's work. In shipping he designed the first Atlantic steamship, the *Great Western* (1854) and was the first to develop the metal hull, which was used on the Atlantic steamship *Great Britain* (1845).

RESERVATION IN NEW MEXICO

An Act of Congress permits President Buchanan to have the New Mexico lands of the Pima and Maricopa tribes near the Gila river surveyed and preserved as a reservation.

THE SOLFERINO LEGACY

A Souvenir of Solferino is published by Swiss philanthropist Jean-Henri Dunant (1828–1910). His scandalized account of the huge losses and inadequate treatment of the wounded at the Battle of Solferino arouses public indignation and leads to the establishment in 1864 by sixteen nations of the International Red Cross.

HIGH WIRE FEAT

French tightrope walker Charles Blondin (Jean-François Gravelet, 1824–97) walks a tightrope across Niagara Falls.

THE RUBAIYAT OF OMAR KHAYYAM

This free translation from the Persian is the only famous work of Victorian writer Edward Fitzgerald (1809–93). The aphoristic style of the verse means that it will be often quoted, and gives many Europeans their first idea of the culture of western Asia.

UNIVERSITY MUSEUM, OXFORD

A masterpiece of Gothic, designed by Benjamin Woodward (1815–61) and Sir Thomas Deane (1792–1871) under the influence of John Ruskin, this building is famous for its fine detail, the discerning selection of different stones used in its construction, and its iron and glass roof. The last is rendered Gothic with the use of rich ornament.

DARING YOUNG MAN

The first-ever flying trapeze circus act is performed with only mattresses to cushion falls at the Cirque Napoleon in Paris by French performer Jules Léotard. His name is given to the costume he wears.

Above: *A model farm in England. The buildings are expensive. Farming has become agribusiness.*

Above and below: *The botanist Charles Darwin.*

Above: *Charles XV of Sweden who succeeds to the throne this year, and his brother Prince Oscar.*

THE ORDEAL OF RICHARD FEVEREL

This, the fifth major novel by English writer George Meredith (1828–1909) is successful with readers and critics, although its theme — the mishaps brought about by an oppressive upbringing — causes scandal.

OBLOMOV

The greatest novel by Russian writer Ivan Goncharov (1812–91) plays out the theme of the conflict between traditionalism and practicality. Russians recognize in the main character's inertia the worst traits of the Russian aristocracy, but the novel transcends its setting and will later become more widely popular.

BREEDING LIKE RABBITS

Australian landowner Thomas Auston imports 24 English rabbits to provide sport. However, shooting them is unable to keep pace with their rate of reproduction and the Australian bush is soon overrun.

POLO CLUB

The Cachar Polo Club, the first in the world, is founded by British colonial officers in Assam, India.

Above: *The dramatic Niagara Falls traversed on a tightrope this year by French acrobat Blondin.*

Right: *George Meredith, English writer, publishes a scandalous novel this year.*

Below: *The iron-hulled warship the* Warrior *is built this year, as is the French ship* La Gloire.

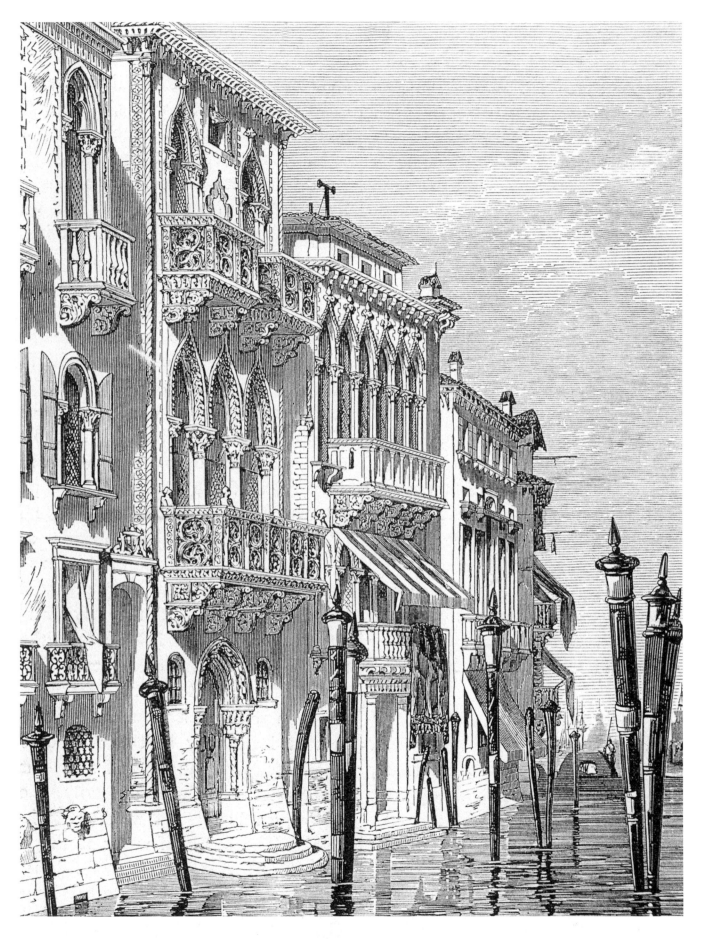

Above: *The canals of Venice, which is still an Austrian possession despite struggling for independence.*

INDEPENDENCE FOR ITALY

AFTER THE FAILURE of 1849, when Austria and the Papacy regained control of most of Italy, only Sardinia keeps its independent constitution. Now it becomes the focus for Italian dreams of independence. Count Cavour, prime minister of Sicily, forms an alliance with Napoleon III. Austria fears it is losing Italy and so declares war on Sardinia in 1859. The combination of French and Sardinian armies defeat the Austrians at Magenta and push them eastwards. Meanwhile, Giuseppe Garibaldi returns, leading a thousand volunteers, known as the "Red Shirts", lands in Sicily to support the Sicilian bid for freedom, then crosses to the mainland and captures Naples and the rest of southern Italy. In 1861, Victor Emmanuel, king of Sardinia, declares the Kingdom of Italy, over which he will rule. Only Venice and Rome remain separate.

★ Key Dates ★

● **SOLFERINO June 24, 1859**
A battle fought between 150 000 Austrians under their Emperor Franz Joseph with Generals Wimpffen and Schlick and the French and Piedmontese under Napoleon III and Victor Emmanuel with generals MacMahon, Niel (1802–69) and d'Hilliers in command. By the end of the day the Austrian centre has been broken and Franz Joseph is in retreat. The Austrians suffer 22 000 casualties and the Allies 18 000 casualties; France withdraws from the war. The battle marks the first extensive troop movements to the front by railway.

● **CALATAFIMI May 15, 1860**
Garibaldi's volunteers with Sicilian help fight 4000 Neapolitan troops commanded by General Landi and for the loss of eighteen killed and 128 wounded drive them back to Palermo.

● **MILAZZO July 18, 1860**
Fought between the Italian volunteers under Giuseppe Garibaldi and the Neapolitans under General Bosco. Though the Neapolitans are in a strong position, they are outflanked. Garibaldi then crosses the Straits of Messina to the mainland.

● **GAETA November 3, 1860–February 13, 1861**
Francis II of Naples with 12 000 troops makes a last stand against Garibaldi's "Red Shirts" and 10 000 other Italian troops. The siege is directed by Colonel Enrico Cialdini (1811–92), a Piedmontese who is assisted by Piedmontese warships. The defeated Francis is exiled.

● **ASPROMONTE August 29, 1862**
Garibaldi sets out on an ill-advised freelance mission to capture Rome. He is wounded and captured after a short fight with Royalist troops under General Pallavinci. He lives to fight another day.

Left: *Zouaves led by French officer charge the Austrian lines at the Battle of Solferino.*

Above left: *The Battle of Solferino, so terrible that it prompts the founding of the Red Cross.*

Above right: *Fearful struggle between Austrians and Italians at the Battle of Magenta.*

Right: *Nationalist hero Giuseppe Garibaldi, who returns with his volunteer troops to continue efforts to build a unified Italy.*

Left: *Garibaldi's signature on a note to his sister discussing his many campaigns.*

THE FIGHT FOR FREEDOM

*T*HE STRUGGLE FOR FREEDOM and self-determination reaches new heights. Civil war rocks the emergent United States as the northern Union fights the southern Confederacy over the question of slavery. Italy becomes one nation and Prussia begins its expansion into a unified Germany. Denmark loses Schleswig-Holstein. Austria and Hungary unite to carve out space in central Europe. France loses its toe-hold in Mexico, and Central and South American colonies claim autonomy from their colonial masters. In New Zealand, Maoris rebel against encroaching settlers and Canada fights its dominion status almost as soon as it is granted. The power structure in Japan shifts just as the West is gaining an insight into Japanese culture and art. Abraham Lincoln, Giuseppe Garibaldi, Robert E Lee, Ulyssses S Grant and Otto von Bismarck are the personalities of the decade. Kansas and Nebraska join the United States.

1860–1869

KEY EVENTS
of the
DECADE

UNIFICATION OF ITALY FINALIZED

CIVIL WAR IN AMERICA

PRINCE ALBERT DIES

GETTYSBURG ADDRESS

ABRAHAM LINCOLN ASSASSINATED

PONY EXPRESS FOUNDED

MEXICO AND FRANCE AT WAR

EARLY BICYCLE AND MOTOR CAR

SALVATION ARMY FOUNDED

MATTERHORN CLIMBED

SLAVERY ABOLISHED

MENDEL PUBLISHES WORK ON GENETICS

ALASKA PURCHASED

DOMINION OF CANADA FORMED

THE FIGHT FOR WOMEN'S SUFFRAGE

THE PERIODIC TABLE DEVISED

DIAMOND RUSH IN SOUTH AFRICA

WORLD POPULATION

1340 MILLION

(ESTIMATE)

Riots in Jamaica as the British Governor General imposes an unnecessarily harsh regime.

The Seven Weeks' War between Prussia and Austria.

Advertisement for bathroom fixtures and fittings, now widely available.

THE YEAR OF THE THOUSAND RED SHIRTS

Above: *Italian patriot Giuseppe Garibaldi.*

GARIBALDI IS THE MAN OF THE YEAR when his band of red-shirted patriots take Sicily and Naples, and Victor Emmanuel becomes king of a unified Italy. In America, abolitionist Abraham Lincoln becomes president of the Union and the Pony Express makes its first delivery. War breaks out in New Zealand but ends between France and Morocco. Harriet Tubman makes her last trip to conduct slaves to freedom on the Underground Railroad.

❊ 1860 ❊

JAN	20	Count Cavour returns to power as prime minister of Sardinia
FEB	2	US Senator Jefferson Davis demands a code for protection of property in slaves
MAR	17	Second Maori War in New Zealand
	24	France annexes Savoy and Nice
APR	13	In the USA, the first Pony Express reaches Sacramento, California
	26	Franco-Moroccan War ends
MAY	5	Giuseppe Garibaldi and his 1000 Red Shirts sail from Genoa to Sicily
	27	Garibaldi captures Palermo, Sicily, and sets up a provisional government
JULY	9	Muslim mob begins massacring Christians in Damascus, Syria
AUG	22	Garibaldi lands in mainland Italy
SEP	5	Western powers' treaty with Turkey restores order in Damascus
	7	Garibaldi captures Naples
	11	Victor Emmanuel II of Sardinia invades the Papal States
OCT	21	People of Naples and Sicily vote to join Sardinia
	26	Garibaldi hails Victor Emmanuel as king of Italy
NOV	6	Abraham Lincoln (Republican) elected as US president
DEC	20	South Carolina secedes from the Union in protest at Lincoln's election

ITALY VOTES FOR UNION

Plebiscites held throughout northern Italy are in favour of union with Sardinia-Piedmont. In June, Garibaldi captures Sicily and in September, Naples, and threatens to march on Rome. He is pre-empted by Piedmont invading the Papal States and uniting most of Italy except Rome and Venice under Victor Emmanuel, who becomes the first king of Italy in February 1861.

LINCOLN FOR PRESIDENT

Abraham Lincoln (1809–65) of Illinois wins the presidential election for the newly formed Republican Party; vice-president is Hannibal Hamlin of Maine. Lincoln faced a divided Democrat opposition, pro-slavery elements of which warned that southern states would secede from the Union of the anti-slavery states if Lincoln won.

LABOUR-SAVING DEVICES

The Oneida Community, a religious society of Perfectionists in central New York State, established in 1848 by John Humphrey Noyes (1811–86), invents a steel trap which becomes commercially successful. To relieve them of domestic duties, the members invent machines for washing dishes and preparing vegetables for cooking.

Above: *Anti-Christian riots in Damascus, a reaction to Western intervention in Turkey's invasion of Syria.*

SECESSION AND UNION

South Carolina leaves the Union in protest against the election of Lincoln as president. By the following June, a further ten states join with South Carolina, setting up their own Confederacy with its capital at Richmond, Virginia. All wish to continue to keep slaves, although three slave states — Missouri, Kentucky and West Virginia — remain in the Union. Meanwhile, the free state of Kansas joins the Union as the 34th state.

THE CIVILIZATION OF THE RENAISSANCE IN ITALY

Swiss historian Jacob Burckhardt (1818–97) publishes this classic of history. It defines the Renaissance as a historical period in its own right, demonstrates its influence over modern life and events, and makes a vivid case for the writing of cultural history.

NEW WATERWAYS FOR THE NETHERLANDS

The Dutch decide to improve their access to the sea by excavating the New Waterway (Nieuwe Waterweg) from Rotterdam to the coast, and the North Sea Canal (Noordzee Kanaal) to Amsterdam.

THE COLLEEN BAWN
The most famous play by Irish playwright and actor Dion Boucicault (1822–90) is produced. He is known for a style of rollicking drama that is highly fashionable in the late nineteenth century, and which will influence later writers such as Sean O'Casey (1884–1964).

THE RED HOUSE
This house in Bexleyheath, Kent, England is designed for the artist and craftsman William Morris (1834–96) by Philip Webb (1834–96). It is in an eclectic Gothic style, in brick, with pointed windows and high-pitched roofs. Its interior and furnishings reflect Morris's interests, and will influence the later Arts and Crafts Movement, in which he is a dominant figure.

EARLY TELEPHONE
The principle of the telephone is first demonstrated to a fascinated public by German inventor, Johann Phillip Reis, in Frankfurt. Using sausage skin for a diaphragm, it is a crude version of the telephone eventually developed by Alexander Graham Bell (1847–1922).

THE SELF-ADHESIVE ENVELOPE
The self-adhesive envelope is designed by a British publisher, Jeremiah Smith.

Above: *Garibaldi and Victor Emmanuel meet to discuss tactics for the last stages of the struggle for unification.*

THE A T STEWART STORE, NEW YORK CITY
Built of prefabricated iron units, which repeat across the façade to make a series of bays in Renaissance style, this department store, designed by John Kellum (1807–71), shows a notable coming-together of modern materials and building methods with decoration based on antique models.

MAX HAVELAAR
Under the pseudonym Multatuli ("I have suffered much"), Dutch author Eduard Douwes Dekker (1820–87) writes his masterpiece, an attack on the exploitation of colonial commercialism. The book causes much controversy, offending many Dutch people, who are seen as the smug and hypocritical exploiters of the peoples they rule.

NAVAJO ATTACK
One thousand Navajo Indians attack Fort Defiance, New Mexico, in retaliation against soldiers from the fort who have shot their sheep and goats, but they are driven off by musket fire.

Left: *Members of the Westward Ho Ladies' Golf Club enjoy a fashionable pitch and putt.*

Right: *The Minerva printing machine, which can be worked by hand, treadle or steam power.*

FASTER-FIRING ARTILLERY

The Armstrong 18-pounder becomes the first breech-loading artillery weapon to be fired in anger. Used in Sinho, China, it revolutionizes the nature of field warfare by considerably increasing the rate at which guns are reloaded and fired.

FAST TRACK

The first Pony Express takes eleven days to reach Sacramento from St Joseph, Missouri; a distance of 3200km (2000mi). The riders of the Pony Express carry mail and newspapers at a gallop and switch horses every 19km (12mi).

TUBMAN'S LAST TRIP

Harriet Tubman (1821–1913), a runaway slave who, helped by slaves and Quaker sympathizers, escaped to Philadelphia along the Underground Railroad in 1849, makes her last trip south to conduct fugitives to safe havens. Since 1850, when she returned to Maryland to liberate her sister, she has helped more than 200 slaves to freedom in the northern USA and Canada. She becomes known as "the Moses of her people".

EDUCATION IN THE USA

All US states now have some tax-supported free elementary schools, but it is still illegal to educate black people and slaves. However, a Washington DC Department of Education surveys the nation's high schools and finds that more than half of them are in the northern states.

DEADLY ADDITIVES

An Adulteration of Food Law is passed in Britain after physician and scientist Edwin Lankester (1814–74) reports green blancmange coloured with arsenite of copper and buns coloured yellow with sulfide of arsenic. Consciousness about the composition of foodstuffs was raised in 1855 by a report in *The Lancet* medical journal, "Food and Its Adulterations", denouncing the use of poisons such as lead and mercury to preserve and colour food and drinks.

THE SOURCE OF THE NILE — OR IS IT?

British explorers John Speke (1827–64) and James Grant (1827–92) probe west of Lake Victoria and then make their triumphant descent of the Nile. They have, however, not followed the river all the way from Lake Victoria and rival traveller Richard Burton (1829–90) challenges their claims very publicly.

DUTCH AGAINST SLAVERY

The Dutch extend their anti-slavery policies, introduced in 1812 in their African colony of St George del Mina, to the East Indies.

NURSING SCHOOL

The Nightingale School for Nurses — the world's first secular nurse-training school — is established in London by Florence Nightingale (1820–1910). It is paid for by public funds subscribed to commemorate her work during the Crimean War.

PRESS-STUDS

English inventor John Newman designs an alternative to buttons — the press-stud fastener or popper. It becomes popular because it works well and is also very simple.

TITLE FIGHT

The world championship fight between English champion Tom Sayers (1826–65) and American John Camel Heenan, the "Benicia Boy", is the first to capture the imagination of boxing fans on both sides of the Atlantic Ocean. The contest, held in Farnborough, England, on April 17, ends in a draw after 42 rounds amid much confusion, and interference from the rowdy crowd of fans.

FIRST GOLF MAJOR

The Open, formally The Open Championship of the British Isles, is the first of the modern golf "Majors" to be established.

THE UNION AND THE CONFEDERACY

WAR BREAKS OUT BETWEEN the northern emancipation states and the southern slave states of America. Victor Emmanuel declares Italy united and officially becomes king of the new country. France and Mexico go to war and a new nation, Romania, is created in the Balkans. The first recognizable bicycles appear in France, Louis Pasteur puts forward his new germ theory and Czar Alexander II abolishes serfdom in Russia.

Above: *Unionist General Philip Sherman.*

❧ 1861 ❧

JAN	2	Frederick William IV of Prussia dies; succeeded by brother William I	JUNE	6	Italy's Count Cavour dies, aged 50
	29	Kansas becomes the 34th US state	JULY	21	Confederates win First Battle of Bull Run (Manassas)
FEB	4	Seven seceding states form the Confederate States of America			
	9	Jefferson Davis chosen as president of the Confederate States of America	NOV	8	The Trent affair: Unionists seize two Confederates from a British ship; they are subsequently released
	18	An Italian parliament proclaims Victor Emmanuel king of Italy	DEC	14	Death of Britain's Prince Consort, Albert, aged 42
MAR	4	Abraham Lincoln inaugurated as sixteenth US president			
	19	Maori War ends in New Zealand			
APR	14	Confederates capture Fort Sumter, South Carolina			
	19	President Lincoln proclaims a blockade of the Confederate States of America			

A New Nation

A new Balkan nation of Romania is created when Moldavia and Wallachia unite. The two provinces had been ruled by the Ottomans but were invaded by Russia during the Crimean War and declared independent. A local prince, Alexander Cuza, is elected as ruler.

Reform in Russia

Czar Alexander II emancipates the Russian slaves, freeing millions of serfs tied to the land. Other reforms overhaul the archaic administrative structures, which were revealed to be inefficient during the Crimean War.

A State of Insurrection

Civil war breaks out as Confederate forces bombard the Union-held Fort Sumter in Charleston Harbor, South Carolina. In response, President Abraham Lincoln declares a "state of insurrection", not war, and issues an appeal for 75 000 volunteers to protect the Union.

War between Mexico and France

Napoleon III hopes to build an empire in Mexico and struggles to do so between 1861 and 1867. After initial military setbacks the French, under General Elie Forey (1804–72), enter Mexico City on June 7, 1863. The Austrian Archduke Maximilian (1832–67) is made emperor of Mexico. However under pressure from the USA, Napoleon deserts Maximilian and withdraws troops in 1867. The most notable incident is the Battle of Camerone, which takes place on April 30, 1863. A French Foreign Legion convoy escort, commanded by Captain Danjou and consisting of two officers and 62 legionnaires, fights to the death against 800 Mexican cavalry and 1200 infantry. The anniversary of the battle becomes the Legion memorial service and festival.

Wallpaper and Tapestry

Inspired by the craftsmanship of the Middle Ages, designer William Morris (1834–96) decides to make household items that are both aesthetically pleasing and inexpensive. He co-founds Morris, Marshall, Faulkner and Company and begins to make his first products.

Colour Photography

Thomas Sutton of Jersey, Channel Islands, produces the first-ever photograph in colour, rather than black and white. With the help of scientist James Clerk-Maxwell (1831–79), he uses liquid filters of red, green and blue to produce a colour transparency of a piece of tartan ribbon.

Apache Raids

The Apache Indians begin raids to drive settlers from Arizona after their chief Cochise is taken prisoner and subsequently escapes.

A New Sport

Frenchman Pierre Michaux adds pedals and a crankshaft to a "Hobby Horse" to create the "Vélocipede" — the first popular bicycle. The sport of bicycling or "wheeling" explodes in popularity in the late nineteenth century. Early designs, many of which feature an enormous front wheel, are often difficult to control and stop, and cause many casualties.

Above: *The funeral of Prince Albert, who dies on December 14 at Windsor Castle, England.*

His Royal Highness the Prince Albert
1819–1861

The Prince Consort has died at an early age of a serious illness, and Her Majesty the Queen enters a prolonged state of mourning occasioned by the most sincere grief. Prince Albert, whom she married in 1840, was her cousin, the son of the Duke of Saxe-Coburg-Gotha, and has been her staunchest supporter and adviser. He was particularly interested in the industrial arts and the progress of technology, and had been the organizer of the Great Exhibition of 1851.

Left: *Troops massing on the square in front of the palace in Mexico City, preparing for war with France.*

Below: *Fort Bowie, Arizona, raided by Apache Indians in retaliation for the capture and imprisonment of their chief, Cochise.*

Great Expectations

During his last great creative period (the 1850s and early 1860s see the creation of *Bleak House, Hard Times, Little Dorrit* and *Our Mutual Friend*), English writer Charles Dickens (1812–70) produces one of his best-loved works, which revisits some of his favourite themes — the poor boy making his way in the world, the individual at sea in society, the contrasting worlds of country and city and the disillusion of the idealist.

Pneumatic Drill

Frenchman Germain Sommelier invents a drill powered by compressed air for hewing rock. It is used with considerable effect in the construction of the Mont Cenis rail tunnel, linking France with Italy. In fact, work proceeds at three times the usual pace.

Weather Forecast

The Daily News in England becomes the first paper to publish regular prognoses for the weather. Data are taken from a number of meteorological stations, spread over Great Britain, and telegraphed to the Greenwich Observatory to be processed and analyzed before release.

Practical Training

The first Netherlands trade school to teach practical skills opens in Amsterdam. It is based on the Workers' Schools formed earlier in the century to teach spinning and weaving to the poor.

Pretzels for All

The first commercial pretzel factory is founded in Lititz, Pennsylvania, by Julius Sturgis and Ambrose Rauch.

Pasteur's Progress

French chemist Louis Pasteur (1822–95), who in 1857 showed that a living organism causes milk to ferment, and in 1860 sterilized it by heating it to 125°C (257°F) at a pressure of 0.5 atmospheres, publishes a paper refuting the theory of spontaneous generation and proposing the germ theory of disease.

Left: Archduke Maximilian of Austria, set up by Napoleon III as emperor of Mexico, but abandoned by his mentor.

Right: William I, who takes over the Prussian throne on the death of his brother Frederick William IV.

Mrs Beeton

English writer and magazine publisher Isabella Beeton (1836–65) publishes *The Book of Household Management*, giving practical information on running a household, together with precise recipes and cooking instructions. The book has previously appeared in serial form, between 1859 and 1860, in the magazine produced by Isabella's husband, Samuel Orchard Beeton.

Camillo Cavour
1810–1861

The Italian statesman Camillo Benso, Conte di Cavour, has died in the midst of negotiating the separation of Church and State with the pope. Cavour, who was premier of Piedmont-Sardinia, was a progressive nationalist, and had been the leading force in creating a united Italy. As a young man he was a republican and had some contact with the Carbonari, a secret revolutionary organization guided by Mazzini. On leaving his career in the army in 1831 he was found a post by his father as mayor of a village near Turin. He also took the opportunity to travel, and his visits to England left him in admiration of the liberal institutions in that country as well as developments in industry and the railways. In 1835, no longer espousing republicanism, he returned a dedicated patriotic nationalist and European, and founded the journal *Il Risorgimento* which made propaganda for war with Austria to reassert Italian independence. From 1847 he held various political appointments, becoming prime minister of Sardinia in 1852. He was closely involved in the handling of the war, and largely through his political efforts, the first parliament of a united Italy, with King Victor Emmanuel II of Sardinia-Piedmont at its head, met in Turin in 1861.

CIVIL WAR IN AMERICA

THE WAR IS FOUGHT between the north, or Union, and the south, or Confederacy, of the newly emergent United States. The southern states, under President Jefferson Davis (1808–89), wish to secede. The north, under President Abraham Lincoln, wants to keep the United States intact and also offers liberty to the black slaves employed in the southern plantations. The south hopes that France and Britain will support it, because of the cotton trade that supplies the European textile industry with southern cotton, but the north, with a powerful industrial base and larger population, is bound to win in time. The war starts on April 9, 1861, when southern forces fire on the north's Fort Sumter, and ends four years later, almost to the day, when General Robert E Lee (1807–70) of the Confederacy surrenders to General Ulysses Simpson Grant (1822–85) of the Union at the Appomattox Courthouse in Virginia. It is the first "modern war" in which trench warfare, mines, telegraphy, photography, rail transport, repeating rifles, breech-loading weapons and balloon observation all play a part, as does the compulsory drafting of troops on both sides. In all, about a million soldiers lose their lives and much of the land and the infrastructure of the south is destroyed.

✶ Key Dates ✶

The war is fought mainly on two fronts: the eastern front stretches from the Appalachian mountains to the coast, and the western front between the mountains and the Mississippi river. Many battles become known by two names, as the Union side names battles for the nearest stretch of water, while the Confederates name them after the nearest town.

- **FORT SUMTER April 12–14, 1861**
Held by Major Robert Anderson (1805–71) and 76 men of the northern states, the fort is surrounded by Confederates under General Pierre Gustave Toutant Beauregard (1818–93), who fires 4000 shells in 36 hours. Although it suffers no casualties, the Union garrison surrenders.

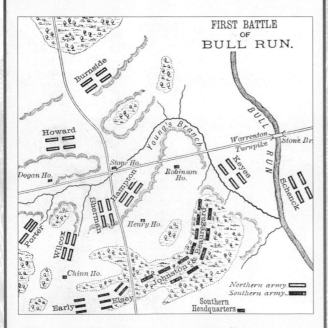

Above: *Troop positions at noon at Bull Run.*

- **FIRST BATTLE OF BULL RUN (Manassas) July 21, 1861**
This battle sees the first tactical delivery of troops to the fringe of a battlefield by railway, as 1900 Confederates reach Manassas Junction. A major Confederate victory: 30 000 Confederates under Beauregard hold 14km (9mi) of the Bull Run river. The 40 000 Union troops attack and are counter attacked, losing 1492 casualties and 1600 prisoners to the Confederates' 1982 casualties.
- **THE MONITOR AND THE MERRIMACK March 8–9, 1862**
The *Merrimack* is a sunken Unionist ship which the Confederates raise, clad with iron plates and use to destroy two Union ships at Hampton Roads. The Union's own ironclad, the *Monitor*, challenges the *Merrimack*. Neither ship wins the ensuing battle but the *Merrimack* successfully blocks Union entry to the James river, the route to the Confederate town of Richmond. This is the first sea battle in which both ships move under steam power.
- **YORKTOWN April 4, 1862**
A holding action by 12 000 Confederates under General Magruber, who convinces McClellan, with 45 000 soldiers, that he has a larger force. He conducts regular siege operations against Yorktown, which allows the Union troops time to prepare the defences of their capital Richmond.
- **SHILOH (Pittsburg Landing) April 6–7, 1862**
Fought between 43 000 Confederates under General Joseph J Johnston and 42 000 Union troops under General Grant. A confused battle in which the Union suffers 13 087 casualties, including 1754 killed, and the Confederates 10 697, including 1723 killed.
- **NEW ORLEANS April 24–May 1, 1862**
A Federal fleet of 30 armed steamers under Commodore David Glasgow Farragut (1801–70) bombard Forts Jackson and Mary for nine days and then force a passage up the Mississippi river to New Orleans, which surrenders on May 1.

- **BATTLE OF FAIR OAKS (Seven Pines) May 31–June 1, 1862**
Advancing on Richmond, the Union forces, under McClellan, are attacked by Johnston's forces and driven back 3km (2mi). The following day McClellan recovers the lost territory but the Confederates are able to withdraw, having suffered 4500 casualties to the Union's 7000. The battle sees the first use of the manual machine gun.

- **SEVEN DAYS June 25–July 1, 1862**
MECHANICSVILLE OR BEAVER DAM CREEK June 26, 1862
FRAYSER'S FARM (Glendale) June 30, 1862
A series of actions fought by General Robert E Lee with 100 000 Confederates against the Union force of 95 000 under General George Brinton McClellan (1826–85). By the close of the fighting the Confederates have suffered 20 000 casualties and the Union 16 000.

- **SECOND BATTLE OF BULL RUN August 30, 1862**
CHANTILLY September 1, 1862
Union troops under General John Pope attack the Confederates under General Thomas "Stonewall" Jackson (1824–63). Jackson counter attacks at the close of the day and takes 7000 Union prisoners.

- **ANTIETAM (Sharpsburg) September 17, 1862**
Fought between 35 000 Confederate forces under Lee and 95 000 Union troops under McClellan. The casualties are the heaviest experienced in a day's fighting in the war, the Union suffers 12 140, including 2108 killed, and the Confederates 13 724, including 2700 killed.

- **FREDERICKSBURG December 13, 1862**
A major battle between 150 000 Union troops under General Ambrose Everett Burnside (1824–81) and 80 000 Confederates under Lee, who hold positions on a range of heights. The Confederates lose 1800 and are in no condition to follow up, having caused the Union 13 771 losses.

- **CHANCELLORSVILLE May 2–4, 1863**
Under the command of General Joseph Hooker (1814–79), 120 000 Union troops are attacked by 53 000 Confederates under Lee. In the fighting "Stonewall" Jackson is mortally wounded by friendly fire. Superior tactics give the Confederates the victory although they suffer 10 000 casualties. The Union side has 18 000 casualties and 7650 are taken prisoner.

- **VICKSBURG May 7–July 4, 1863**
Vicksburg is a Confederate fortress, with a garrison of 25 000 under General Pemberton, which blocks Union attempts to control the Mississippi. The Union campaign prosecuted by Grant and General Philip Henry Sherman (1831–88) includes a clash at Champion's Hill that costs the Confederates 3851 casualties. The Siege of Vicksburg, which is now defended by 30 000 Confederates but surrounded by 75 000 Union troops, ends on July 4 when the garrison is starved out. The Confederacy is now split in half and doomed.

- **GETTYSBURG July 1–3, 1863**
A major battle between the northern Army of the Potomac under General George Gordon Meade (1815–72) and the Army of Virginia under Lee. Both sides lose 20 000 men, and Lee withdraws safely.

- **CHATTANOOGA (or Missionary Ridge) November 23–25, 1863**
Fought between 80 000 Union troops, under Grant, and the 64 000-strong Confederate Army of the West under General Braxton Bragg (1817–76). The Confederates are heavily attacked and spend two days in rearguard actions: they suffer 361 killed and 2160 wounded and lose 4000 prisoners and 40 guns. The Union loses 753 killed, 4722 wounded and 349 missing.

- **FORT PILLOW April 12, 1864**
A Union fort on the Mississippi held by 262 black and 295 white soldiers is attacked by Confederates under General Nathan Bedford Forrest (1821–77); fourteen men are killed and 86 wounded. After they surrender, many of the black troops are reportedly massacred: of the garrison, 231 are killed, 100 seriously wounded and 226 captured.

- **WILDERNESS CAMPAIGN May 4–June, 1864**
The Union, under Grant and Meade, with 120 000 men and 316 guns, outgun and outnumber the Confederates under Lee with 64 000 men and 274 guns. After punishing fighting, Grant is able to withdraw, having inflicted 2246 killed and 12 073 wounded on the Union for 7750 casualties on the Confederate side.

- **PETERSBURG June 15–18, 1864 and June 30, 1864–April 3, 1865**
The initial attack by Grant against Confederate troops under Beauregard, reinforced by Lee, is beaten back at a cost of 1688 killed, 8513 wounded and 1185 captured. In a second assault, the Union side blows up a mine, killing or wounding 278 Confederates and creating a huge crater.

- **ATLANTA July–September 1864**
PEACH TREE CREEK July 20, 1864
The Confederates lose 2600 men and the Union 1600. Sherman's 224km (140mi) drive from Chattanooga to Atlanta inflicts 27 565 casualties for 21 656, but destroys the south's main port and further divides the Confederacy.

- **FORT STEDMAN March 25, 1865**
The Union loses 2000 men but inflicts 4400 casualties on the southerners. On April 1 the Confederates, outnumbered and outgunned, withdraw. The fighting has cost the north 42 000 men; the south has lost 28 000, but is broken.

Above: *The Confederate flag.*

CIVIL WAR IN AMERICA

Left: *The Confederate warship* Alabama, *built in Birkenhead, England, is sunk in the English Channel by a British ship before she reaches America.*

Below: *Roanoke Island falls to the Unionists after a bitter struggle.*

Below left: *The Battle of Shiloh, where General Grant is almost overwhelmed by Confederate forces but reinforcements turn the tide of battle his way.*

Below right: *The First Battle of Bull Run results in victory for the Confederates.*

Left: *The fall of Vicksburg to the Union after a siege lasting two months in the summer 1863.*

Above: *General Ulysses S Grant, military leader of the Union side.*

Above: *General Robert E Lee, military leader of the Confederate side.*

Below: *General Lee surrenders to General Grant at the Appomattox Courthouse, Virginia, on April 9, 1865.*

HMP

STARS AND WEATHER

THE NINETEENTH CENTURY'S love affair with technology continues as instruments are built to track the stars and measure the weather. A new astronomer royal, Sir William Christie, will introduce new instruments at London's Royal Observatory, establishing the pattern for modern astronomy.

Right: *The Royal Observatory at Greenwich, London, designed and built by Sir Christopher Wren in 1675, and home to Greenwich Mean Time and the Greenwich meridian (0°).*

✲ *Measuring the Weather* ✲

The English obsession with the weather is reflected in the number of thermometers, barometers, wind glasses and storm glasses to be found in the average English home. Many of them are beautifully designed and are art objects in themselves, regardless of function.

Barometer and storm glass.

Centigrade thermometer.

Double scale thermometer.

Fahrenheit thermometer.

Combination scale thermometer.

IRON CHANCELLORS AND IRONCLAD SHIPS

THE CIVIL WAR CONTINUES in America and Lincoln declares that all slaves shall be free after the first day of 1864. In Prussia, Otto von Bismarck becomes the new chancellor and begins to lay his plans for a unified Germany. France expands its empire in Southeast Asia. The first motor car is seen, and Livingstone plunges into the heart of Africa.

Left: *Abraham Lincoln, president of the Union.*

✳ 1862 ✳

FEB	6	In the American Civil War, Unionists capture Fort Henry, Tennessee
	15	Unionists capture Fort Donelson, Tennessee
MAR	9	Ironclad ships *Monitor* (Unionist) and *Merrimack* (Confederate) fight
	10	Britain and France recognize Zanzibar as independent
APR	7	Battle of Shiloh, Tennessee: Unionist victory
MAY	1	Unionists capture New Orleans
	6	US writer Henry David Thoreau dies at 45
JUNE	5	France annexes Cochin China, Southeast Asia
	15	Turks bombard Serb rebels in Belgrade

AUG	2	France and Russia sign a trade treaty
	29	Italian troops capture Giuseppe Garibaldi, but soon free him
	30	Unionists defeated at Second Battle of Bull Run
SEP	17	Confederates defeated at Antietam (Sharpsburg)
	22	Otto von Bismarck becomes Prussian prime minister
	22	President Lincoln proclaims that all slaves shall be free from January 1, 1864
OCT	22	Greeks depose their king, Othon (formerly Prince Otto of Bavaria)
DEC	13	Confederates heavily defeat the Unionists at Fredericksburg, Virginia

THE IRON CHANCELLOR
Otto von Bismarck becomes prime minister of Prussia, stating that "blood and iron" will be needed to unify Germany under Prussian leadership. He enlarges and reorganizes the Prussian army and begins to challenge Austria for supremacy in Germany.

MACHINE GUN
The rapid-fire machine gun is revealed by two American inventors, independently. One is designed by Wilson Agar, but it is the design of Richard Gatling (1818–1903) that is adopted for military use. The Gatling gun will change the nature of warfare altogether.

MOTOR CAR
Jean-Joseph Etienne Lenoir, a French engineer born in Luxembourg, introduces a major new form of transport. Having made a 1.5 horsepower internal combustion engine fuelled by a hydrocarbon liquid, he fits it to a carriage and drives the first car. Overland travel will never look back.

THERMOPLASTIC
A substance named "Parkasine" is invented by English chemist Alexander Parkes (1813–90). The material, eventually known as "celluloid", is the first thermoplastic, meaning that it can be reworked into different shapes with the action of heat. It is demonstrated at this year's International Exhibition in London.

ANOTHER EXHIBITION
The second International Exhibition, a world trade fair, opens in London. It features displays of Japanese arts and crafts, which stir up a demand for Japanese artefacts. An American, Ferdinand PA Carre, manufactures blocks of ice to demonstrate his mechanical refrigerator in which he uses liquid ammonia for compression.

Above: *French writer Victor Hugo produces his greatest work,* Les Miserables, *this year.*

Right: *Drilling machine made by Whitworth & Company and shown at the International Exhibition.*

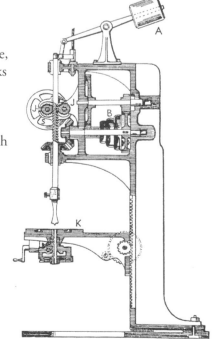

Henry Thoreau
1817–1862

Henry David Thoreau, the American journalist, essayist, poet and lecturer — and disciple of Emerson — has died, aged only 45. In the new age of the machine and industrial labour, his idealistic desire to live the simple life led him to build a cabin near Concord, Massachusetts, where he lived from 1845 to 1847. His book *Walden* records the experience. During that time he was imprisoned for refusing to pay poll tax. His reflections on government and individual liberty are published under the title *On the Duty of Civil Disobedience* and will be one of the most influential works of the nineteenth and twentieth centuries.

PEABODY PHILANTHROPY

George Peabody (1795–1869), an American financier who has settled in London, establishes a trust to build sound housing for the London poor. Peabody has financed the American exhibits at the Great Exhibition of 1851, education schemes in the southern USA, and endowed the archaeological museum at Harvard and the museum of physical sciences at Yale. The housing situation for London's poor is appalling and the homeless are commonly found dead on the streets.

EDUCATION GRANTS

The US Land-Grant Act sponsored by Justin Smith Morrill (1810–98), the representative for Vermont, is signed by the president, donating 30 000 acres of land to each state to build higher education institutions offering courses in agriculture, technology and industrial subjects such as engineering.

NATIVE AMERICAN REBELLION

A mass hanging is held in Minnesota, USA, of Sioux Indians, whose uprising was suppressed at Wood Lake by General Sibley. In 1850 they had ceded their lands in Iowa and some in Minnesota to the government, in return for the right to live on their Minnesota reservation, but found themselves surrounded by hostile white settlers. In August they rebelled under Chief Little Crow, killing more than 400.

WHOLESALE CO-OPERATION

The Co-operative Wholesale Society is established in England to supply the scores of co-operative societies that have sprung up since the movement was founded in 1844.

A GREAT GAME FROM INDIA

Modern polo is born when British cavalry officers stationed in India take up the game, taught by tribal horsemen. They will introduce it in England in 1869. Polo is thought to have originated in ancient Persia 4000 years ago.

Above: *Otto von Bismarck, Prussia's new prime minister, intent on the unification and expansion of Germany.*

FATHERS AND SONS

Liberal Russian writer Ivan Turgenev (1818–83) reaches the peak of his career with his novel *Fathers and Sons*; the work is given a hostile reception by the critics at home but is well received elsewhere.

SARAH BERNHARDT'S DEBUT

At the Comédie Française, French actress Sarah Bernhardt (1844–1923) plays Iphigénie, starting her off on a sixty-year international career. The début does not attract widespread notice, but Bernhardt will soon be admired for her voice and her great range as an actress.

ONLY ONE WIFE

Polygamy is prohibited in the US territories in an act aimed at the polygamous Mormons in Utah. The authority of the Mormon Church to regulate and perform marriages is annulled.

EDUCATION FIRST FOR WOMEN

Julie-Victoire Daubie becomes the first woman to pass the French baccalauréat.

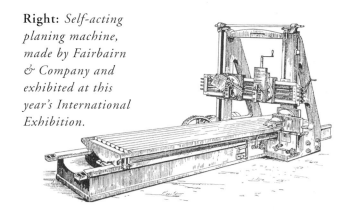

Right: *Self-acting planing machine, made by Fairbairn & Company and exhibited at this year's International Exhibition.*

LIFE WITH THE GREAT BEAR

THROUGHOUT THE CENTURY Europe and Russia have confronted each other in a series of wars, alliances and periods of uneasy peace. Russia features in the European mind as a bear, powerful and unpredictable.

Europe appears to Russia to form a conspiracy to prevent legitimate expansion. The Russian empire expands and contracts throughout the century, but life for the people who live there stays much the same.

Right: *A welcoming wayside inn in the grip of a Russian winter. The steeply pitched roof allows snow to slide off easily.*

Below: *Boatmen on the Volga river, the great artery of trade and communication that runs 3880km (2425mi) from the Valdai hills northwest of Moscow to the Caspian sea.*

Left: *A temporary village of yurts, tent like dwellings used by the nomadic peoples of southeastern Russia.*

Below: *Fierce cossacks from southern and eastern Russia demonstrate a traditional standing riding position that makes them such outstanding cavalry troops.*

Below: *The Volga delta at Astrakhan in southern Russia, where wild horses and ponies breed.*

GETTYSBURG AND THE RED CROSS

Above: Confederate General Thomas "Stonewall" Jackson.

ABRAHAM LINCOLN DELIVERS the Gettysburg Address and institutes the tradition of thanksgiving in America. In Switzerland, the Red Cross is founded in response to the horrors of war. Poland makes a bid for freedom. The first submarines plunge under the ocean wave, Nobel invents dynamite, Napoleon III invents the Salon des Refusés to comfort spurned artists and John D Rockefeller takes his first steps on the path to outrageous fortune.

✺ 1863 ✺

JAN	1	Emancipation Proclamation frees all slaves in the USA
	22	Poles rebel against Russian rule
MAR	4	Confederates defeat Unionists at Chancellorsville, Virginia
	4	More Maori rebellions in New Zealand
JUNE	6	Prince William of Denmark becomes King George of Greece
	20	West Virginia becomes the 35th US state
JULY	3	Confederates are heavily defeated at Gettysburg, Pennsylvania
	4	Unionists capture Vicksburg, Mississippi, after a long siege
SEP	20	Confederates defeat the Unionists at Chickamauga, Georgia
OCT	26	The International Red Cross organization is formed in Switzerland
	26	In Britain the Football Association is formed
NOV	13	Danes declare the Duchy of Schleswig part of Denmark
	15	King Frederik VII of Denmark dies; succeeded by Christian VIII
	19	President Lincoln delivers his Gettysburg Address
	25	Unionists win Battle of Chattanooga, Tennessee

THE RED CROSS

The International Red Cross is formed in Geneva, Switzerland. The following year, twelve nations sign the Geneva Convention "for the amelioration of the condition of the wounded and sick of armies in the field", the basic international agreement concerning treatment of casualties during war, which grants neutral status to Red Cross personnel.

A PROCLAMATION OF EMANCIPATION

President Lincoln signs the Emancipation Proclamation, freeing all slaves in both the Confederate and Union states. Although Lincoln does not have the constitutional authority to act in the Union states nor the power to do so in the Confederate states, the proclamation gives the Union moral authority in the Civil War.

POLAND'S BID FOR FREEDOM

A national insurrection begins when the National Committee issues an independence manifesto, attempting to free Poland from Russian, Austrian and Prussian rule. The revolt is put down by both Russia and Prussia, working in alliance.

THE GETTYSBURG ADDRESS

President Lincoln dedicates a cemetery at the battlefield of Gettysburg, Pennsylvania, making a simple speech much derided at the time. In retrospect, the Gettysburg Address, which called for "a new birth of freedom", defined the principles for which the Union states were fighting.

LONDON UNDERGROUND

A 6km (4mi) tunnel from Farringdon Street to Paddington in London is opened as the first "tube" line. The journey along the Metropolitan Railway takes some 33 minutes and the tunnel is gaslit. The engine, however, is steam-powered and the damp smoke makes travelling a rather dirty business.

LINOLEUM

Londoner Frederick Walton invents a floor covering by applying a mixture of cork, linseed oil and rosin to jute matting. Linoleum becomes popular as it is easy to clean and maintain. It can also be pigmented and patterned to suit differing tastes and is easy to disinfect.

THE ALBERT MEMORIAL

In England, the architect Sir George Gilbert Scott (1811–78) wins the competition to design a memorial for Prince Albert. The spired and pinnacled canopy for the statue is a typical example of Gothic design in the High Victorian period.

Thomas Jonathan "Stonewall" Jackson
1824–1863

The tough and brilliant commander (with Robert E Lee) of the Confederate southern states in the ongoing American Civil War has died in the Battle of Chancellorsville. He was named "Stonewall" because of his resolute stance in the Battle of Bull Run at the beginning of the war (1861). He was professor at the Virginia Military Institute from 1851 to 1861, leaving to take command of Confederate troops when Virginia seceded from the Union. His death is a blow to his side (he was accidentally killed by his own troops) and after it the Confederates are increasingly less able to hold their own.

SUBMARINE VESSEL

The American Confederates Navy becomes the first to own self-propelled submarine vessels. They are designed to do battle with the Union Navy's *Goliath*. The seamen inside have to crank shafts with a propeller at the rear to drive the vessels — known affectionately as "Davids".

BIG BANG

Swedish chemist, Alfred Nobel (1833–96), invents dynamite. It is made from nitroglycerin, stabilized by using an absorbent clay medium. It proves to be a great advance for mining and quarrying, but also marks the beginning of high-explosive applications in warfare.

STAR MATTER

William Huggins (1824–1910), a British astronomer, discovers that stars contain the same essential elements as those comprising the Earth. It is yet another piece of evidence that the universe is a uniform and scientifically understandable phenomenon.

THE LIFE OF JESUS

French linguist and professor Ernest Renan (1823–92) produces this, his most famous work, in which he applies modern methods of scholarship to the Christian story. The Clerical Party refuses to confirm his appointment as Professor of Hebrew at the Collège de France.

SCHOOLS IN SCANDINAVIA

The first fifteen Folk High Schools, started by Bishop Grundtvig, open in rural Denmark. They are weekly boarding schools for farmers' sons and women, open from three to five months a year, and prove immensely popular and influential, spreading through Denmark to Norway and Sweden.

DEJEUNER SUR L'HERBE

French artist Edouard Manet (1832–83) repeats a traditional classical subject, but instead of having all the picnickers naked or draped, in the Renaissance style, clothes the two men in contemporary suits while leaving their female companion naked. The public is scandalized by this "immoral" treatment. Meanwhile artistic traditionalists are shocked by Manet's use of realistic daylight in the picture.

SALON DES REFUSES

In the midst of an ongoing argument about which artists' work is accepted for exhibition in the official Salon in Paris, Napoleon III orders the setting up of a "Salon des Refusés" (Gallery of Rejects), at which artists such as Manet and Whistler may exhibit. Later refusés will include Picasso and Cézanne. This is a turning point in the development of modern art.

CLIFTON SUSPENSION BRIDGE

After a long period of design and construction, this great bridge over the River Avon in Bristol, England, is completed after the death of its engineer, Isambard Kingdom Brunel (1806–59). It is admired for its daring, since many doubted that such a large bridge in such a difficult position could be safe. It remains an object-lesson in bridge-building.

CRICKET ACE

William Gilbert Grace (1848–1915), who will dominate cricket for 40 years, plays his first first-class game at age 15 for Bristol and District against an All-England side. He scores 32 runs. Grace becomes the personification of cricket in the Victorian age, scoring a hundred centuries before he retires from the game.

HEINRICHSHOF, VIENNA

This vast apartment block, one of many such buildings created during the reign of Franz Joseph, is ornamented in a variety of Renaissance styles. Its grand appearance reflects the grandeur of contemporary Vienna.

HOMES IN THE WEST

The Homestead Act becomes law, declaring that any US citizen or anyone intending to become a citizen may have 160 acres of western land for a $10 registration fee and $1.25 per acre, provided the purchaser makes improvements and lives on the land for five years.

CELEBRITY WEDDING

The marriage takes place in New York between Charles S Stratton, "General Tom Thumb", who is 86cm (35in) tall, and Lavinia Warren, who is 80cm (32in) tall. The wedding is organized by showman PT Barnum (1810–91).

SOCIAL REFORM IN THE NETHERLANDS

A new type of secondary school, the Higher Citizens' School (HBS), in which emphasis is not on the classics, is introduced in The Netherlands by liberal Prime Minister Jan Rudolf Thorbecke. He also makes the authorities responsible for public health and for preventing industrial misuse of child labour, and standardizes medical practice, excluding anyone without a medical degree from practising medicine.

RUGBY RIFT

In England, the Rugby Union splits from the Football Association. The unionists continue with a handling rather than a kicking game leading to the survival of the very different games of rugby and football.

Left: *Maori war canoe; Maoris of New Zealand's North Island are not willing to sell land to the white immigrant settlers and there is tension and trouble for the next decade.*

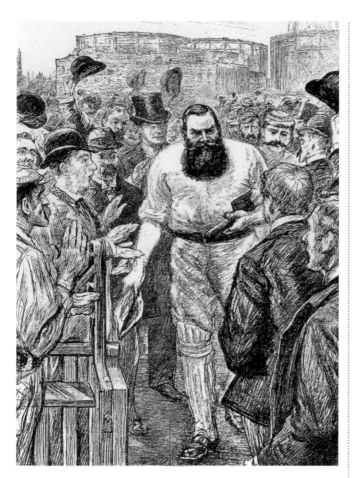

Above: *This year sees the beginning of the meteoric career of Dr WG Grace, cricketing phenomenon.*

AN ABOLITIONIST RETURNS

Abolitionist Harriet Tubman (1821–1913) abandons her retirement from conducting runaway slaves along the Underground Railroad to lead black soldiers up the Combahee river to plantations where they free some 800 slaves.

A TRADITION IS SET

President Lincoln proclaims the first national Thanksgiving Day, October 3, and sets aside the last Thursday of November to commemorate the feast given by the Pilgrims in 1621 for the Wampanoag Indians who helped them survive.

RUBY VALLEY TREATY

The Nez Percé Indians in the northwest of the USA are forced to sign a treaty agreeing to vacate lands coveted by whites. The Ruby Valley Treaty signed with the Shoshone, Washoe and other tribes in Nevada leaves them mainly desert for their reservation.

HORSE-RACING AT SARATOGA

Thoroughbred horse-racing takes place in America for the first time at Saratoga Springs, New York.

PLAGUES AND PESTILENCE

A worldwide cholera epidemic begins, and an epidemic of scarlet fever strikes Britain. A epizootic (epidemic) of cattle diseases also occurs, decimating herds of Dutch milking cows, and in the USA the worst winter in years affects cattle on the Texas plains, resulting in widespread cattle rustling.

FIRST WOMAN PRIEST

Olympia Brown, who in 1860 became the first woman to study theology alongside men, becomes the first woman to be ordained in the USA.

THE FOUNDATION OF A FORTUNE

John Davison Rockefeller (1839–1937) enters the oil business, investing $4000 in the lard oil refinery of a candle-maker, Samuel Andrews.

GET YOUR SKATES ON

Roller skates with four wheels are patented by New York inventor James L Plimpton. The wheels are made of boxwood and cushioned with rubber pads, making it possible to maintain balance and execute intricate manoeuvres.

FOOTBALL RULES

The English Football Association is created on October 26 and on December 1 publishes the Association Rules for the game.

Eugène Delacroix
1798–1863

The French Romantic painter Ferdinand Victor Eugène Delacroix has died, perhaps the greatest figure in French nineteenth-century art. He painted huge canvases on classical or historical themes, and also used literature as a source for his works. One of his first great paintings was *Dante and Virgil in Hell* (1822) and this was followed by *The Massacre at Chios* (1824), which was bought by the government. He was also commissioned to produce works for panels in the Chambre des Deputés in the parliament building, yet despite this he was never wholly approved of, for there was something non-conformist about his sense of drama, his rather loose drawing style and brilliant use of colour, and the energetic character of the man himself.

TOLSTOY, TCHAIKOVSKY AND SCHLESWIG-HOLSTEIN

ANOTHER PRESIDENTIAL TERM FOR LINCOLN as Denmark, Austria and Prussia wrestle with the Schleswig-Holstein question. Maximilian of Austria becomes Napoleon III's short-lived puppet emperor in Mexico. Russia begins to clamp down on Poland. It is a good year for the Russian arts, with Tolstoy and Tchaikovsky producing major works. Native Americans are massacred and cheated once again and there are riots in Belfast, Northern Ireland. A new steam whaling ship shakes up the whaling industry.

✤ 1 8 6 4 ✤

JAN	16	Austria and Prussia call on Denmark not to incorporate the Duchy of Schleswig
FEB	1	Austrian and Prussian armies enter Schleswig
MAR	29	Britain hands over the Ionian islands to Greece
APR	10	Maximilian of Austria accepts the throne of Mexico as emperor
	25	Conference of Austria, Britain, France, Prussia and Russia to solve the Schleswig problem begins in London
MAY	5	Indecisive Battle of the Wilderness, Virginia
	19	US author Nathaniel Hawthorne dies at 59
	22	Battle of Spotsylvania Courthouse also ends indecisively
JUNE	25	London Conference ends without a decision
SEP	15	Italy renounces its claim to Rome
OCT	30	Denmark surrenders Schleswig-Holstein and Lauenburg to Austria and Prussia
	31	Nevada becomes the 36th US state
NOV	8	Abraham Lincoln is re-elected as US president
DEC	16	Confederates are defeated in the Battle of Nashville, Tennessee
	21	Unionists capture Savannah, Georgia

Right: *Riots break out in Belfast in response to the erection of a monument to Daniel O'Connell in Dublin. Effigies of O'Connell are carried through the streets to be burnt or hanged.*

PRUSSIA AND RUSSIA SEIZE DANISH TERRITORY
Prussia and Austria invade the Duchy of Schleswig-Holstein, ruled by Denmark, and by agreement the following year divide the duchy between them. This acquisition gives Prussia the strategic Kiel Canal connecting the Baltic to the North Sea.

OVERTURE TO ROMEO AND JULIET
One of the first works by Russian composer Piotr Ilych Tchaikovsky (1840–93) to prove popular, this overture is remarkable for its singing melodies and lush orchestral writing. The work will remain one of the most popular by a Russian composer.

ANOTHER TERM FOR LINCOLN
President Lincoln wins re-election for the Republicans, defeating the Democrat George B McClellan. Andrew Johnson of Tennessee — a southerner, a Democrat and a former slave owner — becomes vice-president.

WAR AND PEACE
Russian novelist Leo Tolstoy (1828–1910) embarks upon his great novel, a huge canvas which portrays a whole society. Its epic sweep combined with telling details, and its well-drawn characters make it a landmark work, in which all human life, all aspirations and fears, all triumphs and tragedies, can be found.

APOLOGIA PRO VITA SUA
Catholic Cardinal John Henry Newman (1801–90) writes his spiritual autobiography to defend himself from charges of untruthfulness. The work is soon recognized as a masterpiece of English prose.

MAN WITH A BROKEN NOSE
French artist Auguste Rodin (1840–1917) begins to show the way forward for sculpture — his work has a new sense of life, but does not fall into traditional classical sculptural modes. Rodin finds it hard to make his way at this early stage in his career.

MICROSTRUCTURE
The structure of steel on a microscopic scale is discovered and described by British geologist, Henry Sorby (1826–1908). The relationship between the iron and carbon atoms explains the high strength of steel and initiates interest in the microstructure of other materials.

ISLANDS FOR GREECE
Britain agrees to cede the Ionian islands, including Corfu, to Greece.

Nathaniel Hawthorne
1804–1864

The American writer Nathaniel Hawthorne, author of *The Scarlet Letter* (1850), has died. This is his best-known work, and with its radical morality it will be increasingly valued during the twentieth century. Hawthorne was a hard-working writer who produced numerous short stories, magazine articles, children's stories and several other novels, including four written during the years 1851–52.

Above: *Russian composer Pyotr Ilych Tchaikovsky writes his* Overture to Romeo and Juliet *this year.*

DRIVING CHAIN
Belt-driven machinery in factories sees the introduction of the driving chain. Englishman James Slater fits it to textile machinery. Stronger and more hardwearing than belts, the chains result in faster production with fewer interruptions for maintenance.

RUSSIAN OPPRESSION IN POLAND
The Russian language is made obligatory in Polish schools, and the authority of Polish Roman Catholic clergymen is challenged after Russia suppresses the widespread insurrection that began in Poland in 1863.

WHALING SHIP
Sven Foyn of Oslo, Norway, launches his steam whaling ship *Spes e Fides*. The introduction of steam power to whaling marks a new era in which previously numerous species will be over-hunted for products to supply the burgeoning cosmetics industries.

MASSACRE AND MALTREATMENT
The Cheyenne Indians are massacred by US troops under John Chivington at Sand Creek in Colorado after they go on the warpath, supported by Arapahoe, Apache, Comanche and Kiowa. The Navajo, forced last year to make a long march 480km (300mi) to a New Mexico reservation, are now being resettled by Kit Carson (1809–68), who imposes so harsh a regime that hundreds die of disease and starvation.

Above: *Norwegian whaler Sven Foyn using the harpoon cannon mounted on his steam whaling ship.*

ONWARD CHRISTIAN SOLDIERS
The Salvation Army is founded as a mission in Whitechapel, East London, by William Booth (1829–1912), an English religious revivalist.

EARLY ECOLOGIST
Man and Nature is published by US ecologist George Perkins Marsh, who warns that the ravages of man are destroying the balance of nature.

BEAUTY PRESERVED
The Yosemite valley in California is made a preservation area by a Congressional Bill introduced by landscape architect Frederick Law Olmsted (1822–1903) which protects the valley as a national scenic preserve. Olmsted is the first person to describe himself as a landscape architect.

A NEW BREW
Gerard Adrian Heineken, a Dutch brewer, acquires the 272-year-old De Hooiberg brewery and develops a new yeast, which gives Heineken beer a distinctive taste.

Above: *The Amalienborg Palace, Copenhagen, Denmark. Prussia and Austria seize Danish territory of Schleswig.*

Above: *William Booth, founder of the Salvation Army, which provokes mixed reactions among the public (left).*

MOTOR BOAT

Just as an internal combustion engine is added to a carriage to invent the car, so one is added to a rowing boat to invent the motorboat. Jean-Joseph Etienne Lenoir (1822–1900) fits a gas-fuelled, two horsepower engine, with a propeller shaft, to his boat and tests it on the Seine in Paris.

PULLMAN COACH

American cabinet-maker, George Pullman (1831–97), designs and builds his railway sleeping car. The Pullman coach becomes a standard feature of rail travel, especially in America where journeys can cover many hundreds of kilometres.

PUNDITS IN TIBET

Between now and 1866, the British recruit Asian explorers to probe into Tibet after the border is closed to Europeans to prevent spying. The nickname of Nain Singh — "The Pundit" — becomes the generic term for these adventurers. Singh maps the route to Lhasa while posing as a trader. He fixes the position of Lhasa accurately and, on a second trip, locates the gold mines of Tibet.

NEW RULE FOR CRICKET

Overarm bowling in cricket is legalized.

Right: *A group of Cheyenne Indians; after many Cheyenne are massacred this year, members of the tribe retaliate by going on the warpath.*

Victory and Assassination

*T*HE CIVIL WAR IN AMERICA comes to an end at last, but Abraham Lincoln is assassinated. The Thirteenth Amendment is passed, officially abolishing slavery in America. The Schleswig-Holstein question is answered. There is war between Spain and her former colony Peru, as South America begins to shake off the shackles of colonial rule. The Matterhorn is conquered.

Above: *Lord Palmerston, who dies this year.*

❧ 1865 ❧

Feb	18	Charleston, South Carolina, surrenders to the Unionists
Mar	18	Paraguayan dictator Francisco López leads his country into war with Argentina, Brazil and Uruguay
Apr	9	Confederate General Robert E Lee surrenders to Unionist General Ulysses S Grant at Appomattox Courthouse
	14	US President Lincoln is assassinated; succeeded by Vice-President Andrew Johnson as seventeenth president
May	11	Confederate president Jefferson Davis is captured
	26	US Civil War effectively ends as most of the Confederate army surrenders
July	14	British mountaineer Edward Whymper is the first person to climb the Matterhorn
Aug	14	Austria takes Holstein, Prussia takes Schleswig and buys Lauenburg
Sep	2	Maori War in New Zealand ends
Oct	18	British prime minister, Lord Palmerston, dies; succeeded by Earl (formerly Lord John) Russell
Dec	10	King Leopold I of Belgium dies; succeeded by his son Leopold II
	18	The Thirteenth Amendment to the US Constitution formally abolishes slavery

CONFEDERATE SURRENDER

Confederate General Robert E Lee surrenders to Union General Ulysses S Grant at the Appomattox Courthouse, Virginia, ending four years of war. The last of the Confederate troops surrender in New Orleans in late May.

Above: The American Civil War ends when General Robert E Lee signs a formal surrender.

Lord Palmerston
1784–1865

The octogenarian British prime minister, statesman, and grand old man of politics, Henry John Temple, third Viscount Palmerston, has died while still in office. He first entered Parliament, where he served for most of his life, in 1807. He was controversial, high-handed, brusque and assertive and earned himself the nickname "Firebrand". He gained a reputation as a gunboat diplomat during his long stints in the foreign office and was generally conservative in domestic policy, though he lost office with his fellow Whigs in 1841 over their support for the repeal of the corn laws. His aim was to lead a nation and not a party and he generally had wide electoral support.

Left: Caricature of the English poet Algernon Swinburne whose work is considered decadent by some.

Death of a President

President Lincoln is assassinated by John Wilkes Booth while attending the theatre in Washington, DC, just as the Civil War is drawing to a close. Andrew Johnson (1808–75) becomes president, and begins the task of uniting the country after the war; he faces a difficult task, not least because of the immense popularity of his predecessor.

Germ Warfare

Carbolic acid, otherwise known as phenol, is discovered to have antiseptic and disinfectant properties by English chemist Frederick Crace Calvert (1819–73). Its ability to kill pathogens, without poisoning people, means that its use marks a breakthrough in the promotion of healthcare and general cleanliness.

Carving up Europe

Prussian statesman Otto von Bismarck (1815–98) and Napoleon III meet at Biarritz. The French emperor agrees to a united Italy and Prussian supremacy in other German states, clearing the way for Prussia to unify Germany.

War between Spain and Peru

In 1864, Spain invaded the Chincha islands off Peru, the site of Peru's greatest natural resource, guano. This year, Peru unites with Bolivia, Chile and Ecuador (none of whom want to see Spanish dominance return to South America) and declares war on Spain. The Spanish try to invade but are turned back by Peruvian forces, and a truce is brokered in 1871 by the USA. In 1879, Spain will recognize Peru's independence.

Abraham Lincoln
1809–1865

The sixteenth president of the United States (since 1860) has died in the year the Civil War (begun in 1861) ends, shot by actor/gunman John Booth while at the theatre in Washington. Two days earlier, Lincoln made his last speech, calling for peace. He passionately believed in the Union and had also been an early leader of the Republican party, opposed to slavery. The way to abolition was opened when he pronounced in 1863 that freedom would be granted to slaves in rebel states, and the Thirteenth Amendment to the Constitution prohibited slavery shortly after his death. He had been born the son of a pioneer, in a log cabin, and studied law and grammar to prepare himself for a political career. A powerful speaker, he stood for "government of the people, by the people, for the people".

Above: *President Lincoln, assassinated just after orchestrating victory for the Union in the Civil War.*

ALICE'S ADVENTURES IN WONDERLAND

This, the most famous book by English writer and mathematician Lewis Carroll (Charles Lutwidge Dodgson, 1832–98) begins as a story told to the daughters of one of his friends. It creates a bizarre, unique world, which will live on, supported by the illustrations of John Tenniel (1820–1914). It breaks the mould of children's books at the time because it is not trying to teach or point a moral.

THE END OF SLAVERY IN THE USA

The Thirteenth Amendment to the US Constitution is agreed, making slavery illegal throughout the USA. In July 1868, the Fourteenth Amendment is carried, making black Americans full citizens of the USA.

PRISONERS FROM THE FRONT

Winslow Homer (1836–1910), a great American painter who remains true to his roots and works mostly in his homeland, is employed to paint pictures of the Civil War for *Harper's Weekly*. These, including *Prisoners from the Front*, become his first well-known oils. Their realism, strong lines and composition, show the way his art will develop.

OLYMPIA

French artist Edouard Manet courts scandal once again by giving a "classical" subject a modern setting. His Olympia is a courtesan who seems to be welcoming the spectator into her boudoir.

EARLY FAX MACHINE

A simple facsimile machine known as the "pantelegraph" is invented by Italian, Giovanni Caseli. A telegraph line between Paris and Lyon is used to demonstrate the device. Recording paper, soaked in potassium cyanide, changes colour to reveal the message as the electrical signals pass through it.

ESSAYS IN CRITICISM

This is the first series of essays in criticism by English writer and poet Matthew Arnold (1822–88), and his first book of essays in which he systematically pulls apart the materialism and coarseness of contemporary British intellectual life. His work will prove influential on some of the most important literary figures in the English-speaking world.

ATALANTA IN CORYDON

This Ancient Greek-style drama brings first fame to English poet Algernon Charles Swinburne (1837–1909). Above all, critics praise the poet's skill in handling rhythms, something which will become something of a Swinburnian trademark.

Above: *Paraguayan and Brazilian warships in conflict on the Amazon river.*

TUBERCULOSIS

A connection between the disease tuberculosis and its spread through contact is made. Wilhelm Wundt (1832–1920), a German physician, announces that tuberculosis is a highly contagious disease, catalyzing the introduction of isolation procedures with those infected.

OIL PIPELINE

The infrastructure for the petrochemical industry begins with an 8km (5mi) pipeline in America. The sections of pipe are made from cast iron, with a diameter of 600mm (24in). This marks the beginning of an industry to rival that of electricity.

EDUCATION IN THE USA

Many coeducational Higher Education colleges have been established during the American Civil War, when fee-paying women enrolled to replace men who joined the armies. Vassar Female College, Poughkeepsie, New York, is the first all-women's college founded in the USA. European immigrant groups are establishing many private colleges in the Midwest.

Above: *Steam and sail in the English Channel; steam is gradually taking over from sail power, but for a time, both are used together.*

Above: *Kingston, Jamaica, where British Governor Eyre is illegally using torture on political enemies.*

Above: *Lewis Carroll, writer and amateur photographer, publishes his classic* Alice in Wonderland.

The Klan Comes together

A secret club for young men is formed in Tennessee, USA. It is called the Ku Klux Klan. Members ride out at night in sinister hooded white robes and terrorize blacks. The organization quickly evolves into a white supremacist secret society.

Keeping the Red Flag Flying

The Red Flag Act is passed in England, brought about by coaching interests opposed to the highly successful steam vehicles. A man carrying a red flag must walk in front of the steam engines as a warning to pedestrians.

Big Hat

The Stetson 10-gallon hat is made by Philadelphia milliner John Batterson Stetson (1830–1906), who modifies a Mexican sombrero. The 10cm (4in) brim can carry ten *galions* or ribbons.

Alps Vanquished

Wood engraver and mountaineer Edward Whymper (1840–1911) of Britain is the first to scale the Matterhorn on July 14. His party sets off from Zermatt in a race of 4478m (14 692ft) to the top of the Swiss peak against Frenchman Antoine Carrell. Whymper wins, but four of his companions slide to their death on the descent. The Matterhorn is the final goal in the Alps and Whymper's success marks the end of the "Golden Age" of climbing in Europe.

PRUSSIA, AUSTRIA AND ITALY GO TO WAR

EUROPE BREAKS OUT IN a rash of wars again as Prussia, Austria and Italy wrangle for territory. Further south, Crete rebels against Turkey. In the USA, civil rights are granted to nearly all men, prompting the founding of the Equal Rights Commission by Lucretia Mott. Pioneering cattle trails are blazed across the American west. The torpedo is invented and speedy clipper ships race to bring tea from China.

Above: *Count von Moltke, Prussian military leader.*

✳ 1866 ✳

JAN	14	Peru declares war on Spain
JUNE	8	Prussia annexes the Duchy of Holstein
	13	Congress passes the Fourteenth Amendment to the US Constitution, defining civil rights
	14	Seven Weeks' War in Europe begins
	20	Italy declares war on Austria
JULY	3	Battle of Sadowa (Königgrätz): Prussia defeats Austria
	26	Prussia and Austria make peace
	27	First successful transatlantic cable is laid between Ireland and Newfoundland
AUG	10	Bolivia cedes territory to Chile
	12	Armistice between Austria and Italy
	23	Peace of Prague settles many points of the Seven Weeks' War

SEP	2	Crete rebels against Turkish rule
	6	Three clipper ships racing from China with tea arrive at London, England, within a few hours of each other
	20	Prussia annexes Hanover, Hesse, Frankfurt and Nassau
OCT	3	Treaty of Vienna ends the Austro-Italian War
DEC	24	Prussia annexes Schleswig-Holstein duchies

FENIAN UPRISING

Fenian campaigns against British rule in Ireland lead to the suspension of all civil liberties in Ireland. In the following year, Fenian risings take place in several Irish towns, and Fenians attempt to seize Chester and to free prisoners from Clerkenwell gaol in London; twelve people are killed in the explosion.

PRUSSIAN POWER

Prussia ends the German Confederation and invades Saxony, Hanover and Hesse. Simultaneously, Italy declares war on Austria; Prussia joins in and defeats the Austrian army at Sadowa (Königgrätz) in July. By the Treaty of Prague, Austria is excluded from Germany and Prussia gains extensive lands at the expense of Austria and Saxony; many independent German principalities and duchies are swallowed up by Prussia. The north German states form a confederation under Prussia in April 1867; the three southern states of Bavaria, Baden and Württemberg remain independent.

PEACE FOR ITALY

The Treaty of Vienna ends the war between Italy and Austria; a plebiscite in the state of Venezia leads to union with the rest of Italy.

THE WHITEHEAD TORPEDO

English engineer and inventor Robert Whitehead (1823–1905) invents the torpedo named after him. The weapon is 4m (14ft) long and has a 9kg (20lb) warhead. Driven by a compressed-air motor, it runs at six knots for 700m (778yds).

A NEW DIRECTION FOR DEGAS

With their unconventional compositions (figures cut off at the edges of the frame), the pictures of dancers produced by French artist Hilaire Germain Degas (1834–1917) show a new direction for painting. They are controversial at first, but Degas insists on the classicism of his subjects' movements.

THE BARTERED BRIDE

Czech composer Bedrich Smetana (1824–84) creates his comic masterpiece. He brings the richness of Czech/Bohemian music into the Western sphere for the first time, but integrates folk music much more seamlessly than nationalist composers from Russia and elsewhere.

CITIZENSHIP FOR NEARLY ALL

The US Congress passes the Equal Rights Act giving full citizenship to all persons born in the US, excluding Indians, who are not taxed. However, attempts to introduce black suffrage into the Louisiana Constitution causes a race riot in New Orleans.

LETTRES DE MON MOULIN

These famous sketches of Provençal life by Alphonse Daudet (1840–97) appear in the French newspaper *Le Figaro*. They are important for bringing regional culture to the centre stage in Paris.

CRIME AND PUNISHMENT

Beset by gambling debts and personal problems, Russian writer Fyodor Mikhailovich Dostoyevsky (1821–81) completes his first great novel, establishing him as a major figure in world literature. He explores the individual's plight in a claustrophobic society and the psychological impact of social restrictions.

POEMES SATURNIENS

French poet Paul Verlaine (1844–96) is established with his first book of poems. He appears as a member of the Parnassians, but with hints of a looser personal style which he will develop further later.

MENDEL'S HEREDITARY THEORY

Austrian monk Gregor Johann Mendel (1822–84), publishes the first results of his work on heredity using pea plants. Although laying the foundations for modern genetic study, his work remains unrecognized until the turn of the century, with the general acceptance of Darwinian theory.

RADIO TELEGRAPHY

American Mahlon Loomis invents a means for conveying electrical signals through the air. He uses two kites, 22km (14mi) apart, carrying copper-wire gauzes attached, by electrical wire, to galvanometers. Pulse signals are transmitted from one kite and received at the other.

EQUAL RIGHTS CONVENTION

The American Equal Rights Convention is formed in May to promote suffrage for blacks and women. Lucretia Coffin Mott (1793–1889) is president and Elizabeth Cady Stanton (1815–1902) vice-president.

OPTICAL RECEPTORS

A German zoologist, Max Schultze (1825–74), discovers the differentiation between rod and cone cells in the retina of the mammalian eye. The primary, central cells are "cones", responsible for perception of colours, while the peripheral "rods" detect differences in light from black to white.

UNDERSEA CABLE

The first successful transatlantic cable is completed. The cable on the sea floor allows instant communication by telegraph between Europe and North America for the first time.

Right: *The Chincha islands off the coast of Peru, a rich source of guano. Spain seized the islands in 1865 but Peru unites with other newly independent South American countries and asserts its independence.*

BLAZING TRAILS

The Chisholm cattle trail from Texas north to the Kansas railheads is blazed by the half-Cherokee scout Jesse Chisholm, who drives a wagon loaded with buffalo hides through the hostile Indian territory of Oklahoma, making deep ruts in the ground which will be followed by cattle herders. Charles Goodnight and Oliver Loving blaze the Goodnight-Loving cattle trail from Texas to Wyoming.

CLINICAL THERMOMETER

Having made a connection between body temperature and illness, English physician Thomas Allbut (1836–1925) invents the clinical thermometer. Its introduction is a simple but important contribution to the diagnosis and prognosis of disease.

EUROPEAN IN SOUTHEAST ASIA

French sailor Francis Garnier (1839–69) and Doudart Lagree explore the Mekong river, following it through

Above: *Kilmainham jail in Dublin. Fenian uprisings mean that civil rights are suspended.*

Southeast Asia. They leave the river, which they had hoped would lead to China, and cross into China overland. Lagree perishes but Garnier brings back huge amounts of information on previously unexplored territory.

BUFFALO PLAN

Civil War veteran on the Union side, General Philip Henry Sheridan (1831–88) reports sighting 100 million head of buffalo between Fort Dodge, Kansas, and the Indian Territory. He proposes exterminating them in order to rob the Plains Indians of their livelihood.

CHOCOLATE TO DRINK

Pure cocoa powder is produced for the first time by the Cadbury Brothers of Birmingham, England, who discover a way of eliminating excess cocoa butter from the crushed bean. The powder is used for cooking and making drinks.

THE 40TH PARALLEL

Congress places the 25-year-old Clarence King in charge of the geological exploration of the 40th Parallel to pave the way for a trans-continental railway across America. King and Jerry T Gardner survey the area from the Pacific Ocean to the Great Plains.

RACING FOR TEA

Three clipper ships racing to be the first to bring tea from China arrive within hours of each other in London. The clippers, which are built for speed with slender hulls and large sail areas, had all set off from Foochow in China during the space of two days.

Above: *Reform leaguers clash with police at Marble Arch in London.*

THE SEVEN WEEKS' WAR

FOUGHT BETWEEN AUSTRIA and Prussia, hostilities are initiated by Otto von Bismarck to break the hold of Austria over the German Confederation and unite the German states under Prussia. Prussia is successful and becomes the dominant power in Europe.

Right: *The Battle of Langensalza.*

Left: *Armies confront each other across the plain at the Battle of Königgrätz.*

Below: *Prussians close in on the village and woods of Sadowa, where the Austrian troops make a heroic last stand but are ultimately defeated.*

Above: *Prussian batteries are pushed into action at the Battle of Königgrätz.*

Below: *Chancellor Otto von Bismarck, initiator of the Seven Weeks' War.*

✷ Key Battles ✷

- **KÖNIGGRÄTZ (Sadowa) May 19, 1866**

The Austrians deploy 200 000 men and 600 guns under Marshal Ludwig von Benedek (1804–81), and the Prussians about an equal force under Prince Frederick-Charles and Crown Prince Frederick. After initial setbacks, the Prussians triumph, albeit at a cost of 10 000 casualties. The Austrians lose 20 000 casualties, 20 000 prisoners and 174 guns.

- **LANGENSALZA June 27, 1866**

Major General Flies, with 12 000 Prussians, attacks an equal number of Hanoverians under George, king of Hanover (1819–78). Though the Prussians lose 1400 casualties and 900 prisoners, George surrenders on June 29.

- **MÜNCHENGRATZ June 28, 1866**

The Prussian advance guard of Prince Frederick-Charles (1828–85) defeats the Austrians under Count Clam-Gallas, inflicting 300 casualties and taking 1000 prisoners.

REFORM AND RECONSTRUCTION

*A*USTRIA AND HUNGARY UNITE to form a formidable new power in Europe. The British Dominion of Canada is formed and the United States expands by purchasing Alaska from Russia. The Second Reform Act, passed in Great Britian after much agitation, gives more men the vote. Fenian rebels in Ireland meet with small success and begin a bombing campaign in England. While trying to take Rome, Garibaldi is captured at Mentana and in Mexico, Emperor Maximilian is executed. Japanese art astounds artists and aesthetes in the West.

✹ 1867 ✹

FEB	17	Dual monarchy of Austria-Hungary is formed
MAR	1	Nebraska becomes the 37th US state
	5	Fenians (Irish nationalists) rebel in Ireland, with no success
	29	The Dominion of Canada is formed from New Brunswick, Nova Scotia, Ontario and Quebec
	30	The USA buys Alaska from Russia
APR	1	Straits Settlements (now Malaysia) become a British crown colony
	16	Prussia forms the North German Confederation
JUNE	19	Deposed Mexican Emperor Maximilian is executed
AUG	15	Reform Act in Britain gives more people the vote
OCT	27	Italian patriot Giuseppe Garibaldi leads a march on Rome
NOV	3	Garibaldi's force is defeated at Mentana, and he is captured
DEC	13	Bomb planted by Fenians kills twelve people in London

Above: *Alaska becomes American property.*

Above: *Countries of the world unite as Franz Joseph I, emperor of Austria, is crowned king of Hungary.*

Left: *Even when slavery is illegal in the USA, working conditions for the ex-slaves in the southern states can be just as gruelling.*

REBIRTH OF THE AUSTRO-HUNGARIAN EMPIRE
Following the Austrian defeat by Prussia, the Hungarian parliament meets and reinstates the constitution of 1848, under which Austria becomes a dual monarchy, with Hungary governing all the non-German parts of the empire; foreign and defence policies remain under joint control.

EXECUTION OF AN EMPEROR
Archduke Maximilian, the Hapsburg prince installed as Emperor of Mexico by the French in 1864, is captured and executed by Mexican troops after the French army withdraws. His death marks the end of French imperial ambitions in the region, and seriously weakens Napoleon III.

CANADA ESTABLISHED
The British North America Act sets up the independent Dominion of Canada, created by the union of Quebec, Ontario, Nova Scotia and New Brunswick.

ALASKA AND NEBRASKA
The expansion of the USA continues as the colony of Alaska is purchased from Russia for $7 million. Nebraska is admitted as the nation's 37th state, continuing the expansion of the USA westwards.

LAST TRANSPORTATION
The last convict ship leaves England for Western Australia, ending transportation as a punishment for crime in Britain.

Reconstruction Enforced

The Third Reconstruction Act is passed by the US Congress, establishing full control by the Union government over the defeated Confederate states. After the war, many former Confederate leaders were pardoned and re-elected to power; southern legislatures began to pass the so-called Black Codes, which restricted the rights of freed slaves, in effect re-introducing slavery. Angry at continued southern resistance, Congress agrees this new, draconian act to enforce reconstruction throughout the south.

Pacific Pitstop

The Midway islands, two tiny islands and an atoll in the Pacific Ocean, 2080km (1300mi) northwest of Hawaii, are annexed by the USA for use as a coaling station for trans-pacific steamships.

Japanese Art Goes West

With Japan open to Western trade for more than a decade, Japanese painting and prints start to appear on the Western market. An exhibition of "floating world" (*ukiyo-e*) prints is held at the World's Fair in Paris. European artists begin to be influenced by the Japanese flair for composition, selection of essential subject matter and portrayal of nature.

Tickertape

The equivalent of the first "plain-paper" fax machine, known as "tickertape" is invented. The Gold and Stock Telegraph Company install their device in a New York office. The machine prints out translated telegraph data on to a continuous ribbon of paper — the tickertape.

Above: *Philosopher, MP and radical reformist John Stuart Mill supports the Second Reform Bill.*

Above: *Mark Twain, the celebrated creator of* Tom Sawyer *and* Huck Finn, *starts his literary career.*

Therese Raquin

This is the first important novel by Emile Zola (1840–1902). It launches him on a career of exploration of society through fiction, for which Zola claims quasi-scientific status. He is also remarkable for opening up areas of subject matter and society that have been only rarely covered in fiction before.

The Celebrated Jumping Frog of Calvaleras County and Other Sketches

This collection, named for one of its pieces, a retelling of an old folk tale, wins recognition for Mark Twain (Samuel Langhorne Clemens, 1835–1910) as a leading American humorist.

Right: *Fenians attack a police van in Manchester, England, taking their protest to the mainland.*

Above: *Supporters of the Second Reform Bill gather at the "Reformers' Tree" in London's Hyde Park.*

Above: *The waltz, based on an Austrian folk dance, sweeps the dancefloor.*

THE BLUE DANUBE

This glorious waltz by Johann Strauss the Younger (1825–99) is one of some 400 (plus numerous polkas, marches, gallops and operettas) that he composes to entertain the Viennese. His music defines the culture — leisured, easy-going, moneyed — that dominates Vienna at the time.

PEER GYNT

This is the first major play by Norwegian dramatist Henrik Ibsen (1828–1906), a mythical, poetical drama unlike his later realist works. It establishes him as a uniquely Scandinavian voice and is frequently revived.

RAPE

The lumpy brushwork, thick paint and, above all, sensational subject matter of some of the early works of French artist Paul Cézanne (1839–1906) establish him as a troubled master. He seeks the "realism" that his friend Zola aspired to in fiction, but comes up with a still darker vision than Zola's. At this time, his work is regularly refused at the Salon.

GALLSTONE OPERATION

Mary Wiggens of Indiana, USA, becomes the first person to undergo a gallstone operation. The procedure is performed by Dr John Strugh Bobbs. The condition is painful, and the operation is very unpleasant and dangerous, with analgesics and antiseptics in an early stage of development.

ANTISEPTIC SURGERY

English surgeon Joseph Lister (1827–1912) performs the first operation under "relatively" antiseptic conditions, using carbolic acid to sterilize the instruments and theatre. The patient is his sister, on whom he performs a mastectomy.

AUTOMATED VENDING

German inventor Carl Ade introduces his automatic vending machine to the world. It is designed to dispense all manner of goods, including cigarettes and confectionery. A wide variety of vending machines will be introduced for the convenience of the public as the century advances.

ARTIFICIAL MILK

A substitute for mothers' milk is devised by German chemist, Baron Justus von Liebig (1803–73). Wet-nursing for the middle classes is brought to an end by his invention, which comprises exactly the same chemical make-up as breast milk.

CHRISTMAS SHOPPING

Macy's department store in New York, opened in 1858 by Rowland Hussey Macy, stays open until midnight on Christmas Eve.

Charles Baudelaire
1821–1867

The avant-garde French poet, author of the infamous *Les Fleurs du Mal (The Flowers of Evil)* (1857) has died in a wretched state induced by long-term use of opium and absinthe. After a period of travel (on which he was sent by his stepfather) he returned to settle in Paris in 1843. There became a member of the artists' circle and devoted himself to writing. He published several art criticisms in 1845–46 and his autobiographical novel *La Fanfarlo* in 1847. He introduced the works of Thomas De Quincey and Edgar Allan Poe to France through his translations.

BARNARDO'S FOUNDATION

Irish medical student Thomas Barnardo (1845–1905) founds the East End Mission for Destitute Children in London. It is his response to the growing problem in the city of children abandoned on the streets following the criminalization of abortion and of child employment.

GENDER-FREE EQUALITY

A plea for equal treatment of homosexuals is put before the Congress of German Jurists by Karl Ulrichs, a Hanover lawyer and author of a pioneering study of homosexuality in which he argues that homosexual people constitute a third sex. In supporting his action a Hungarian writer, KM Kertbeny, later coins the term "homosexual" in an open letter to the Prussian minister of justice.

MARXIST ANALYSIS

Das Kapital, the first volume of a new analysis of political economy by the German journalist Karl Marx (1818–83), is published in London. Marx argues for an end to private ownership of public utilities, transportation and means of production.

EDUCATION FOR BLACK AMERICANS

Howard University for Negroes is founded by white Congregationalists outside Washington DC; the founders include General Howard, director of the Freedmen's Bureau. In Georgia, Morehouse College has opened in Augusta, and Atlanta University is founded in Georgia and will become a leading institution for the higher education of black Americans.

GOETHE IN YOUR POCKET

The world's first paperback book is an edition of Goethe's *Faust* issued by the Reclams Universal Bibliothek in Leipzig, Germany.

CONSTITUTIONAL CRITIQUE

The English Constitution published by Walter Bagehot (1826–77), an editor at *The Economist* in London, is an immensely influential examination of Britain's unwritten constitution and the role of government and monarchy.

QUEENSBERRY RULES

Sir John Sholto Douglas, the Eighth Marquis of Queensberry (1844–1900), sponsors new rules for boxing. Among many changes, gloves are required and rounds last for three minutes followed by a minute's rest. It will be many years before all bouts are fought under the new rules.

Impeachment and Imperial Power

A PRESIDENT IS IMPEACHED and a Civil War hero gets to the White House. Maoris on New Zealand's North Island fight back against white settlers. In Japan, the military rule of the shogunate is dismantled and an emperor takes over. The bathroom comes inside the house and hot running water becomes the new status symbol. The first sneakers are invented, making it easier to play the new game of badminton. Grape phylloxera blights the wine harvest of France.

❋ 1868 ❋

JAN	3	Rule of the shoguns is abolished in Japan; power reverts to Emperor Mutsuhito, who takes the reign name Meiji
FEB	24	US President Andrew Johnson is impeached for opposing Congress
	28	Benjamin Disraeli (Conservative) becomes Britain's prime minister after the resignation of Lord Derby
MAR	12	Britain annexes Basutoland (now Lesotho)
	13	Trial of President Andrew Johnson begins
MAY	12	Russians occupy Samarkand (now in Uzbekistan)
	26	President Johnson is acquitted
JUNE	10	Serbian ruler Mihailo III is assassinated; succeeded by Milan IV
JULY	28	Another Maori war breaks out in New Zealand
SEP	30	Queen Isabella II of Spain is deposed; General Francisco Serrano takes over as regent
NOV	3	Ulysses S Grant (Republican) wins the US presidential election
DEC	3	In the British general election, Liberals defeat the Conservatives; Prime Minister Benjamin Disraeli resigns and William Gladstone (Liberal) forms a government

Above: Emperor Theodore of Abyssinia kills himself when his fort is stormed by the British to rescue hostages.

JOHNSON IS IMPEACHED

President Johnson survives an impeachment trial in the Senate after the House of Representatives finds him guilty of "high crimes and misdemeanours" for dismissing the Secretary of War in violation of Congress, among other offences. Johnson becomes the first US president to face such a trial.

REVOLT IN SPAIN

A Liberal revolt against Queen Isabella II (1830–1904) by leading army and navy officers causes Isabella to flee to France. In her absence, she is deposed and a new, liberal constitution is drawn up providing for the continuation of the monarchy.

GRANT FOR PRESIDENT

General Ulysses S Grant, the victor of the Civil War, stands as a Republican and becomes the eighteenth president of the USA, easily defeating his Democratic opponent, Horatio Seymour of Indiana. The vice-president is Schuyler Colfax of Indiana.

PIANO CONCERTO IN A MINOR

Norway's nationalist composer Edvard Grieg (1843–1907) writes his masterpiece, a virtuoso piano concerto that stands out from the many other such pieces written in this period because of its distinctive melodies.

THE MOONSTONE

This, the most famous novel by British writer William Wilkie Collins (1824–89), introduces the figure of Sergeant Cuff, and confirms Collins' status as the first author in English to write full-length detective novels. His *The Woman in White* (1860) is generally considered to be the first of the genre.

Above: Writer Wilkie Collins, considered to be the inventor of the crime thriller. His book The Moonstone *is published this year.*

LITTLE WOMEN

Suffragist, reformer, friend of the Transcendentalists, American writer Louisa May Alcott (1832–88) finds fame and fortune with her story of four sisters, which becomes one of the most popular children's books ever published. It recalls Alcott's own upbringing.

THE RING AND THE BOOK

This is the largest work of the English poet Robert Browning (1812–89). It is a multiple retelling, from different points of view, of a murder story set in Rome in the late seventeenth century. The work is a great success with both critics and readers, and makes Browning's reputation. Its craggy style, its poetic transmutation of fact into poetic narrative, and its multiple viewpoints make it a milestone in poetry.

Above: Thanks to high-tech plumbing, bathrooms and lavatories can now be built inside the house.

Hot Water
The separate, permanent bathroom is introduced to homes with the invention of the gas-fuelled water heater. Londoner, Benjamin Waddy Maughan, invents the appliance which ends the tradition of filling the tin tub in front of the fire in the living room, bedroom or kitchen.

Traffic Lights
London is the first place to receive a signalling system for controlling the flow of traffic. A gas-lit lantern displaying a red and a green glass window is turned manually. Red means stop, while green advises caution.

Air Brakes
With locomotives increasing in size and momentum, a new means for braking is warranted. American engineer George Westinghouse (1846–1914) introduces pneumatically operated brakes to an engine and finds that the stopping distance is reduced by a considerable amount.

Earthquake Damage
A San Francisco earthquake causes more than $3 million damage. In August, earthquakes struck Ecuador and Peru, killing 25 000 people.

Above: *Fighting in the streets of Malaga, Spain, in protest against Queeen Isabella and the monarchy.*

First Sneakers
Shoes with rubber soles and canvas uppers are invented by the Candee Manufacturing Company of America. Dubbed "sneakers" because they are designed for light stepping whilst playing croquet, they see footwear step towards specific designs for particular sports.

Votes for All (except Women)
The Fourteenth Amendment to the US Constitution is formally ratified, giving black citizens the vote. Martial law is imposed in the south until all states agree to ratify the amendment. The suffragist Elizabeth Cady Stanton (1815–1902) had protested in 1866 against the wording of the amendment, which excludes women from the vote.

New Ancestors
Cro-Magnon Man is discovered by French archaeologist Edouard Armand Isidore Hippolyte Lartet (1801–71), who explores a cave near Périgueux in the Dordogne area of France and finds four adult skeletons and one fetal skeleton dating from some 40 000 years ago.

Gioacchino Antonio Rossini
1792–1868

The composer Rossini, one of the founders of the Italian operatic style, has died. His operas, and particularly the comic operas, are immensely popular in Italy, France, Austria and England, and although he had composed very little for many years, he remained at the centre of artistic and intellectual life. As early as 1802 his opera — *La Pietra del Paragone* — was performed at La Scala and by 1814 he was music director of the two great opera houses in Naples, where he wrote *The Barber of Seville* (*Il Barbiere di Siviglia*) in 1816 and *Cinderella* (*La Cenerentola*) in 1817, and married the soprano Isabella Colbran. From 1824 he was director of the Italian Theatre in Paris, for which he wrote *William Tell* in 1829. As a young man he often produced three operas a year (sometimes writing one in only two weeks) but he had almost ceased to compose after *William Tell*. In 1836, after political upheavals in France, he became honorary president of the Liceo Musicale in Bologna, but had lived in France again from 1855.

Above: *A youthful portrait of Benjamin Disraeli, who becomes the British prime minister this year aged 64.*

WOMEN'S WORK

An employment agency, The Association for the Promotion of the Employment of Women, is set up in London by Barbara Leigh Smith and Bessie Rayner Parks to assist unmarried middle-class women into new types of work. Women are branching out from teaching and nursing. This year Elizabeth Lynn Linton is the first woman to be employed as a feature writer on an English newspaper.

NAVAJO TREATY

Navajo chiefs sign a treaty agreeing to live on reservations and cease opposition to whites. The treaty establishes a 3.5 million acre reservation on their old domains, but most is desert and semi-desert and the 200 000 sheep they owned before military internment have dwindled to 940.

THE SIOUX WAR

A treaty with the Sioux ends a war which began in 1866 when braves led by Chief Red Cloud ambushed and massacred a force of 80 soldiers in Idaho Territory. The Sioux were retaliating against miners heading for the Montana gold fields, encroaching on their sacred hunting-lands reserved for them by treaty. Forts have been built along the trail and wagon trains attacked.

WALKING ACROSS AMERICA

John Muir (1838–1914) a Scots-born American naturalist, arrives in the Yosemite valley in California and begins to sketch and study its natural phenomena. Last year he walked 1600km (1000mi) through Kentucky, Tennessee, Georgia and Florida, taking notes on their physical geography, flora and fauna.

A COMPLETE ENCYCLOPEDIA

Chambers Encyclopedia, written and published by the Scottish authors William and Robert Chambers, is now completed with the publication of the tenth volume. The encyclopedia was begun in 1832 by William and several editions have been produced.

POWER SHIFT IN JAPAN

The shogunate, or military dictatorship, is abolished and power restored to the Meiji dynasty in Japan. The change marks the start of a massive reform programme which transforms Japan into a major Asian power by the end of the century. The capital is moved from Kyoto to Edo, renamed Tokyo.

Above: Croquet is favoured by young persons who find it a splendid way to meet friends and flirt with admirers.

A NEW GAME

Badminton, a game played on an indoor court with rackets and a feathered shuttlecock, is invented at Badminton Hall, Gloucestershire, England, the residence of the Duke of Beaufort.

DINING ON TRACK

The Pullman Palace Car Corporation, formed last year when Andrew Carnegie (1835–1918) and George M Pullman (1831–97) merged their railroad sleeping-car companies, introduces a dining car on the Union Pacific Railroad, adding to the luxury of carriages fitted with ingenious folding upper berths, and seat cushions which extend to form lower berths.

CHILLED TRANSPORT

A refrigerated railcar cooled by tanks filled with cracked ice is patented by Detroit inventor William Davis. Railcars using cooling devices have begun to transport fish, fresh meat and fruit across the USA, and in England, milk is mechanically cooled to be delivered by rail to cities.

WINNER ON WHEELS

Dr James Moore of Britain wins the first bicycle race. The event, held in Paris, France, is over 2km (1¼mi).

INDOOR GAMES

The New York Athletic Club organizes the first indoor athletics meet.

WINE BLIGHT

Grape phylloxera, a form of plant lice, carried to Europe in fruit consignments from the USA, begins to devastate the European vineyards. Resistant roots from New York State vineyards will be grafted onto French stock to halt the destruction.

Right: Superseding croquet is a brand new game called badminton. It is a great hit with both ladies and gentlemen.

Above: *Sir Robert Napier, who deals with Britain's problems with Emperor Theodore in Abyssinia.*

Above: *The shoguns who have ruled Japan for so long are driven out and the emperor returns.*

Above: *President Andrew Johnson, vice-president to the assassinated Lincoln, is the first president to be impeached.*

Above: *Maori warlord Te Kooti leads a final raid on British troops and then escapes into the bush.*

Above: *William Gladstone, Liberal, who replaces the Conservative Disraeli as British prime minister.*

CANALS, DIAMONDS AND VOTES FOR WOMEN

Above: *Ulysses S Grant, hero of the Civil War, is installed as president this year. He serves two terms.*

THE SUEZ CANAL IS OPENED, linking the Mediterranean and the Red Sea and cutting thousands of kilometres from the route from Europe to India. Wyoming is the first state to grant women the vote, encouraging the growth of more associations for the promotion of female suffrage in the USA. Diamonds are found in South Africa and the first ecologist presents his studies to the world.

❧ 1869 ❧

FEB	6	Turks force Greeks to leave Crete
	26	Congress passes the Fifteenth Amendment to the US Constitution, which states that no one must be denied the right to vote on account of race or colour
MAR	4	Ulysses S Grant is inaugurated as the eighteenth US president
MAY	10	The first transcontinental railroad is completed in the USA
JULY	12	In France, Napoleon III adopts a parliamentary system of government
OCT	11	Red River Rebellion begins in Canada
NOV	17	The Suez Canal is opened to traffic
	19	The Canadian government purchases territory from the Hudson Bay Company

Above: *Ernst Heinrich Haeckel, inventor of the concept and terminology of ecology.*

Above: *Science-fiction writer Jules Verne, author of* From the Earth to the Moon, *writes another tale this year.*

TRANSCONTINENTAL RAILWAY

A golden rail spike is ceremoniously hammered home at the junction of the Union Pacific and Central Pacific railroads at Promontory Point, Utah, connecting the east and west coasts of the USA by railroad for the first time.

THE SUEZ CANAL

Empress Eugénie of France opens the Suez Canal, connecting the Mediterranean to the Red Sea and shortening the sea route from Europe to Asia.

VOTES FOR WOMEN AT LAST

The territory of Wyoming, not yet a state of the Union, becomes the first area in the world to grant women the vote. Mrs Louisa Swain becomes the first woman elector when she — and 1000 other women — votes in elections in September 1870.

THE OUTCASTS OF POKER FLAT

This short story, plus a number of others which appear at around this time, make Bret Harte (1836–1902) one of the most highly regarded American story-writers.

Below: *Thousands of hopeful miners gather along the Vaal river, South Africa, looking for diamonds.*

DAS RHEINGOLD

German composer Richard Wagner (1813–83) continues his operatic revolution with the production in Munich of *Das Rheingold*, the first part of the Ring cycle. (The entire cycle will be experienced in 1876, when the operas are performed at Wagner's new Bayreuth theatre.) Wagner brings to fruition his ideas of the *Gesamtkunstwerk*, his incorporation of the orchestra into the drama, his use of the *Leitmotiv* (key musical themes for particular characters or ideas), and so on. All this will have an incalculable influence on future composers.

TWENTY THOUSAND LEAGUES UNDER THE SEA

The tale of the adventures of Captain Nemo aboard the submarine *Nautilus*, one of the most successful books by French writer Jules Verne (1828–1905) is written this year and will be published in 1870.

THE PERIODIC TABLE

As elements have similarities and differences, Russian chemist Dmitri Ivanovich Mendeleev (1843–1907) devises a table to arrange them according to these properties. Those in horizontal "periods" have sequentially similar atomic numbers, those in vertical "groups" possess similar properties.

POPE AGAINST ABORTION

Pope Pius IX prohibits deliberate destruction of the unborn child as a sin punishable by excommunication. Until now, the Catholic Church did not count the fetus as human life. Following new medical discoveries and legislation in progressive Western states to outlaw abortion, the Vatican declares that the fetus has a soul from conception.

MARGARINE INVENTED

With butter being an expensive and perishable substance, French chemist Hippolyte Mege-Mouries invents a substitute for the French Navy. Margarine comprises a blend of vegetable and animal fat, with smaller amounts of milk, salt, vitamins and yellow colouring.

AMERICAN WOMEN MOBILIZE

The American Woman Suffrage Association (AWSA) is founded in Boston, Massachusetts, by feminist Lucy Blackwell Stone (1818–93) and her husband, Henry Brown Blackwell, while Susan Brownell Anthony (1820–1906) and Elizabeth Cady Stanton (1815–1902) found the more radical National Woman Suffrage Association (NWSA). Mary Ashton Livermore founds *The Agitator*, a journal aimed at promoting voting rights for women.

Above: *The railway station at Omaha in the Midwest. Railways now cover the US from coast to coast.*

Below: *A type-composing machine of the period, built along the lines of an organ. Typesetting is regarded as a suitable job for a woman.*

Above: *Bird's-eye view of the Suez Canal, opened this year. It links the Mediterranean and the Red Sea.*

Below: *The city of Cincinnati, Ohio, home to the first professional baseball team in the USA.*

Full-metal Jacket
With an increase in required velocity of bullets and shells by using higher charges, Englishman, EM Boxer, develops the all metal gun cartridge or "full-metal jacket". First adopted for the Martini-Henry rifle, it is able to withstand high forces and also protects the charge from moisture.

Along the Colorado
John Wesley Powell (1834–1902), Professor of Geology at the Illinois Wesleyan College, travels by boat along the Colorado river through the Grand Canyon, USA, as part of his geological expeditions in Colorado and Utah, begun in 1867.

Deoxyribonucleic Acid
The substance from which all cell nuclei are made, deoxyribonucleic acid (DNA), is discovered by Swiss biochemist, Johann Friedrich Miescher (1844–95). Although the actual chemical make-up and structure are yet to be revealed, it is an important advance.

The Fifteenth Amendment
The first National Convention of Colored Men is formed in Washington under the leadership of Frederick Douglass (Frederick Augustus Washington Bailey, 1817–95), promoting suffrage. In February, Congress passes the Fifteenth Amendment directly stating the right of all male citizens of the USA to vote. The amendment is needed because the southern states have circumvented the terms of the Fourteenth Amendment.

Kidney Removal
Margaretha Kleb becomes the first person to have a diseased kidney removed. She is operated on by German physician Gustav Simon. It is known that people could survive with only a single kidney, as a small percentage of the population are born with just one.

Diamond Chasers
Prospectors and miners from around the world converge on southern Africa after the discovery of diamonds in the Vaal river and gold nearby. The area in question is claimed by a number of African tribes, the new Boer Republics and Britain.

The Red Stockings Score
The Cincinnati Red Stockings, the first true professional baseball team in the USA, record 56 wins and one tie in their first year of playing.

Housewife's Friend
The first vacuum cleaner is patented by W McGaffey, an American inventor.

The First Ecologist
The term "ecology" is coined to describe the concept of biological balance in the environment by Ernst Heinrich Haeckel (1834–1919), Professor of Zoology at the University of Jena, Germany, the leading institution for study of the biological sciences. Haeckel is an advocate of Darwin's theories of evolution.

Nachtigal in Africa
German traveller Dr Gustav Nachtigal (1834–85) makes his reputation as one of the great African explorers during five years of wandering. Setting out from Tripoli he heads south to Lake Chad and then east through uncharted territory to the Nile at Khartoum in the Sudan.

Australian Tourists
A team of Aboriginal cricketers from Australia is the first team to tour Britain.

Above: *The Sudan, North Africa, one of the goals of the German explorer Gustav Nachtigal this year.*

NATIONHOOD AND IMPERIALISM

NATIONALISM CONTINUES TO HOLD SWAY in Europe. The first years of the decade are marked by the unification of Germany and Italy and their emergence as two new and significant nations. British imperialism is felt in Egypt, Africa (particularly South Africa) and India, which by the late 1870s has become the "jewel in the crown" of the British Empire. In the United States, which celebrates its centenary in 1876, westwards settlement continues, facilitated by an ever-growing railway network which crosses the continent from coast to coast. Technology increasingly impacts on all areas of daily life. Significant developments include the telephone, the light bulb, the electric motor and dynamo. The first phonogram also appears, as do the first shopping arcades.

∽ 1870–1879 ∽

KEY EVENTS
of the
DECADE

Franco-Prussian War

The Paris Commune

Unification of Germany

The Battle of Little Bighorn

US Centenary Celebrations

Korean Independence

The Annexation of the Transvaal

Home Rule Campaign, Ireland

The Zulu War

The First Successful Telephone Call

Livingstone and Stanley
Explore Africa

Tunnelling Machine Developed

Typewriter Invented

Cable Car Built

Electric Dynamo Invented

Osteopathy Developed

The Impressionists Exhibit

WORLD POPULATION

1420 Million

(Estimate)

Cat and dog butcher in Paris during the siege of the Franco-Prussian War.

Henry Stanley on his own African adventure.

An early bicycle race between Bath and London in Great Britain.

FRANCO-PRUSSIAN WAR DECLARED

*F*OLLOWING MANOEUVERING by German Chancellor Bismarck, France and Prussia go to war. The Prussians defeat the French at Sedan, then move on to beseige Paris. Manitoba becomes part of Canada. Italian forces occupy Rome, completing the unification of Italy. The first Afro-American is elected to the US House of Representatives. The ancient city of Troy is excavated and an underground tunnelling machine is developed.

Above: *WE Foster, whose Education Act leads to free education in England.*

❧ 1 8 7 0 ❧

MAR	1	Paraguay is forced to make peace with Argentina, Brazil and Uruguay
MAY	12	Manitoba becomes a Canadian province; Red River Rebellion ends
JUNE	19	Prince Leopold, a relative of the king of Prussia, accepts the offer of the vacant throne of Spain
JULY	6	France objects to Leopold's candidacy
	12	Leopold's candidacy is withdrawn in secret; meanwhile France demands guarantees from Prussia that he will never be considered
	13	King William I of Prussia refuses, politely; but Bismarck publishes a doctored account to upset the French
	19	France declares war (the Franco-Prussian War)

	28	Doctrine of papal infallability is proclaimed; Austria ends concordat with papacy (30 July)
AUG	4	Prussian army defeats the French at Weissenberg
	6	French defeated at Wörth
	19	French troops withdraw from Rome
SEP	1	French defeated at Sedan; Emperor Napoleon III surrenders next day
	4	Revolt in Paris: the Third French Republic is proclaimed
	19	Germans begin siege of Paris
	20	Italian troops enter Rome
OCT	2	Italy annexes Rome and makes it the capital
NOV	16	Duke Amadeus of Aosta, an Italian prince, is elected king of Spain

Above: *King Victor Emmanuel II in the Corso, Rome, declared the new capital of the unified Italy.*

Left: *The Vatican City; the Vatican Council decrees the infallibility of the pope in matters of faith and morals.*

Below: *A Hudson Bay Company post in Canada. This year, the federal government takes over the company.*

Manitoba Joins Canada

Following a rebellion by the *métis* or half-Indian population in October 1869, Manitoba joins Canada. The Hudson Bay Company's lands in the north are passed over to the new federal government. British Columbia joins in July 1871, and Prince Edward Island in 1873.

Franco-Prussian War Declared

After the Prussian Prince Leopold of Hohenzollern accepts the vacant throne of Spain, France sends Prussia an ultimatum, the Ems telegram, threatening war unless Prussia backs down. When Prussia refuses, France declares war. After a heavy defeat at Sedan in September, the French empire collapses, Napoleon III flees to England, and a republic is established.

Italian Unification Completed

Taking advantage of the withdrawal of French troops guarding the pope in Rome, the Italians occupy Rome, and the remaining Papal States, and make the city the capital of Italy. This completes the unification of Italy.

Coppelia

This ballet score, with its exquisite tunes, earns its creator, Léo Delibes (1836–91), a place amongst the best-known French composers. Delibes helps to keep up the standard of French theatre music (especially the "lighter" vein — ballet and operetta), and *Coppélia* remains popular.

Poems

For many years, painter Dante Gabriel Rossetti (1828–82) has been writing poetry and having it published in periodicals, but this book formally launches his poetic career. It is a critical success (being reviewed by many of his friends) and leads to other literary efforts.

Steam Lorry

Just as the internal combustion engine is being developed, the steam-powered lorry appears. The twin-cylinder engined vehicle is used at Glasgow dock in Scotland to haul marine boilers over a distance of 3.2km (2mi). Although slow, the steam lorry does the work of 400 men.

Cragside, Northumberland

British architect Norman Shaw (1831–1912) develops his "vernacular" style (steep gables, tall chimneys, mullioned windows, half-timbering) in this complex manorial house design. In a more simplified version, this will become one of the most popular styles for smaller houses in the late nineteenth and early twentieth centuries.

Charles Dickens
1812–1870

The English writer Charles Dickens has died suddenly at his home in Gadshill, Kent. As a boy Dickens had to struggle for an education: his father lost his job as an admiralty clerk and was later sent to debtors' jail with his entire family, apart from Charles who was allowed to work. On his release he became a reporter and Charles followed in his footsteps. From 1828 he worked for the *Morning Chronicle* and his first works were sketches published in the *Evening Chronicle* under the pen-name Boz. He married the daughter of the paper's editor in 1836 but, ten children later, they separated. His long novels were largely published in serial form. *The Pickwick Papers* began publication in 1836 and was followed by many works including *Oliver Twist* (1837–39), *Nicholas Nickleby* (1838–39), *David Copperfield* (1849–50), and *A Tale of Two Cities* (1859). His writing vividly portrays aspects of life in Victorian England, and highlights and appeals against the kind of social hardship the author had experienced in his own early life.

Tunnelling Machine

South African engineer, James Greathead (1844–96), develops the "Greathead Shield" system for digging tunnels. It is the first method for producing tunnels without the need for surface excavation and is used for constructing much of the London "tube" network.

Hommage a Manet

Accepted at the Salon while Manet is rejected, French artist Ignace Henri Jean Théodore Fantin-Latour (1836–1904) has already painted his friend's portrait and now creates this homage to Manet. He is becoming famous for single and group portraits and still-lifes.

Typewriter

Pastor Malling Hansen, a Dane, invents the radial-plunger principle typewriter. It is manufactured as the *Skrivekugle* (Writing Ball), and made from brass and steel components. It has 52 keys which, when pressed, swing a type-head to a common printing point.

Metal Bicycle

James Starley and William Hillman demonstrate their lightweight all-metal bicycle by riding it the 155km (96mi) from London to Coventry in one day. Londoner Thomas Sparrow invents rubber tyres with skid-resistant treads in anticipation of this development.

Left: *A Thomson Road steamer in Edinburgh, Scotland. Originally intended to haul freight wagons up steep hills, the steamer has now been adapted to pull an omnibus which can carry 65 passengers: twenty inside and the rest outside.*

CUSTER ATTACKS CHEYENNE AND ARAPAHO

In the Battle of Washita River in Texas, the US Seventh Cavalry under General George Custer (1839–76) strikes a combined force of Cheyenne and Arapaho Indians led by Chief Black Kettle. More than 100 Native Americans and 900 of their horses are killed.

FIRST BLACK CONGRESSMAN

Reverend Hiram Rhodes Revels (1827–1901) of Mississippi becomes the first Afro-American congressman. In December he is joined by Joseph H Rainey (1832–87) who is the first Afro-American to be elected to the US House of Representatives.

BON MARCHE

The *Bon Marché* store in Paris has grown in fewer than twenty years from a small shop into the world's first department store, occupying an entire block. Aristide Boucicaut, a merchant who joined the store in 1852, reduces mark-ups to increase turnover, introduces fixed prices, which he displays on the goods, and begins selling women's ready-to-wear clothing, accessories and even undergarments.

PAPAL INFALLIBILITY

The Vatican Council votes that the pope is infallible when he defines doctrines of faith or morals.

Above: *The Boulevard Montmartre, Paris. Chic Parisiens can now buy high fashion for less at the Bon Marché store.*

Alexandre Dumas
1802–1870

The French writer and creator of the three musketeers, known as Dumas père, has died. To support his career as a writer Alexander Dumas took up work as a clerk in Paris in 1823, and his first success came with the historical drama *Henri lll et sa Cour* (*Henry III and his Court*) in 1829. He was a most industrious writer, producing many popular works of historical romance, including *The Count of Monte Cristo* (1844–45) and *The Black Tulip* (1850), and ten volumes of his *Mémoires*. Dumas was also involved in the political struggles of his time, taking part in the events of July 1830 in Paris which brought about the abdication of Charles X and the installation of a new "citizen king" together with a new constitution. He also fostered the reputation of the Italian nationalist guerrilla fighter, Garibaldi. He earned and lost more than one fortune and, in the end, was penniless.

Schleimann Digs up Troy

German-American businessman Heinrich Schleimann (1822–90), an amateur archaeologist, begins excavating the ancient Greek city of Troy.

Wish You Were here

The British Post Office issues the world's first postcards.

Can-openers

The first can-opener is produced in the USA. Cans are now manufactured from thinner tin sheets with ridges around the top which a can-opener can grip. In 1866 a US patent was issued for a tin can with a key opener.

Central Asia Explored

Nikolai Przhevalsky embarks on a journey that will take him across Mongolia and the Gobi Desert to Peking and then a huge distance west to Lake Koko Nor. He is exploring central Asia for the Russian authorities.

Figure Skating

American ballet dancer Jackson Haines is credited with mixing dance and skating to create figure skating.

Betting System

Pierre Oller invents *pari-mutuel* betting in France. Under this system all money bet on a race is placed in a pool and divided between the backers of the winning horse after expenses are deducted. It is now used all over the world.

Above: *Leon Gambetta (1838–82), minister of war for the provisional Republican government of France declared this year, escapes from a besieged Paris during the Franco-Prussian War to orchestrate his country's defence from the city of Tours.*

Robert E Lee
1807–1870

The great American Confederate general, Robert E Lee, has died. When the Civil War broke out in 1861 he was offered command of the Union forces, but coming from Virginia in the south, felt he had to decline and resign from the army. He then took command of the Army of Northern Virginia and was responsible for Confederate victories at the Second Battle of Bull Run in 1861, the Battle of Fredericksburg in 1862 and the Battle of Chancellorsville in 1863. However he was forced to surrender to Lieutenant-General Grant, commander of Union forces at Appomattox in 1865, bringing about the end of the war. Two days later, President Lincoln offered a peace deal. Like Grant, Lee was a graduate of the military academy at West Point and a veteran of the Mexican War. After the Civil War he became president of Washington College, Lexington.

The Franco-Prussian War

Prussia's Chancellor Bismarck, who is working to bring the independent southern German states into a united Germany, is trying to promote a war with France to strengthen this union. An excuse is provided by the offer of the throne of Spain to Leopold of Hohenzollern, a relative of the Prussian king. France becomes alarmed and Bismarck provokes Emperor Napoleon III into declaring war.

✳ Key Battles ✳

- **Weissenburg August 4, 1870**
The German Third Army composed of 25 000 troops attacks 4000 troops in positions near Weissenburg, and for 1551 casualties, captures the position. The French lose 2300.

- **Worth August 6, 1870**
A tough fight between 38 000 men under Marshal Edmé MacMahon (1808–93) blocking the advance of 77 000 Prussian troops under Crown Prince Frederick (1831–88). They fight for eight hours, with both sides losing about 12 000 men, before the Prussians triumph.

- **Spicheren August 6, 1870**
Fought between 27 000 Prussians, under General Carl Friedrich Steinmetz (1796–1877), and 24 000 French, under General Frossard. The French are driven from their positions and retreat into Metz. The French lose 4000 men and the Prussians 223 officers and 4648 men.

- **Gravelotte-St Privat August 18, 1870**
The French, under General Achille Bazaine (1811–88), and the Prussians, led by Field Marshal Helmuth von Moltke (1800–91), fight a battle in which the Prussians lose 899 officers and suffer 19 260 casualties, and the French lose 13 000 with 5000 prisoners.

- **Mars-la-Tour August 18, 1870**
The Prussians, under General von Alvensleben, are saved by their cavalry and prevent the French, under Bazaine, from breaking out. Casualties on both sides are about 16 000.

- **Sedan September 1, 1870**
Napoleon III leads his army of 130 000 to relieve besieged forces in Metz. The Prussians under von Moltke manoeuvre to trap the French. They lose 9000 casualties; the French lose 3000 killed, 14 000 wounded and 20 000 prisoners. A day later the surviving 82 000 French troops surrender.

- **Paris September 19, 1870–January 28, 1871**
Paris is besieged by the main Prussian army under William I (1797–1888) and von Moltke. The French under General Louis Trochu (1815–96) have a force of 146 000 troops, slightly more than the Prussians, but are ground down. The surrender to the Prussians triggers the revolt of the Paris Commune by National Guardsmen who wish to continue the war. French prisoners are released by the Prussians and, under MacMahon, an army of 130 000 assaults the barricades held by 30 000 National Guardsmen. MacMahon loses 83 officers and 790 men. About 28 000 Communards die and of the 18 000 captured, some are executed after trials.

- **Metz October 26, 1870**
The Prussians besiege the fortress and Bazaine surrenders to Prince Frederick-Charles (1828–85). The French surrender includes 6000 officers, 173 000 men and 622 field guns.

- **Le Bourget October 27–30, 1870**
A French sortie from Paris drives the Prussians out of Le Bourget before a counter attack by the Prussian Guards. The French lose 1200 prisoners and the Prussians suffer 378 casualties.

- **Belfort November 15, 1870–February 1871**
Colonel Pierre Denfert-Rochereau (1823–78), with 17 600 locally recruited troops, holds the fortress until the French General Assembly orders him to surrender. The French suffer 5200 casualties, including civilians, and the Prussians 2000.

- **Bapaume January 3, 1871**
An indecisive battle between the French, under General Louis Faidherbe (1818–89), and Prussians, under von Goeben. The French are prevented from relieving Peronne and suffer 1569 casualties with 550 prisoners; the Prussians have 750 casualties.

- **Le Mans January 10–12, 1871**
The Prussians, under Prince Frederick-Charles, though outnumbered three to one by the French, rout them so completely that they are no longer an effective army. The Germans take 20 000 prisoners.

- **Belfort January 15–17, 1871**
An untrained army of 150 000 French forces under General Charles Bourbaki (1816–97) attempts to relieve Belfort. Though they force the 60 000 Prussian troops under General Wilhelm Werder on to the defensive, Bourbaki bungles the operation, losing 6000 men to the Prussians' 2000. The surviving French troops escape to Switzerland, where they are interned.

- **St Quentin January 19, 1871**
A French force of 40 000 men under Faidherbe attempting to relieve Paris is stopped and decisively beaten by 33 000 Prussians under von Goeben. The French lose 3500 casualties, 9000 prisoners and six guns, the Prussians 96 officers and 2304 men.

Above: *During the siege of Paris the dirigible balloon, devised by Dupuy de Lôme, eludes the Prussian grasp.*

THE FRANCO-PRUSSIAN WAR

Above: *French soldiers in defeat after their surrender at the Siege of Metz in October 1870.*

Prussia is much better prepared for war than France. After three fierce battles which the Prussians win, the tactic is to split the French strength into two and keep the sides apart. One half is besieged and defeated at Metz. The other half is routed at the Battle of Sedan. The French depose Napoleon III and the army, and the people defend the capital, but are defeated in 1871. The Treaty of Frankfurt, May 10, 1871, ends the war.

Left: *Crowds in Paris demonstrating their support for the war.*

Above: *Enterprising telescope owners charge a small fee for a "peep at the Prussians" outside Paris.*

Above: *Marshal Edmé Patrice, Comte de MacMahon, Duke of Magenta, is severely wounded at Sedan.*

Below: *Map of the fortifications surrounding Paris during the siege. The city is more vulnerable on the south side.*

Above: *After a brave fight, Paris yields in 1871 and the Prussians march through the city in triumph.*

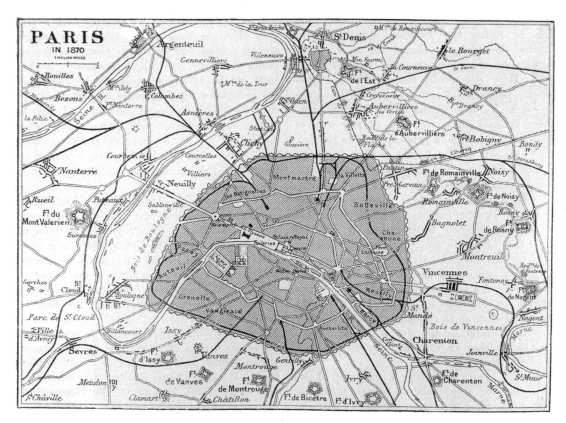

GERMAN UNIFICATION AND PARIS COMMUNE

THE FRANCO-PRUSSIAN WAR ends with the Treaty of Frankfurt. Germany is finally unified and gains Alsace and part of Lorraine from France. William I of Prussia becomes emperor of Germany; Otto von Bismarck is chancellor. Radicals in Paris reject the Treaty and form the Paris Commune. It is brutally suppressed. American showman Phineas T Barnum launches "the greatest show on earth". A newly-developed rock drill boosts the petrochemical industry. The first woman successfully climbs the Matterhorn.

❋ 1871 ❋

JAN	18	Bismarck unites 25 German states, and William I of Prussia is proclaimed Kaiser (emperor) of Germany
	28	Paris, with eight days' food left, surrenders to the Germans
FEB	13	Adolphe Thiers is elected chief executive of France
MAR	26	Paris rebels and sets up a commune
MAY	10	Treaty of Frankfurt: France surrenders most of Alsace and Lorraine to Germany, and agrees to pay an indemnity of 5 billion francs; Germans leave an occupation force
	21–28	Paris Commune defeated after "Bloody Week"

JULY	20	British Colombia joins the Dominion of Canada
AUG	17	The British Army is reorganized: purchase of commissions abolished
	31	Adolphe Thiers is elected president of the French Third Republic
OCT	8	Fire in Chicago kills 300 people and renders 90 000 homeless
NOV	10	Explorers David Livingstone and Henry M Stanley meet at Ujiji, on Lake Tanganyika, Africa

Above: *The famous meeting between "lost" explorer David Livingstone and journalist Henry Morton Stanley.*

Above: *William I, king of Prussia, who becomes emperor, or Kaiser, of a united Germany this year.*

Above: *Alphonse Thiers who is elected president of France after the deposition of Napoleon III.*

Germany Unified

William I of Prussia (1797–1888) is proclaimed emperor of Germany at Versailles Palace, outside Paris. Prussia takes over the remaining independent German states. In April, the new empire approves a federal constitution modelled on that of the now defunct North German Confederation. In May the Treaty of Frankfurt between France and Germany cedes the French provinces of Alsace-Lorraine to Germany. France also agrees to pay a large indemnity and accept an army of occupation until it is paid in full.

Kulturkampf

Bismarck, now chancellor of a united Germany, begins a *Kulturkampf* (cultural struggle) with the German Catholic Church when he suppresses its department for spiritual affairs. Over the next few years, the drive for secularization and the removal of Catholic dominance over education leads to the dissolution of religious orders and other anti-clerical measures throughout Germany.

Steam-powered Battleship

The HMS *Devastation,* a 9330-tonne steam-powered armoured battleship is launched. She is armed with four guns in turrets.

The Greatest Show on Earth

American showman P(hineas) T(aylor) Barnum (1810–91), after a long career as showman, museum proprietor and impresario, launches a circus in New York, USA, which he describes as "the greatest show on earth". It includes the midget "Tom Thumb" and other extraordinary exhibits. In 1881 PT Barnum joins forces with his chief rival James Anthony Bailey.

The Artist's Mother: Arrangement in Grey and Black No 1

American artist James Whistler (1834–1903) causes offence with his provocative title and his insistence that the public should have no interest in whether this is a faithful portrait of his mother — they should be concerned with the composition, and the work's other formal aspects. The affection conveyed in the portrait becomes apparent later.

Rougon-Macquart Series of Novels Begins

The first of twenty novels, *La Fortune des Rougon* begins French author Emile Zola's vast portrayal of French life via the stories of two branches of a family. As time goes on he will tell stories relating to many areas of life among the lower and middle classes, influenced by (but transcending) contemporary theories of heredity.

MIDDLEMARCH

British author George Eliot's masterpiece, *Middlemarch*, begins to appear. It is many things — a portrait of an unhappy marriage, a defence of modern scholarship against narrow-mindedness, a debate about Toryism and Reform, a portrait of a whole society. It takes what Henry James called the "old-fashioned English novel" about as far as it can go and confirms Eliot's position as a writer of major status. George Eliot (1819–80) is the pen-name of Mary Ann (or Marian) Evans.

ROYAL ALBERT HALL

A vast new concert hall, the Royal Albert Hall, opens in London, UK. A conception on the grand scale, it evokes Roman amphitheatres and is decorated with friezes of worthies. Named after Prince Albert, its acoustics are disappointing, but the great arena captures the public imagination and it becomes a centre for all sorts of entertainment.

ROCK DRILL

The search for oil extends to areas where thick layers of bed rock need to be penetrated. American engineer Simon Ingersoll (1818–94) invents a drill tip for this purpose. As a result, the petrochemical industry is able to expand its infrastructure.

MODEL AIRCRAFT

While others are experimenting with manned gliders, Frenchman Alphonse Penavos builds and successfully flies a self-propelled model aeroplane. The rubber-band powered *Phlanaphore* covers a distance of some 70.4m (131ft).

Above: *The main telegraph office in London, staffed by over 500 young women, paid lower wages than men.*

WIND TUNNEL

With advancements in the use of materials for the construction of buildings and bridges, it becomes necessary for engineers to test their ideas before committing to designs. The Greenwich wind tunnel, made by FH Wenham, allows them to test designs for strength in scale model form.

MARGARINE PATENT

Dutch businessman Antoon Jurgens buys the patent for margarine from Hippolyte Mege-Mouries, the French chemist who developed the oil-based butter substitute in 1869, on the orders of Napoleon III. The initial aim was to provision the navy on long voyages. Jurgens markets the product and his output is snapped up by the British. In Paris, the Council of Hygiene rules that margarine may not be sold as butter.

DOCTOR LIVINGSTONE, I PRESUME?

The disappearance of the explorer David Livingstone in Africa causes an outcry in Europe and rescue parties are prepared. Henry Stanley (1818–1904), a journalist for the *New York Herald*, tracks down Livingstone at Ujiji. He introduces himself with the words: "Doctor Livingstone, I presume?" They set off together in 1872 and ascertain that Lake Tanganyika cannot be joined to the Nile. Stanley returns to Europe but Livingstone, ignoring his advice, continues his mission to find the source of the Nile.

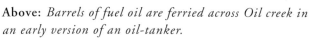

Above: *Barrels of fuel oil are ferried across Oil creek in an early version of an oil-tanker.*

Above: *A steam-powered type composing machine developed this year increases production by 500 per cent.*

Left: *Workers in the London matchmaking trade unite to petition for better working conditions and more pay.*

Charles Babbage
1791–1871

English mathematician Charles Babbage has died. A professor at Cambridge University, he devoted much of his life to developing two calculating machines, the first dedicated to calculating tables of logarithms and the second (known as the "analytical engine") to performing computations, using punched cards as "programmers". His inventions were far in advance of current engineering and their construction was limited by the mechanical devices available. So far they have not found any practical use but will be recognized as early forerunners of the computer.

WOMAN CLIMBS MATTERHORN

British mountaineer, Lucy Walker (1836–1916) becomes the first woman to climb the Matterhorn. An accomplished mountaineer, she began climbing in the Alps with her father and brothers when she was 22.

NATIONAL RIFLE ASSOCIATION

The National Rifle Association is formed in the USA. Its initial role is to implement uniform rules for shooting as a sport.

SLIDING SEAT

A new sliding seat is adopted in rowing.

RUGBY UNION

The Rugby Football Union is founded in England. The first rugby international takes place with England playing Scotland.

CHICAGO FIRE

After a very dry summer, the buildings in Chicago, made mainly from timber, are like tinderwood. A fire, allegedly started in a barn on the southwest side of the city, sweeps north and east. Fuelled by the wooden buildings, the flames even jump the river. The fire burns for more than a day and a night. Over 300 people are killed, 90 000 are made homeless. More than a million acres of forest in Wisconsin and Michigan are lost. In financial terms, the city loses about $2 million. However, the fire gives an opportunity to rebuild in style and the city attracts America's greatest architects. The first skyscraper in the world will be built here in 1884 (designed by William le Baron Jenney).

Above: *A vigorous game of rugby football played at the school from which it takes its name.*

THE PARIS COMMUNE

FOLLOWING A LENGTHY siege by the Prussian army during the winter of 1870–71, and distrust of the new republican government, Parisians rise in revolt. Radical republicans, socialists, anarchists and others set up the Paris Commune. Known as communards and influenced by Proudhon and other thinkers, their aims include economic reform. They throw up barricades, burn the Tuileries Palace and put up a desperate defence, but are ultimately crushed. Savage reprisals follow, during which thousands of communards are executed.

Left: *A cat and dog butcher in besieged Paris. The citizens have already eaten all the animals from the Zoological Gardens; now domestic pets are consumed. The very poor have to eat rats.*

Right: *"Amazons of Commune", the women of Montmartre, defend the barricades against the National Guard.*

Below: *Rioters and* pétroleuses *set fire to public buildings in Paris.*

Smile Please: Photography

Although the principles of photography were established in the 1820s and various developments have occurred since, it is in the latter part of the century that cameras and film become easier to use, cheaper to make and accessible to everybody. People of all classes seize on the new medium with enthusiasm, using it to record the milestones of family life, travel and new experiences. It becomes a new art form.

Above: *An early documentary photograph in progress: Lady Stanley, wife of the local governor-general, records the war dance of the Blackfeet Indians for posterity.*

Left: *A photographer records a happy seaside scene, establishing the tradition for holiday snaps.*

Above: *One for the family album as intrepid trippers are photographed in front of the mighty Niagara Falls.*

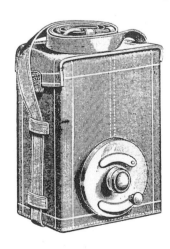

Left: *The British Royal Family pose reluctantly for the camera on the occasion of Prince George's birthday.*

Emperors, Impressionists and Skyscrapers

GERMANY, AUSTRIA AND RUSSIA AGREE on an entente between the three powers. US President Ulysses S Grant is re-elected. Claude Monet unwittingly initiates Impressionism, a new movement in art. The first reinforced concrete building is constructed in the United States. The carpet-sweeper is patented. The volcanic peak in Ecuador, El Cotopaxi, is scaled. American feminist Susan Brownell Anthony attempts to flout the law and cast a vote.

❋ 1872 ❋

FEB	2	Britain buys Gold Coast (Ghana) trading posts from The Netherlands
	8	The Earl of Mayo, Viceroy of India, is assassinated
MAR	1	Yellowstone is opened as first US national park
JUNE	25	Germany expels Jesuits
JULY	18	Secret ballot is introduced for British elections
	28	France introduces compulsory military service
SEP	7	Emperors of Germany, Austria-Hungary and Russia agree on an entente
NOV	5	Ulysses S Grant is re-elected US president
	30	In Britain, the first England-Scotland football match ends in a 0–0 draw

Right: *The first railway opens in Japan. The line runs from Yeddo to Yokahama. This is the opening ceremony; the sparse crowd indicates that railways are not yet of great interest to the general population.*

ENTENTE

The emperors of Germany, Austria and Russia, meeting in Berlin, agree an entente between the three powers, strengthened the following year into a formal alliance.

ILLEGAL VOTING

American feminist Susan Brownell Anthony (1820–1906) persuades two Rochester election inspectors to allow her to sign the electoral register vote in the presidential election. She is arrested for voting illegally. At her trial the judge directs the jury to return a verdict of guilty and fines her $100. She refuses to pay, but he frees her so she cannot appeal.

GRANT RE-ELECTED

US President Ulysses S Grant wins a second term as president, defeating his Democratic opponent, Horace Greeley. The new vice-president is Henry Wilson of Massachusetts.

WOMAN RUNS FOR US PRESIDENCY

American reformer and journalist Victoria Woodhull (1838–1927), the founder in 1870 of a magazine advocating free love, women's suffrage and legalized prostitution, becomes the first woman nominated to run for the American presidency.

Right: *A ladies' game in an American ten-pin bowling alley. Nine-pin bowling has become such a target for gamblers that some states have banned it. The ban is evaded by adding an extra pin to make a "new" game.*

UTOPIAN SATIRE

British author Samuel Butler (1835–1902) publishes his novel *Erewhon* anonymously; it achieves instant success. A Utopian satire, it describes life in a land where illness is a crime, machinery is banned, and cranky philosophers rule.

CONCRETE BUILDING

The era of the skyscraper arrives with the first reinforced concrete building. American, William E Ward, uses a combination of steel and concrete to erect a structure in Connecticut which will influence urban architecture in a seminal way.

Above: *A Monday "Pop". Pops are a series of popular concerts aimed at the British working classes.*

UNDER THE GREENWOOD TREE

This second published novel by British writer Thomas Hardy (1840–1928) is the first of his great works and establishes his literary reputation, although it does not bring him enough money to give up his profession as architect. Hardy's evocation of place (Wessex) and his later increasingly eloquent pessimism will make him unique among English novelists.

AROUND THE WORLD IN EIGHTY DAYS

The most famous of French writer Jules Verne's adventures, describing the round-the-world journey of Phileas Fogg, will remain popular, and will later inspire adaptations and films.

UNWITTING IMPRESSIONIST

Unwittingly, Claude Monet (1840–1926) gives a name to one of the most important of all artistic movements — Impressionism. The title of his painting, *Impressionism, Sunrise*, says that this is a sketch (of the sun rising over a harbour). But Monet and his friends are also exhibiting finished pictures, painted out of doors with similar loose brushwork to capture the fleeting effects of light, and for these, the hostile critics' label "impressionism" sticks.

QWERTY

The "universal" keyboard arrangement for typewriters is devised by American, Christopher Latham Sholes. The arrangement of keys — using QWERTY as the first six — is based on the order of type found in a printers case.

REPEATING RIFLE

The Austrian army is the first to adopt a firearm which has a repeating mechanism. It provides a distinct advantage in the battlefield, because it enables the infantryman to fire a number of shots from his weapon without having to reload.

STEAM TRACTOR

The Thompson steam tractor unit is introduced on to English roads. It is an immensely heavy and sluggish machine with a maximum speed of only 22.5km/h (14mph) but it is ideal for its intended job — hauling large industrial components, typical of the age.

SMUGGLED SEEDS

Seeds from the Brazilian rubber tree, *Hevea brasailiensis*, are smuggled to Kew Gardens in London by the English explorer Henry Wickham. They are transplanted to plantations in colonies in the East.

Right: *English writer Thomas Hardy, seen here in later life, produces his second novel this year.*

Above: *A day in the country for "the really deserving poor" given by the National Sunday Schools Association.*

Above: *The lobby of the Mammoth Hot Springs Hotel, at Yellowstone Park, the first National Park in the USA.*

NATIONAL PARK

Yellowstone in Wyoming, North America, becomes the first American National Park. Even though the country still contains a relatively low population, with vast tracts of wilderness, the encroachment of farming and settlement are seen as a threat to its natural heritage.

ELIAS EXPLORES CENTRAL ASIA

English explorer Ney Elias (1844–97) crosses China, the Gobi Desert, Mongolia, Siberia and the Urals before completing his return to Britain by train in 1873. The trek, one of eight that he makes, covers 8000km (4970.9mi).

BABIES REGISTERED

In Britain, the registration of babies is required for the first time under the Infant Life Preservation Act. This results from campaigning by the Society for the Protection of Infant Life set up in the 1860s by doctors and politicians, for the care of abandoned infants, funds for foundling hospitals, nurseries, and an allowance for poor mothers.

CARPET-SWEEPER

The first carpet-sweeper is patented by MR Bissell, the proprietor of a china shop. He suffers from allergic headaches caused by dust from the straw in which china is packed and invents the sweeper to remove it.

EL COTOPAXI SCALED

German scientist and traveller Wilhelm Reiss, together with AM Escobar, scales El Cotopaxi, the 6003m (19 700ft) volcanic peak in the Andes. They are the first Europeans to do so, various unsuccessful attempts having taken place during the century.

INTERNATIONAL MATCH ENDS IN DRAW

The first international football match between Scotland and England ends in a 0-0 draw in Glasgow.

Below: *Broadway, New York; New Yorkers doing well walk on the west, or sunny, side of the street.*

Above: *A private party in London's Belgravia. Whereas improving entertainment is provided for the working classes, the upper ecehelons have to entertain themselves.*

Giuseppe Mazzini
1805–1872

The Italian nationalist and revolutionary, Giuseppe Mazzini, has died. As a young man he was a member of the Carbonari — a secret revolutionary society — and founded the Young Italy movement. He was exiled in France, and then travelled widely in Europe preaching the republican message and also speaking in favour of women's emancipation. In the revolutionary struggles of 1848 he briefly formed part of a triumvirate at the head of the newly declared republic of Rome after the city had been seized from the papacy. Later, in exile once more, he refused his support for the nationalist movement of Cavour on the grounds that he was a republican and the movement sought to reinstall a king after unification. His writing will have a powerful influence on the growth of the Indian nationalist movement later in the century.

Samuel Morse
1791–1872

Samuel Finley Breese Morse, the American artist who was also a student of chemistry and electricity, has died, leaving the world with his invention, Morse Code. He conceived the idea of a magnetic telegraph in 1832 and struggled for twelve years to patent the idea and gain financial backing to develop it. In 1843 Congress at last granted him financial aid and he developed a telegraph line to operate between Washington and Baltimore, which sent its first message in 1844. The Morse alphabet or code was developed, but not by Morse himself, to be used on the telegraph.

WOMEN AT PLAY

THE CENTURY SEES HUGE LEAPS forward in the emancipation of women. Status is changing, in Europe at least, from "chattel" to person with rights and self-determination. Industrialization means that many women, especially from the 1870s onwards, now go out of the house to work. Laws are passed to give women rights over their own money, and more and more women are fighting their way into universities and colleges. Women also have to struggle to get their share of leisure and sport. The fashion for cumbersome clothes that impede movement, especially running, does not help. In the 1840s and 1850s, Mrs Amelia Bloomer introduces the idea of rational clothing, but it takes some time to catch on. Meanwhile, women begin to have the time and the means to enjoy cycling, hockey, badminton, horseriding and other sports and pastimes.

Left: *Affinity races are extremely popular at gymkhanas in England. Ladies on horseback ride holding the hand of their gentlemen partners, who ride on donkeys. The winner is the lady who gets herself and her partner past the winning post without letting go of his hand on the way.*

Below: *Stoolball, an ancient game rather like cricket, is revived by the gentry in Sussex, England.*

Above: *Battledore and shuttlecock, an early version of badminton, brought to England from India.*

Above: *A Ladies' Hockey Club at spirited play. English women take up the game in 1887.*

Above: *The practice of the Impressionists of drawing "on the spot" becomes very popular with amateur artists.*

Left: *Tricycles are introduced in the 1870s and taken up with enthusiasm by lady cyclists.*

Cable Cars, Mounties and Electric Dynamos

BRITISH TROOPS INVADE the Ashanti kingdom, West Africa. Spain is declared a republic. Travel becomes easier in hilly San Francisco with the arrival of the cable car. The Northwest Mounted Police are formed in Canada to establish law and order. A combined electric motor and dynamo is invented in France. Colour photography becomes possible with the development of the orthochromatic plate.

❄ 1 8 7 3 ❄

JAN	9	Napoleon III of France dies in exile, aged 64
FEB	11	Spain's King Amadeo abdicates
	16	Republic is proclaimed in Spain
APR	23	Royalist demonstrations in Madrid, Spain
MAY	1	Scottish missionary-explorer David Livingstone dies, aged 88
	11	Prussia puts the clergy under state control
	24	President Thiers of France resigns after defeat in the Assembly; he is succeeded by Marshal Marie MacMahon
JUNE	5	Sultan of Zanzibar abolishes slave markets
JULY	1	Prince Edward Island joins the Dominion of Canada
SEP	15	German occupation force leaves France when the French finish paying the indemnity imposed after the Franco-Prussian War
OCT	27	Attempts to restore the monarchy in France fail
NOV	20	Marshal MacMahon is given seven years' presidential powers

Spanish Republic

Following the abdication of Amadeo I — who became king when Prince Leopold of Hohenzollern, the Prussian candidate, refused to take over the throne in 1870 — a republic is declared in Spain. In 1874, Alfonso, son of the deposed Queen Isabella, comes of age and is proclaimed king as Alfonso XII.

Ashanti Revolt

War breaks out in the Gold Coast as Ashantis attack British forts on the coast. British troops soon invade the Ashanti kingdom. They take the capital, Kumasi, in February 1874, ending the revolt and consolidating British power in West Africa.

War in Indochina

France's influence expands into northern Vietnam. A small force captures Hanoi but suffers some setbacks in fighting with the Sino-Vietnamese "Black Flag Pirates".

Un Saison en Enfer

French poet Arthur Rimbaud (1854–91) publishes his first book, in which he uses prose in a poetical manner, asserting the writer's right to create his own forms. This is his lasting legacy, but the volume is panned critically, and Rimbaud turns his back on literature. His work will only be widely appreciated after the end of his short life.

Above: *Napoleon III dies at Chislehurst, Kent, England, where his funeral takes place at St Mary's Chapel.*

Orthochromatic Plate

Hermann Vogel (1834–98), a German chemist, takes photographic science a stage further by inventing the orthochromatic plate. It is the first practicable means for taking full-colour photographs; the plate being coated in a special chemical layer.

Divorced Women Keep Children

In the UK, divorced women win the right to claim custody of their children.

Shoot-out

In the United States, a shooting contest on Long Island draws 100 000 spectators.

Typhoid Fever Is Contagious

In his book *Typhoid Fever: Its Nature, Mode of Spreading, and Prevention*, English physician William Budd (1811–80) proves the contagious nature of the disease. In 1866 he had checked the spread of cholera in Bristol by introducing strict hygiene controls, and stamped out an epizootic (epidemic) of rinderpest in British livestock.

Above: *British army enters Kumasi, capital of the Ashanti kingdom of the Gold Coast, to quash rebellion.*

Above: *Ashanti King Attah of Akim enthusiastically greets the British Commissioners.*

CABLE CAR
Built on an undulating landscape, San Francisco, USA, becomes the site of the world's first cable car. The Clay Street Hill Railroad Company builds the cable car as a solution to the problem of transporting people up and down a very steep incline.

MOTOR/DYNAMO
French engineer, Hippolyte Fontane (1833–1917) invents the combined electric motor and dynamo. The machine can be powered by electricity or generate electricity, and with its dual purpose is employed within France's first electricity supply system.

SLAVE MARKET CLOSES
Zanzibar's public slave markets close by order of Sultan Barghash Sayyid, acting under pressure to prohibit the export of slaves.

SPHAIRISTIKE
Major Walter Clapton Wingfield of Wales invents "Sphairistike", a game in which players use a racket to hit a ball over a net dividing an hourglass-shaped court. The initial name is quickly dropped but lawn tennis becomes a huge hit and is adopted by the All-England Croquet Club in Wimbledon, London.

DEATH OF LIVINGSTONE
Scottish missionary and explorer David Livingstone dies at Chitambo while praying. His heart is buried in the shade of a tree by Susi and Chuma, his African lieutenants. In an incredible act of loyalty, they then transport his corpse and papers to the coast, a distance of 2414km (1500mi). From there Livingstone's body is shipped to England and laid to rest in Westminster Abbey in London.

Right: *Explorer and missionary David Livingstone dies at Chitambo this year.*

John Stuart Mill
1806–1873

The English philosopher and economist, John Stuart Mill, has died in Avignon, having spent his last years in France. As a philosopher he was known for his analysis of the foundations of human knowledge published in *A System of Logic* (1843), and for his development of the theory of utilitarianism in ethics. He emphasized the distinction between quality and quantity of pleasure ("better a man dissatisfied than a pig satisfied"). He was a friend of Jeremy Bentham and fellow founder-member of the Utilitarian Society (1823), which met for discussions at Bentham's home. In his later work *On Liberty* (1859), Mill argued for freedom of thought and discussion, and in *Subjection of Women* (1861, published 1869) he defended women's rights. Mill was arrested for distributing literature on birth control to the London poor in 1824. In 1865, he was elected to Parliament, where he campaigned for women's suffrage and supported the Advanced Liberals. He was "secular godfather" to the British philosopher Bertrand Russell.

Above: *The Shah of Persia, who visits England this year.*

Above: *Colonel Festing wins the Victoria Cross by rescuing his lieutenant under fire from Ashanti troops.*

Above: *Spaniards gather in the streets of Madrid to show their support for the newly declared republic.*

AMERICAN FOOTBALL

Princeton beats Yale 3–0 at the start of the oldest continuous college sports rivalry in the United States.

MOUNTIES

The Northwest Mounted Police are established in Canada to halt trading in alcohol and arms with the Indians of the Northwest Territory, and to bring order to the Canadian west. They will win the nickname "Mounties" for their daring exploits and romantic reputation. In 1920 their official name changes to Royal Canadian Mounted Police.

CAMERON CROSSES AFRICA

Backed by the Royal Geographical Society, explorer Verney Lovett Cameron (1844–94) sets off from Bagamoyo, East Africa to try and meet up with David Livingstone. Cameron encounters Livingstone's associates carrying the explorer's body. He carries on and maps Lake Tanganyika before continuing on to the west coast, which he reaches in 1875, becoming the first European to make an east-west crossing of Africa.

Right: *Hostile crowds at Masindi meet Governor Samuel Baker, who is trying to suppress the African slave trade.*

Below: *Samuel Baker discovers a boatload of slaves being shipped up the Nile in Africa. A chance discovery reveals 150 women and children packed tightly in sacks disguised as a cargo of corn and ivory.*

OSTEOPATHY, BLUE JEANS AND ELECTRIC CARS

SURGICAL OPERATIONS become safer as the practice of sterilizing surgical instruments is introduced. Osteopathy, healing by bone manipulation, is described, adding another to a growing range of healing therapies. The electric car is invented when an electric motor is attached to an engine. The Impressionists hold their first exhibition in Paris. Ancient Pueblo dwellings are discovered in the southwest United States.

✸ 1874 ✸

JAN	3	Marshal Francisco Serrano becomes president of Spain, with dictatorial powers
FEB	16	In the UK, Benjamin Disraeli (Conservative) becomes prime minister, succeeding William Ewart Gladstone (Liberal)
MAR	15	French take control of Annam (now part of Vietnam)
OCT	25	Britain annexes Fiji
NOV	24	Alfonso, son of ex-Queen Isabella II of Spain, comes of age and wins support for a constitutional monarchy
DEC	29	Alfonso is proclaimed king of Spain as Alfonso XII

Above: *Work on the first of the North Tunnels under the Hudson river, New York, is begun this year. Digging stops before the tunnel is finished, but will be restarted in 1902. The tunnel uses a steel tunnel shield and cast-iron lining. Two will be built eventually, finished in 1904. They are used for railroad traffic.*

Right: *A hydraulic erector mounted on a travelling carriage is used to build the Hudson tunnels, once funds are raised to complete the project.*

STERILE INSTRUMENTS

English surgeon, Abraham Groves (1847–1935), establishes the practice of sterilizing surgical instruments and the wearing of sterile rubber gloves during surgical procedures. The mortality rate from post-operative infection falls dramatically as a result.

OSTEOPATHY

American physician Andrew Still (1828–1917) describes osteopathy, the system of healing by the manipulation of parts of the body — especially the bones. It is based on sound scientific experimentation and works by stimulating the body's natural healing mechanisms.

ELECTRIC CAR
Sir David Salomons is the first person to attach an electric motor to a carriage, thereby inventing the electric car. The vehicle has three wheels and is propelled by a single horsepower electric motor, which is fuelled by Bunsen electric cells.

DEWEY SYSTEM
American library pioneer Melvil Dewey (1851–1931) becomes librarian at Amherst College, USA. He evolves a system of book classification, using the numbers 000–999 to cover the major, general, fields of knowledge. Decimals are introduced to focus the numbers on specialized subjects.

Above: *Modest Petrovich Mussorgsky, composer of* Boris Godunov *and* Pictures from an Exhibition.

Above: *A bicycle race is held from Bath to London. Eight riders take part and the winner reaches 16km/h (10mph).*

BARBED WIRE
Joseph F Gliddon patents his invention of barbed wire, inspired by thorned shrubs, for use on the US Plains. The new invention enables ranchers to enclose their territories, greatly facilitating cattle raising.

IMPRESSIONISTS EXHIBIT
The group of artists who are becoming known as Impressionists hold an exhibition at the studio of the photographer Nadar in Paris, France. The exhibition will be one of a series of collective exhibitions which establish and publicize the movement. Among the artists who take part in some or all of these shows are: Claude Monet, Pierre-Auguste Renoir, Camille Pissarro, Alfred Sisley, Berthe Morisot and Mary Cassatt.

BORIS GODUNOV
The masterwork of Russian composer Modest Mussorgsky (1845–81), based on a poem by Pushkin, is performed at St Petersburg after rewritings and cuts. It will go through various other revisions (notably by Rimsky-Korsakov), until it establishes itself as one of the most popular of all Russian operas and a major work of Russian nationalism.

PUEBLO BUILDINGS DISCOVERED
Pueblo Indian cliff dwellings are discovered by government surveyor and photographer WH Jackson in the Mesa Verde area of the southwest United States.

Above: *Sailors and marines who fought in the Ashanti War in a march-past reviewed by Queen Victoria.*

Below: *Oxford undergraduates try to follow John Ruskin's idea that exercise should have some useful purpose.*

MA VLAST (SYMPHONIC POEMS)

This cycle of symphonic poems by Czech composer Bedrich Smetana (1824–84) is an orchestral portrait of his homeland — its woods, fields and the great river, Vltava. Although Smetana will soon be under the shadow of a greater master, Dvorak, this work remains a great symbol of Czech nationalism. "Vltava" is the most popular of all the symphonic poems in the collection.

PARIS OPERA HOUSE

The opera house by French architect Charles Garnier (1825–98), finished this year, is the epitome of the idea of opera as spectacle. Nicknamed the "Palais Garnier", its vast entrance staircase is the place where audience members go to be seen, its stage is where composers want to get maximum publicity for their works.

STANLEY EXPLORES

After his "finding"of David Livingstone, Henry Stanley becomes an explorer in his own right. Over the next three years he circles Lake Victoria and Lake Tanganyika, then crosses to the Congo. The journey down the river is constantly disrupted by attacks and the dangers of rapids and waterfalls. Stanley sets out with 350 people; only 114 survive to reach the Atlantic.

Top and above: *Benjamin Disraeli becomes prime minister of Great Britain this year. Like all politicians, he is caricatured in the press.*

Above: *Temperance ladies in Ohio endeavour to turn whisky drinkers from the alcoholic road to hell.*

HARVARD PLAY MCGILL

In a vital step in the development of American football, Harvard play McGill University of Toronto in a game similar to rugby. The day before, Harvard had won a contest of a more soccer-like sport, but McGill's "rugby" version is hugely popular and so the soccer-style game takes a back seat at Harvard.

HANSEN'S DISEASE

The leprosy bacillus is discovered by the Norwegian physician Arrnauer Gerhard Henrik Hansen (1841–1912) and leprosy is renamed Hansen's disease.

CHAUTAUQUA MOVEMENT

The Chautauqua movement in American education begins as a summer training programme for Sunday School teachers at Fair Point on Lake Chautauqua, New York State. Its founders are Methodist preacher John Heyl Vincent and Lewis Miller, who begin a travelling tent show of lectures.

CAPITALS ONLY

The Remington typewriter is marketed by E Remington & Sons, who initially produce only eight machines. Although the machine is an improvement on the model patented by William Burt in 1829, and on British and French models, it types only in capitals.

RUSSIANS SETTLE IN KANSAS

German-speaking Russians from the Crimea are invited to settle in Kansas by Carl R Schmidt, a Santa Fe railway official, who needs settlers who will produce crops to generate freight revenue. The first Hutterite immigrants to the USA arrive in New York from Europe. A group speaking Tyrolean Hutterische dialect founds the Bonhomme colony at Yankton, South Dakota.

FOOTBALL IN BRAZIL

British sailors introduce football to Brazil when they play a game there. Brazilians take up the game with enthusiasm and soon become very proficient at it. They will eventually produce Pelé, widely considered to be the world's greatest footballer.

RIVETED JEANS

Levi Strauss, the inventor of denim jeans, introduces a new range of work trousers featuring copper rivets. Their purpose is to reinforce the garments at points where they experience the highest levels of wear and tear; particularly the main seam and pocket corners.

CULTURE FOR THE MASSES

PRINCE ALBERT HAD LED THE WAY to mass culture in England. He had understood that technology is the way forward, and that an educated workforce was essential to progress. Culture and education had been the privilege of the rich upper- and middle-class male; now it was to become available for all. Using the money generated by the Great Exhibition of 1851, Albert commissioned museums and colleges open to all. People working to an industrial (rather than agricultural) timetable have time to learn; transport developments allow them to travel to galleries, museums and institutes. Education is making most people literate and numerate and there is a great enthusiasm for "self-improvement" using books and journals, clubs, institutes and evening classes. In the USA, the Chautauqua system of summer schools and correspondence courses is set up this year.

Left: *The Imperial Institute in South Kensington, London, part of the museum complex built at the command of the late Prince Albert.*

Below: *Art students at the Louvre in Paris. Many great artists begin their career copying the works of the Old Masters.*

Above: *The Lecture Room at the Royal Institution, London.*

MUSIC HALLS AND VAUDEVILLE

The late 1800s sees the rise in popularity of music halls. The music hall is an extension of the "singing room" of a public house or tavern, where a variety of acts entertain the drinkers. The first hall in London is the Oxford, opened in 1861. In the USA, vaudeville — song and dance acts usually performed in the breaks between acts in a play — becomes popular in its own right. In 1883, Benjamin Keith opens the first vaudeville house, The Gaiety Museum, in Boston.

Above: *Dan Leno, Marie Lloyd, Fannie Leslie, Little Tich and other stalwarts of the London music hall circuit.*

Above: *A modern London music hall, where the behaviour is more refined than in older halls.*

Above: *Cockney music hall artiste Albert Chevalier entertaining the drawing-room class with his tearful song, "My Old Dutch".*

Above: *Contemporary sketch of bar loungers.*

Right: *A song-and-dance man tries to engage the audience's attention. Such acts in bars and pubs are popular in England and America.*

Above: *The Angel, a popular public house in Islington, London. Men, women and children all go there.*

SHARES SOLD IN SUEZ CANAL

BRITAIN BUYS SHARES in the strategically-placed Suez Canal, becoming the largest shareholder. Attempts at reform are made in China. Dentistry moves into a new age with the development of a battery-powered drill for removing decay. The American author Mark Twain publishes his classic novel, *The Adventures of Tom Sawyer*. Canned baked beans make their first appearance. The US Congress passes a Civil Rights Act.

❋ 1875 ❋

JAN	12	Kuang-Hsu becomes emperor of China	OCT	12	New Zealand government is centralized, and provincial governments are abolished
FEB	6	In Germany, civil marriages are made compulsory	NOV	25	British Prime Minister Benjamin Disraeli buys 176 602 shares in the Suez Canal from the Khedive of Egypt
APR	8	A Berlin newspaper carries an article "Is War in Sight?"; it causes panic in France			
MAY	10	Czar Alexander II of Russia visits Berlin			
AUG	25	Captain Matthew Webb swims the English Channel for the first time			

Above: *The* Castalia, *a twin-hulled steamship, takes just
under two hours to cross the Channel from Dover to Calais.*

REFORMING EMPEROR

Kuang-Hsu becomes emperor of China, although the dowager Empress Tz'u-Hsi remains a powerful presence behind the throne. The new emperor tentatively supports attempts at reform in order to strengthen China in the face of European expansion, but little headway is made.

BOSNIA-HERZEGOVINA

A revolt breaks out in the Balkan province against Turkish rule, leading to an escalating crisis throughout the Balkans.

SUEZ CANAL SHARES

British Prime Minister Disraeli (1804–81) buys 176 602 shares in the Suez Canal from the Khedive of Egypt for £4 million, making Britain the largest shareholder in the Canal Company and hence giving it effective control over the Suez Canal.

DENTAL DRILLS

Dentistry enters the age of whistling drills when American inventor George F Green invents a battery-powered device for the removal of decayed dental tissue. Thankfully, analgesics are also now available to counter the unpleasant consequences of the work of over-enthusiastic dentists.

THE ADVENTURES OF TOM SAWYER

Frontier life is evoked by American author Mark Twain (1835–1910) with a satirical power and a sense of realism unmatched in any other previous work. This book (and its sequel, *The Adventures of Huckleberry Finn*, 1885) earn Twain lasting fame, which he needs when, later in life, he has to earn his keep on the lecture circuit.

THE GROSS CLINIC

American realist artist Thomas Eakins (1844–1916) paints his greatest canvas, *The Gross Clinic*, a portrait of the surgeon Gross performing an operation and describing what he is doing to a group of students. The surgical details are faithfully reproduced. It and similar works lead to Eakins later being considered as America's greatest realist artist.

CANNED BAKED BEANS

Sold as "Boston Beans", the world's first canned baked beans are enjoyed by the Maine fishing fleets. In 1880 a tomato-based sauce is added which helps to popularize them nationally, before their invasion of Europe.

Right: *French balloon the* Zenith *ascends too fast, killing two of its three occupants.*

Above: *Britain's Prince of Wales enters Baroda, India, in grand style during his tour of the country this year.*

Piano Concerto No 1 in B Flat Minor

Russian composer Pyotr Tchaikovsky's first piano concerto establishes itself as one of his most popular works. It is criticized at its première, in New York, but quickly gains a foothold in the repertoire in Europe, where pianists value both the great romantic melodies and the opportunities for the virtuosic display it affords.

Carmen — a Flop?

French composer Georges Bizet (1838–75) thinks he has composed a flop when his masterpiece *Carmen* closes after 48 performances with audiences dwindling. The composer dies soon afterwards, but the opera is taken up and becomes a success, influencing many later composers, especially the *verismo* school.

Corrugated Cardboard

The Thompson and Norris Co., of New York, begins manufacturing packaging material, corrugated paper or cardboard. The product, destined to become a ubiquitous material, makes clever use of paper by exploiting its dynamic strengths without wasting resources unnecessarily.

Civil Rights Act

The US Congress passes the Civil Rights Act guaranteeing black people equal rights in public places and banning their exclusion from jury service.

Above: *Contenders in an amateur bicycle race. Cycling is becoming increasingly popular as a sport.*

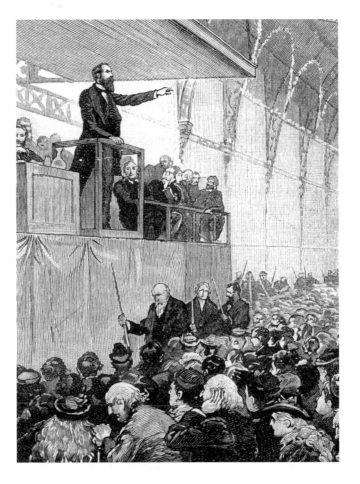

Above: *Cardinal Manning endeavours to persuade the poor Irish in London to forswear the demon drink.*

Right: *American religious revivalists Moody and Sankey tour Great Britain holding packed meetings.*

INDOOR HOCKEY
McGill University students compete in the world's first recorded indoor hockey game at Montreal's Victoria Skating Rink.

WAR WITH SIOUX
White gold prospectors' continual and illegal occupation of Indian lands in Dakota Territory sparks a war with the Sioux nation.

CHANNEL SWIMMER
British swimmer Captain Matthew Webb becomes the first person to swim the English Channel. He takes 22 hours to reach the French coast.

AMERICAN FOOTBALL BORN
A game between the American universities of Harvard and Yale is considered the birth of American football.

KENTUCKY DERBY
The Kentucky Derby horse race is run for the first time.

WHITES SETTLE OREGON TERRITORY
Oregon Territory, occupied under treaty with the Nez Percé Indians, is opened to white settlement. In Texas, the US cavalry capture and destroy the 1400-strong herd of horses of the Comanches, forcing them to end their resistance to settlement of the Texas prairie and move to a reservation.

SWEET CHOCOLATE
The Swiss company Nestl develops milk chocolate for eating by mixing sweetened condensed milk with chocolate. Henri Nestl originally set up his company in 1866 to produce and market a formula milk for infants who cannot take mother's milk.

Hans Christian Andersen
1805–1875

The Danish writer of fairy stories, Hans Christian Andersen, has died. The son of a shoemaker and a washer-woman, he found benefactors in Copenhagen and was educated under the patronage of the king. Their confidence was repaid as he produced poetry, travel writing, plays and novels, and most famously his 150 or more fairy stories which include "The Emperor's New Clothes", "The Little Mermaid", "The Snow Queen" and "The Ugly Duckling".

Right: *The Atlas compression ice machine, this year's improvement on the many previous ice-making machines introduced into industry.*

Below: *Henry Stanley's Anglo-American Expedition to central Africa hits some problems at Bumbireh island, Lake Victoria. After being threatened, the explorer and his team escape with their lives.*

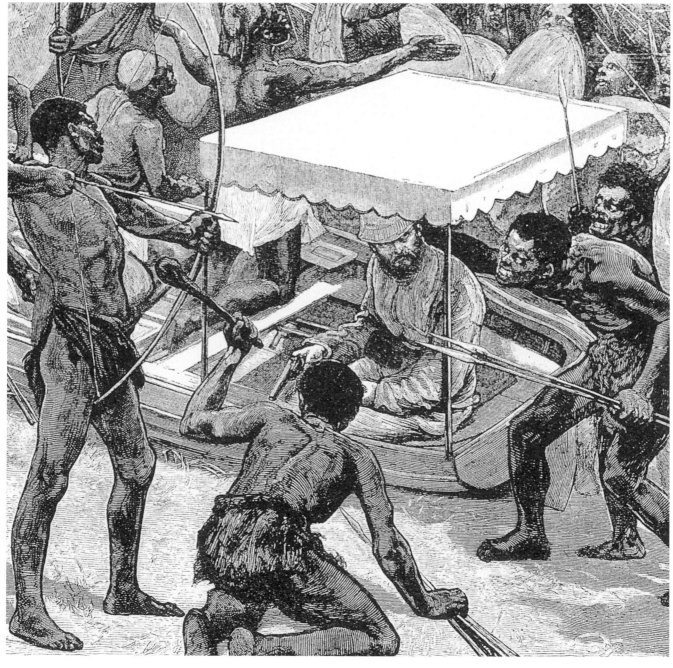

The Telephone is Ringing

Serbia and Montenegro declare war on Turkey. General Custer and the US Seventh Cavalry are wiped out by Sioux and Cheyenne at the Battle of Little Bighorn. The United States celebrates its 100th birthday with a massive exhibition. Rutherford B Hayes is elected US president. Alexander Graham Bell demonstrates the world's first successful telephone. Tomato ketchup and breakfast cereal go on sale.

✺ 1876 ✺

Jan	31	Sultan Abdul Aziz of Turkey promises reforms in the Ottoman Empire, but rebel elements reject them	July	2	Montenegro declares war on Turkey
Feb	26	China says Korea is independent	Aug	1	Colorado becomes the 38th US state
				31	Abdul Hamid II becomes sultan of Turkey
Mar	9–16	Turkish soldiers massacre Bulgarians	Oct	31	Turkey agrees to a six-week armistice
	10	Alexander Graham Bell makes the first telephone call	Nov	7	Samuel Tilden (Democrat) wins the most votes in the US presidential election, but twenty votes are in dispute
May	30	Sultan Abdul Aziz of Turkey is deposed and kills himself			
June	25	Custer's Last Stand: American General George Custer and many of his regiment are slain by Sioux and Cheyenne forces at the Battle of Little Bighorn	Dec	23	New Turkish constitution is proclaimed
	30	Serbia declares war on Turkey			

KOREA INDEPENDENT

China declares Korea independent, ending a lengthy period of Chinese rule over the country.

WAR WITH TURKEY

After Turkish troops massacre numerous Bulgarians, causing huge controversy throughout Europe, Serbia and Montenegro declare war on Turkey. In August, Sultan Murad V is declared insane and replaced by Abdul Hamid II, who grants Turkey a constitution in December.

ARTIFICIAL FLAVOURING

Vanilla pods, coming from exotic, tropical shores, are very expensive and difficult to obtain. To overcome this, Germans William Harman and Karl Reimer invent a synthetic vanilla essence. It is eagerly adopted by a German chocolate producer.

HAYES ELECTED PRESIDENT

Rutherford B Hayes (1822–93) becomes US president after a closely fought contest against the Democrat Samuel J Tilden of New York. Initially Tilden had led his Republican opponent, but twenty disputed electoral college votes went to Hayes, ensuring his election. William A Wheeler of New York becomes vice-president.

US CENTENNIAL EXHIBITION

The United States Centennial Exhibition opens in Philadelphia. Exhibits extol America's progress in agriculture, industry and the arts, including the largest steam engine ever built, the Corliss centennial engine, and a rotary printing press. Budweiser beer, developed by Adolphus Busch of E Anheuser & Co wins a competition; rootbeer, a drink made from dried roots, barks and herbs, is marketed by Charles E Hires; and bread is raised with compressed yeast produced by Gaff, Fleischmann and Co. Halls exhibit the products of more than 30 nations and colonies.

TELEPHONE CALL

Scotsman Alexander Graham Bell (1847–1922) invents the first telephone capable of conveying sustained articulate speech, thanks to various other scientists having developed the constituent parts. Bell transmits the first successful sentence via his telephone and demonstrates his invention, first in Boston to the American Academy of Arts and Sciences and then at the international exhibition at Philadelphia. His telephone has a profound effect on global communication.

Left: American author Henry James publishes his first important novel and moves to Paris where he lives for a year.

Gaugin Exhibits

French artist Paul Gaugin (1848–1903) begins to exhibit landscapes at the Paris Salon while still following his professional career as a stockbroker. The bold colours and direct style of his works will soon start to influence the group of artists who will become known as the Post-Impressionists.

Britain and France Control Egypt

After a British government report that Egypt is near bankruptcy, Britain and France establish dual control over Egypt's finances.

Roderick Hudson

This first important novel by Henry James (1843–1916) establishes him as America's foremost writer of fiction. Like many of his works, it describes the interaction between America and Europe, chronicling the fate of an American who moves to Rome but fails to adjust to his new home.

Funicular Railway

Scarborough, in England, sees the first funicular railway, for scaling the cliff face. The railway works on the principle that one car uses its weight to pull another up, as it descends on the other end of a cable. The required weight is gained and lost by filling and emptying water tanks.

L'Apres-midi d'un Faune (Poem)

Written some ten years earlier, this modernist masterpiece by French poet Stéphane Mallarmé (1842–98) is published. The compression of the language and the intellectualism of the verse will be highly influential on later modernist writers.

Women's Declaration

American feminists Elizabeth Cady Stanton and Matilda Joslyn Gage compile The Declaration of Rights of the Women of the United States. Stanton presents it to the acting US vice-president on July 4 at Philadelphia.

The Age of Bronze

One of the most influential sculptures by French sculptor Auguste Rodin (1840–1917) is unveiled. In breaking up the smooth surface of the traditional sculpted nude, and in giving the figure a sense of animation, Rodin points the way forward for future sculptors. The figure also courts controversy because some argue (patently absurdly) that the figure is so realistic that Rodin must have cast a live model.

Breezing Up

The picture of boys enjoying themselves sailing a dinghy wins American painter Winslow Homer (1836–1910) great popularity when it is exhibited this year. The vigour with which the sea and clouds are painted is particularly successful.

Torpedo Boat

The British 19-knot HMS *Lightning* is designed and built. It is armed with a bow-mounted swivelling torpedo tube. A year later, the French build a 14-knot boat with two underwater axial tubes.

Dona Perfecta

The Spanish novelist Pérez-Galdós is the writer of two vast sequences of novels. *Doña Perfecta* is one of the main works in the second (and greater) of the two sequences, *Novelas españolas contemporáneas*. It deals with the life of a young liberal in a hostile environment. The works of Pérez-Galdós show him capable of creating a fictional world that is as true to Spain as Balzac's is to France, or Dickens' to England.

First Polo in the USA

The first game of polo in the United States is played indoors in New York City.

Right: Rutherford Birchard Hayes, the nineteenth president of the USA. He bans liquor from the White House.

Above: *Constantinople, the major city and port of Turkey, where there is a great deal of trouble this year.*

Mikhail Bakunin
1814–1876

Russian revolutionary anarchist Mikhail Aleksandrovich Bakunin has died. In 1848 he took an active part in revolutionary activity in Paris and Germany. Sentenced to death in 1849, he was instead returned to Russia and imprisoned for six years before being sent to Siberia. He escaped on an American frigate and travelled to England. He joined the First International in 1863, forming within it a semi-secret group called the Social Democratic Alliance. Bakunin preached the use of violent means to overthrow the existing order, and vigorously rejected centralization and subordination to authority. However, he believed that Communism was merely a necessary step towards anarchism, and in 1872 was expelled for his views.

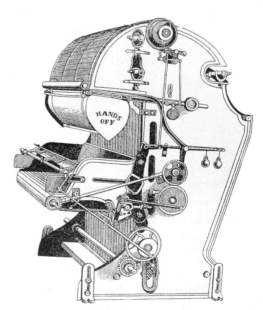

Above: *Bramwell's Automatic Weighing and Feeding machine, used in the woollen industry.*

TOMATO KETCHUP
F & J Heinz, a company established in 1875 by HJ Heinz of Pittsburgh with his brother and cousin to pack and market pickles and other foods, introduces tomato ketchup, a condiment made with tomato, vinegar and a very high percentage of sugar additives.

BREAKFAST CEREAL
The first cold cereal breakfast food is made and marketed by Harvey Kellogg, a surgeon, manager of the Western Health Reform Institute in Michigan, Seventh Day Adventist and vegetarian. He combines wheat, oatmeal and cornmeal and bakes the mixture into thick biscuits which he grinds and sells in packages. He also develops peanut butter and other vegetarian foods.

GERONIMO
Chiricahua Apache leader Geronimo (1829–1909) leads his warriors into Mexico from where he terrorizes settlers in the southwest after attempts to move his people to a reservation.

BASEBALL CLUB FORMED
The National League of Professional Baseball Clubs is formed. It will survive in the future as the National League of Major League Baseball.

Above: *The promenade at Brighton, England, a popular resort thanks to the railways.*

TRAVELS IN ARABIA
English traveller Charles Doughty (1843–1926), considered one of the finest of the Arabian explorers, details his work in his book *Travels in Arabia Deserta*. He travels openly and without great resources for 21 months.

PLIMSOLL LINE
Ships are found to have varying buoyancy depending on the density of the water they are floating in. Samuel Plimsoll (1824–98) introduces a series of marks on the side of ships to indicate safe loading levels of cargo, taking this into account. The Plimsoll line is adopted in Britain; all British merchant ships are to be marked with a Plimsoll line so that none can sail with an overweight cargo.

Left: *Samuel Plimsoll, known as the "Sailor's Friend", because the Plimsoll line makes their work a great deal safer.*

Above: *The main street of Cetinje, capital of Montenegro, the Balkan country which declares war on Turkey this year.*

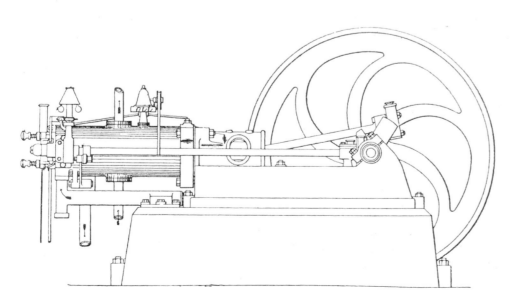

Left: *The Otto horizontal gas engine. German Nikolaus Otto patents the first gas-operated four-stroke internal combustion engine this year.*

LIFE IN AUSTRALIA

In 1770, explorer James Cook had claimed the part of Australia called New South Wales for Great Britain. A settlement was established at Sydney in 1788, and for some time Australia became the place to which British convicts were sent. This practice stopped in the 1850s and 1860s, after the discovery of goldfields. Australian states remain separate until 1891, when they unite to form a commonwealth with its own constitution.

Above: *Rough justice in the colonies. In the tough new country physical punishment is easier than jail sentences.*

Above: *Immigrants from Europe arrive in Australia. There are few home comforts to help them settle in.*

Above: *Locals gather at the general store in Tambo, Queensland. Bushmen and stock riders meet and talk.*

Left: *Shepherds and stockmen in a Queensland tavern. They frequently bring in their pay, give it to the barman, and keep drinking until the money runs out. This is called "doing your pile".*

Right: *Great Bourke Street, Melbourne; a visiting Englishman, complete with monocle, is causing amusement.*

Left: *For some people, Australia is not a young land full of opportunity, but an ancient one, imbued with tradition. The aboriginal Australians, whose way of life has been the same for thousands of years, have their rights and rituals overturned by the white settlers.*

THE BATTLE OF LITTLE BIGHORN

URING A CAMPAIGN to try to force them on to reservations, Sioux and Cheyenne people are being rounded up by the US army. General George A Custer (1839–76) and his regiment come across a village in the valley of the Little Bighorn river, where almost 5000 hostile Native Americans are gathered. Custer orders an immediate attack and in the Battle of the Little Bighorn he and over 260 of his troopers die.

Left: *A Sioux cemetery. The Sioux resent white American attempts to confine them to reservations and suppress their native culture.*

Below: *In the thick of the battle between the Sioux and a regiment of the US Cavalry under General Custer.*

THE JEWEL IN THE CROWN

BRITAIN'S QUEEN VICTORIA is proclaimed empress of India. Russia declares war on Turkey and invades Romania. Britain annexes the Transvaal. Irish nationalist Charles Stewart Parnell leads the Home Rule for Ireland movement. The phonogram, a forerunner of the gramophone, is invented by American Thomas Edison. A new industrial process, welding, is developed. The first-ever Wimbledon Lawn Tennis Championship is held.

❖ 1877 ❖

JAN	1	Britain's Queen Victoria is proclaimed empress of India
	29	US electoral commission decides that the presidential election has been won by Rutherford B Hayes (Republican)
FEB	5	Turkey and Serbia sign peace treaty
MAR	4	Rutherford B Hayes is inaugurated as the nineteenth US president
	31	The European Powers demand that Turkey undertakes reforms
APR	24	Russia declares war on Turkey, and invades Romania
MAY	2	General Porfirio Diaz becomes president of Mexico
	6	Britain warns Russia not to blockade the Suez Canal
	21	Romania enters the war against Turkey and declares independence from Russia
DEC	10	Russians capture Plevna, Bulgaria
	14	Serbia declares war on Turkey

Empress of India

Queen Victoria of Britain is declared empress of India as British influence continues to expand throughout the Indian subcontinent. For the British, India is their "jewel in the crown" and a much-loved colonial possession.

Russia Declares War on Turkey

After an attempt by Britain and other powers to mediate between Russia and Turkey fails, Russia declares war on Turkey and invades Romania in retaliation for Turkish atrocities against fellow Slavs in the Balkans. Turkey eventually sues for an armistice in January 1878 after suffering a number of heavy defeats.

Transvaal Annexed

Britain annexes the Boer Republic of Transvaal on the grounds of bankruptcy and threats from Basutos and Zulus.

Reconstruction Ends

In the United States, the last federal troops leave the southern states, ending the era of Reconstruction begun after the defeat of the Confederacy in the Civil War.

Home Rule Campaign

Charles Stewart Parnell (1846–91), MP for County Meath in Ireland, becomes president of the Home Rule Confederation and leads the Home Rule for Ireland campaign against British rule, making the Irish Question a major political issue in Britain.

Symphony No 2 in B Minor

The Russian Alexander Borodin (1833–87), part-time composer and Professor of Chemistry, will produce few works, but in this symphony he creates a finely orchestrated Russian sound-world which haunts listeners.

Galleria Vittoria Emanuele

An arcade with a fine iron and glass roofed atrium, the Galleria, in Milan, has a lasting influence on shopping malls in both Europe and North America. This is not the first, but one of the best and most striking designs.

Trinity Church, Boston

The church in Boston by American architect Henry Hobson Richardson (1838–86) is completed and confirms his reputation. Its massive Romanesque forms and details, the choice of red granite, and the encaustic interior decoration by Lafarge make it one of the most memorable nineteenth-century buildings in the USA.

Boston Switchboard

Only one year after the introduction of Bell's telephone, a switchboard is set up in Boston. The Holmes Burglar Alarm Company connect up to five of their clients, who use the wire for making calls during the day and as a burglar alarm telegraph during the night.

Below: *Edison's invention, the phonogram, is exhibited in London. The poet Tennyson witnesses the demonstration.*

PORTRAIT OF IDA
American Impressionist Mary Cassatt (1844–1926) exhibits this portrait, which attracts the interest of Degas. The French artist invites her to exhibit with the Impressionists in Paris, which she will do in 1879. She gains a reputation for portraits and domestic scenes in the Impressionist style.

LIQUID OXYGEN
Oxygen in liquid form is obtained by the fractional distillation of liquid air. Raoul Pictet, a Swiss physicist, finds that by compression-cooling air into liquid, he can then evaporate the nitrogen and other trace gases, thereby leaving the 21 per cent atmospheric oxygen as a pale blue liquid.

YWCA
The Young Women's Christian Association is formed from a number of institutions for women that have opened since 1855, when a London boarding house was founded by philanthropist Lady Kinnaird, to supply accommodation for women living away from home.

PHONOGRAM
American inventor, Thomas Alva Edison (1847–1931), invents an early version of the gramophone. The phonogram translates sound vibrations into a track scribed onto the surface of a wax-coated cylinder. It can thus record and then play back sound waves.

Above: *A pow-wow in British Columbia between Sitting Bull, the Sioux chief, and British and US ambassadors.*

ARC WELDING
American engineer, Elihu Thomson (1853–1937), exploits the heat energy produced by an electric arc to invent a machine for welding. Welding quickly replaces the traditional use of forged rivets for joining industrial metal components — being far stronger and airtight.

JEWISH CITIZENSHIP
In Switzerland, an Emancipation Law gives full citizenship to Jewish people in that country.

CHIEF JOSEPH SURRENDERS
Nez Percé Indian Chief Joseph surrenders to General OO Howard in Montana and declares that he will cease fighting. In May, Crazy Horse, one of the leaders behind the Custer massacre last year, surrenders peacefully at Camp Robinson, Nebraska.

TENNIS AT WIMBLEDON
Wimbledon, a croquet club in the UK, hosts the first Lawn Tennis Championships. By now the hourglass-shaped court laid down by Walter Wingfield has become a rectangle and scoring has taken the modern form. In 1882, the net will be lowered and the measurements of the tennis court become fixed.

THE RUSSO-TURKISH WAR

THIS IS THE FOURTH AND LAST war fought between Russia and Turkey this century. The two countries have been at loggerheads since the 1600s. After the Crimean War (1853–56) Russia lost strategic territory in the Balkans and around the Black Sea. This war is fought to regain those losses. Most of the action takes place in Plevna, where there are two battles and a siege. The war ends in 1878 with the Russians victorious.

Above: *General Mikhail Dmitrievich Skobeleff (1843–82) who plays an important role in the Battle of Plevna.*

Right: *The* Russia *captures the Turkish vessel the* Mercene *in the Dardanelles.*

Left: *The Russians crossing the Danube at Simnitza.*

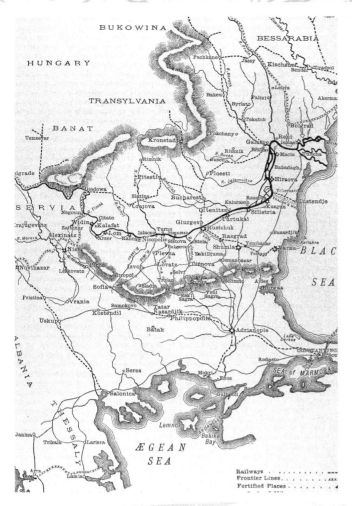

Above: *A map showing the war zone.*

Above: *Turkish leader Osman Pasha and his troops try to cut their way out of trouble at the Battle of Plevna.*

Left: *The Russians cross the Balkans under General Gourko.*

VICTORIA, EMPRESS OF INDIA

After the debacle of the Sepoy Rebellion, in the mid-1850s, the British government took over the control of India from the East India Company. Twenty years later, Queen Victoria is proclaimed the empress of India, during the Conservative administration of Benjamin Disraeli, a politician with whom Victoria is in great sympathy. As empress, the queen now makes more public appearances, which she had largely given up since the death of Prince Albert in 1861. This improves her standing with the public, who will celebrate her Golden Jubilee in 1887 with gusto, establishing the pomp and ceremony that becomes the British Royal tradition.

Above: *Queen Victoria visits her favourite minister, Benjamin Disraeli, at his home in Hughenden.*

Above: *A Hindu fakir, a holy man of India.*

Opposite: *The official proclamation of Queen Victoria as empress of India.*

Left: *Hindu workers harvest rice. Victoria's empire will bring a great wealth of commodities.*

LIGHT BULBS AND FROZEN MEAT

THE BALKAN WARS END with the Treaty of Berlin. Montenegro, Serbia and Romania become independent. The Second Afghan War breaks out. Lighting is revolutionized with the invention of the incandescent light bulb. Frozen meat is transported successfully by sea. Cleopatra's Needle arrives in London from Egypt. The first psychology laboratory is established in Germany. Eccentric frontierswoman Calamity Jane nurses smallpox sufferers. Tchaikovksy's ballet *Swan Lake* is performed.

✳ 1878 ✳

JAN	9	Turkey asks Russia for an armistice
	9	Victor Emmanuel II of Italy dies; succeeded by son Umberto I
	31	Turks and Russians sign an armistice
FEB	2	Greece declares war on Turkey
	15	British fleet arrives at Constantinople (Istanbul)
MAR	3	By the Treaty of San Stefano, Russia and Turkey end their war; Montenegro, Serbia and Romania become independent
	27	Britain sends Indian troops to Malta, fearing Russian aggression
JUNE	4	By a secret pact with Turkey, Britain promises to defend it against Russia, and is allowed to occupy Cyprus
JULY	13	Under the Treaty of Berlin, Bulgaria is divided in three, and Montenegro gains independence
OCT	17	Conservatives win general election in Canada: John A McDonald becomes prime minister
NOV	21	British troops invade Afghanistan

Right: *The Radziwill Palace in Berlin, where the Congress meets to draw up the Treaty of Berlin, which ends the current Russo-Turkish War.*

TREATY OF BERLIN
The Treaty of Berlin ends the Balkan Wars. Romania, Montenegro and Serbia become independent, and Montenegro and Romania gain territory. Austria is given a mandate to occupy Bosnia and Herzegovina, Britain gets Cyprus. Russia gains lands in the Caucasus and Bessarabia from Romania. Bulgaria becomes autonomous, and Turkey introduces reforms.

SECOND AFGHAN WAR
British troops invade the country after Emir Shere Ali refuses to receive a British envoy in the capital, Kabul. The Second Afghan War continues until May 1879, when Britain agrees to pay an annual subsidy to occupy the strategic Khyber Pass and gains the right to send an envoy to Kabul. The peace stabilizes the northwest frontier of the Indian empire, although fighting continues in Afghanistan until British troops are finally withdrawn in April 1881.

Above: *Zealous young British patriots, known as jingoists, agitate for war with Russia.*

CLEOPATRA'S NEEDLE
Famous for kindling interest in Ancient Egypt, Pharaoh Tuthmosis III's obelisk finally reaches London from Alexandria, having been presented to Britain by the Turkish viceroy of Egypt, Mohammed Ali. The Needle is also known as an early example of a "time capsule". Beneath it are buried a selection of items, including a morning's newspapers, *Bradshaw's Railway Guide*, coins, four Bibles (in different languages), and photographs of twelve of the "best-looking Englishwomen" of the day.

INCANDESCENT LIGHT BULB
Both Thomas Edison and Joseph Swan (1828–1914) invent versions of the safety light bulb. The filament is a carbonized cotton thread held within a sealed glass bulb filled with an inert gas that prevents the filament from oxidizing as it glows, and prevents any risk of fire.

SWAN LAKE
This is the first of Tchaikovsky's three famous ballets. It pleases audiences with its beautiful tunes and enchanting story, while the composer revolutionizes ballet by working closely with his choreographer to create a dramatic, almost operatic, structure.

MICROPHONE
Based on the principle used in Bell's telephone mouthpiece, a microphone for addressing audiences is demonstrated by Professor DE Hughes at the Submarine Telegraph Company office in London. Public address, recording and radio will all benefit from its development.

TIFFANY GLASSWARE
American craftsman Louis Comfort Tiffany sets up a glassware factory in New York. Tiffany glass becomes famous for its iridescent colours and Art Nouveau style.

FROZEN MEAT

The SS *Paraguay* carries the first-ever cargo of frozen meat. A shipment of 5500 mutton carcasses is made from Buenos Aires in Argentina to Le Havre in France. The transportation of perishable goods over long distances is now possible.

ARCTIC EXPLORATION

Swedish explorer Nils Nordenskjöld (1832–1901) sails along the northern coast of Russia and Siberia in the steam-powered ship *Vega*. Thick ice forces him to overwinter for nearly 300 days, but his crew uses the time for scientific observations. In July 1879 the *Vega* reaches the Bering Strait and the Pacific. Nordenskjöld returns to Europe via the Pacific and the Suez Canal.

THE BENDS

French physiologist Paul Bert (1833–86), discovers the cause of "the bends" suffered by deep-sea divers. It is more properly known as decompression sickness. Bert discovers that nitrogen absorbed into the blood whilst at depth, has a tendency to form bubbles before it is released from the blood if the diver rises too quickly.

ELECTRIC RAILWAY

German engineer, Werner von Siemens (1816–92), pioneers the development of electrically-powered public vehicles by building an electric tramway in the streets of a Berlin suburb. The motors are supplied by overhead wires to prevent the electrocution of pedestrians.

Above: *Maoris gather to commemorate a historic war, their celebrations shared by white immigrants.*

Pius IX
1792–1878

The Italian pope (since 1846), born Giovanni Maria Mastai Ferretti, has died in the Vatican. Early in his papacy he instituted many reforms. These included introducing two chambers of papal government, one of which was elected by the people, and restoring rights to Jews. However in refusing to side against the Austrians in the struggle for Italian independence, he lost popular support. In 1848 a republic was proclaimed in Rome, and the pope was forced to flee. Papal government was restored in July 1849, and thereafter Pius IX became rigidly conservative. Under his rule, the Vatican Council of 1869–79 proclaimed papal infallibility. When Victor Emmanuel II's soldiers took over Rome in 1870 after the withdrawal of the French garrison that had been keeping it separate from Italy, the papacy effectively lost its last piece of territory and only the Vatican City remained.

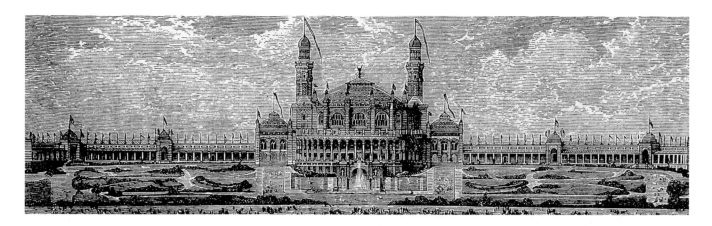

Above: *The magnificent Trocadero building, home to the Paris Exhibition of 1878.*

CALAMITY JANE

More than 14 000 die of Yellow Jack — a yellow fever epidemic in the southern USA. In Deadwood, Dakota Territory, an eccentric frontierswoman, Martha Jane Canary, nurses people through a smallpox epidemic while dressed in men's clothes. She is nicknamed "Calamity Jane".

HEADLINE COURT CASE

Modern art hits the news following a headline court case. English art critic John Ruskin, in one of his sillier moments, calls the American artist James Whistler (1834–1903) a "cockscomb" for asking money for his work, described by Ruskin as "throwing a pot of paint in the public's face". The insult provokes a lawsuit; Whistler wins but is awarded only a farthing damages, a derisory sum showing the court's sympathies.

BICYCLE RACE

CA Parker triumphs in the first bicycle race on American soil. He covers 4.8km (3mi) of Beacon Park, Boston, in 12 minutes 27 seconds.

JEHOVAH'S WITNESSES

Charles Taze Russell establishes the Jehovah's Witnesses, first known as Russellites, as an independent church. In 1872, in Pennsylvania, Russell predicted Christ's second coming in the year 1874, and the subsequent establishment of Christ's kingdom on Earth.

PSYCHOLOGY LABORATORY

The first experimental psychology laboratory is established at the University of Leipzig, Germany, by Wilhelm Max Wundt (1832–1920). It is a landmark in the establishment of psychology as a science.

BERLITZ LANGUAGE SCHOOL

German emigré Maximilian Delphinius Berlitz opens a language school in Rhode Island, USA, and develops a method that allows non-native speakers to teach any language.

Left: *Lord Beaconsfield (Benjamin Disraeli) attends the Berlin Congress and holds a reception for the key players at the British embassy in Berlin.*

ELECTRICITY: THE NEW POWER

ALTHOUGH THE PRINCIPLES OF ELECTRICTY have been known of since the 1700s, its use in the home as a source of light is a new phenomenon. Many inventors have tried to design a suitable light bulb, and in 1879, Edison will invent the incandescent lamp, using carbonized thread as a filament. Edison is also the first person to build an electrical power plant, on Pearl Street, New York City in 1882, to generate electricity for domestic lighting. Insurance companies plan to charge higher premiums on electrically-lit homes.

Left: *Domestic electricity demonstrated in a splendid suite of rooms at the Crystal Palace Electrical Exhibition in London. Mr Edison's newest glow lamps are used.*

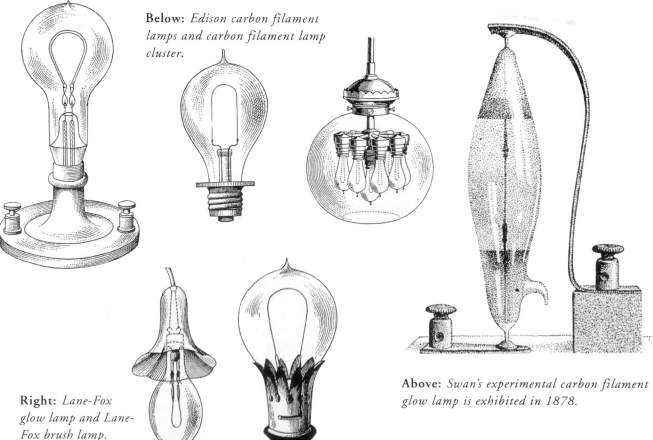

Below: *Edison carbon filament lamps and carbon filament lamp cluster.*

Right: *Lane-Fox glow lamp and Lane-Fox brush lamp.*

Above: *Swan's experimental carbon filament glow lamp is exhibited in 1878.*

TROUBLE IN AFGHANISTAN

AFGHANISTAN, WHICH LIES BETWEEN India and Russia is the scene of many conflicts throughout the century, as Great Britain and Europe try to contain Russian expansionism and Russia tries to contain the imperial ambitions of British India. There are four wars between Britain and Afghanistan and some further fighting between Britain and Russia using Afghanistan as a battlefield. The hostile terrain and difficult access makes all fighting dangerous and costly. The guerrilla tactics of the Afghanis also make them fierce enemies.

Above: *The Battle for Ali Musjid; the British finally win through after a very long struggle.*

Above: *Elephants are used to haul the 40-pounders, guns deployed by General Roberts to destroy Ali Musjid.*

Above: *Fort Ali Musjid, which guards the entrance to the Khyber Pass, the easily defended path to Kabul.*

Above: *Shere Ali, the emir of Kabul since 1863. His refusal to receive a Britsih envoy triggers war.*

ZULUS AND BRITISH AT WAR IN SOUTH AFRICA

THE BRITISH FIGHT THE ZULUS in South Africa, defeating them and gaining control over Zululand. The Irish Land League is formed. Steel production is boosted by the invention of an electrically-heated steel furnace. The world's first birth control clinic opens in The Netherlands. Frank Woolworth opens a Five and Ten Store in Pennsylvania as the era of low-cost consumer goods begins.

✺ 1879 ✺

JAN	12	Anglo-Zulu War begins in South Africa
	22	Zulus annihilate British force at Isandhlwana
	30	Jules Grévy (Conservative Republican) elected president of France
FEB	22	Bulgaria gains a constitution
APR	5	Chile declares war on Bolivia and Peru (beginning of the War of the Pacific)
JULY	4	British troops defeat the Zulus at Ulundi
AUG	28	British capture Zulu leader Cetewayo

SEP	1	Treaty ends Zulu War
	3	Afghans massacre the British Legation at Kabul
OCT	29	Irish Land League is founded in Dublin, with Charles Stewart Parnell as its president
	19	Afghanistan's Emir Shere Ali abdicates and surrenders to the British

Left: *Irish politician Charles Parnell addresses an anti-rent meeting in Limerick. High rents and absentee British landlords are causing unrest.*

WAR IN SOUTH AFRICA

War breaks out between Britain and the Zulus as Britain tries to control the warrior state. After a heavy defeat at Isandhlwana and a close contest at Rorke's Drift, the Zulus are finally overwhelmed at Ulundi in July. The war ends in September with Britain taking full control over Zululand, which it formally annexes in June 1887, thus blocking Transvaal's access to the coast.

WAR IN SOUTH AMERICA

The Bolivian government cancels the concession of a Chilean company mining for nitrates in the Bolivian-controlled Atacama Desert. In April, Chile occupies the area and also declares war on Peru, which it believes incited the Bolivian action. The war between the three continues until 1883, when Chile gains the entire Bolivian coastline, denying the country access to the Pacific, and a part of Peru.

DUAL ALLIANCE

Germany and Austria-Hungary sign a treaty of Dual Alliance, which ties the countries together until 1918.

NATIONAL LAND LEAGUE

Irish nationalist Michael Davitt (1846–1906) forms the Irish National Land League in Dublin to campaign for land reform and an end to absentee landlords and high rents. The campaign begins in County Mayo, where tenants ostracize Captain Charles Boycott, an agent for Lord Erne. The tactics of "boycott" soon gain wide acceptance throughout Ireland.

VOTIVKIRCHE

Heinrich von Ferstel's *Votivkirche* is completed. It is especially notable for its highly ornate version of the Gothic revival style, with openwork belfries and spires.

DONA LUZ

Spanish novelist Juan Valera (1824–1905) publishes one of his best novels, about the conflicts between pride and idealism. This, and his other novels of this period, are singled out by some critics for their alleged attacks on Catholic extremists.

CHURCH OF CHRIST, SCIENTIST

American religious leader Mary Baker Eddy (1821–1910) and her followers found the Church of Christ Scientist. In 1875 she published *Science and Health* in which she established the principles of her church. Her ideas have been influenced by the healer, Phineas Quimby, who believes that all illness originates in the mind. She was his student between 1862 and 1866, since when she has redefined her beliefs.

LES BEATITUDES

Belgian composer César Franck (1822–90) produces what he views as one of his most important pieces, the major choral work *Les Béatitudes*, a grand statement by a composer of chamber music and organ pieces. But he can only get it performed in his own apartment. It is not performed publicly until after his death.

VIOLIN CONCERTO FOR JOACHIM

German composer Johannes Brahms (1833–97) writes this masterwork of the classical repertory, one of the great works from the composer's mature years. Brahms finds the composition taxing and is helped by the violin virtuoso Joseph Joachim (1831–1907), for whom the piece is written.

BROTHELS REGISTERED

The compulsory registration of all brothels in The Netherlands is introduced by the government.

James Clerk Maxwell
1831–1879

The Scottish theoretical physicist and mathematician, James Clerk Maxwell, has died. His greatest contribution was probably his work on electromagnetic radiation, which developed Michael Faraday's theory of electrical and magnetic forces and hypothesized that there are many electromagnetic wave frequencies and that light consists of electromagnetic waves. Maxwell suggested that these waves could be produced in a laboratory, and will be later vindicated, in 1887, by the work of Heinrich Hertz. This will lead to wireless telegraphy and also paves the way for Einstein's theories. Other work, which came out of his theoretical study of the energies of gas molecules, led to the theory of mathematical probability, and helped to found the science of statistics.

FIRST BIRTH CONTROL CLINIC
The world's first birth control clinic is opened in Amsterdam by Aletta Jacobs, the first Dutch woman to qualify as a doctor and practise in The Netherlands. It operates illegally but no steps are taken to close it or restrict its activities.

SCHOOL FOR NATIVE AMERICANS
The Carlisle Training and Industrial School for Indians is established in Carlisle, Pennsylvania, with an intake of Sioux children in a scheme by Richard Henry Pratt, a former US army officer and amateur anthropologist, to assimilate Indians into white society.

MUNICIPAL LIGHTING
The world's first municipal electric lighting systems are installed in Cleveland, Ohio, and in San Francisco, USA, using carbon-arc street lamps invented by the scientist Charles F Brush of Cleveland, and produced by his company, the Brush Electric Light Co.

ARC FURNACE
A steel furnace heated by electrical arc is invented by German engineer Wilhelm Siemens (1823–83). It has the advantage over combustion-heated furnaces, because enormous amounts of energy can be introduced far more quickly, so accelerating the furnace process.

MILK BOTTLES
The Echo Farms Dairy Company of New York is responsible for the introduction of the milk bottle. It is just one of many inventions introduced for consumer convenience, as a part of the developing modern infrastructure.

PHOTOGRAVURE PLATE
Karl Klic shows off his invention, the photogravure plate, at the Vienna Photographic Society. It is a metal plate which has a negative photographic image etched into its surface and can thus be used to print the image on to paper.

VASELINE
Having heard from an oil worker that a residue found on drill shafts had the power to heal cuts and sores, American chemist, Robert Cheseborough, begins marketing the substance as "Vaseline". The product is a translucent gelatinous ointment, otherwise known as petrolatum or petroleum jelly.

Left: *New York's new elevated railway has its critics, who fear it will frighten the horses and worry about the danger of falling cinders.*

Five and Ten Store

Frank W Woolworth, a failed bank clerk, opens a Five and Ten Store in Pennsylvania in an attempt to launch mass-market, low-cost merchandizing. Goods at five cents are displayed on one side of the store, goods at ten cents on the other. His Great Five Cent Store in Utica, New York, failed this year, but Woolworth sees this new venture in Lancaster as the beginning of an empire.

Global Hunger

Worldwide hunger has resulted from failed harvests in Britain, Ireland and Asia. Millions have died in India and China alone.

Fertilization

Herman Fol, a Swiss scientist, observes a single sperm penetrating an egg and confirms the view of the German embryologist, Oscar Hertwig, published in 1875, that fertilization is accomplished by a single male cell.

Archery Association

The National Archery Association is formed in the United States. The organization helps to popularize the sport.

Mme Charpentier and her Children

French artist Auguste Renoir (1841–1919) begins to paint his famous family group portraits. Their charm, bright colours, and soft brushwork make them popular with many bourgeois families.

Above: *Archery competition at Wimbledon, near London.*

Above: *Bad behaviour at the new Suez station, opened this year.*

Below: *An attack on the British Residency in Kabul during the Afghan War.*

THE ZULU WARS

THE BRITISH, WHO annexed the Transvaal from the Boers, come into dispute with the Zulus under King Cetewayo. When the British invade they are met by ill-armed but warlike and highly disciplined Zulu forces.

• ISANDHLWANA **January 22, 1879**
The Zulus under Matyana overwhelm and massacre six companies of the British 24th Regiment with two guns and a small force of Natal volunteers.

• RORKES DRIFT **January 22, 1879**
Chief Cetewayo's 4000 Zulu warriors attack a force of 137 men, mostly from the 24th Regiment, holding a farm. The small force, commanded by two lieutenants, holds out for a day and a night, inflicting 400 killed on the Zulus for 25 casualties and winning eleven Victoria Crosses.

• ULUNDI **July 4, 1879**
Though the Zulu base is held by 20 000 warriors, the British force of 5000 men under General Garnet Wolseley (1833–1913) and General Thesiger (1827–1905) is well armed and for 15 killed and 78 wounded kill 1500 warriors, breaking Cetewayo's power.

Above: *The British break through with their colours at the Battle of Isandhlwana.*

Above: *The charge of the 17th Lancers at Ulundi.*

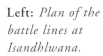

Left: *Plan of the battle lines at Isandhlwana.*

Left: *Cetewayo, king of the Zulus, surrenders to the British after the Battle of Ulundi.*

Right: *The morning after the attack at Rorke's Drift.*

THE SCRAMBLE FOR AFRICA

IN EUROPE, IMPERIALISM IS THE KEYNOTE of the decade. By the mid-1880s the major European powers are dividing Africa between them in what becomes known as the "scramble for Africa". Germany, France, Britain, Portugal and Belgium all gain territories, and by the end of the 1880s, Africa has been truly carved up. The United States is gaining in power, wealth and global influence, and becomes the focal point for increasing numbers of immigrants who flood into the country in their thousands every year. A distinctive American way of life is also emerging, characterized by the world's first skyscraper, and Bloomingdales department store. Impressionism is the innovative art movement of the decade, and the age of motoring begins with the invention of the first petrol-powered car.

⟅ 1880–1889 ⟆

KEY EVENTS
of the
DECADE

FIRST BOER WAR

NATIONALIST REVOLT IN EGYPT

PHOENIX PARK MURDERS

THE SCRAMBLE FOR AFRICA

INDIAN NATIONAL CONGRESS FORMED

HOLY WAR IN THE SUDAN

ITALO-ETHIOPIAN WAR

STATUE OF LIBERTY UNVEILED

FIRST IMPRESSIONIST EXHIBITION

EIFFEL TOWER CONSTRUCTED

STEAM TURBINE INVENTED

SACCHARIN DISCOVERED

BERLIN PHILHARMONIC ORCHESTRA
FOUNDED

BROOKLYN SUSPENSION BRIDGE
OPENED

PETROL-FUELLED CAR DEVELOPED

VAN GOGH'S SUNFLOWERS

WORLD POPULATION

1485 MILLION

(ESTIMATE)

General Gordon makes his last stand at Khartoum in the Sudan.

Westerners are invited to China.

Threshing is mechanized by steam engines in California, USA.

REVOLT IN TRANSVAAL, THE FIRST BOER WAR

*T*HE FIRST BOER WAR BREAKS OUT between Britain and the Boers in the Transvaal. James A Garfield is elected president of the USA. France annexes Tahiti. Outlaw Ned Kelly is hanged. An American amateur astronomer predicts the existence of the planet Pluto. The typhoid bacterium is discovered. The first radio telephone is invented. Cologne cathedral is completed after more than 400 years.

❖ 1880 ❖

MAR	24	Britain, Germany and the USA sign trade treaties with the independent kingdom of Samoa
APR	18	Liberals defeat Conservatives in British general election; Lord Beaconsfield resigns as prime minister
	28	William Gladstone (Liberal) becomes Britain's prime minister
MAY	3	Atheist British MP Charles Bradlaugh refuses to take the oath and demands the right to make an affirmation
JUNE	23	Bradlaugh is arrested and excluded from the House of Commons
	25	Cape parliament rejects a plan for a South African federation
	29	France annexes Tahiti

OCT	13	Boers in Transvaal declare independence from British rule
NOV	2	James A Garfield (Republican) wins US presidential election
	8	Civil war breaks out in Samoa
DEC	30	Paul Kruger proclaims a Boer republic in Transvaal

Left: *Captain Charles Boycott (1832–97) gathers his harvest and gives the language a new word. He is an English land-agent for Lord Erne in County Mayo, Ireland, and is so harsh and cruel to his employer's tenants that local people refuse to have anything to do with him.*

FIRST BOER WAR

The First Boer War breaks out between Britain and the Transvaal as resentment against the British annexation of the Transvaal turns into a revolt led by Paul Kruger and General Piet Joubert. Britain suffers defeats and, in April 1881, agrees to recognize the independent Boer Republic of the Transvaal, ruled, after April 1883, by President Paul Kruger (1825–1904). The major battles are Laing's Nek and Majuba Hill. Laing's Nek is fought on January 28. British General Sir George Colley (1835–81) leads 1100 men on a suicidal frontal attack on Boer positions. The Boers suffer 41 casualties, the British 198. At Majuba Hill, fought on February 27, 647 British troops under Colley hold Majuba Hill. However, skilful tactics and accurate shooting by the Boers force them to retire. Colley is killed and the British lose 223 casualties and 50 prisoners. An armistice with the Boers follows.

FRANCE ANNEXES TAHITI

During the year, France annexes the South Pacific island of Tahiti as European domination of the region becomes almost total. The annexation follows Britain's take-over of Fiji (in 1874), and of other islands.

BEN HUR

American novelist Lewis Wallace (1827–1905) writes his historical novel, *Ben Hur*, about early Christianity. In the twentieth century (1925) it will become the subject of a famous silent movie.

PIANO QUINTET

Now a naturalized Frenchman, Belgian-born composer and organist César Franck (1822–90) produces one of his most famous works. The sheer beauty of the sound he creates is widely admired — and haunts the French novelist Marcel Proust.

CARDBOARD CARTONS

Robert Gair, the Scots-born American who invented the paper bag, begins manufacture of cardboard cartons. He has recently begun printing merchants' names on his paper bags.

GARFIELD WINS US ELECTION

The Republican candidate James A Garfield (1831–81) wins the US presidential election by only 9464 popular votes against his Democratic opponent Winfield Scott Hancock of Pennsylvania, although he comfortably wins the vote in the electoral college. The new vice-president is Chester A Arthur.

SACCHARIN

The discovery of saccharin is published by American chemist Ira Remsen (1846–1927) at Johns Hopkins University, while investigating coal tar products. His German research student files a patent claim in his own name, Constantin Fahlberg.

Left: *William Ewart Gladstone, the Liberal politician who becomes prime minister of Great Britain this year.*

Left: *Radical free-thinker Charles Bradlaugh (1833–91) is elected MP for Northampton, but is thrown out of the House of Commons in London after being refused the opportunity to make an affirmation of allegiance, rather than swear the parliamentary oath as he is an atheist. In spite of being re-elected three times, it is not until 1886 that he is allowed to take his seat.*

George Eliot
1819–1880

English writer Mary Ann (Marian) Evans, better known as George Eliot, has died. Reared in the Midlands, she was liberated by her father's death in 1849 and travelled in Europe, returning to write for the *Westminster Review*. She formed a relationship with the writer GH Lewes which lasted for over twenty years, until his death, and in the year of her death married her friend John Walter Cross. Her first novel *Adam Bede* (1859) was immediately successful and was followed by many other works of stature, including *Middlemarch* (1871–72) and *Daniel Deronda* (1876).

Gustave Flaubert
1821–1880

The French novelist, best known for his book *Madame Bovary* (1857), has died. Flaubert was the son of a doctor. His contribution to the development of modern literature was great, despite his relatively small output. *Madame Bovary*, which describes the restlessness and eventual suicide of a country doctor's wife, was his first book and was condemned for its immorality. It was followed by various works, including *Salammbo* (1862), *Sentimental Education* (1869), and *The Temptation of St Anthony* (1874), as well as a number of stories.

COLOGNE CATHEDRAL COMPLETED

Although begun in 1388, Cologne's great Gothic cathedral was never completed during the medieval period. Building begins again in the nineteenth century, when the fashion for Gothic is at its height, and the building, with its twin spires, at 157m (515ft) the tallest such structure, is finally finished.

RADIO TELEPHONE

The first radio telephone capable of sending and receiving articulated speech is invented by Charles Sumner Tainter and Alexander Graham Bell. Using simple transmitters and receivers they manage to convey a spoken message over a short, direct air space.

NED KELLY HANGED

In Australia, the famous outlaw Ned Kelly is hanged in Melbourne, Victoria. Kelly was a bushranger, a convict who escaped into the outback and outwitted the police for two years before being captured and imprisoned.

PHOTOPHONE

Alexander Graham Bell (1847–1922) invents a communications device which uses pulses of light. Only with the development of optical fibres in the 1980s would his basic idea become a reality, with the ability to send light signals around bends.

SAFETY RAZOR

The safety razor is patented by the Kampfe Brothers in New York. It consists of a blade inserted into a frame to prevent accidental cuts.

Above: *General Sir Frederick Roberts, who leads 10 000 men to relieve Kandahar, Afghanistan, in August.*

Below: *The notorious Ned Kelly, held at bay by constables who capture and hang him this year.*

WOMAN PREACHER

Anna Howard Shaw (1847–1919), an English-born American who graduated in theology in 1878, is ordained by the Methodist church. She becomes the first ordained Methodist woman preacher.

CHIMBORAZO SCALED

English mountaineer Edward Whymper, the first man to climb the Matterhorn, scales Chimborazo — 6297m (20 561ft) — and most of the other major mountains in Ecuador.

Lucretia Coffin Mott
1793–1880

American abolitionist and women's rights campaigner, Lucretia Mott (born Lucretia Coffin), has died at an advanced age. She was one of the founders of the American Anti-Slavery Society and, with feminist Elizabeth Cady Stanton, organized the first Women's Rights Convention, which was held in 1848.

Left: *The Prince and Princess of Wales, leaders of London's fashion scene.*

Below: *Steam power is now used to drive the winding gear for mines.*

RUGBY SCRIMMAGE

Walter Camp, "The Father of American Football," introduces the scrimmage to replace the rugby scrum. American football continues to evolve, and the forward pass, which will become its dominant feature, is not introduced until 1906.

24–26 CARRER DE LES CAROLINES, BARCELONA

Maverick Barcelona architect Antoni Gaudí (1852–1926) creates his first building. A suburban villa influenced heavily by traditional Spanish building styles, it nevertheless has elements, such as multicoloured tiling, which the architect will develop in his later works.

Above: *Women unite for the vote; meetings are attended by women from all sections of society.*

TYPHOID

The bacterium that causes typhoid is discovered by German bacteriologists, Karl Eberth (1835–1926) and Robert Koch (1843–1910). Typhoid is a serious disease which claims many lives, so this development is of great importance.

PLANET X

American engineer and amateur astronomer, George Forbes (1849–1936), predicts the existence of the planet Pluto, labelled planet "X". It will take a further 50 years before the planet is visually located, and given its name, by Clyde Tombaugh (1906–97).

Left: *Fire engines drawn by hand are gradually being replaced by steam driven engines. Steam can also be used to pump water.*

US PRESIDENT AND RUSSIAN CZAR ASSASSINATED

A NATIONALIST REVOLT BREAKS OUT in Eygpt against European influence. Russian Czar Alexander II is assassinated. So too is US President James A Garfield. Russia, Germany and Austro-Hungary set up the League of Three Emperors Alliance. In the USA, the so-called "Jim Crow" laws introduce racial segregation on public transport. Norwegian Henrik Ibsen completes his ground-breaking drama *Ghosts*.

❖ 1881 ❖

JAN	28	Rebel Boers in Transvaal defeat the British at Laing's Nek	JUNE	18	Austria, Germany and Russia sign a secret alliance for three years
				28	Austria and Serbia form an alliance
FEB	27	Boers defeat the British at Majuba Hill	JULY	2	An unemployed man shoots US President James Garfield
MAR	2	Detention without trial is temporarily introduced in Ireland	AUG	2	Irish Land Act guarantees fair rents for land
	4	James A Garfield is inaugurated as twentieth US president			
	12	France occupies Tunis	SEP	9	Arabi Pasha leads a rebellion in Egypt
	13	Terrorists assassinate Czar Alexander II of Russia; he is succeeded by his son Alexander III		19	President Garfield dies, and is succeeded by Vice President Chester A Arthur as the 21st president
APR	5	Britain accepts the independence of the South African Republic (Transvaal)	OCT	13	Irish nationalist Charles Stewart Parnell is arrested for opposition to the Land Act
MAY	12	Tunis agrees to accept French protection			

Above: *British General George Colley in the thick of battle at Majuba Hill, during the Boer War.*

Above: *Irish politician Charles Parnell is removed from the House of Commons, along with 27 other Irish members, for disregarding the authority of the Speaker of the House.*

FRENCH OCCUPY TUNISIA
Following raids on French settlers by local tribes in Algeria, French troops occupy Tunisia, which becomes a French protectorate in May.

FIRE SPRINKLER
Due to the volatile nature of the materials used by the Edinburgh Rubber Works, the factory warrants the invention of a fire sprinkler system. Any large building containing flammable materials or furnishings will soon benefit from a similar device.

Above: *President James Garfield, who is assassinated at Washington DC railway station this year.*

Above: *Charles Parnell, arrested this year for making "incendiary speeches" in support of the Land League.*

CZAR ASSASSINATED

The day after calling an assembly of Russian nobles, Alexander II is assassinated. He is succeeded by his son, Alexander III (1845–94), who begins to reverse many of his father's more enlightened policies. Anti-Jewish pogroms begin throughout western Russia as anti-Semitism is encouraged.

US PRESIDENT ASSASSINATED

President Garfield is assassinated by a hardline Republican, Charles Guiteau. He is succeeded by the vice-president, Chester Arthur.

LEAGUE OF THREE EMPERORS

Russia, Germany and Austro-Hungary establish the secret League of Three Emperors Alliance for three years. The alliance is initiated by Bismarck to reassure Russia after the establishment of the Dual Alliance between Germany and Austro-Hungary in 1879. All three agree to remain neutral if one goes to war with a fourth country.

SAGESSE

One of French poet Paul Verlaine's best-known volumes, *Sagesse,* appears after the poet's return to the Catholic Church. It also shows a return to more conventional verse-forms, but still with a certain freedom.

GHOSTS

At the height of his powers, Norwegian dramatist Henrik Ibsen (1828–1906) completes *Ghosts*, one of his most daring social dramas, in which the effects of congenital syphilis throw their shadow across the whole cast. The frankness of the play shocks audiences; its dramatic power, with psychological discoveries pushing the plot along, keeps it in the theatre.

Fyodor Dostoyevsky
1821–1881

Fyodor Mikhailovich Dostoyevsky, the Russian novelist, has died. His father, a Moscow doctor, was murdered by serfs, but Dostoyevsky joined a socialist circle, for which he was condemned to death in 1849, despite being already well known and admired through the success of his first work, the short story "Poor Folk". The sentence was commuted and instead he spent five years in a Siberian jail, where he read Dickens and was converted to Russian Orthodox Christianity. His writing looks at the dark side of late nineteenth-century life, with novels such as *Crime and Punishment* (1866), *The Idiot* (1868), and *The Brothers Karamazov* (1880).

Above: *Women at the new Central Telephone Exchange in London; the female workforce is gradually increasing.*

Egyptian Nationalism

Nationalist revolt led by Ahmed Arabi (Arabi Pasha) breaks out against European influence in Egypt, imitating the fundamentalist Mahdi revolt in the Sudan. In September 1882, the British army defeats the Egyptians at Tel-el-Kebir and occupies Cairo, establishing full Anglo-French control of the country. Faced with the more powerful revolt in the Sudan, Britain decides, in November 1883, to withdraw from the Sudan.

Black Colleges

The Atlanta Baptist Female Seminary (Spelman Institute) opens in Georgia, USA, and becomes the leading American college for black women. Booker T Washington (1856–1915) founds the Tuskegee Institute, a pioneering school enabling black Americans to learn practical skills.

"Jim Crow" Laws

The first "Jim Crow" law is enacted in Tennessee, introducing segregation for black people on public transport. The laws are tolerated by the US Congress provided that "equal carriage space is made available for whites and Negroes". The term "Jim Crow" is taken from a popular "nigger minstrel" song.

Portrait of a Lady

Of the early works by American novelist Henry James (1843–1916), the novel *Portrait of a Lady* will prove the most enduring success. It describes in telling detail the fate of various Americans transplanted to Europe.

An Asylum for Old Men

Max Liebermann (1827–1935) brings a new realism to German painting, taking as his subjects the inmates of asylums and orphanages in Amsterdam and the peasants in the fields of Germany.

Savoy Theatre

The Savoy Theatre is the first public building in England to be lit by electricity. Electric lighting will have an enormous impact on the theatre, transforming the way plays look on stage, and giving directors a new vocabulary of scene-setting and mood-creation. The first, albeit simple, electric lighting appears at the Savoy.

Blueprints

The term "blueprint" is coined as the result of a copying process invented by Marion & Co. of London, UK. The "ferro-prussiate" process results in documents which show white details on a blue background, hence the common name.

Lesbian Nightclubs

The first lesbian nightclubs and restaurants in the Western world are reported in Paris, France.

HYDRAULIC EXCAVATOR

Alexandra dock in Hull, England, witnesses the first application of an excavating machine operated by the pressure of liquid. Hydraulics, which translate mechanical energy via the pressurization of water or other liquids to remote workings, will become a commonplace phenomenon.

ELECTRIC POWER STATION

The inauspicious town of Godalming in Surrey, England, becomes the location of the first station for the production of electrical power. The generator, built by Siemens, is turned by the waters of the River Wey, to produce electricity for public and domestic consumption.

SMASH SHOT

Ernest and William Renshaw burst upon the tennis scene with the unknown smash shot. They help to boost the sport's popularity during a decade of dominance at Wimbledon. This year too sees the creation of the United States National Lawn Tennis Association.

ICE YACHTING

The Ice Yacht Challenge Pennant, America's most prestigious prize for ice yachting, is introduced. The sport, pioneered by the Dutch in the eighteenth century, is popular among the rich along the Hudson river. It spreads to the Great Lakes, where smaller yachts, mounted on skates to ride on the ice, are used.

Mary Seacole
1805–1881

Crimean nurse Mary Seacole has died. She was born in Kingston, Jamaica, the child of a Scottish man and his freed-slave wife. Mary's mother taught her the arts of Creole midwifery and herbal medicine, which she had learnt in Africa. She cared for patients during the Panamanian cholera epidemic of 1850 and immediately volunteered for service when the Crimean War broke out in 1853. After initial rejection, she managed to set up a canteen for British regiments in Balaclava and became known for the brave way in which she cared for the sick and the dying on the battlefield, giving not only medical care but also much needed human comfort. After the war she spent her life between Kingston and London, and became masseuse to the Princess of Wales.

Below: *Queen Victoria presents honours to the British veterans of the Zulu Wars and the Afghanistan campaign.*

LEISURE AND PLEASURE

THE WEALTHY HAVE always enjoyed leisure, but the late 1800s sees the increase of leisure time for the working and middle classes. In the UK, bank holidays, which were introduced in 1871 and 1875, give everyone time off to enjoy themselves with their families. The rise of affordable transport, courtesy of the railway, and the advent of the bicycle means that communal days out in the country or at the seaside are regular treats for all but the most desperately poor. The racecourse becomes a favourite venue for people from all walks of life.

Above: *A day out in the country for children who live the rest of the year in towns.*

Above: *The Sport of Kings at Ascot racecourse.*
Below: *Crowds on their way back from Derby Day.*

Above: *Learning to swim at Brighton.*
Below: *The Milk Fair in St James's Park, London.*

Left: *Messing about in boats during the annual regatta held at Henley-on-Thames.*

Below: *A large crowd spending a quiet Sunday in the park.*

Below: *The diving raft, central to a good holiday by the sea.*

THE PHOENIX PARK MURDERS

ENIANS, IRISH NATIONALISTS, murder the chief secretary and under-secretary of Ireland. Congress imposes immigration restrictions on Chinese labourers entering the United States. An underground telephone cable is laid in Massachusetts, USA. The first standardized camera film is invented. Counselling as a therapy for emotional trauma is pioneered. The Berlin Philharmonic Orchestra is founded. Evolutionist Charles Darwin and Italian nationalist Garibaldi die.

⇝ 1882 ⇜

JAN	22	Italy introduces electoral reform
MAR	29	France makes primary education free and compulsory
MAY	2	In Ireland, Charles Parnell is freed from jail
	6	Fenian extremists assassinate Lord Frederick Cavendish, chief secretary of Ireland, and his under-secretary in Phoenix Park, Dublin
	6	Chinese Exclusion Act restricts Chinese immigration into the USA
	20	Italy joins an alliance with Austria and Germany
	22	USA secures trade rights in Korea
JUNE	12	Arabi Pasha leads riots in Alexandria, Egypt

AUG	29	Australia defeats England in cricket test match: a bail is burned to signify the "ashes of English cricket"
SEP	13	Arabi Pasha's forces are defeated by a British army
	15	British occupy Cairo, Egypt
NOV	9	Dual Franco-British control of Egypt is ended

Above: *A lunatic makes a failed attempt on Queen Victoria's life.*

FRENCH EDUCATION

France introduces non-sectarian, free, compulsory primary education in an effort to remove Church influence from daily life and to ensure the country keeps up with the expanding and economically powerful German empire.

PHOENIX PARK MURDERS

The chief secretary of Ireland, Lord Frederick Cavendish, and the under-secretary, TH Burke, are both murdered in Phoenix Park, Dublin, by Fenians campaigning for an independent Ireland. The murders force the British government to maintain coercion in Ireland, overturning the Kilmainham Agreement of March 1881 with Parnell, leader of the Irish nationalists, which was designed to bring peace in return for land reform.

SUBTERRANEAN CABLE

The Telephone Despatch Co. of Massachusetts lays an 8km (5mi) stretch of telephone cable underground. Despite the work involved, subterranean cables are less susceptible to damage than those elevated on poles and become an essential feature of the communications infrastructure.

Above: *The Highlanders charge at Tel-el-Kebir, Egypt, bringing victory to the British side.*

WOMAN TO INVESTIGATE NATIVE AMERICAN CONDITIONS

American writer Helen Hunt Jackson, author of *A Century of Dishonour*, an influential book describing the abuse of Native Americans by the US government, is appointed special commissioner to investigate living conditions among the Mission Indians of California.

US RESTRICTS IMMIGRATION

The Chinese Exclusion Treaty is signed between the US and Chinese governments to restrict the entrance and naturalization of immigrants into the USA from China. Academics and travellers are not affected, but the treaty severely restricts the influx of labourers, who have been entering at a rate of 10 000 a year since 1870. The US Congress prohibits Chinese immigration for ten years, and, in August, bars criminals, paupers and the insane from entering the country. Both measures reflect national unease about the extent of unlimited immigration and its impact on jobs.

Above: *Ahmed Arabi Pasha, who declares a Holy War against Egypt and invokes the wrath of the British.*

Below: *British General Sir Garnet Wolseley (in glasses) sends telegrams to England announcing victory in Egypt.*

AIRBRUSH
The principle of applying paint using a fine jet of air is invented by American Abner Peeler. Having sold the idea to form the Rockford Airbrush Co., its first application is for tinting monochrome photographs, previously coloured using hand brushes.

CAMERA FILM
The first standardized film for cameras is invented and manufactured by Alfred Pumphrey, English photographer. Using a gelatine emulsion coating, his film plates can be used in any plate camera and go a long way towards making photography more convenient and therefore more popular.

FAMINE AND DROUGHT
Crop failures cause famine in Japan, and drought continues for the second year in the USA.

CURING HYSTERIA
Josef Breuer (1842–1925), an Austrian physician, pioneers the cathartic method of curing hysteria — encouraging patients to relive traumatic scenes from their past — and creates a landmark in the treatment of mental illness.

BROOKLYN SUSPENSION
Brooklyn Bridge over New York's East river is the first significant suspension bridge that has cables of parallel steel wires spun *in situ*, a method that will be used on many other suspension bridges in years to come.

BAR AT THE FOLLIES-BERGERES

French artist Edouard Manet (1832–83) cleverly uses a mirror to show the nightclub setting of his painting, while concentrating on the foreground figure of the bar-maid. He provides a new take on the social setting of the Impressionists.

TRIPLE ALLIANCE

Germany, Austro-Hungary and Italy sign the Triple Alliance, tying the countries closely together. The alliance will remain in force until 1915.

BERLIN PHILHARMONIC ORCHESTRA FOUNDED

An orchestra that will dominate the life of classical music in Europe is founded. The Berlin Philharmonic will attract some of the world's greatest conductors, such as Nikisch, Furtwängler and Karajan.

LECTURES ON THE DECORATIVE ARTS

Irish playwright Oscar Wilde (1854–1900) explains the aesthetic movement in his lectures. The notions he explains, such as the idea of art for art's sake, although not new, attract attention and are the key to much cultural activity at the turn of the century.

TERRE VERGINE

Italian writer and political leader Gabriele D'Annunzio (1863–1938) publishes his first collection of short stories and is established as a writer of note, of the realistic tradition in Italy. A (second) volume of poems also appears this year.

Above: *Innovative cables of steel wire are put in place on the Brooklyn Suspension Bridge.*

Charles Darwin
1809–1882

The English naturalist Charles Robert Darwin has died. Having initially studied medicine, Darwin considered entering the Church but his interest in natural history led to his being recommended to join a scientific survey on HMS *Beagle* in South American waters (1831–36) and he never looked back. His studies of flora and fauna led him to develop the theory of natural selection or evolution. Other scientists were independently coming to similar views at the time, and Darwin and Alfred Wallace published their theories in papers read to the Linnaean Society on the same day in 1858. Darwin's great work on evolution, *The Origin of Species by Means of Natural Selection*, was published in 1859. His later work *The Descent of Man and Selection in Relation to Sex* (1871) places man in relation to the apes. Darwin also published several works on plants and *The Formation of Vegetable Mould through the Action of Worms* (1881), which describes the work of the earthworm, "nature's ploughman".

Guiseppe Garibaldi
1807–1882

The Italian nationalist and popular hero Garibaldi has died. He learned the art of guerrilla fighting while in exile in South America from 1836–48, and the Battle of Sant' Antonio of 1846 earned him fame in Europe, partly fanned by the writer Alexandre Dumas. Returning home with his volunteer army, Garibaldi aligned himself with Mazzini in the Italian independence struggle. From 1858, with the backing of Cavour, he became a nationalist leader of the Risorgimento, and at the head of his army of the One Thousand Red Shirts fought to reunite Italy. A military alliance under Victor Emmanuel II of Sardinia eventually secured unification, with Garibaldi conquering Naples and Sicily for the king in 1860. Towards the end of his colourful life he had begun to espouse pacifism, disillusioned with the way in which war seldom achieves the effects desired. He championed the rights of workers and women, was in favour of racial equality and against capital punishment, and was a religious free-thinker.

Above: *Success for the first lady wrangler (qualified mathematician) at Newnham College, Cambridge.*

Above: *Pifre's power plant harnesses solar power to drive a small printing press.*

Above: *The tourist becomes part of the scenery. Personally conducted guided tours, as here in Paris, are proving very popular with British holiday makers.*

AMERICAN FOOTBALL GAINS DOWNS

The concept of downs enters American football. Teams now have three opportunities — downs — to move the ball 4.5m (5yd) or they have to surrender possession to the other side.

BIRTH OF THE "ASHES"

Australia hands England their first-ever defeat in a test match. The death of English cricket is proclaimed, a bail is burnt and the ashes placed in a vial. For years to come English and Australian cricketers will continue to compete for the "Ashes".

Henry Wadsworth Longfellow
1807–1882

The American poet Longfellow has died. He was educated at Bowdoin College in Brunswick, Maine, where he was in the same class as writer Nathaniel Hawthorne. He spent three years in Europe before becoming Professor of Foreign Languages at Bowdoin College from 1829–35. Subsequently he was Professor of Modern Languages and Literature at Harvard from 1836–54. One of his best-known works is the epic poem *The Song of Hiawatha*, written in the metre of a Finnish epic. Poems such as *The Village Blacksmith* and *The Wreck of the Hesperus* ensure him a place in every golden treasury.

THE AGE OF MOTORING BEGINS — SLOWLY

THE FIRST PETROL-DRIVEN CAR JOURNEY takes place in France. The spark plug, essential to successful motoring, is invented. The first successful appendectomy is carried out. The machine gun is invented. "Buffalo Bill" Cody's Wild West Show goes on the road. German philosopher Friedrich Nietzsche publishes *Thus Spake Zarathustra*, and influental political thinker Karl Marx dies in London.

✳ 1883 ✳

JAN	16	USA begins reform of its civil service
APR	16	Paul Kruger becomes president of the South African Republic
	24	Germany begins colonizing South West Africa (now Namibia)
JUNE	1	France goes to war with Madagascar
AUG	25	Annam and Tonkin, in Indochina, become French protectorates
	27	Krakatoa volcano explodes, Indonesia; resulting tsunami kills 36 000 people
OCT	20	Peru cedes territory to Chile
	30	Austria and Romania form a secret alliance against Russia
NOV	5	The Mahdi, a Sudanese prophet, defeats an Egyptian army under British command at El Obeid

Above: *Queen Mohilla of Madagascar protected by her attendants.*

Right: *The trial in Dublin of the men involved in the Phoenix Park murders, the fatal stabbing of Lord Frederick Cavendish, the Irish chief secretary, and TH Burke, his under-secretary. The accused men, members of a gang known as the "Invincibles" are betrayed by their leader, James Carey.*

METROPOLITAN OPERA

The Metropolitan Opera House in New York opens with Gounod's *Faust*. The most important opera house in the United States, it is funded initially by William H Vanderbilt. The Metropolitan will soon be attracting the world's greatest singers and establishing itself as one of the world's top operatic venues.

FRENCH INDOCHINA

Fighting between the French and Sino-Vietnamese forces, including the bombardment of Hue, finally results in the establishment of French Indochina.

PETROL-FUELLED CAR

The first petrol-fuelled car hits the road. Frenchman Edouard Delamare-Debourteville (1856–1901) modifies an eight-horsepower gas engine to accept a vaporized jet of petrol or gasoline and takes his "car" on a shaky journey down a country lane.

SPARK PLUG

The essential component of the petrol engine, the spark plug, is invented by Frenchman Etienne Lenoir (1822–1900). The significance is that it is a standardized component for his engine, making it easy to replace with a new one during running repairs.

Karl Marx
1818–1883

The German political theorist Karl Marx has died in London. As a young militant atheist, he lived in Paris (1843–45) where he met his associate Friedrich Engels, joined the communists, and began to develop his analysis of capitalism and its internal contradictions. Marx and Engels drafted the *Communist Manifesto* (published 1848), with its clarion call, "the workers have nothing to lose but their chains". In 1849, Marx and his family became refugees in England, where he was a founder of the International Workingmen's Association (the First International) in 1864 and toiled daily in the British Museum Library on his critique of capitalism, *Das Kapital,* (volume 1 published in 1867, volumes 2 and 3 edited and translated by Engels and published after his death). His core theory was that class struggle is the agency of historical change, and that capitalism will be succeeded by Communism which, out of historical necessity, will become a dominant force in world history.

Above: *Queen Victoria and her highland ghillie John Brown, who becomes her trusted adviser.*

THUS SPAKE ZARATHUSTRA

The influential German philosopher Friedrich Nietzsche (1844–1900) publishes *Thus Spake Zarathustra*, his best-known book. In it, he outlines the key concepts for which he will remain famous — the superman, the will to power and the death of God.

RAILWAY LINKS COLONIES

Eventual union of the British colonies is advanced by the opening of a railway connecting Melbourne in Victoria and Sydney in New South Wales, the first rail link between any of the colonies.

TREASURE ISLAND

This romantic adventure story is one of the books that establishes the name of Scottish author Robert Louis Stevenson (1850–94). *Treasure Island* introduces a host of characters, from the marooned seaman to the one-legged pirate, that will influence future stories of the sea and entertain young people for decades.

RHAPSODY ESPANA

The high spirits of composer Alexis Emmanuel Chabrier (1841–1940) bring something new to French music. As well as an appreciation of other cultures, Chabrier's music brings a style that will influence later composers such as Ravel.

KRAKATOA EXPLODES

The Krakatoa volcano, in the Sunda strait between Java and Sumatra, erupts in the biggest known explosion of modern times.

BOYS' BRIGADE

The Boys' Brigade, the first youth organization, is founded in Glasgow, Scotland, by William Smith, a Sunday School teacher, who applies military organization to boys attending his Sunday schools.

Richard Wagner
1813–1883

The German composer and conductor Richard (Wilhelm) Wagner has died in Venice. Wagner made a unique contribution to music, conceiving huge and ambitious operatic works that enfold his principles of the essential unity of music and drama. Despite some early achievements as a conductor, and successful performances of his works, it was not until he was in his 50s that true recognition and more consistent success came to him. Apart from *The Ring* his works include *Rienzi* (1838–40), written in a debtors' jail in Paris, *The Flying Dutchman* (1841), *Tristan and Isolde* (1857–59), *The Mastersingers of Nuremberg* (1862–67) and *Parsifal* (1878–82). In 1870, after the death of his wife Minna, he married Liszt's daughter Cosima, who was already the mother of his three children. Wagner wrote several works of music theory (including *Opera and Drama*, 1850–51, and *The Music of the Future*, 1860), as well as developing the themes of his operas and writing the poetical libretti himself. The theatre he created in Bayreuth, which opened in 1876 with a complete 15-hour performance of his operatic cycle *The Ring (Der Ring des Nibelungen)*, is a living memorial to his work.

LES FLAMANDES

Belgian poet Emile Verhaeren (1855–1916) launches his career with this volume. It contains realistic descriptions of Flemish peasant life, on which he will build in later socially concerned, and socialist, verses.

WILD WEST SHOW

"Buffalo Bill" Cody (1846–1917), former Indian fighter, buffalo hunter and rider for the Pony Express, opens a Wild West Show in Nebraska, staging sharpshooting, cattle-handling and mock hold-ups of stagecoaches.

Right: *French illustrator, painter, sculptor and caricaturist Gustave Doré dies this year aged 51.*

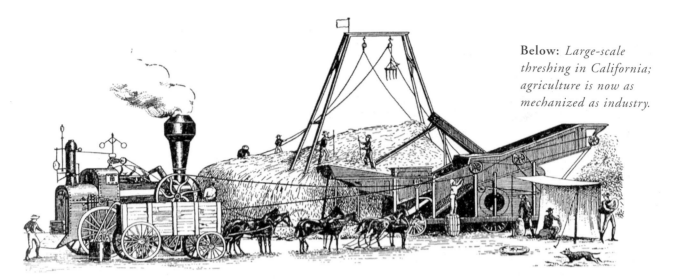

Below: *Large-scale threshing in California; agriculture is now as mechanized as industry.*

APPENDECTOMY

A twelve-year-old boy becomes the first person to have his life saved by the removal of his infected appendix. Dr Abraham Groves (1847–1935) performs the operation in Ontario. It is a complete success but is not hailed as a significant breakthrough at the time.

ARTIFICIAL FIBRE

Sir Joseph Swan (1828–1914) invents an artificial fibre from cellulose whilst working on alternative filaments for his electric light bulbs. His "artificial silk" sees some experimental application, but will be superseded by superior synthetics before any commercial application is considered.

VASECTOMY

French surgeon, Felix Gruyon, inadvertently invents this means of birth control whilst performing a prostate operation. He snips the man's vas deferens, believing it may help limit any post-operative problems, not realizing the contraceptive consequences of his actions.

Above: *The wide prairies of Dakota. The US, Canada and Australia are producing wheat on a huge scale.*

STOUGHTON HOUSE

HH Richardson (1838–86) clads this large, timber-framed house in wooden shingles. Shingle-clad houses have been popular for some time, but Stoughton House in Cambridge, Massachusetts, is one of the biggest, showing the influence of a vernacular style on larger buildings.

MACHINE GUN

Hiram Maxim (1840–1916) patents the first fully automatic machine gun.

Sojourner Truth
c. 1797–1883

American civil rights and women's suffrage activist Sojourner Truth has died. Born a slave in Ulster County, New York State, she became an evangelist preacher after she gained her freedom and settled in New York, changing her name (originally Isabella Van Wagener) in 1843. She soon took up the causes of abolition and women's rights and always drew crowds to listen to her compelling speeches. After the Civil War, Abraham Lincoln made her counsellor to the freed slaves of Washington. She finally retired in 1875, aged nearly 80.

Above: *Testing the Maxim gun, a water-cooled, belt-fed weapon with 7.69mm (.303in) ammunition.*

EUROPE BEGINS TO CARVE UP AFRICA

ORTUGAL AND BRITAIN settle their differences over colonial possessions in Africa. European powers at an international conference in Germany carve up Africa between them. Democrat Grover Cleveland wins the US presidential election. The first controlled glider flight takes place and a high-speed steam turbine is invented. The anaesthetic properties of cocaine are discovered. A roller-coaster draws the crowds at Coney Island, near New York.

✺ 1884 ✺

JAN	18	British General Charles Gordon arrives in Egypt to supervise the Egyptian evacuation of Sudan; the Mahdi refuses talks
	27	Britain redefines the status of the South African Republic, saying it cannot make treaties without British consent
MAR	17	Austria, Germany and Russia renew their alliance
APR	4	Bolivia yields the Atacama region to Chile
MAY	17	The USA puts Alaska under the same laws as Oregon

JUNE	28	International conference lasting until August 2 discusses Egyptian finances
OCT	13	The Mahdi captures Omdurman, in Sudan
NOV	4	Grover Cleveland (Democrat) is elected US president
	15	Berlin conference agrees to abolish slavery in Africa
DEC	10	General Porfirio Diaz becomes president of Mexico

Above: *Biodegradable wicker coffins are exhibited by Seymour Haden, an early conservationist.*

Above: *The vogue for lawn tennis has not faded, and the Wimbledon tournament attracts up to 3000 spectators.*

EUROPEAN POWERS DIVIDE UP AFRICA

Britain and Portugal agree to settle their colonial differences in Africa in order to forestall German expansion in Africa, although Germany takes over the Cameroons and South West Africa during the year. In July, Britain establishes a protectorate over Somalia in order to protect sea routes to India from possible German expansion in East Africa. Over the next seven years, a number of agreements between Portugal and Britain define their colonial boundaries across southern Africa. In November, the European powers, meeting in conference in Berlin, carve up Africa between them, settling control of the Congo, slavery and other issues. In February 1885, Leopold II of Belgium establishes the Congo as his personal state.

DIAZ REGAINS POWER

Porfiro Diaz, president of Mexico from 1876 to 1880, regains power and intensifies his drive to modernize Mexico by introducing liberal economic policies while at the same time keeping strong control over the government and the army, thus ensuring stability.

CLEVELAND WINS

Democratic candidate Grover Cleveland (1837–1908), governor of New York, wins the US presidential election against his Republican opponent, James Blaine of Maine. In the highly personal campaign, Republicans attack Cleveland, a bachelor, for having an illegitimate child. In June 1886, Cleveland marries the young daughter of his former business partner, 25 years his junior.

Left: *Stephen Grover Cleveland is elected president; he will serve two non-consecutive terms.*

CONTROLLED GLIDER FLIGHT

John Montgomery of California makes the first controlled glider flight. He flies some 183m (200yd) at a speed of approximately 29km/h (18mph), but evidently he is not taken by the experience as it is recorded as his one and only flight. It is left to others to develop aviation techniques.

STEAM TURBINE

A seminal moment in the generation of energy occurs with the invention of the high-speed steam turbine by Charles Parsons of Gateshead, England. The conversion of combusted energy into steam, and then into mechanical energy by turning a turbine, is still used for producing electricity.

Gregor Johann Mendel
1822–1884

Abbot Mendel, the Austrian monk and botanist, has died. As a result of experiments with plants in the monastery gardens, Mendel formulated the Law of Independent Assortment (known as Mendel's Law) and the Law of Segregation. The significance of his understanding of organic inheritance and the behaviour of cells in reproduction, first published in 1865 as the result of studies performed on the hybridization of peas, is unrecognized at his death, but will prove to be the basis of the science of genetics.

Above: *Demonstrations in support of the Third Reform Bill currently going through the British parliament.*

Above: *Science is being taught in English state schools and the relevant equipment is provided for keen learners.*

The Adventures of Huckleberry Finn
American novelist Mark Twain produces a masterwork in this novel, his sequel to *Tom Sawyer*. In *The Adventures of Huckleberry Finn*, Twain pushes forward American fiction in several ways — adding to the myth of the frontier, and analyzing slavery and other American ways of life, using the "innocent" narrator.

Une Baignade, Asnieres
This is the first major pointillist picture by French artist Georges Seurat (1859–91). Working on a huge scale, Seurat applies paint in tiny dots of colour which, according to the scientific theory current at the time, are supposed to blend "in the eye". The painting puts Seurat firmly at the head of the avant-garde.

Cocaine
Austrian Karl Koller discovers anaesthetic properties of cocaine whilst working with the drug as a treatment for morphine addiction. The substance will be used ubiquitously for analgesic purposes until more sophisticated chemical compounds are developed.

Manon
In his greatest opera, *Manon*, composer Jules Massenet (1842–95) introduces Wagnerian techniques such as the *leitmotiv* to France, but clothes them in melodies and harmonies that are typically French.

A Rebours
Joris Karl Huysmans' character Des Esseintes becomes the archetype of decadence, a man who overcomes boredom by trying more and more exotic pleasures. The work sets the style for a literary movement. It also bolsters the reputation of Mallarmé, whom Des Esseintes reads.

Wolf's Comet
German astronomer, Max Wolf (1863–1932) discovers a little-known comet named after him. The comet has a period (the time span for it to complete one elliptical orbit of the sun) of only seven years, which is incredibly short in relative terms.

Greenwich Mean Time
Greenwich, near London, England, is designated the site of the Earth's prime meridian, longitude 0°, by the International Prime Meridian Conference in Washington, USA. All longitudes and times will be calculated in relation to a line through Greenwich.

Fungal Control
Bordeaux mixture, invented by a French botanist, Pierre M Alexis Millardet (1838–1902), proves to be effective against fungal diseases which attack vines, and against potato blight.

King Cophetua and the Beggar Maid
Sombre colours, graceful composition, and fine detail show the French influence on Edward Burne-Jones (1833–98) in this famous canvas, based on an old ballad. He conjures up a dream world far away from the bright colours of Pre-Raphaelitism.

Roller-coaster
The first roller-coaster, invented by a schoolteacher, Lemarcus A Thompson, opens at Coney Island, a recreation centre near New York.

Fountain Pen
The first practical fountain pen with capillary feed is invented by a US insurance man, Lewis E Waterman.

Cetewayo
c. 1826–1884

The last king of the Zulus has died. Having victoriously led his spear-wielding army in the defence of Zululand against the British in 1879, he was captured at Ulundi later that year and held prisoner. He begged to be allowed to plead to Queen Victoria for freedom and for the Zulu cause, and in England he impressed all with his dignity. In 1883 he was restored as king to a diminished territory from which he was promptly driven out by new chiefs who refused to accept his authority. He became a fugitive and died of a heart attack seeking the protection of British residents of Eshowe. His grave in the forest of Nkandla will become a Zulu sacred place.

HOLY WAR IN THE SUDAN

AFTER RAISING A REVOLT against Anglo-Egyptian rule of the Sudan in 1881, Muhammad Ahmad Ibn 'Abdallah (1840–85), or the Mahdi — the "divinely guided one", as he is known — sweeps the whole country before him, encircling the British army of General Charles "Chinese" Gordon (1833–85), who has been sent to evacuate British residents from Khartoum. A British relief force arrives two days after Gordon's death, and evacuates the Sudan, which becomes independent of all foreign control.

Above: General Gordon departs from London's Charing Cross on his mission to the Sudan.

Right above: General Gordon arrives at Khartoum. His orders are to evacuate the British citizens there.

Above: British cavalry visit the site of a battlefield in the Sudan.

Right below: Gordon's last stand. The Mahdi's troops storm Khartoum and Gordon is killed.

✶ Key Battles ✶

• ABU KLEA **January 17, 1885**
While attempting to reach Khartoum, a force of 1500 troops under Sir Herbert Stewart (1843–85) is attacked by 5000 Mahdists from a force of 12 000. In the fighting, the British suffer 168 casualties, one of whom is Colonel Frederick Burnaby (1842–85). The Mahdists suffer 1100 killed.

• KHARTOUM **January 26, 1885**
Having surrounded Khartoum, the Mahdists storm it and kill General Gordon. A British relief force in gunboats arrives two days later.

• KIRBEKAN **February 10, 1885**
General William Earle (1833–85) leads 1000 troops in a charge against a strong Mahdist force holding the heights of Kirbekan. The British carry the heights for 60 killed, including the general.

• TOFREK **March 22, 1885**
About 5000 Mahdists attack 2000 British and Indian troops under General McNeill (1831–1904) and break into their improvised position. In a violent 20-minute battle they are repulsed, suffering 1500 killed to British casualties of 470.

Above: General Gordon's head is cut off after his death as a trophy for the supporters of the Mahdi.

THE SIEGE OF KHARTOUM

EUROPEAN POWERS, INCLUDING GERMANY, Britain, and France continue to seize possessions in Africa in what becomes known as the "scramble for Africa". General Gordon is killed at the Siege of Khartoum, which is recaptured by a British relief force. Serbia invades Bulgaria but is repulsed. Austrian intervention ends the fighting. The Indian National Congress is formed. Pasteur successfully uses an anti-rabies vaccine.

Above: Lord Salisbury takes over from Gladstone as British prime minister.

❧ 1885 ❧

JAN	26	Dervishes led by the Mahdi take Khartoum, Sudan, killing General Charles Gordon
	28	British relief force recaptures Khartoum
FEB	2	Belgian Congo founded as personal possession of Leopold II
	25	Germany annexes Tanganyika and Zanzibar
MAR	4	Grover Cleveland is inaugurated as the 22nd US president
MAY	17	Germany annexes Bismarck Archipelago and northern New Guinea
JUNE	19	In Britain, Prime Minister William Gladstone (Liberal) resigns
	22	The Mahdi dies, aged 40; succeeded as Dervish leader by the Khalifa, Abdullah el Taashi
	24	Lord Salisbury (Conservative) becomes British prime minister
JULY	23	Former US President Ulysses S Grant dies
	30	Dervishes take Kassala, and now control most of Sudan
OCT	22	King Thibaw of Burma rejects British request to stop interfering with trade; Third Burmese War begins
NOV	13	Serbia invades Bulgaria
	23	Liberals gain most seats in British general election, but do not have an overall majority; Lord Salisbury remains prime minister
	28	British capture Mandalay, Burma; Thibaw surrenders
DEC	18	Indian National Congress is formed

INDIAN NATIONAL CONFERENCE
During the year, the first meeting of the Indian National Congress is held. The idea of forming an organization to regenerate and unify India came in a speech by a retired British civil servant, AO Hume, at Calcutta University in 1883. The new organization is initially dominated by Anglo-Indians and is conservative in its approach, but it slowly begins to become more radical in its demands.

LAND-GRABBING IN AFRICA
Germany annexes Tanganyika and Zanzibar, establishing a large colonial presence in the region. A scramble for colonies in Africa and the Pacific occurs as Britain annexes Bechuanaland, and later Nigeria. France grabs Madagascar and Germany takes northern New Guinea and many Pacific islands.

AUSTRALIAN TROOPS LEAVE FOR THE SUDAN
Troops leave Australia for the Sudan to fight against the Mahdi. They are the first Australian troops sent overseas to fight for the British Empire.

BRITISH INVADE BURMA
Following the Burmese confiscation of Bombay traders' property, the British invade and occupy Upper Burma. They annexe the entire country in January 1887.

Above: *Russia clashes with Afghanistan in a border dispute which is settled by negotiation in 1886.*

SERB-BULGARIAN WAR
Serbia, unhappy with its territorial boundaries, demands that Bulgaria give up territory. A Serbian force under King Milan I invades Bulgaria. The Bulgarians under Prince Alexander and General Stambolov counter attack and drive the Serbians back. Austria, as Serbia's protector, intervenes and is able to bring a halt to the fighting.

DICTIONARY OF NATIONAL BIOGRAPHY
English philosopher Leslie Stephen (1820–1904) begins the *Dictionary of National Biography*, one of the greatest reference-publishing projects ever. The Dictionary aims to chronicle notable Britons and sets the style for biographical recording everywhere.

RABIES VACCINE
Louis Pasteur (1822–95), French microbiologist, injects his vaccine for the deadly disease hydrophobia or rabies into the stomach of Joseph Maister of Alsace, and succeeds in curing him. One of the most feared diseases has been beaten.

Above: *Inspired by Wimbledon, ladies and gentlemen all over England take up the sport of tennis.*

Above: *The Home Insurance Building, Chicago, built using steel made by the Bessemer process.*

WOMAN DRYING HER FEET

French artist Edgar Degas (1834–1917) develops the use of the pastel medium in apparently offhand but wonderfully evocative drawings such as this. Both the "casual" subject matter, and the pastel technique are new.

HOME INSURANCE BUILDING, CHICAGO

As the first true skyscraper, a tall building with a metal framework structure which takes the weight, this is one of the most influential of all buildings. It also establishes Chicago (already a centre of new buildings after the 1871 fire) as the major centre of American architecture.

EVAPORATED MILK

The Helvetia Milk Condensing Co. in the USA starts the first commercial production of evaporated milk.

THE ARABIAN NIGHTS

Explorer and adventurer Richard Burton's celebrated translation of *The Arabian Nights*, a vast collection of Arabic popular stories, fuels the current fashion for things oriental and is highly successful. His work of translation will continue until 1888.

Above: *The powerhouse of Paddington station. The generators are used to produce electricity for light.*

JOHN TWACHTMAN RETURNS TO NORTH AMERICA

After a period of study in Europe, American artist John Twachtman (1853–1902) returns to the USA, where he paints in a style derived from both the Impressionists and his fellow-countryman James McNeill Whistler. Twachtman becomes known as one of the most prominent US Impressionists.

SAVE WILDLIFE

The National Audubon Society is organized by an American naturalist, George Bird Grinnell, to protest against the commercial hunting of birds and the indiscriminate slaughter of wildlife.

Above: *General Gordon, whose death at Khartoum inspires much public outrage and distress.*

Above: *War correspondent for the* Daily News, *Mr HH Pearse, gets first-hand experience of his subject.*

TINNED TREACLE
Abram Lyle, Scottish sugar refiner, of Tate and Lyle fame, produces canned treacle for the first time. It is marketed as "golden syrup" and becomes a highly valued product at a time when sugar in pure form is a relatively unfamiliar concept.

FINGERPRINTING
A fingerprint identification system is devised by an English scientist, Francis Galton (1822–1911), who demonstrates that people have the same fingerprints for life, and that no two people have the same fingerprints.

WOMEN AT WIMBLEDON
Women tennis players compete for the first time at the All-England Championship at Wimbledon. Their movement is limited by their dress: petticoats, stiff collars and cuffs, and long skirts.

RIJKSMUSEUM, AMSTERDAM
The Dutch national museum, which has existed for some decades as a collection, is given its permanent home and is officially opened as the Rijksmuseum. Its collections of Dutch art are unparalleled.

Left: *Battle of Little Red Deer River, part of the rebellion led by the French Canadian Louis Riel.*

HOCKEY ASSOCIATION FOUNDED
The Amateur Hockey Association of Canada is founded in Montreal.

CREMATORIUM
With the growth of populations it becomes inevitable that a clinical means for the disposal of corpses is developed. Woking, a town in southern England, sees the first purpose-built crematorium, but the idea of burning remains takes a while to become accepted as ethically sound.

CARBURETTOR
One of the most fundamental components of the petrol engine, the carburettor, is developed by German engineers, Karl Benz (1844–1929) and Gottlieb Daimler (1834–1900). It mixes vaporized petrol with air to provide the ideal mixture for efficient internal combustion.

VICTORIAN WOMEN

THE CENTURY SEES a huge change in the way people dress. In the early 1800s, all but the most reactionary of men give up knee breeches and take to the full-length trouser. Women begin the century literally caged in the hoops of their crinoline costumes, but fashions change radically over the years so that by the end of it, they too, are wearing the trousers. Fashion's "whim" is actually dictated by huge technological and sociological changes. Industrialization, urbanisation and the advent of official "leisure time" for all classes play their part.

Above: *Victorian fashion styles from the crinoline of 1884 (left) to the "aesthetic"dress of the 1890s (right).*

Above: *After Sunday church, the fashionable classes meet to exchange greetings and show off their fine clothes.*

Left: *Fierce corsets create the desired silhouette of the late 1800s, a tiny waist and a generous bosom.*

Above: *A debutante of the 1890s tries on some "fascinating hats" to wear at a Royal charity bazaar.*

Left: *Princess Mary (1867–1953) who is to marry Prince George (later George V) in 1893, buys her wedding trousseau under the sartorial guidance of her mother.*

Below: *A selection of corsets, basques and "unmentionable" underwear worn by the fashion-conscious Victorian woman.*

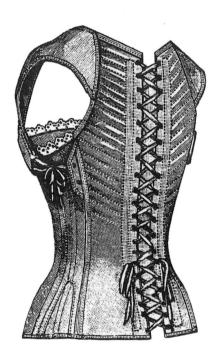

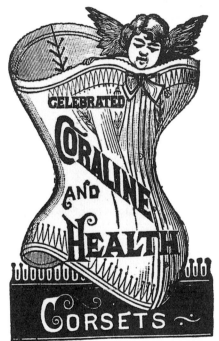

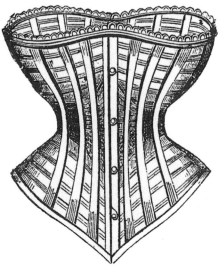

GIVE ME YOUR TIRED, YOUR POOR

THE STATUE OF LIBERTY, with its inscribed plaque welcoming immigrants to the United States, is unveiled in New York harbour. The Home Rule Bill for Ireland is defeated in the British parliament, sparking a political crisis. In the US, Apache chief, Geronimo, finally surrenders, bringing to an end the last major Indian War. An automatic dishwasher is invented. Bloomingdales opens.

❧ 1886 ❧

JAN	1	Britain annexes Upper Burma
	27	British Prime Minister Lord Salisbury resigns after defeat in Parliament
FEB	1	William Gladstone (Liberal) becomes Britain's prime minister again
MAR	3	Serbia and Bulgaria make peace
JUNE	8	Gladstone's government is defeated on Irish Home Rule Bill
	23	France banishes the Bonaparte and Orléans (royal) families
SEP	3	Ruling Prince Alexander of Bulgaria is forced to abdicate
OCT	28	Statue of Liberty (the gift of France) is dedicated in New York harbour

DEC 30 Germany and Portugal agree on frontier between Angola and German South West Africa (now Namibia)

Above: *Raffles Hotel, the crowning glory of the colony of Singapore.*

HOME RULE BILL DEFEATED

The Home Rule Bill, establishing a parliament in Ireland, is defeated in the British parliament, with 93 Liberals voting with the Conservative opposition against their own government. British Prime Minister William Gladstone (1809–98) resigns, and in the following general election, the Conservatives are returned with a huge majority, ushering in a period of continuous Conservative government that will last until 1905.

Above: *Rioting in Belfast, Northern Ireland, as Protestants insist on marching through "Catholic" streets.*

PEARY EXPLORES GREENLAND

American explorer Robert Peary (1856–1920) and his colleague, Matthew Hanson, travel inland from Disko bay over the Greenland ice sheet for 161km (100mi) to 2286m (7500ft) above sea-level.

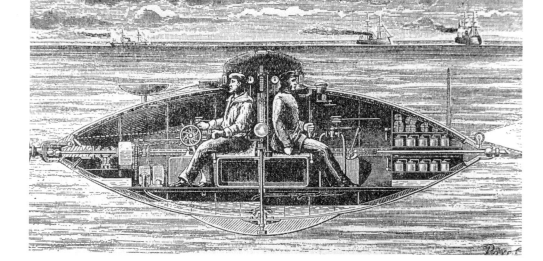

Right: *An electrically-driven submarine. It can remain underwater for eight hours, using the telegraph system to communicate with the surface world.*

Statue of Liberty

The Statue of Liberty, designed by Auguste Bartholdi, built by Gustav Eiffel, and paid for by France, is unveiled and dedicated on Beldoe's island in New York harbour, welcoming the millions of immigrants pouring into the USA from Europe every year.

Federation of Labor

The American Federation of Labor (AFL) is formed out of the Federation of Trades and Labor Unions. The AFL soon becomes the major trades union force in the USA, using the weapon of strikes to improve working conditions for its members.

Geronimo Surrenders

The last major Indian War in the USA ends when the Apache Chief Geronimo surrenders at Skeleton canyon after a decade-long campaign of terror to discourage settlers in New Mexico and Arizona. He and his tribe agree to move to Florida.

Schloss Linderhof, Oberammergau

Georg von Dollmann designs this pseudo-German Rococo house for Ludwig II of Bavaria, the king who adores fantasy palaces and castles.

Above: *Emigrants travelling to the USA in search of opportunity, wealth and happiness.*

Electric-powered Submarine

Constructed by Lieutenant Isaac Peral of Spain, the first electric-powered submarine is launched. In 1887 the Russians will produce a torpedo armed submarine and periscopes will be introduced in other countries.

Final Impressionist Exhibition

The eighth — and final — Impressionist Exhibition takes place. By this time, the Impressionists are looking less united and more diverse. They are still producing good work, but the movement has lost the artistic initiative and the way is open for the various Post-Impressionist styles to flourish.

King Solomon's Mines

A fascination with landscape, wildlife, history, and all that is "other" fuels the adventure novels of British writer H Rider Haggard (1856–1925). *King Solomon's Mines*, probably his best-known work, makes him famous. His books will remain popular for decades.

Above: *The French flag is hoisted on the New Hebrides in the Pacific Ocean.*

Above: *American poet Emily Dickinson dies this year, her work as yet unknown to the public.*

Emily Dickinson
1830–1886

The American recluse Emily Elizabeth Dickinson has died, leaving a huge volume of unpublished poetry, most of which she produced between the ages of 23 and 35. Some poems have been published anonymously, but in general her work is unknown. Her sister publishes three poems in 1890, 1891 and 1896, making Emily's reputation; further volumes are published later. Her mystical, unrhyming lyrics are to have a great influence on modern poetry.

Above: *William Gladstone reaches the climax of his speech in favour of the Home Rule Bill, defeated in Parliament.*

LE SYMBOLISTE

This year sees the founding of *Le Symboliste*, review of the Symbolist movement. The French poets of the Symbolist movement use dreamlike imagery, subjective viewpoints, and musical effects in their work, reacting against the realism and naturalism that has been fashionable in France. They open up a literary route deep into the psyche.

RAFFLES HOTEL

The Raffles Hotel opens in Singapore for the use of colonial administrators from Britain, who have developed the area since 1819 and have made it one of the world's major ports, exporting tin and rubber. The hotel is named for Sir Thomas Stamford Raffles (1781–1826), former governor, who founded the city.

Above: *Joseph Chamberlain, radical Liberal, resigns this year over the Home Rule for Ireland question.*

SMALLBORE CARTRIDGE
The French adopt the first military smallbore smokeless-power cartridge.

ALUMINIUM UTENSILS
With improved methods for producing aluminium, kitchenware is made available, using the "new" metal. Charles Martin Hall brings a range of products onto the market. They are sold as "Wear Ever Cooking Utensils".

DISHWASHER
A machine for cleaning dishes automatically is invented by Mrs WA Cochran of the United States. Having developed the design over a ten-year period, using a steam engine, she finally sells the manufacturing rights to the Crescent Washing Machine Co., in 1889.

ABORTION ILLEGAL
The Netherlands becomes one of the last Western states to make abortion illegal.

FIRST CHESS CHAMPION
Chess master Wilhelm Steinitz, from Bohemia, becomes the world's first chess champion at a world championship held in London, UK.

BRAIN TONIC
John Pemberton of Atlanta, invents his "Esteemed Brain-Tonic and Intellectual Beverage", a liquid containing sugar, extract from coca leaves and other secret ingredients. His product will eventually seduce the global village as Coca-Cola.

BLOOMINGDALE'S OPENS
The three Bloomingdale brothers, who have built up a drapery business, now open Bloomingdale's department store in New York, USA.

WAX POLISH
Johnson's Wax for polishing wood is introduced by an American parquet flooring salesman, Samuel C Johnson.

BAYONET LIGHT BULB
Having independently invented the incandescent filament light bulb, Edison and Swan, working in partnership — United Electric Light Co. — develop their product to be more convenient. The two-pinned bayonet fitting makes their bulbs quick and easy to change.

Franz Liszt
1811–1886

A virtuoso pianist who began performing in public at the age of nine, the Hungarian-born Ferencz (baptized Franciscus) or Franz Liszt has died. Liszt was taught as a young child by Salieri, the teacher of Beethoven and Schubert. He was a performer of massive talent, and also something of a showman; his amours and later adoption of holy orders (1865) were the talk of Europe. He lived in Paris, Weimar and Rome, but also travelled widely. While living in Weimar, he conducted the first performance of Wagner's *Lohengrin*. He was also a much-admired composer. Among his many piano works the *Hungarian Rhapsodies* will be remembered, along with his piano transcripts of operas by Donizetti, Mozart, Tchaikovsky, Verdi and others.

Above: *Prince Alexander of Bulgaria signs his abdication.*
Bulgaria is still part of the Ottoman Empire.

ESPERANTO, ELECTROCARDIOGRAMS AND ETHIOPIA

Q UEEN VICTORIA'S GOLDEN JUBILEE attracts all the major European leaders to celebrations in London. Italy and Ethiopia go to war over Italian imperial ambitions in Ethiopia. Photographic studies of animals in motion are published for the first time. The electrocardiogram, for measuring the activity of the heart, is invented. A universal language, Esperanto, is devised with the hope that it might encourage world peace.

✳ 1887 ✣

JAN	11	Chancellor Otto von Bismarck calls for a bigger German army
	26	Ethiopians defeat Italians at Battle of Dogali
FEB	12	Britain and Italy agree to maintain the status quo in the Mediterranean
	20	Austria, Germany and Italy renew their Triple Alliance
JUNE	17	In The Netherlands, electoral reform doubles the number of voters
	21	Britain's Queen Victoria celebrates her Golden Jubilee
	21	Britain annexes Zululand
JULY	4	Bulgaria elects Ferdinand of Saxe-Coburg as its ruling prince

NOV	13	"Bloody Sunday" in London: Irish agitators riot in Trafalgar Square
DEC	1	China cedes Macao to Portugal
	12	Austria, Britain and Italy agree to maintain the status quo in the Near East

Above: *The first Bloody Sunday at Trafalgar Square, London. Troops suppress an unemployment rally.*

Left: *A billiard saloon for the gold-diggers of Barbeton, South Africa. Often, more money is made by those entertaining the miners than the miners themselves make by digging up nuggets.*

BOULANGER'S COUP FAILS

General Georges Boulanger (1837–91) stages a coup in an attempt to overthrow the republican government. Briefly minister for war in 1886–87, Boulanger gained popularity for his strident attacks on Germany, but his coup fails when it is discovered that despite radical support, he is financed by conservative royalists. The strength of pro-Boulanger sentiment reveals the weakness of political institutions in France.

ITALO-ETHIOPIAN WAR

Italy's colonial ambitions lead to war between Italy and Ethiopia. Italian troops are defeated at the Battle of Dogali but the Italians strengthen their position by backing Meneluk, king of Shoa, against Ethiopian King John IV. In 1889, Italy establishes a protectorate over Ethiopia, with Meneluk becoming Ethiopian emperor.

Jenny Lind
1820–1887

Opera singer Jenny (Johanna) Lind, "the Swedish nightingale", has died in England. A child prodigy, she made her first stage appearance in Stockholm when aged only ten and had her operatic début there in 1838. Her performances caused a sensation wherever she appeared, from Hamburg to Vienna and London, but she retired from opera in 1849 and restricted her performances to oratorios and concerts. She married the conductor Otto Goldschmidt and helped him to found the Bach Choir in London in 1876. After her final retirement in 1870, she continued to teach, and to work for charity, becoming Professor of Singing at The Royal Academy of Music, London, in 1883.

GOLDEN JUBILEE

On the occasion of Queen Victoria's Golden Jubilee, the leaders of the British Empire meet in London, the first of many colonial and imperial conferences held to tie the British Empire closer together.

LA TOSCA

Victorien Sardou (1831–1908), a brilliant technician and dramatic constructor whose plays are often lacking in life, produces one of his most successful works, the vivid melodrama *La Tosca*. The drama will become more famous when Puccini composes his opera on its story.

ANIMAL LOCOMOTION

Since the 1870s Eadweard Muybridge (1830–1904) has been producing photographic studies of animals in motion, using special equipment which he designed in order to freeze movement. Now he publishes *Animal Locomotion*, the first book to show the fruits of his work *en masse*, no less than 781 groups of frames that give scientific information about motion and indicate one route towards the movies.

ELECTROCARDIOGRAM

London physiologist Augustus Waller successfully records the electrical activity of the heart, and in so doing invents the electrocardiogram. The embryonic science of cardiology is brought into the "modern" era of medicine with this development.

SPEAKING ESPERANTO

Polish linguist Dr Ludovic Zamenhof (1859–1917) invents Esperanto, a new language which he describes as his "universal tongue". Zamenhof's initial intention is to initiate better relations between the various ethnic groups living in his Polish town, who include Russians, Germans and Jews, but he also hopes that Esperanto will be a way forward to world peace.

Above and right: *Queen Victoria celebrates her Golden Jubilee Year by emerging from mourning for Albert.*

Photo Ad
The Harrison Patent Knitting Machine Co. becomes the first company to use photography for advertising purposes. A photograph of their display stand and staff is published in a local humorous Manchester periodical called the *The Parrot*.

Record Player
Emile Berliner, a German inventor based in America, invents the gramophone disc record player. Using Edison's phonograph principle, he devises flat shellac discs which rotate on a turntable, thereby bringing the record player into existence.

Stanley's Final Journey
Henry Morton Stanley sets out on his final African journey to rescue Dr Emin, a German scientist, from the shores of Lake Albert. In crossing Africa from west to east, Stanley maps the Semliki river from Lake Edward to Lake Albert, the last piece of the puzzle of the source of the Nile.

TEXTILES AND TECHNOLOGY

THE TEXTILE INDUSTRY was the first to become mechanized, and to organize itself into factories. The eighteenth century saw huge leaps forwards in the design and building of textile machinery and this tradition is carried on in the nineteenth century, with refinements and modifications producing machines that can weave anything from a delicate silk scarf to a heavy carpet. In Europe, the industry is boosted by cheap supplies of raw materials provided by the colonies and dominions of the various European powers.

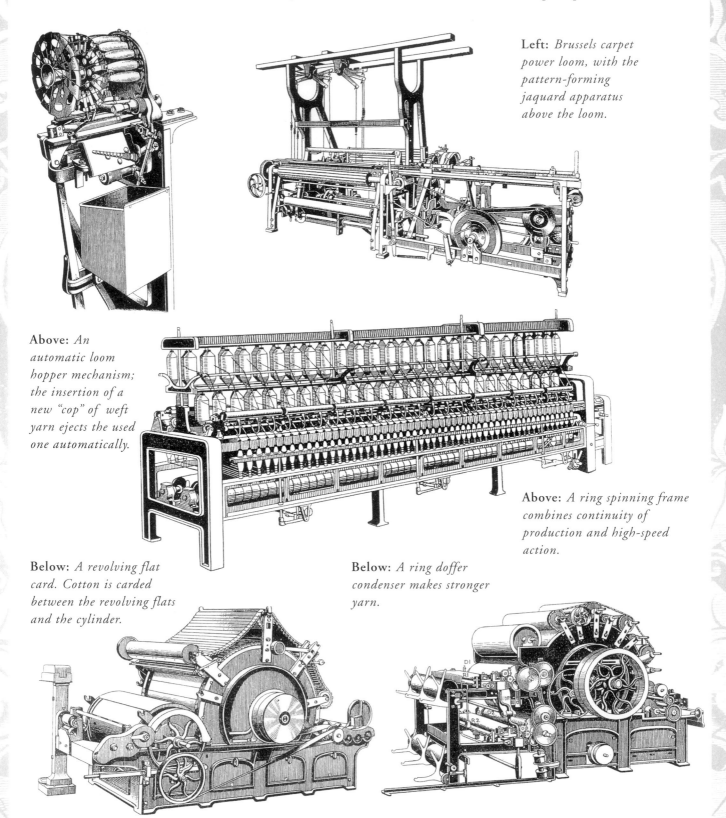

Left: *Brussels carpet power loom, with the pattern-forming jaquard apparatus above the loom.*

Above: *An automatic loom hopper mechanism; the insertion of a new "cop" of weft yarn ejects the used one automatically.*

Above: *A ring spinning frame combines continuity of production and high-speed action.*

Below: *A revolving flat card. Cotton is carded between the revolving flats and the cylinder.*

Below: *A ring doffer condenser makes stronger yarn.*

Above: *Overcome by the vast crowds, many young people faint or fall ill during the procession for the Queen's Golden Jubilee in Trafalgar Square, London.*

Tennis Star
Lottie Dodd wins the first of her five All-England titles at age 15. She will never lose at Wimbledon and becomes an international hockey player and English golf champion after retiring from tennis when she is 21.

Football Star
John William Heisman plays American football for Brown University. For 36 years he is an innovative coach, and the trophy for the outstanding player of each college season is named after him.

One Million Dead
Famine in China kills almost one million people after the Huanghe (Yellow river) floods.

Above: *An Ethiopian soldier sings a war song. Italy goes to war with Ethiopia (also called Abyssinia) this year.*

Left: *South African gold-diggers enjoying a "bull dance". There are few ladies in the gold fields and so the men have to dance with each other, which sometimes ends in a fight.*

SUNFLOWERS, A YELLOW CHAIR AND RADIO WAVES

RAZIL ABOLISHES SLAVERY. This finally brings an end to to slavery throughout the American continent. Benjamin Harrison is elected US president. The theory of radio waves is revealed. George Eastman markets his "Kodak No. 1" snapshot camera. Karl Benz begins manufacture of the first commercially practicable motor car. The first experiments with contact lenses take place. Vincent van Gogh reflects the light of Provence in his painting *Sunflowers*.

❧ 1888 ❧

JAN	28	Italy promises military aid to Germany if war with France breaks out	AUG	9	Britain establishes county councils
FEB	3	Bismarck warns Russia that Germany and Austria have a pact	SEP	8	The Football League is set up in Britain
	11	Matabeleland (now part of Zimbabwe) accepts British protection	OCT	30	South African statesman Cecil Rhodes acquires mining rights in Matabeleland
MAR	9	Willliam I of Germany dies; succeeded by son Frederick III, son-in-law of Britain's Queen Victoria	NOV	6	Benjamin Harrison (Republican) wins US presidential election
	17	Britain establishes a protectorate over Sarawak			
MAY	12	Britain establishes a protectorate over Brunei and North Borneo			
	13	Brazil abolishes serfdom (slavery)			
JUNE	15	Frederick III of Germany dies; succeeded by his son Wilhelm II			

Brazil Abolishes Slavery

The Brazilian government finally abolishes slavery, 38 years after the abolition of the slave trade to Brazil. With the gradual abolition of slavery throughout Latin America in the 1850s and 1860s and its abolition in the southern states of the USA in 1865 and Cuba in 1886, only Brazil had retained slavery on its plantations. The decision of the Brazilian government finally removes the institution of slavery from the American continent, more than four centuries after the first slaves were brought over from Africa.

Harrison Wins Presidential Election

Benjamin Harrison (1833–1901), grandson of the ninth president, William Harrison, wins the presidential election for the Republicans, defeating the incumbent president, Grover Cleveland, the Democratic candidate. Levi Morton of New York becomes vice-president.

Sunflowers and The Yellow Chair

Dutch artist Vincent van Gogh (1853–90) has a unique vision, which is summed up in his paintings *Sunflowers* and *The Yellow Chair*. They show the impact of the bright sunlight of Provence, where van Gogh is now living. More than any of his other famous works, these canvases will come to symbolize the directness of his vision and the loneliness of the misunderstood artist on the borders of sanity. In 1889 he is placed in an asylum; the following year he commits suicide.

Britain Establishes a New Protectorate in Southeast Asia

Britain establishes a protectorate over Sarawak, North Borneo and Brunei. This protects British trade routes in the China sea and expanding British influence in Southeast Asia.

German Emperors

Following the death of Emperor William I, his son, the liberal-minded Frederick II, becomes emperor of Germany. In June, however, he suddenly dies, and is succeeded in turn by his son, William II.

Left: Frederick II of Germany, whose reign as emperor lasts for only a few months.

Above: *Leading prima donna Christine Nillson performs a farewell concert at the Albert Hall in London.*

Don Juan

With its large orchestra, romantic changes of pace and melody, and romantic subject matter, German composer Richard Strauss's tone poem, *Don Juan*, is a breakthrough for the composer. He is seen as the successor of Liszt and the person who will take orchestral writing into the twentieth century. This work will be followed by a string of further tone poems, which extend the genre.

Long-recoil Cylinder

Konrad Haussner develops the long-recoil cylinder. This absorbs the energy of the recoil in artillery, allowing guns to be laid and fired quickly and accurately.

Miss Julie

Swedish playwright August Strindberg (1840–1912) produces *Miss Julie*, his most famous play. His frank portrayal of the war of the sexes, brought to life with Strindberg's own bleak brand of psychological analysis (he was widely read in psychology), makes the writer famous throughout Europe.

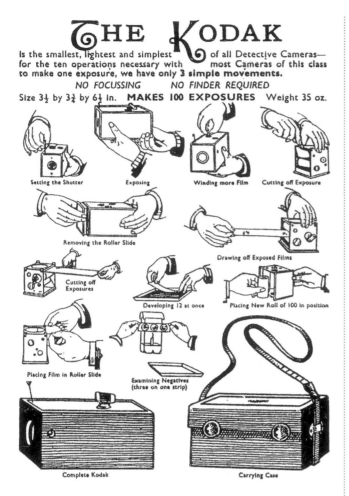

Above: *Advertisement for the instantly popular box camera introduced by American George Eastman.*

SNAPSHOT CAMERA

George Eastman (1854–1932) of New York markets his "Kodak No. 1" snapshot camera for the masses. The camera can take one hundred circular pictures and has to be sent back to the factory to have the film removed and processed. The camera is then returned with a new film loaded.

RADIO WAVES

German electrical scientist, Heinrich Hertz (1857–94), reveals his discovery of radio waves. Radio signals have already been sent and received, but the knowledge of their wave form introduces the concept of wave frequency and is thus a significant step forwards in radio communication.

CONTACT LENSES

Swiss opthalmologist Dr Adolph Frick, begins trials with the concept of viewing lenses that are in direct contact with the eyeball. Six patients are fitted with glass lenses of 14mm (½in) diameter. The lenses are held in place by the eyelids, and being so heavy, can only be worn for short periods.

MOTOR CAR PRODUCTION

Karl Benz (1844–1929) begins production of a two-horsepower motor car, with three wheels and two seats. The vehicle, manufactured by his company Rheinische Gasmotoren Fabrik, is the very first efficient and commercially practicable motor car.

GESTETNER STENCIL

The first typewriter stencil is invented by a Hungarian, David Gestetner, living in London.

REVOLVING DOOR

The world's first revolving door is installed in an office building in Philadelphia, USA, by inventor Theophilus Van Kannel.

THE REVOLUTION IN TANNER'S LANE

With its sympathetic depictions of dissenters, radicals and workers of the earlier nineteenth century, Mark Rutherford's novel adds to the breadth of the English novel, which had often been scathing of such groups.

FOOTBALL LEAGUE

In the UK, a group of football clubs form the Football League and play each other on a fixed schedule. Preston North End wins the first title.

Above: *President Benjamin Harrison, the grandson of William Henry Harrison, president for 30 days in 1841.*

Left: *Government House, Melbourne, Australia. The newly established Australian parliament decides to exclude Chinese immigrants this year.*

Above: *William II of Germany reviews his hussars. He has expansion on his mind.*

KEEP THE RED FLAG FLYING

SOCIALISM AND MILITANT TRADE UNIONISM sweep through sections of the labour movement in Britain. France expands its influence in West Africa. Britain, Germany and the USA divide up Samoa. A major international exhibition is held in Paris to celebrate technology and the 100th anniversary of the Revolution; the Eiffel Tower is completed for the exhibition. Mata Hari buys a newly-invented brassière.

❧ 1889 ❧

JAN	19	France establishes protectorate over Côte d'Ivoire (Ivory coast)	AUG	19	London dock strike begins (lasts until September 14)
	30	Crown Prince Rudolf of Austria commits suicide	OCT	5	Two Germans climb Mount Kilimanjaro, Tanzania
FEB	11	Japan sets up a two-chamber parliament	NOV	2	North and South Dakota become the 39th and 40th US states
MAR	4	Benjamin Harrison is inaugurated as 23rd US president		8	Montana becomes the 41st US state
				11	Washington becomes the 42nd US state
MAY	2	Italy claims protectorate over Ethiopia		15	Brazil deposes its emperor, Pedro II, and becomes a republic with Marshal Deodora de Fonseca as president
	31	Britain starts to build more warships to make its fleet equal to those of its rivals			
JUNE	14	Britain, Germany and the USA agree to divide up Samoa	DEC	6	Coalition of Calvinists and Catholics is elected to power in The Netherlands

Left: *The Chinese boy emperor receives the ladies of the diplomatic corps. This is the first time foreign women have been to the Imperial Court.*

FRENCH PROTECTORATE ESTABLISHED

France establishes a protectorate over the Ivory coast, consolidating its power and influence in West Africa.

WAR BETWEEN DAHOMEY AND FRANCE

Britain cedes the city of Cotonou and Dahomey in West Africa to the French. The Dahomeyans, including formidable female warriors, and commanded by King Behanzin, attack the French when they land. French discipline and fire-power eventually force King Behanzin to cede Cotonou and another coastal city in return for an annual payment.

JAPAN AGREES NEW CONSTITUTION

After many years of controversy and debate, a new constitution is agreed, setting up a two-chamber representative parliament but with the emperor retaining extensive powers.

NAVAL DEFENCE ACT

In Britain, the Naval Defence Act establishes the principle of the "two-power standard". This states that the British Navy will be "at least equal to the naval strength of any two other countries". The act is designed to ensure the supremacy of the British Navy against Germany.

SAMOA DIVIDED

Britain, Germany and the USA agree to divide up the islands of Samoa between them, removing a potential colonial flashpoint in the Pacific after US and German warships faced each other in Appia harbour.

REPUBLIC OF BRAZIL

After the abdication of Emperor Pedro II, Brazil becomes a republic.

STATES JOIN THE UNION

The four western states of Washington, Montana, and North and South Dakota join the Union. The following July, both Idaho and Wyoming join the Union, bringing the total number of states to 44.

THE RED FLAG

The anthem of the British labour movement, and symbol of international socialism, *The Red Flag*, is written by Jim Connell. It coincides with an upsurge of militant trade unionism and socialism in Britain and Europe, and is written after a major, and successful, dock strike which takes place in Britain this year. The dock workers' victory follows a successful strike by match-girls in 1888. Aided by Annie Besant (1847–1933) and other socialists, the match-girls won their fight against miserable pay and conditions.

MT KENYA CONQUERED

Halford Mackinder, Cesar Ollier and Joseph Brocherel conquer Mt Kenya.

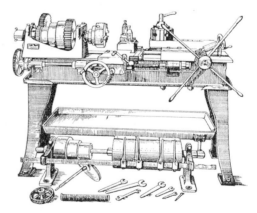

Above: *A capstan lathe showing the level of sophistication reached on machine tools near the end of the century.*

EXHIBITION AND EIFFEL TOWER

A great exhibition is held in Paris to celebrate the French Revolution of 1789 — and modern technology. The tower is the lasting monument to the exhibition, and a symbol of Paris and all France. Another feature of the exhibition is the Galerie des Machines. A revolutionary building built with modern materials, it has vast metal arches supporting a glass roof covering an enormous span, making it perfect for the display of machinery featured in the exhibition.

THE WANDERINGS OF OISIN

WB Yeats (1865–1939), already well known as a dramatist and collector of Irish folktales and legends, publishes his first volume of poetry, starting him on the course for which he will be remembered. The book, and those that follow, will be famous for their Irish themes.

READY-MIX PANCAKES

The first ready-mix food, Aunt Jemima pancake flour, a self-raising flour for pancakes, is produced in Minnesota, USA.

Above: *The Eiffel Tower, star of the Paris Exhibition. It is 300m (984ft) tall and made from iron and steel.*

DATA COMPUTER

A machine for processing data is patented by Herman Hollerith of New York. It is used for a census questionnaire by means of punched cards containing the recorded information. It is able to make instant tabulations using an electric impulser.

LAND RACE

In a massive "land race", Oklahoma District, land formerly belonging to Native Americans is given away to settlers and speculators. An estimated 200 000 people enter Oklahoma on the first day to claim the plots marked out by the government. The scramble, in which the first to reach a plot could claim it, is thought to be the fairest way to distribute the territory. Previous distributions of land in the West had been plagued by corruption and cheating.

BEFORE DAWN

German writer Gerhardt Hauptmann's reputation is made with this, his first play. It shocks audience with its hero's doctrine of determinism, and its portrayal of alcoholism. The play marks the beginning of naturalist drama in Germany.

EXTERNAL SCREW-TOP

The ubiquitous external screw-top lid, seen on all manner of bottles and jars, is invented by Dan Rylands at the Hope Glass Works in Yorkshire, England. Vessels and containers for liquids will never look back.

FREE ASSOCIATION OF WOMEN

Dutch feminist Wilhelmina Drucker sets up the Free Association of Women (Vrie Vrouwen Vereeniging), the first women's organization with socialist backing.

Above: *William Butler Yeats, the Irish poet and dramatist, publishes his first significant work this year.*

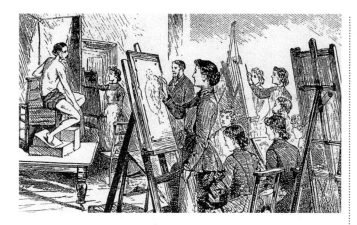

Above: *Art schools are among the first educational establishments to accept women as equal pupils with men.*

BRASSIERE
Mata Hari (1876–1917), celebrated spy and *femme fatale*, is one of the first to purchase the new undergarment for holding the bosom without the need for a corset. The brassière is invented by Parisian corset maker, Hermenie Cadolle.

LAST BARE-KNUCKLE BOXING
American John L Sullivan (1858–1918) claims the heavyweight title by beating Jake Kilrain. It is the last bare-knuckle heavyweight championship fight. Kilrain's seconds throw in the towel after 75 rounds, lasting over two hours 16 minutes.

KILIMANJARO SCALED
Hans Meyer, a German geographer, and Ludwig Purtscheller, are the first to scale Kilimanjaro. The Tanzanian peak, which reaches a height of 5895m (19 341ft), had defeated many prior attempts at reaching the summit.

TRACTOR
The first tractor to be powered by an internal combustion engine is manufactured by the Charter Engine Co. of Chicago. The "Burger" tractor is a converted Rumely Steam Traction Engine, using a single-cylinder gasoline engine.

RSPB
The Royal Society for the Protection of Birds (RSPB) is founded in Britain as a result of harm caused to bird populations worldwide by agents employed by the millinery trade.

Above: *The Florence Maybrick Trial, a notorious British murder case which is never satisfactorily solved.*

SURGICAL DILATOR
The Hegar Dilator, a surgical instrument produced by the gynaecologist Hegar, makes obstetric operations, including abortion, much more accurate and safer, especially when used with antiseptic techniques.

Below: *Activist John Burns addresses a rally of striking dockers, signalling the rise of socialist militancy.*

FROM WOUNDED KNEE TO THE HAGUE

As the century ends, the United States is established as a major world force. White settlers have finally overcome Native American resistance and the US population has topped 50 million. Like major European nations, the USA has adopted imperialism, making inroads into Southeast Asia and the Caribbean. The British Empire is still the largest the world has ever seen, but Britain's industrial and trading role in the world is being overtaken by the United States and Germany. China and Japan have emerged from centuries of isolation and are beginning the process of modernization. Railroads have appeared on all continents, gas and electricity are established power sources, and medicine has improved enormously. War is still a global feature, but in 1899 nations meet at the first-ever peace conference.

1890–1899

KEY EVENTS
of the
DECADE

Battle of Wounded Knee

Panama Canal Scandal

Sino-Japanese War

The Dreyfus Affair

Jameson's Raid

Italo-Ethiopian War

War in the Sudan

Spanish-American War

Second Boer War

Votes for Women in New Zealand

Controlled Glider Flights

The First Airship

Radio Communication Developed

X-Rays Used

Chemotherapy Developed

First Virus Identified

Diesel Engine Invented

Freud Founds Psychoanalysis

First Modern Olympic Games

WORLD POPULATION

1650 Million

(Estimate)

British soldiers at war in Africa.

Trouble in Benin.

The first glider briefly takes to the air.

THE BATTLE OF WOUNDED KNEE

Above: *Cecil Rhodes, prime minister of the Cape Colony.*

*T*HE FINAL BATTLE in the long series of Indian Wars takes place at Wounded Knee, Dakota. Nearly 200 Sioux are massacred. The electric chair is used for the first time in New York, as a supposedly more humane form of capital punishment. The first electric underground railway opens in London. Java Man, a prehistoric fossil and ancestor of modern humans, is discovered.

✽ 1 8 9 0 ✽

MAR	20	German emperor William II dismisses his chancellor, Otto von Bismarck
JUNE	18	Germany declines to renew its treaty with Russia
JULY	1	Britain exchanges Heligoland, in the North Sea, for Zanzibar and Pemba off East Africa
	2	Sherman Anti-Trust Act seeks to curb "restraint of trade" in the USA
	3	Idaho becomes the 43rd state of the USA
	10	Wyoming becomes the 44th state of the USA
	17	In South Africa, Cecil Rhodes becomes prime minister of Cape Colony
AUG	17	Czar Alexander III of Russia fails to persuade Germany to make a new treaty

SEP	12	Founding of Salisbury (now Harare, Zimbabwe)
NOV	23	Death of William III of The Netherlands and Luxembourg; succeeded in The Netherlands by his ten-year-old daughter, Wilhelmina
	23	Adolphe, Duke of Nassau, becomes Grand Duke of Luxembourg because William III had no male heir
DEC	18	Buganda (now part of Uganda) comes under British control
	29	US cavalry massacres Sioux tribespeople at Wounded Knee

Above and left: *The Forth Rail Bridge, Scotland, officially opened by the Prince of Wales this year.*

BISMARCK RESIGNS

German Chancellor Otto von Bismarck is forced to resign by the new German emperor, William II, who wishes to take control of policy himself. Over the next few years, William introduces an increasingly personal style of government.

BATTLE OF WOUNDED KNEE

The last major Native American resistance to white settlement takes place at Wounded Knee in northwest Dakota. After Chief Sitting Bull is killed for resisting arrest, the Sioux under Chief Big Foot flee and are captured by the US Seventh Cavalry. At Wounded Knee creek, where they are to be disarmed, nearly 200 Sioux, including many women and children, are massacred by cavalry. White settler domination of the Great Plains is now almost total.

ELECTRIC CHAIR

Thomas Edison supplies the equipment for the electric chair, which is used in New York for the first time for capital punishment. William Kemmler is the first murderer to be executed. He takes eight minutes to succumb to the electrical current, which burns the flesh where the electrodes are in contact with his body.

Right: *The dangers of traffic in London, made faster and more silent by the tarmacadam roads, are a source of anxiety. Traffic police and traffic islands in the road are introduced to make crossing the street less hazardous.*

POPULATION REACHES 50 MILLION

The US population is now 50 million. A growing percentage of immigrants is arriving from Eastern Europe. Croats, Volga Germans and Russians dominate the western states; more than two million Jews, mainly from Russia and Romania but also from Germany and Poland, have arrived since 1880, and Scandinavian immigration has reached a peak.

CAVALLERIA RUSTICANA

This short one-act opera by Italian composer Pietro Mascagni, inaugurates the *verismo* school of opera. In this type of work, humble characters, violent action, and often contemporary settings are portrayed in highly emotional music. The mode will be taken up by other composers, notably Puccini.

HUNGER

Norwegian writer Knut Hamsun (1859–1952) reacts against other Scandinavian writers such as Ibsen, who, in their quest for realism, ignore the subconscious. *Hunger* is Hamsun's first important novel.

HELIGOLAND CEDED TO GERMANY

Britain cedes the North Sea island of Heligoland to Germany in return for the islands of Zanzibar and Pemba off the East African coast.

AMERICAN INDUSTRIAL SOCIETY DESCRIBED

How the Other Half Lives by Jacob Riis, a New York journalist, is a pioneering social analysis of the new industrial society of the USA by an immigrant from Denmark, who describes slum life in the cities.

KELMSCOTT PRESS
Socialist and craftsman William Morris founds the Kelmscott Press to print his own works and those of others in specially designed type (plus ornaments and borders also designed by Morris). Classics, notably the *Kelmscott Chaucer*, also appear. Morris brings to the printed book something of the visual quality of medieval illuminated manuscripts.

ELECTRIC UNDERGROUND
The City and South London Railway — now the Northern Line — becomes the first electrified underground railway line or "tube". It marks the true beginning of a new era in metropolitan transport, previously having been powered by very dirty steam locomotives.

THE GOLDEN BOUGH
The first volume of this vast survey of human belief, thought and ritual appears. Scottish folklorist James George Frazer (1854–1941) aims to show how humankind has progressed from magical, through religious, to scientific modes of thought. The argument is less influential than the mass of detail that Frazer collects and which will influence many later writers. Publication of *The Golden Bough* continues until 1914.

Above: *Pioneers of the British South Africa Company (run by Cecil Rhodes) in Mashonaland.*

Heinrich Schliemann
1822–1890

The German archaeologist and discoverer of Homer's ancient Troy has died. As a young man Schliemann went into business specifically to raise money to enable him to carry out the archaeological researches of which he dreamed. He retired at the age of 41 to begin this work. He dug at a site overlooking the Dardanelles and uncovered Troy. His enthusiasm led to mistakes of interpretation, but he was rigorous and careful in his methods and record-keeping, and made astonishing discoveries. Between 1871 and 1890 he not only discovered and excavated the nine superimposed cities on the Troy site, but also explored the site of Mycenae, all his work supporting the historical truthfulness of many classical Greek legends.

Auditorium Building, Chicago

Dankmar Adler and Louis Sullivan's Auditorium Building is multi-storey but has load-bearing walls. It is thus a backward-looking building, but its imposing façades and fine detailing make it one of the best-loved of all Chicago's buildings.

Commercial Battery

The famous brand of battery (correctly called an electric cell) by Ever Ready is first marketed by the National Carbon Co., USA. It is an indication of the increasing popularity of electricity, especially for powering gadgets and labour-saving devices.

Psychology Principles

William James, an American philosopher, publishes *The Principles of Psychology*, the first comprehensive academic work on psychology. A lecturer in the department of psychology and philosophy at Harvard since 1880, James is the son of the Swedenborgian theologian Henry James and brother of the novelist of the same name.

Around the World in 72 Days

American journalist Nellie Bly (1867–1922) succeeds in travelling around the world in 72 days, 6 hours and 11 minutes. An adventurer, who specializes in exposing terrible social conditions, she was born Elizabeth Cochrane but took the pen name Nellie Bly after a popular music hall song.

Left: Explorer Henry Morton Stanley, who will later travel through South Africa during 1897 and 1898.

Java Man

Eugene Dubois, a Dutch military surgeon and palaeontologist, at Kedung Brebus, Java, discovers Java Man, the first fossil of *Homo erectus*, ancestor of modern humans.

Port Sunlight

A modern industrial town, Port Sunlight, is built near Liverpool, England, by William H Lever, around his Sunlight Soap factory. It includes housing and amenities such as a library and an art gallery.

Lipton's Tea

Thomas Lipton buys tea to sell in his 300 grocery stores to satisfy the rising demand for tea in the UK. Coffee rust, which began in Ceylon in 1869, has destroyed the eastern coffee crops, creating a coffee shortage and high coffee prices.

Hockey Introduced into India

Lord Harris, governor of Bengal, encourages Indians to take up hockey. The game flourishes on baked mud pitches, which encourage skilful play.

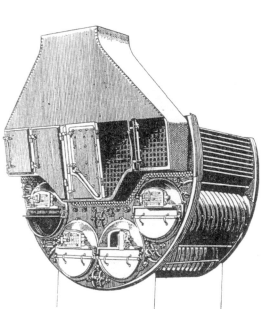
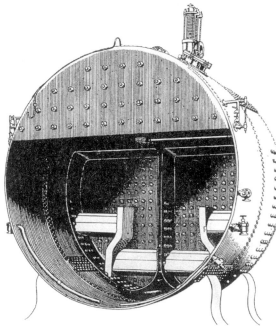

Left: The "Scotch" marine boiler, cylindrical in shape, is now the boiler of choice for the engines of naval and mercantile vessels.

Above: *The Princess of Wales fires the first shot at Bisley, the British army's weapons training ground.*

BLACK COLLEGES
The US federal government grants land for public colleges for black citizens; the colleges emphasize manual and industrial education.

ELEVEN CITIES ON ICE
The Eleven City Ice Skating Tour — *Elfstedentocht* — is first mentioned in Dutch newspapers. Skaters visit eleven cities in the Friesland area in a loop beginning and ending in Leeuwarden. To prove the competitors have made the trip, innkeepers sign a piece of paper for the skaters. In 1909 the Elfstedentocht becomes an official event and continues to be held each year, provided the ice is thick enough.

THE BIRD MAN SOARS

*F*RANCE AND RUSSIA SIGN AN ENTENTE as Germany, Austro-Hungary and Italy become closer allies. Carnegie Hall opens in New York. Otto Lilienthal makes a successful controlled glider flight. An incubator for premature babies is developed. The world's first old-age pensions are introduced. World-famous fictional detective Sherlock Holmes solves his first baffling case with characteristic cunning and observation. The electric kettle is one of many new labour-saving devices.

❋ 1891 ❋

JAN	31	Civil war breaks out in Chile
FEB	9	Emperor Menelek of Ethiopia objects to Italian claims on his country
MAR	24	Britain and Italy agree on boundaries of their Red Sea territories
MAY	6	Austria, Germany and Italy renew their alliance for twelve years
JUNE	10	Dr Leander Starr Jameson becomes governor of the South Africa Company's territories
	17	Josia Lawlor wins single-handed transatlantic yacht race
	20	Britain and The Netherlands agree on the boundaries of their Borneo territories
SEP	19	President José Balmaceda of Chile commits suicide after losing the civil war; succeeded by Jorge Montt
NOV	23	President Deodora da Fonseca of Brazil is deposed; succeeded by Marshal Floriano Peixoto

Above: *Czar Alexander II inspects the French Fleet
visiting the Russian naval base on the Gulf of Finland.*

Left: *Arthur Conan Doyle, medical man and inventor of the great sleuth of Baker Street, Sherlock Holmes.*

FRANCE AND RUSSIA SIGN ENTENTE

As relations between Germany, Austro-Hungary and Italy grow closer, France and Russia sign an entente linking their two countries together. In January 1893 the two sign a formal alliance.

BIRD MAN

German flight pioneer Otto Lilienthal (1848–96) makes the first of his controlled glider flights. Over five years, until his eventual death by crashing, he completes 2000 flights from a hilltop, using his body movements to control the glider.

RUSSIAN FAMINE

Famine spreads across the rural areas of Russia after the crops fail, but the US sends aid in the form of wheat.

CARNEGIE HALL OPENS

Industrialist and philanthropist Andrew Carnegie (1835–1918) gives New York its first purpose-built symphony-concert hall. Tchaikovsky conducts part of the opening concert. The hall is just one of countless donations in the cause of education, the arts and peace, made by Carnegie.

TESS OF THE D'URBERVILLES

Thomas Hardy's story of Tess, whom he calls "a pure woman" in his subtitle, creates a stir on publication. Many find the work immoral (because Hardy defends a woman who has been seduced) and pessimistic. But it is later accepted as a classic, one of his greatest novels, and a work that pushes the boundaries of fiction in the English language.

INCUBATOR

Frenchman Dr Alexandre Lion devises the baby incubator. As well as regulating the temperature of the child via a thermostatic control, it also supplies filtered air. At his base in Nice he experiments and has a 72 per cent success rate with premature and sickly newborns.

PAUL GAUGIN SETTLES IN TAHITI

Escaping from Europe in search of a simpler life, French artist Paul Gaugin (1848–1903) discovers the subjects that will inspire his greatest paintings. His life in Tahiti however, explodes any remaining myths of the nobility of the European amongst the "savages".

OLD-AGE PENSIONS

The world's first old age pension, introduced by Bismarck into Germany in June 1889, becomes effective. Workers aged over 16 who are fully employed and earn more than 2000 marks a year must contribute to the scheme and their employers must contribute equal amounts. People who have paid premiums for at least 30 years may claim from the age of 70.

NEW GRUB STREET

This, the most famous novel by English writer George Gissing (1857–1903) appears. Its portrayal of the negative side of the literary world bolsters Gissing's reputation as a realist novelist in the European vein.

TROTTING SULKY

The low-wheel sulky replaces the high-wheel version in the sport of harness-racing or trotting.

Above: *Alfred, Lord Tennyson, Britain's poet laureate, a few months before his death.*

Left: *Sydney Harbour, Sydney, Australia, viewed from South Head. The First Australian Federal Convention meets in Sydney this year.*

Herman Melville
1819–1891

The American author Herman Melville has died, not yet secured of the place he will eventually hold in world fiction. His novel *Moby Dick* (1851) was written from his own experience, Melville having left his job as a bank clerk to be a seaman on a whaler and a man-of-war. Around 1850 he settled with his wife on a farm in Massachusetts, near his friend the writer Nathaniel Hawthorne, and began to write. In 1866, too impoverished to continue his attempt to live by his writing, he took a job as a customs official. He wrote novels and short stories (including "Bartleby the Scrivener"), and also poetry. A later short novel, *Billy Budd,* will be published successfully after his death (1924).

Above: *Australian statesman Sir Henry Parkes chairs the first Australian Federal Convention, held in Sydney.*

Above: *General William Booth, founder of the Salvation Army, exhorts the public to spend two days with God.*

Madame Blavatsky
1831–1891

Helen Blavatsky (originally Hahn), the Russian spiritualist, has died. From 1848 Madame Blavatsky travelled widely and claimed to have spent long periods studying under Hindu mahatmas while in India and Tibet. Her travels took her to the United States, where with her student Henry Steel Olcott and others she founded the Theosophical Society in 1875. Theosophy was said to be derived from Brahman and Buddhist sacred scripts, and was a spiritual religion but with no personal god. Madame Blavatsky's claims to have psychic powers were investigated by the London Society for Psychical Research in that year and she was found by the researchers to be a sham. She left India and lived in Germany and Belgium before settling in London and working on her writing. Her books include *Isis Unveiled* (1877), *The Secret Doctrine* (1888) and *The Voice of Silence* (1889).

PEARY ATTEMPTS NORTH POLE

US naval commander Robert Edwin Peary (1856–1920) makes his first attempt at reaching the North Pole. He fails, but becomes the first to achieve the feat with a highly organized expedition in 1909.

A NEW KETTLE

Labour-saving devices are beginning to become all the rage as electricity is made available domestically. The electric kettle is just one of many useful new inventions which do indeed save a lot of inconvenience and effort.

MUSIC HALL POSTERS

French artist Henri de Toulouse-Lautrec (1864–1901), at home amongst the music-hall artistes of Paris, paints some memorable posters and spearheads a general raising of standards in the graphic arts.

SPRING'S AWAKENING

This is the first notable play by German dramatist Frank Wedekind (1864–1918). It is a tragedy of an adolescence ruined by convention. Wedekind's work foreshadows both expressionist drama and the much later Theatre of the Absurd.

SHOSHONE NATIONAL FOREST

The US Congress authorizes the president to set aside forest lands for preservation. The Shoshone National Forest in Wyoming is the first national forest preserve to be established and steps are taken by New York State to create a huge second preserve, Adirondack Park.

Phineas Taylor Barnum
1810–1891

The octogenarian American showman, co-founder of the Barnum and Bailey Circus, has died. Phineas Taylor Barnum traded in the weird and the wonderful, starting his career with a touring exhibit of an Afro-American woman said to be the 160-year-old nurse of the young George Washington. He opened Barnum's American Museum in New York City and also travelled the United Sates and Europe showing "General Tom Thumb", a man who was 62.5cm (25in) high until manhood and who grew to only 100cm (40in) tall, and a woman billed as the "Fiji mermaid", among other human curiosities. He coined the phrase "the greatest show on earth" for his own circus, but in a loftier vein had also handled the tour of the singer Jenny Lind in 1850.

Above: *Stalwart recruiting sergeants try to stop one in three to persuade them to enlist in the British army.*

TRANSATLANTIC YACHT RACE

Americans Bill Andrews and Josia Lawlor agree to tackle the Atlantic in 4.5m (15ft) yachts for a prize of £1000. Lawlor wins the first single-handed transatlantic race in 43 days. His rival abandons the race after only a few days.

ADVENTURES OF SHERLOCK HOLMES

Arthur Conan Doyle (1859–1930) begins his stories about the detective Sherlock Holmes, who becomes so mythic that many people assume he is a real person. The ruthless logic of his detective powers inspires many imitators in the growing genre of detective fiction.

ETHICAL PROBLEMS

The British writer John Addington Symonds prints 50 copies of *A Problem in Modern Ethics,* a review of the existing scholarly literature on homosexuality, in which he sets out fourteen propositions for refuting prevailing attitudes to homosexuality, including decriminalizing it.

THE OPENING OF ELLIS ISLAND

_E_LLIS ISLAND OPENS TO RECEIVE European immigrants, who are pouring into the United States. A scandal breaks in France over the financing of the Panama Canal. French forces occupy Dahomey, West Africa, in the second Dahomey War. Fingerprints are used successfully to convict a murderer. The vacuum flask is invented. A world fair opens in Chicago, USA. The world's first sociology department opens.

❊ 1 8 9 2 ❊

JAN	7	Khedive Tewfik of Egypt dies; succeeded by son Abbas Hilmi II
	15	Rules of basketball are first published at Springfield, Massachusetts
FEB	1	Germany signs trade treaties with Austria-Hungary, Belgium, Italy and Switzerland
AUG	11	British Prime Minister Lord Salisbury (Conservative) resigns
	15	William Gladstone (Liberal) forms his fourth government
SEP	7	First heavyweight boxing match under the new Queensberry rules at New Orleans; Jim Corbett defeats John L Sullivan
NOV	8	Grover Cleveland (Democrat) wins the US presidential election
	10	Panama Canal scandal: French engineer Ferdinand de Lesseps and others accused of corruption
	17	Following slavery raids, the French occupy the capital of Dahomey, West Africa
	22	Belgians put down rebellion of Arab slavers in the Congo

Above: *Sunday evening at the Anarchist's Club, a pro-Marxist group of socialist workers in east London.*

Above: *The Canadian Houses of Parliament at Ottawa.*

I PAGLIACCI

This short opera, by Italian composer Ruggiero Leoncavallo (1858–1919) enjoys immediate success and soon becomes paired with Mascagni's *Cavalliera Rusticana*. The two operas will remain together in the repertoire.

CLEVELAND WINS BACK PRESIDENCY

Grover Cleveland wins back the US presidency, defeating the Republican incumbent, Benjamin Harrison, who defeated him four years ago. Adlai Stevenson of Illinois becomes vice-president.

CHICAGO WORLD FAIR

The World's Columbian Exposition opens in Chicago on the 400th anniversary of the "discovery" of America; the official opening will take place in May 1893. The architect Louis H Sullivan builds a "White City" overlooking Lake Michigan and, with Dankmar Adler, designs the functional Transportation Building. The world's first ferris wheel is built by engineer Washington Gale Ferris. The first moving walkway, the first zip fastener and a long-distance telephone line are exhibited.

PANAMA CANAL SCANDAL

A scandal in France concerning the financing of a project to build a canal in Panama intensifies national mistrust of big companies, as the company goes bankrupt and many workers lose their lives from malaria and yellow fever, while building the canal. The failure of the project implicates radical politicians, and leads to an increase in anti-Semitism in France.

THE CHILDREN OF THE GHETTO

With immigration a subject of much current discussion in London, Jewish writer Israel Zangwill (1864–1926) produces a popular novel, *The Children of the Ghetto*, which gives a sympathetic portrayal of the poorer part of the Jewish community in London.

SECOND DAHOMEY WAR

Following slavery raids and attacks on a French gunboat, a Franco-Senegalese army pushes as far as the Dahomeyan capital, Abomey, entering in November. King Behanzin finally surrenders in 1894 and is exiled to Martinique.

PELLEAS ET MELISANDE

Belgian poet and symbolist Maurice Maeterlinck (1862–1949) produces his most famous play, *Pelléas et Mélisande*. It is typical of his style, which blends symbolism, enigma and the mysterious workings of fate. Debussy's music adds to the misty atmosphere.

OCHRE COURT, NEWPORT

American architect Richard Morris Hunt (1828–95) blends a range of architectural sources from England, Germany and France to create a romantic architecture ideally suited to lavish country houses. One of the most famous is Ochre Court, Rhode Island. It is famed for its steep roofs and ornate dormers, which create a striking, romantic silhouette.

MUNICH SECESSION

An exhibition of paintings by Norwegian artist Edvard Munch (1863–1944) is forcibly closed in Munich. This results in a group of German artists breaking away from the establishment in protest, forming the first of a number of secessions, break-away movements that form nurturing-grounds for the radical and new in art.

ELLIS ISLAND

The Federal Bureau of Immigration opens the new receiving station of Ellis Island in New York harbour, USA. The island office becomes the main receiving point for the many thousands of immigrants pouring into the USA from Europe each year.

CONVICTION BY FINGERPRINTS

Buenos Aires in Argentina becomes the first place to witness a conviction for murder using the evidence of fingerprints. A woman named Francisca Rojas is proven to have killed her own children in an attempt to seduce her lover into living with her.

BASKETBALL DRAW

The first organized game of basketball ends in a 2–2 draw at the Springfield YMCA. Dr James Naismith (1861–1939) invented the sport last year as an indoor pursuit to be played during harsh New England winters. It rapidly becomes very popular, but many YMCAs ban the game because it reduces the number of people who can use a gymnasium at any one time.

THERMOS

Scottish physicist Sir James Dewar (1842–1923) successfully demonstrates the use of a vacuum for insulation by inventing the thermos flask. The bottler has a double skin with a near-vacuum between the layers, eliminating air molecules which would otherwise disperse the heat outwards. Known as the Dewar bottle, it is the precursor of the Thermos flask.

COMPRESSION IGNITION

Richard Hornsby and Herbert Akroyd Stuart of England experiment with an engine, which will later be perfected by German engineer Rudolph Diesel (1858–1913). The fuel spontaneously ignites under high pressure to drive the piston, with the aid of a heating element to get the engine warmed up initially.

FIRST SOCIOLOGY DEPARTMENT

The world's first sociology department opens at the newly established coeducational University of Chicago in the USA, founded largely through gifts from industrialist and philanthropist John D Rockefeller.

SKATING COMPETITION

The first international speed and figure skating competition is held in Vienna.

CORBETT BEATS SULLIVAN

American pugilist "Gentleman Jim" Corbett beats an unfit and unready John L Sullivan in New Orleans, La., in a huge upset. It is the first heavyweight title fight contested under Queensberry rules.

ESCALATOR

New Yorker Jesse W Reno unveils his "Reno Inclined Elevator". It is a looped "continuous" belt made from wooden slats fixed to rubber-covered cleats and powered by an electric motor at a rate of 2.4km/h (1.5mph).

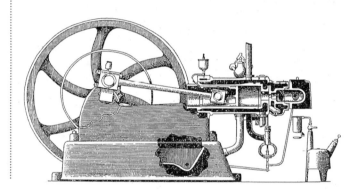

Above: *The Hornsby oil-engine, precursor of the Diesel, showing the vaporizer.*

Left: *Arab slavers are attacked by British and African forces in an attempt to sabotage the North African slave trade.*

Diesel Engine, Automatic Firearms and the Zip Fastener

*F*RANCE GAINS MORE COLONIAL POSSESSIONS in Southeast Asia and West Africa. Rudolf Diesel perfects a version of the internal combustion engine. The first automatic firearm is designed and the invaluable zip fastener is invented. An American architect, Frank Lloyd Wright, produces his first significant work. Dvorak's *New World Symphony* gains popularity. And Victorian lady traveller, Mary Kingsley, explores West Africa.

❧ 1 8 9 3 ❧

JAN	17	Hawaii is proclaimed a republic
MAR	3	Grover Cleveland is inaugurated as the 24th US president — his second term
	8	Trial of Ferdinand de Lesseps and others for corruption over the Panama Canal
	10	French establish colonies of French Guinea and the Ivory coast
	21	De Lesseps is sentenced to five years' jail
MAY	10	Natal in South Africa is given self-government
AUG	6	Corinth Canal in Greece is opened
SEP	8	British House of Lords rejects the Irish Home Rule Bill
NOV	13	Britain agrees to annexation of Swaziland by Transvaal
	17	Dahomey becomes a French protectorate

Above: *Mashona pioneers in South Africa on the track of Lobengula, leader of the people with whom they are at war.*

IMPERIALISM IN AFRICA
Britain acquires Uganda and in May grants self-government to Natal. In West Africa, France formally establishes the colonies of French Guinea and the Ivory coast. Britain and Germany settle their colonial differences in Cameroon.

HOTEL TASSEL, BRUSSELS
No. 6, Rue Paul-Emile Janson, Brussels, also known as the Hôtel Tassel, is the first great domestic building by Art Nouveau master Victor Horta (1861–1947). Its stunning use of the whiplash curve in its interior decoration, the free-flowing use of wrought iron, and other decorative elements, make it an archetype for later Art Nouveau design.

WINSLOW HOUSE, RIVER FOREST, ILLINOIS
This simple house is the first significant work of American architect Frank Lloyd Wright (1867–1959), who will later transform American architecture. The house shows a stress on horizontal lines which Wright will later develop in other, more individual, buildings.

WOMAN LAWYER
Cornelia Sorabji passes the Bachelor of Civil Law examination in London and returns to India to become the first practising woman lawyer there.

FRANCE GAINS LAOS
During the year, France acquires Laos, adding to its possessions in Southeast Asia.

MARY KINGSLEY EXPLORES WEST AFRICA

Mary Kingsley (1862–1900), British ethnologist and naturalist, niece of the writer Charles Kingsley, explores West Africa, painting, photographing and recording undiscovered species of wildlife. She returns in 1894, then sets out again. Dressed in the garments of a well-brought up Victorian lady, she travels up the Ogowe river and through the forests and swamps of West Africa.

KARELIA SUITE

One of the greatest of Finland's composers is Jean Sibelius (1865–1957). This orchestral suite is inspired by Karelia, in southern Finland, where the composer spent his honeymoon the previous year, and which is a rich repository of traditional Finnish tunes. *The Karelia Suite* confirms Sibelius's position as Finland's foremost composer and places him at the centre of a group of nationalist artists in Helsinki.

Left: *The citadel of Cairo. It is ten years since the British occupied Egypt, stamping their authority on this area of North Africa. Meanwhile, the French are expanding their colonial possessions in West Africa, Natal is granted autonomy and British traveller Mary Kingsley explores Gabon.*

DIESEL ENGINE

German engineer Rudolf Diesel (1858–1913) develops and perfects his version of the compression-ignition internal combustion engine. Able to run reliably on low-octane diesel oil, rather than petrol or gasoline, it is particularly suitable for large engines to drive machinery and trains.

FILM STUDIO

Thomas Edison becomes the first to devise a purpose-built film studio. It is dubbed the "Black Maria", being a timber frame covered with black cloth. It is designed to revolve so that the maximum use of available sunlight can be made during the day.

AUTOMATIC FIREARM

The first automatic firearm is the "Prometheus" designed by German, Bor Chardt. It is automatic, as it uses some energy from the previously fired round to reload the next, therefore creating a perpetual readiness to fire. It has a magazine containing eight rounds.

ZIP FASTENER

Whitcomb L Judson becomes the unsung hero of the clothing industry, by inventing the "zip" fastener. Originally intended for boots and shoes, it cleverly causes identical pegs to engage with one another in a single and simple action by pulling a tab.

AMERICAN FRONTIER

Historian Frederick Jackson Turner reads *The Significance of the Frontier in American History*, a paper acknowledging the end of the frontier era, to the American Historical Association during the Chicago World Fair. His paper paves the way for new areas of historical study.

HANSEL AND GRETEL

The famous fairy-tale opera, *Hansel and Gretel*, has its first production. Its success brings German composer Engelbert Humperdinck (1854–1921) fame, and he will write several other operas based on folktales. But none is as successful as this.

VOTES FOR WOMEN

New Zealand gives votes to women; the first country in the world to do so. This follows more than a decade of petitioning and agitation by women of New Zealand for voting rights. (In 1889, the New Zealand government had given votes to all men over 21.) In the coming year, 1894, South Australia will also give votes to women.

LADIES' GOLF CHAMPIONSHIP

The first British Ladies' Amateur Golf Championship is held.

SYMPHONY (NOW NO. 9) "FROM THE NEW WORLD"

Czech composer Antonin Dvorák (1841–1904) travelled to New York in 1892 to head up a National conservatory. He wrote the "From the New World Symphony" during his stay there, and the work soon gains popularity. Although inspired by American themes, including spirituals, its Bohemian spirit shines through the music.

THE SECOND MRS TANQUERAY

Already famous for his farces, British playwright Arthur Wing Pinero (1855–1934) turns to more serious drama in the 1880s and 1890s. This is his most long-lasting success, a play which deals with the double standards prevalent for men and women.

DUTCH UNION FOR CARE OF SICK

The Dutch Union for the Care of the Sick is established by Jeltje de Bosch Kemper, the country's foremost advocate of professional nursing, to provide medical services for the poor, especially in country areas. It follows the establishment in 1875 of the White Cross (*Het Witte Kruis*) district medical organizations.

Pyotr Tchaikovsky
1840–1893

The Russian composer and conductor has died in St Petersburg, among controversial rumours of suicide and homosexual liaisons. His sudden death came a few days after a less than fulsome reception for his new Sixth symphony, which Tchaikovsky deemed his best work. A man of extreme Russian temperament, the composer had always been prey to moods of despair about his work, and restlessness in his life. He was highly popular in Britain and the United States as well as in his homeland, having given acclaimed conducting tours in Europe in 1888 and 1889, and in the USA in 1891. He contributed numerous compositions for orchestra and piano, chamber works, songs, two Russian Orthodox choral works, operas (including *Eugene Onegin* of 1877–78, *Queen of Spades*, 1890), and the ballet music (*Swan Lake*, 1875–76, *Sleeping Beauty*, 1888–89, *Nutcracker*, 1891–92) which ensures his immense popularity.

THE BEARDSLEY PHENOMENON

THE STUDIO, a periodical with drawings by Aubrey Beardsley, spreads the fashion for Art Nouveau. Beardsley's combination of influences — Japanese art, Celtic, Rococo, Greek ceramics — fuses into a unique style which he uses in subject matter that encapsulates decadence.

Right: *Covers of* The Studio *magazine.*

Below: *One of Beardsley's illustrations for the title page of a book.*

Above: *Self-portrait of Aubrey Beardsley.*

Above: *One of Beardsley's illustrations for the published script of Oscar Wilde's shocking play* Salomé.

Japan and China Go to War

Japan declares war on China, achieving a victory over the Chinese at Port Arthur. In France, Captain Dreyfus is unjustly charged with espionage. Nicholas II becomes czar of Russia. Italian inventor Marconi works on practical radio equipment that will revolutionize global communications. Moves are made to revive the ancient Olympic Games. A new dessert — Pêche Melba — is created by a chef at London's Savoy Hotel.

❖ 1894 ❖

Feb	10	Germany and Russia sign a trade treaty
Apr	11	Britain declares Uganda as a protectorate
June	22	Dahomey becomes a French colony
	24	Anarchist assassinates President Carnot of France, who is succeeded by Jean Casimir-Périer
July	23	Japanese soldiers capture Seoul, Korea
	27	Regent of Korea declares war on China
Aug	1	Japan declares war on China
Sep	25	In South Africa, the British annex land connecting Cape Colony and Natal
Oct	15	In France, Captain Alfred Dreyfus is unjustly accused of treason

Nov	2	Czar Alexander III of Russia dies; succeeded by his son Nicholas II
	21	Japanese defeat Chinese at Port Arthur
Dec	22	Alfred Dreyfus is convicted of treason and sent to Devil's Island, French Guiana

Above: *The baptism of Prince Edward of England.*

Above: *Funeral of the French President Marie François
Sadi Carnot, stabbed to death by an anarchist in Lyon.*

Olympic Games To Be Revived

Delegates invited to a meeting at the Sorbonne in Paris, France, by Pierre de Coubertin (1863–1937) endorse his concept of reviving the Olympic Games. The meeting founds the International Olympic Committee (IOC) to oversee the project. De Coubertin, who first floated his idea for the Olympics two years ago, made a study of the effects of sport and the role it played in society. He combines the sporting ideals of Ancient

---

Amelia Bloomer
1818–1894

The American women's rights activist and inventor of the cycling knickers that bear her name has died. Amelia Bloomer championed women's rights, and dress reform was part of this campaign. For six years (1849–55) she edited *The Lily*, the feminist journal she helped to found. Bloomers began to be widely worn by emancipated women in the 1850s. Ironically, bloomers — which are knee-length, voluminous and gathered in at the knee — are named after Mrs Bloomer's husband; Amelia's maiden name was Jenks.

Above: *Captain Alfred Dreyfus, accused of spying, is stripped of his rank and honours before his army peers.*

Greece with modern beliefs on sport that have flourished under British teachers such as Dr Thomas Arnold. The original Greek games are believed to have started as early as 2000 BC. In AD 391 they were banned as a pagan ritual by Emperor Theodosius I of Rome. Olympia, the site of the games, had been discovered in 1776 but was not fully investigated until the 1870s.

Japan Declares War On China

Japan declares war against China after the Chinese intervene in Korea to suppress a revolt. Chinese forces prove no match for the Japanese, who quickly overrun the country. By the Treaty of Shimonoseki, signed in April 1895, China recognizes the independence of Korea, cedes Taiwan and other islands to Japan and opens further ports to Western traders. The war reveals the weakness of China and leads to increasing calls for reform.

Dreyfus Court-Martialled

Captain Alfred Dreyfus (1859–1935) is arrested in France and charged with spying. In December he is convicted of treason by court martial and imprisoned for life on Devil's Island, off French Guiana.

Above: *British troops retreat after a failed attempt to storm the encampment of the King of Matabeleland.*

NICHOLAS II BECOMES CZAR
On the death of Alexander III, Nicholas II (1868–1918) becomes czar of Russia and continues the autocratic, conservative and anti-Semitic policies of his father.

A PENNY BAZAAR
Michael Marks, a Polish immigrant to the UK, opens the Penny Bazaar in Manchester, England, in partnership with his colleague, Thomas Spencer. Goods range from haberdashery and hardware to household goods and toys, all costing one penny.

L'APRES-MIDI D'UN FAUNE
Many hear the beginnings of modern music in the languorous phrases and harmonies of the famous *Prelude* to this piece by French composer Claude Debussy (1862–1918). It rewrites the rules of orchestral music and marks a profound turning point.

SEAL HUNTS
Fur seal catches from the Pribilof herds in the Bering Sea reach a peak of 143 000 animals. The herds, whose numbers have fallen by 50 per cent since 1786 to five million in 1886, are now reduced even more.

RELIANCE BUILDING, CHICAGO
Burnham and Root build this block initially as a four-storey metal frame structure; but in 1894 it will be extended to sixteen storeys. In its extended form it becomes one of the archetypal skyscrapers, tall, elegant, with large windows and restrained terracotta decoration.

RADIO COMMUNICATION
Italian inventor Guglielmo Marconi (1874–1937) makes his important contribution to communications technology by developing a practicable radio signalling and receiving apparatus. Over the next few years, he will succeed in sending wireless messages 4800km (3000mi) across the Atlantic. The world will seem a much smaller place after his achievements.

BUBONIC PLAGUE
The bacterium that causes bubonic plague is identified by French bacteriologist, Alexandre Yersin (1863–1943) and independently by Japanese bacteriologist, Shibasaburo Kitasato (1856–1931). The plague still affects some areas, so the discovery is an important breakthrough.

Opening of Tower Bridge

Tower Bridge opens in London. Its centre span — 61m (200ft) — across the River Thames can be raised to allow tall vessels to pass through.

Diva Dish

French chef Auguste Escoffier (1846–1935), working at the Savoy Hotel, London, invents Pêche Melba, in honour of the Australian opera singer Nellie Melba.

Golfing Events

The United States Golf Association is formed. Also this year, members of the Shinnecock Hills Golf Club, on Long Island, play the Tuxedo Golf Club of New York in the first inter-club contest in the United States.

Bulletproof Vest

Representatives of the British army and navy have the first bulletproof vest demonstrated to them in London by Herr Dowe. With the significant advances in firearms, it is considered a necessary part of the kit for modern battle.

Ice Hockey

The ice hockey team of the Montreal Amateur Athletic Association wins the first Stanley Cup as Canada's champions. The prize is donated by Lord Stanley of Preston, the governor general of Canada.

Above: *English author Rudyard Kipling produces his best-loved work,* The Jungle Book, *this year.*

The Jungle Book

Rudyard Kipling (1865–1936), already known as a writer who has chronicled the world of colonial India, publishes his most enduring work, the story of Mowgli's upbringing by wolves and his education by Baloo the bear in the ways of the jungle.

Montessori Begins Work with Children

Maria Montessori (1870–1952) becomes the first woman in Italy to be awarded a medical degree; she begins work as a psychiatrist specializing in children with learning disabilities at the University of Rome.

Lajos Kossuth
1802–1894

The Hungarian revolutionary, Lajos Kossuth, has died. A lawyer and journalist, he was imprisoned for three years for issuing a left-wing paper but on his release, a popular hero, he was given editorship of an extreme liberal paper, *Pesti Hirlap*. A stirring speaker, Kossuth became leader of the opposition in 1847. Inspired by the French Revolution of 1848, he persuaded the National Assembly to declare Hungarian autonomy from the Hapsburg Empire and became provisional governor of a free Hungary in 1849. When this revolt was suppressed by Russian armies later that year, he was interned in Turkey. He taught himself English by studying the Bible and Shakespeare, and escaped to the United States, where he gave stirring speeches in his newly acquired language. He then settled in England, where he kept the Hungarian resistance movement going, but finally retired disheartened to Turin, where his last years were spent in sickness, loneliness and poverty. His burial in Hungary provokes nationwide mourning.

Above: *Women in New Zealand get the vote years before their European sisters. A woman is elected mayor.*

Below: *The Chinese warship* King-Yuen *at the Battle of Yalu, where Japanese naval forces defeat the Chinese.*

PSYCHOANALYSIS, MOVIES AND X-RAYS

STARR JAMESON LEADS an abortive raid into the Transvaal in an attempt to overthrow the Boer government. An independence movement re-emerges in Cuba. Italy and Ethiopia go to war. The Lumière brothers open the first "cinema", marking the birth of the movies. Psychoanalysis too is born with the publication of Sigmund Freud's *Studies in Hysteria*. X-rays are successfully used to examine a gunshot wound.

❋ 1895 ❋

JAN	13	General strike planned in France; President Casimir-Périer resigns
	17	Félix Faure becomes president of France
FEB	12	Japanese defeat Chinese at Wei-hai-wei (now Wei-hei)
MAR	25	Italians advance into Ethiopia
APR	17	China and Japan recognize independence of Korea; China cedes Formosa (Taiwan) to Japan
MAY	2	British-held territory south of the Zambesi river is reorganized as Rhodesia (now Zimbabwe)
JUNE	28	El Salvador, Honduras and Nicaragua unite
OCT	1	Turks massacre Armenians in Constantinople (Istanbul)
	8	Wife of King Kojong of Korea is assassinated
DEC	7	Ethiopians defeat Italians at Amba Alagi
	29	British statesman Leander Starr Jameson leads raid into Transvaal to support a revolution that did not happen

JAMESON'S RAID

Dr Starr Jameson, an administrator of Cecil Rhodes's British South Africa Company, leads 600 mounted men into Transvaal to overthrow the Boer government under President Paul Kruger. The raiders hope that the *uitlanders*, or foreigners, working in the Transvaal gold mines will rise in their favour, but the uprising does not take place and Jameson is defeated at Krugersdorp on January 1, 1896. The failure of the raid embitters Anglo-Boer relations yet again, causing a diplomatic rift between Britain and Germany when William II sends a congratulatory telegram to President Paul Kruger. Cecil Rhodes (1853–1902), being found guilty of connivance in the raid, is forced to resign, ending his domination of South African politics. The Boers arm themselves against further British incursions.

USA INTERVENES IN BRITISH GUIANA

Tension between Britain and Venezuela over the latter's claim to large parts of British Guiana leads to the intervention of the USA, which demands international arbitration. Britain rejects any US involvement, causing widespread anti-British feeling in the USA. The boundary dispute is eventually settled in 1904.

BRITAIN PUTS PRESSURE ON TURKEY

Britain leads the Great Powers in putting pressure on the Sultan of Turkey to end the massacre of Armenians seeking an independent homeland.

Above and below: *The racy petrol-driven gig (top) and the robust steam-driven "Milord" phaeton.*

ITALO-ETHIOPIAN WAR

A conflicting interpretation of a treaty leads Italy to expand into Ethiopia, causing friction with Emperor Yohannes's successor, Menelik. When Italian forces occupy Tigre, the Ethiopians attack and defeat them. This prompts the Italians to send reinforcements into Ethiopia. At Aduwa in March 1896, a force of 20 000 Italians meets 80 000 Ethiopians, who score an overwhelming victory. A subsequent treaty recognizes Ethiopia's independence.

Above: *Lord Salisbury gives warning to the Sultan of Turkey that Europe is equal to the challenge of war.*

CUBAN INSURRECTION

Promised reforms by the Spanish colonial administration having failed to materialize, a new revolutionary movement breaks out in Cuba with the ultimate aim of independence. The insurrection will continue into 1897–98, the Spanish use of ruthless measures gaining American support for the Cubans.

PROMENADE CONCERTS

British conductors Henry Wood (1869–1944) and Robert Newman launch their series of Promenade concerts. They bring a popularity to the concert world — but without dumbing down: there are many first performances and explorations of unusual works. The concerts will continue into the 21st century.

MOVIE MAGIC

Lumière brothers, Auguste and Louis, reveal their Cinématograph — a combined movie camera and projector. The sixteen frames per second of moving footage is shown to an amazed public and they open the first cinema in the basement of a café in Paris.

LORRY AND BUS

Both the motor lorry and motor bus are invented. With the invention of the internal combustion engine it is inevitable that its application for the haulage of people and goods on public highways will follow the motor car, which is still confined to the wealthy.

PNEUMATIC MOTOR TYRE

Air-filled rubber tyres are fitted to a Peugeot motor car for the first time. The invention, by Edouard Michelin, improves the road holding of the vehicle up to 25km/h (40mph) and the cushioning it provides makes for a much more comfortable ride for the driver and passengers.

X-RAYS

German physicist Wilhelm Roentgen (1845–1923), having discovered X-rays, invents the first successful X-ray machine. Following the discovery, Franz Exner of Vienna, Austria, successfully makes an X-ray examination of a gunshot wound.

SYMPHONY NO. 2

This is the second symphony by Austrian composer Gustav Mahler (1860–1911), but his first truly revolutionary work, which, with its vast scale, use of the orchestra and chorus, extends the scope of the classical symphony as Beethoven's works had done before.

THE BIRTH OF PSYCHOANALYSIS

The beginnings of psychoanalysis are marked by the publication of *Studies in Hysteria* by Austrian neurologist Sigmund Freud (1856–1939) and his collaborator Jean Martin Charcot (1825–93). In it they outline their use of talking to effect diagnosis and cure.

THE TIME MACHINE

This is the first science fiction novel by HG Wells (1866–1946) which, in a way, begins the new genre. The book, set far in the future, depicts two classes, underground workers and a decadent leisured class. The social interest of his fictional worlds sets Wells apart.

CALORIE CONTENT

The calorie is invented by Professor Silbur Olin Atwater of the US Department of Agriculture, who establishes the kilocalorie or large calorie as a way of measuring the energy content of food.

Above: *Oscar Wilde writes his best-known and much-performed* The Importance of Being Earnest *this year.*

THE IMPORTANCE OF BEING EARNEST

Oscar Wilde's comedy, *The Importance of Being Earnest*, is perhaps his finest work. Its linking of the trivial and serious is exemplified in its subtitle (*A trivial comedy for serious people*). The play's distinctive qualities are its brilliant epigrammatic style and its telling social observation. This year too, Wilde brings an unsuccessful libel action against the Marquess of Queensberry, putting his personal life into the news.

EXHIBITION OF 150 PAINTINGS BY CEZANNE

French artist Paul Cézanne (1839–1906) wins artistic recognition at last with Vollard's Paris exhibition of his work. But he still works slowly and deliberately, seeing life as a struggle to get the three-dimensional world on to a flat canvas. Only in the twentieth century will he be widely seen as one of the founders of modern art.

BOOMING ROTTERDAM

Rotterdam, in The Netherlands, is booming now that new harbours have opened at Feijenoord, Delftshaven and Katendrecht. An oil terminal was built after the discovery of oil in the East Indies in the 1880s, and Maashaven, begun this year, is the largest project.

NANSEN ATTEMPTS THE NORTH POLE

Norwegians Fridtjof Nansen (1861–1930) and Hjalmar Johansen use dog sledges to try to reach the North Pole. Nansen had already undertaken great scientific work in the Arctic but was defeated by conditions.

FIRST CAR RACE

Emile Levassor wins the first ever car race. He covers the 1178km (732mi) from Paris to Bordeaux and back in just over two days without using relief drivers. The contest, organized by automotive pioneer Count Jules de Dion (1856–1946), draws 21 entries.

AUTOMOBILES RACE, USA

The Chicago Times-Herald sponsors the first automobile race in the USA. Jerry O'Connor wins $2000 for being the first to complete the course from Chicago to Evanston in Illinois and back.

RUGBY LEAGUE CREATED

In the UK, a "Great Split" in the game of rugby creates Rugby League when northern rugby clubs break away over payment to players. Rugby Union will remain a strictly amateur game for another century.

VOLLEYBALL INVENTED

William G Morgan of Holyoke, Massachusetts, invents volleyball, an indoor or outdoor ball game involving two opposing teams of six players each.

Louis Pasteur
1822–1895

The great French chemist and bacteriologist has died. Pasteur discovered that fermentation is caused by the spontaneous growth of micro-organisms, leading to his "germ theory" of infection and the science of bacteriology. As a result of his work we have the process of pasteurization, by which milk and other foods are preserved through being heated and then rapidly cooled. Pasteur was also responsible for saving French vineyards from phylloxera in the 1860s and for isolating the bacterium responsible for disease in silkworms, thereby saving the French silk industry.

OLYMPIC GAMES REVIVED

CRETANS REVOLT AGAINST Turkish rule. Cecil Rhodes resigns as prime minister of Cape Colony. Gold in the Klondike sparks a second gold rush. Britain invades the Sudan. Radiation is used for the first time to treat cancer. Alfred Nobel dies, leaving money for prizes named after him. The first modern Olympic Games are held in their ancient home in Greece. Parisians are shocked by "*merde*" in the theatre.

❊ 1896 ❊

JAN	2	Boers from the Transvaal capture Starr Jameson (who is later jailed)
	3	Emperor William II of Germany sends congratulary telegram to the Boers; this strains Anglo-German relations
	4	Utah becomes the 45th state of the USA
	6	Cecil Rhodes resigns as prime minister of Cape Colony because of the Jameson Raid
MAR	1	Ethiopians defeat Italians at Adowa
	12	Britain begins reconquest of Sudan
MAY	1	Shah Naser od-Din of Persia (Iran) assassinated; succeeded by son Mozaffar od-Din
	24	Cretans revolt against Turkish rule
JUNE	29	Dutch Liberal government increases the number of people eligible to vote

JULY	3	Turkey proposes self-government for Crete
AUG	17	Gold is found at Bonanza Creek, Klondike, Yukon Territory
	18	France annexes Madagascar
OCT	28	Italian protectorate of Ethiopia is cancelled
NOV	3	William McKinley (Republican) wins US presidential election

Right: *William McKinley, 25th president of the USA.*

Above: *In Britain, Joseph Chamberlain, colonial secretary, argues the case for fighting the Boers in South Africa.*

Above: *Keen prospectors at Dawson City, on the way to the Klondike goldfields via what is known as the All-Canadian route.*

Left: *On the way to the goldfields, a difficult journey fraught with betrayal and peril.*

CRETANS REVOLT

A revolt breaks out in Crete against Turkish rule, leading to Crete declaring union with Greece in February 1897. In April, Turkey declares war on Greece and defeats Greek invading armies in Thessaly in May. By a peace agreement in December 1897, the Turkish garrisons are withdrawn and the island is administered by the son of the Greek king. Crete remains under nominal Turkish sovereignty until joining Greece in December 1913.

WAR IN THE SUDAN

Britain begins to re-occupy Sudan to prevent France gaining access to the Nile and the Red Sea, thus threatening the sea route to India. In July 1898 French troops occupy Fashoda in southern Sudan. A year later, the British government establishes an Anglo-Egyptian condominium as Lord Kitchener defeats the Sudanese army at Omdurman in September, and captures the capital, Khartoum.

THE SEAGULL DIVES

The first well-known play by Russian author Anton Chekhov (1860–1904) is a flop when it opens (later it will be a success at the Moscow Art Theatre). The actors in this first performance do not understand the work and audiences are turned off by the pessimistic tone. But Chekhov perseveres, creating ever better dramas.

Above: *Cecil Rhodes goes unarmed into Matabele country to resolve policing problems and stop further fighting.*

ITALY DEFEATED

Italian attempts to conquer the independent African nation of Ethiopia end in defeat at Adowa. Emperor Menelik of Ethiopia continues to expand his control throughout the Horn of Africa.

McKINLEY WINS PRESIDENTIAL ELECTION

William McKinley (1843–1901), former governor of Ohio, wins the US presidential election on behalf of the Republicans, defeating his Democratic opponent William Jennings Bryan. Garret Hobart of New Jersey becomes vice-president.

PHILIPPINE INSURRECTION

Opposed to the corrupt Spanish administration, many Filipinos join the Katipunan, a secret revolutionary society founded by Andres Bonifacio. Power passes to Emilio Aguinaldo, who fights a guerrilla campaign but is defeated. At the Pact of Biak-na-bato on December 15, 1897, together with other leaders, he accepts 400 000 pesos and goes into exile in Hong Kong. He later returns to the Philippines following the American victory.

Right: *British troops carry abandoned babies across to safety after a campaign against the Dinizulu in Africa.*

LA BOHEME

With its poignant music and fine construction, *La Bohème* is Puccini's best opera and confirms his already high reputation. He finds unique musical ways to tug the audience's heartstrings, and makes the *verismo* style his own.

A SHROPSHIRE LAD

Classical scholar AE Housman (1859–1936) publishes his first collection of poetry, poems of love and death so simple, yet so effective that they sell in large numbers. Their simplicity also makes them an instant hit with composers, and Housman-setting becomes a cottage industry in English musical life. A whole generation reads the poems without realizing that Housman is gay.

GLASGOW SCHOOL OF ART

Charles Rennie Macintosh brings to Scotland a style influenced by Art Nouveau and modern Viennese architecture, to begin one of Scotland's finest buildings.

BRUCKNER LEAVES UNFINISHED SYMPHONY

Having brought the subtleties and strengths of the Wagnerian orchestra to the symphony, writing longer symphonies than anyone before, Austrian composer Anton Bruckner (1824–96) dies three-quarters of the way through his ninth.

SECOND KLONDIKE GOLD RUSH

The discovery of nuggets of gold in Klondike Creek in the Yukon sparks another gold rush 50 years after prospectors had swarmed to California. Prospectors face extremely harsh winter conditions.

JAPANESE EARTHQUAKE

A huge earthquake hits Japan, killing more than 20 000 people.

UBU ROI

The outrageous play, *Ubu Roi,* by French writer Alfred Jarry (1873–1907) causes controversy in France when people hear the word "*merde*" on stage for the first time. The violence of the play's action and language shock, but open up what is possible in the theatre, and the piece looks forward to modern movements such as the Theatre of the Absurd.

NOBEL PRIZE

Annual prizes for physics, physiology or medicine, chemistry, literature, and the furtherance of peace are established under the will of Swedish chemist Alfred Nobel, who dies this year. They are first awarded in 1901.

CHEMOTHERAPY

Radiation is used for the first time in the treatment of a cancer. Emile Grubb of Chicago exposes a Mrs Rose Lee to a dose of radiation in an attempt to treat a carcinoma growing in her breast. The growth of the cancer is successfully halted by the radiation.

HEART SURGERY

A 22-year-old man, stabbed through the heart, becomes the first person to successfully undergo emergency heart surgery. Louis Rehn, working in Frankfurt, goes on to establish a 40 per cent success rate out of some 124 cardiac patients.

IQ TEST

Parisian psychologist Alfred Biney, influenced by the work of English scientist Francis Galton, devises a scale for the assessment of sensory perception. The "Intelligence Quotient" scale is based on the idea that a score of 100 represents an average intelligence level.

WHITES ONLY

The US Supreme Court backs segregation of black people in public places in the USA in a case in which a black man from New Orleans, Homer Plessy, is fighting for his right to sit in a section of a railcar designated for whites only.

London to Brighton Tour
A London to Brighton tour, technically not a race, takes place to celebrate the repeal of a ban on automotive racing on British roads.

First Modern Olympics
The first modern Olympics are staged in the cradle of the ancient games, Greece. Athletes from fourteen countries compete at tennis, athletics, swimming, fencing, weightlifting, cycling, shooting, wrestling and gymnastics. Rowing and sailing competitions do not take place due to bad weather while football and cricket fail to attract enough participants. Most of the 200 competitors are Greek and no women are allowed to compete. The American team does best but Carl Schumann of Germany claims three gymnastics titles and the wrestling prize. For his wins, Schumann and all victors receive an olive branch and a silver medal. Laurel sprigs and copper medals are given to those coming second, but there is no recognition of a third place.

Greek Athletic Success
To the delight of the home crowd a Greek athlete rescues the nation's pride with a triumph in the last event of the Athens games. Spyridon Louis wins the marathon, held in tribute to Phaedippides, the messenger who ran to Athens to announce victory in the Battle of Marathon in 490 BC.

First Motorcycle Race
The first motorcycle race, over 152.9km (95mi), is run as part of the Paris-to-Marseilles car race.

Alfred Nobel
1833–1896

The Swedish chemist, explosives expert and inventor Alfred Nobel has died, leaving much of his enormous fortune as funds for the Nobel Prizes (for physics, chemistry, physiology, literature and peace). Nobel founded a huge chemical industry based on the manufacture of his less than peaceful-sounding inventions, including the stable form of nitroglycerin known as dynamite, a smoke-free gunpowder and gelignite. He was born in Sweden, but spent his childhood and early youth in Russia, Paris and the US, returning to Sweden in 1859. In his private life, Nobel seems to have been the classic "lonely millionaire", leaving few to mourn him.

AIRSHIPS, ELECTRONS AND ULTRAVIOLET

*T*HE FIRST RIGID-FRAME AIRSHIP is built — forerunner of airborne craft. Electrons are discovered, stimulating the development of sub-atomic physics. A Danish physician realizes that ultraviolet light can be used to treat skin disorders. The Vienna Secession is founded, uniting artists, architects and designers. The British Empire is at its height — the largest empire the world has ever seen.

❧ *1897* ❧

FEB	6	Crete announces union with Greece
MAR	4	William McKinley inaugurated as 25th US president
	18	Allied powers blockade Crete
APR	6	Sultan of Zanzibar abolishes slavery
	7	Turkey declares war on Greece
MAY	12	Turks defeat Greeks in Thessaly
	19	Armistice halts Graeco-Turkish war
JUNE	22	Britain's Queen Victoria celebrates her Diamond Jubilee in London
NOV	25	Spain offers Cuba some self-government, but the Cubans want complete independence
	28	Germany occupies Kiaochow, China
DEC	13	Russians occupy Port Arthur

Right: *Queen Victoria shown here at her coronation, celebrates her Diamond Jubilee this year.*

Above: *A British mission comes under fire in Benin, West Africa. Only two survive the massacre.*

DIAMOND JUBILEE

Queen Victoria's Diamond Jubilee — 60 years on the throne — is celebrated in Britain. She now rules the largest empire the world has ever seen.

KIAOCHOW OCCUPIED BY GERMANY

Germany occupies the Chinese port of Kiaochow, establishing a powerful presence in northern China.

VIENNA SECESSION FOUNDED

Perhaps the most famous and influential of the various secessionist movements, the Vienna Secession unites artists, architects and designers, and produces a new style that has wide influence. Included in the movement are architects Josef Olbrich (1867–1908; Secession Building) and Otto Wagner (1841–1918; Karlplatz Railway Station) and artist Gustav Klimt (1862–1918).

THE NIGGER OF THE NARCISSUS

Joseph Conrad (1857–1924) emerges as one of the great storytellers in this early work. Henry James will praise it as the greatest-ever story of the sea, and it sets a theme and a style which Conrad will make his own.

CYRANO DE BERGERAC

This poetic drama by French writer Edmond Rostand (1868–1918) brings to life the seventeenth-century soldier and duellist Cyrano in a romantic persona. His greatest work, it combines dazzling language with a larger-than-life character to produce a memorable work that sticks in the imagination.

DAS JAHR DER SEELE

The lyrics in this collection by German poet Stefan George (1868–1933) represent some of his best work, bringing a new perfection of form to German poetry.

ELECTRON

Sub-atomic physics takes a quantum leap with the discovery of electrons orbiting the nuclei of atoms. British physicist Joseph John Townsend (1856–1940) makes the discovery and gives them the initial name "corpuscles" in reference to tiny blood cells.

FIRST AIRSHIP

The very first airship with a rigid frame is built by German engineer, David Swarz. Later designs by Ferdinand Zeppelin (1838–1917) will dominate the skies of Europe until the advent of the aeroplane, although the hydrogen used to fill the ships will be very dangerous.

ULTRAVIOLET DISCOVERY

Danish physician, Niels Finsen (1860–1904), discovers that ultraviolet light can be used for the treatment of the skin disorder lupus vulgaris, which eats away the epidermis. The UV light kills the lupus bacillus which is very similar to that of tuberculosis.

BARIUM MEAL

American physician, Walter Cannon (1871–1945) develops the barium meal, which is opaque under X-ray. Having been swallowed, it can therefore be used to search for abnormalities in the intestinal tract.

Above and left: *The* Turbinia, *the first ever vessel to be propelled by turbine power, shows her paces at a naval review at Spithead, England. With her powerful engine (left) she reaches a speed of 34.5 knots.*

GAY CIVIL RIGHTS

The Scientific-Humanitarian Committee, the first social organization working to advance the civil rights of homosexuals, is founded in Berlin by physician Magnus Hirschfeld, publisher Max Spohr, lawyer Erich Oberg and novelist Franz Josef von Bulow. The Committee begins campaigning for the abolition of legal penalties for homosexuality.

WILDE RELEASED FROM PRISON

Oscar Wilde, the leading British playwright, is released from prison in Britain. He was imprisoned for homosexuality in 1895 as a result of the 1885 Act of Parliament criminalizing homosexuality. He now seeks refuge in Paris where the laws and social norms are more liberal.

ZIONIST CONGRESS

The first Zionist congress takes place in Basel, where Theodor Herzl raises support for a Jewish homeland in Palestine to be a refuge for oppressed Jews.

PRO-ABORTIONISTS

German socialists and Communists argue in favour of decriminalizing abortion, which has been forbidden by the German Reich since 1871.

DURKHEIM LECTURES IN SOCIAL SCIENCE

Emile Durkheim (1858–1917), the French sociologist who published *The Rules of Sociological Method* in 1895, becomes the first lecturer in social science at the University of Bordeaux in France, proposing that the scientific method can be applied to the study of society.

ACONCAGUA CLIMBED

Mattias Zurbriggen, a Swiss guide, climbs Aconcagua, at 6959m (22 835ft), the highest peak outside Asia.

UNPLANNED WINTER IN ANTARCTICA

Belgian Adrien de Gerlache is leading an exploration of Antarctica's west coast when his ship, the *Belgica*, is trapped by ice, becoming the first vessel to spend an unplanned winter in Antarctica.

FIRST BOSTON MARATHON

The inaugural Boston marathon is raced over a 40.2km (25mi) course. The idea for the race, the world's oldest annual marathon, is taken back to the United States by athletes who competed in the Olympics last year.

Below: *Panning for gold in South Africa. Over the next hundred years, South Africa will become the world's leading gold producer.*

THE DREYFUS AFFAIR AND THE FASHODA CRISIS

SPAIN AND THE UNITED STATES go to war. The USA gains Guam, the Philippines and Puerto Rico. Cuba gains independence. In France, writer Emile Zola is imprisoned for defending Captain Dreyfus. France and Britain come close to war in the Sudan. A naval arms race begins between Britain and Germany. The first virus is identified and the cathode ray tube is invented.

❖ 1898 ❖

JAN	11	Major MC Esterházy is acquitted of forging documents in the Alfred Dreyfus treason case
	13	In an open letter French novelist Emile Zola accuses the Dreyfus court martial of violating the rights of the defence
FEB	15	US warship *Maine* explodes in Havana Harbour, Cuba; Americans blame Spain
	23	Zola is sent to prison for writing his letter
MAR	27	China leases Port Arthur to Russia and Wei-hai-wei to Britain
	28	Germany announces expansion of its navy
APR	8	British defeat the Dervishes at the Atbara river in Sudan
	19	USA sends ultimatum to Spain to relinquish Cuba
	24	Spain declares war on the USA
	25	USA declares war on Spain
MAY	1	Americans destroy a Spanish fleet at Manila, Philippines
JULY	3	US wins naval battle at Santiago
	10	French soldiers occupy Fashoda, Sudan
	25	Americans invade Spanish island of Puerto Rico
	26	Spain sues for peace
AUG	12	USA annexes Hawaii
	30	Forged document admitted in Dreyfus case
SEP	2	British defeat the Dervishes at Omdurman
NOV	4	French evacuate Fashoda, in Sudan
	25	Union of El Salvador, Honduras and Nicaragua breaks up
DEC	10	Spanish-American War ends: Spain yields Cuba, Guam, the Philippines and Puerto Rico to the USA for $20 million

Above: Americans buy war bonds to fund the war that breaks out between Spain and the USA this year.

THE DREYFUS AFFAIR

In France, tension mounts over the conviction of Captain Dreyfus. Convinced of Dreyfus's innocence, and suspicious of the refusal of the French army to acknowledge the fact, the French author Emile Zola (1840–1902) writes *J'accuse*, an open letter to the French president. He is imprisoned. The crisis shows the extent of anti-Semitism in France — Dreyfus is Jewish — and the inability of the army to reform itself.

SPANISH-AMERICAN WAR

The mysterious explosion that destroys the USS *Maine* in Havana harbour as well as the brutal treatment of Cubans by the Spanish, including the use of concentration camps, prompts the United States to declare war on Spain. This is the first major American conflict since the Civil War. In May, Admiral Dewey destroys the Spanish in the Philippines, and later captures the island of Guam and then Manila, the Philippine capital. In December, the Treaty of Paris ends the war. By its terms, the USA gains the Philippines, Guam and Puerto Rico, in exchange for $20 million, and Cuba gains independence.

HUNDRED DAYS REFORM

In China, Emperor Kuang Hsu starts the Hundred Days Reform, with the aim of beginning the process of modernizing Chinese education, government administration and industry. The reforms are designed to strengthen the country against foreign imperial expansion. However, in September, the Dowager Empress Tz'u-hsi seizes power and stops all reforms.

EUROPEAN RIVALRY IN CHINA

Following Russian-Chinese treaties in 1896 recognizing Russia's position in Korea and Manchuria, Russia acquires a lease on Port Arthur on the Dairen Peninsula, opposite Korea. In response, Britain leases Wei-hai-wei opposite Port Arthur, for as long as Russia holds that port. European rivalry over control of the collapsing Chinese empire intensifies. In June, Britain acquires a 99-year lease on the New Territories in Hong Kong.

SLOCUM RETURNS

American sailor Joshua Slocum (1844–c. 1910) returns to Newport, Rhode Island, USA, having completed the first solo circumnavigation of the globe. Slocum had set off in his sloop *Spray* in 1895 and survived numerous adventures, among them repelling a boarding by bare-footed Patagonians, which he did by sprinkling tacks on the deck.

USA TAKES HAWAII

The USA takes over the Pacific island chain of Hawaii, ending hopes of restoring the monarchy and independent rule. Conflict between the monarchists and republicans had raged for some years, with the imprisonment for treason in January 1895 of former Queen Liliuokalani and her overthrow by republican leader Sanford Ballard Dole, who becomes the first US governor.

THE BALLAD OF READING GAOL

Having been imprisoned in Reading Gaol for his homosexuality, Oscar Wilde, now released and living in France, writes this poem based on his time in prison. It is valued for its meditations on the life of the prisoner, and on the human condition in general.

VIRUS

The first virus is identified by Dutch botanist Martinus Beijerinck, although he doesn't realize the significance of his discovery. The "tobacco mosaic virus" is thus the first of a whole group of new organisms to be discovered, explaining many mysterious diseases.

HOOF-AND-MOUTH

German bacteriologists, Friedrich Loffler and Paul Frosch discover that the serious bovine disease "hoof-and-mouth" or "foot-and-mouth" is caused by a virus rather than a bacterium. This prompts a series of preventative measures to be introduced, with no cure.

CATHODE RAY TUBE

The essential component of televisions and monitors, the cathode ray tube, is invented by German physicist Karl Ferdinand Braun (1850–1918). It is evolved from the Crookes tube, designed for studying the emission of electrons as they hit a fluorescent screen.

ASTRONOMY

Stargazers continue to make more discoveries about our solar system. Phoebe, the ninth moon of Saturn, is sighted by American astronomer, William Pickering (1858–1938), whilst the asteroid Eros is spotted by German astronomer, Carl Witt.

ROUTES TO THE POLE

American explorer Robert Peary begins a two-year expedition to reconnoitre routes to the North Pole from Etah in Inglefield Land, northwest Greenland, and Fort Conger, Ellesmere Island, in the Canadian Northwest Territories.

VISCOSE RAYON

The production of viscose rayon is pioneered at a pilot plant in London by CH Stearn, a British chemist who has devised a method to produce a yarn that can be woven and dyed.

BASKETBALL LEAGUE

The National Basketball League in the Philadelphia area, USA, is the sport's first professional league.

CHIROPRACTIC
The first school of chiropractic is opened in Iowa, USA, by Canadian-American healer Daniel David Palmer (1845–1913). He has developed a system for manipulating the bones of the spine and the joints. He claims that many illnesses are caused by misalignment of joints.

THE FASHODA CRISIS
General Herbert Kitchener (1850–1915), leading the British conquest of Sudan, arrives in Fashoda to find the French army already there and claiming the region for France. The two countries come close to war but, in November, France agrees to recognize British control over Sudan. In March 1899 the two countries settle their many colonial differences in Africa.

HIAWATHA'S WEDDING FEAST
Having attracted public attention at the prompting of Elgar, British composer Samuel Coleridge-Taylor (1875–1912) composes the first of his large choral-orchestral works on the Hiawatha story. The work gains huge public popularity and is widely performed.

PLAGUE, FAMINE AND FLOODS
An outbreak of bubonic plague kills millions in China, which also suffers serious famine in the north. In the south the Huanghe (Yellow river) overflows its banks.

ESCALATOR IN HARRODS
Harrods department store, which opened in 1849 in London's Knightsbridge, now has the first escalator in London. Harrods motto is "Harrods serves the world."

BROADLEYS, LAKE WINDERMERE
British architect CFA Voysey (1857–1941) creates an influential style of domestic architecture, based on the vernacular (traditional materials, big hipped roofs, mullioned windows, white rendered wall outside, plain decoration within) that will be taken up in many places on a smaller scale. This is one of the best examples of a large house built in this style.

GROWTH OF GERMAN NAVY
The first German Navy Bill, introduced by Alfred von Tirpitz (1849–1930), begins a rapid German naval expansion, threatening British dominance of the seas.

Left: *General Kitchener of Britain and Major Marchand of France meet on the SS Dal to avert war over the Fashoda question.*

PEACE CONFERENCE AND BOER WAR

THE FIRST-EVER INTERNATIONAL Peace Conference is held at The Hague in The Netherlands. Years of tension in South Africa finally explode into war between the British and the Boers. The Philippines revolts against US control. In France, Captain Dreyfus is pardoned. Suffragists from all over the world attend the first congress of the International Council of Women. The Moscow Art Theatre is founded. Aspirin becomes available.

✤ 1899 ✤

JAN	19	Britain and Egypt establish joint rule over Sudan
FEB	4	Filipinos led by Emilio Aguinaldo revolt against US rule
MAR	21	Britain and France resolve the Fashoda dispute
	24	Johannesburg *Uitlanders* send a petition to Queen Victoria complaining of unfair treatment by the Boers
JUNE	3	Retrial of Alfred Dreyfus is ordered
SEP	19	Dreyfus is pardoned by presidential decree after retrial still finds him guilty

OCT	9	President Paul Kruger of the South African Republic sends an ultimatum to Britain to withdraw troops from its borders
	12	South African (Boer) War begins; Boers win battle at Laing's Nek
	13	Boers besiege Mafeking and Kimberley
	30	Boers defeat British at Nicholson's Nek
NOV	2	Boers besiege Ladysmith
DEC	10–11	Boers defeat British at Magersfontein
	24	The Netherlands adopts proportional representation for elections

Revolt in the Philippines
A revolt against US rule in the Philippines is put down by General Arthur MacArthur, who establishes complete control over the islands by April 1900. The take-over of the Philippines arouses considerable hostility among anti-imperialist sections of US society.

Peace Conference
At the suggestion of Czar Nicholas II of Russia, 26 nations meet, in May, at The Hague in The Netherlands at the first-ever Peace Conference to extend the Geneva Convention to naval warfare, explosive bullets and poison gas, and to set up a permanent International Court of Arbitration.

Whitechapel Art Gallery, London
Charles Harrison Townshend creates his own British blend of Art Nouveau and American styles for this and other London public buildings. The solid-looking masonry, horizontal lines, semi-circular arches and imaginative use of space make these buildings memorable and influential.

Moscow Art Theatre
Russian actors Konstantin Stanislavsky and Nemirovich-Danchenko found the Moscow Art Theatre, which aims to present new plays staged naturalistically. Successful productions of Chekhov are followed by other works that represent the best in modern Russian theatre, as the Moscow Art Theatre establishes itself as one of the world's most forward-looking playhouses.

Dreyfus Pardoned
At a retrial in Rennes, Captain Alfred Dreyfus (1859–1935) is condemned with "extenuating circumstances", but immediately pardoned by presidential decree. A full and unconditional pardon does not come until July 1906, more than eleven years after Dreyfus's initial arrest and trial.

International Council of Women
The first congress of the International Council of Women is held in London, England, and attended by suffragists from all over the world. The American feminist, Susan Brownell Anthony, makes her last public appearance.

Enzymes
German chemist Emil Fischer (1852–1919) proposes the "lock and key" mechanism operated by enzymes. The understanding that enzymes are required for the functioning of biological processes is of fundamental importance to the modern era of medicine and related sciences.

Woman Racing Driver
Madame Labrousse becomes the first woman to compete in a car race when she enters the Paris-to-Spa event.

Left: *Paul Kruger, president of the South African Republic, holds council at Pretoria.*

Oxo Refuse Act
The US Congress passes the Refuse Act, the first legislation enabling polluters to be prosecuted and introducing fines of up to $2500 for oil spills and other acts of pollution.

Croquet Becomes Roque
Roque, an American variant of croquet, is invented. The game's name is croquet, minus the first and last letters.

Cubes
Fray Bentos of Uruguay begins production of cubes of dried beef or ox stock known as Oxo. Although the invention of mechanical freezing has enabled the export of beef carcasses, it is still cheaper and easier to supply a concentrated form of nutrition to North America and Europe.

Natural Pace Maker
The natural mechanism — known as the sino-atrial node — for setting the pace of the heart is discovered by British anatomists, Arthur Keith and Martin Flack. It regulates the heart by supplying electrical pulses to the heart muscles.

School and Society
The US philosopher and educationalist John Dewey (1859–1952) publishes *The School and Society*, in which he challenges authoritarian teaching and emphasizes experimentation and practice as the most effective method of learning. He argues that education is a tool through which people integrate with their culture.

Variations on an Original Theme (Enigma)
This series of variations for orchestra is the first work by British composer Edward Elgar (1857–1934) to be highly successful with audiences and critics. A deeply personal work (its movements are a series of musical portraits of Elgar's friends), it is also easily accessible by the public. Variations in the "noble" style, such as "Nimrod", soon make Elgar a kind of musical spokesman for England but he is also widely appreciated in Europe.

Lesbian Poet
American heiress, Natalie Barney (1876–1972), writer and founder of a highly influential salon of independent, creative women in Paris, submits *Quelques Portraits — Sonnets de Femmes* for publication, a collection of poems expressing her explicitly lesbian affair with the writer Liane de Pougy. Her intellectual circle creates a new, consciously lesbian woman.

Sticking Plaster
Johnson & Johnson, who introduced the first ready-to-use surgical dressings in 1886, produce zinc oxide adhesive plasters with good sticking qualities. They are protected in sterile sealed envelopes, and used for dressing wounds.

Aspirin
Off-the-shelf analgesics become available with the marketing of powdered aspirin. Bayer Co. of Germany make the drug, acetylsalicylic acid, available as a remedy for pain, fever and colds. Before long it is used worldwide.

THE SECOND BOER WAR

THE SECOND BOER WAR breaks out between Britain and the Boer republics after the Boers refuse to give rights to the *Uitlanders* (foreigners) living in their country; the war is the result of increasing tension throughout the region between British and Boers. The war sees the first use by both sides of bolt-action, magazine-fed rifles. The British deploy the first radios in the field — on a cart drawn by bullocks. At the beginning, the British have only about 25 000 men available and are considerably outnumbered by the Boers.

✱ Key Battles ✱

- **TALANA HILL (or Dundee) October 20, 1899**
The Boers under Meyer are dislodged from the heights of Dundee, but the British lose their commander General William Penn Symons (1843–1899), 162 casualties and 331 prisoners.

- **ELANDSLAAGTE October 21, 1899**
The Boers under Koch hold a strong position on high ground near the Ladysmith-Dundee railway track but are dislodged by three battalions, five squadrons and twelve guns commanded by General Sir John French (1852–1925). The British suffer 254 casualties and the Boers 450.

- **NICHOLSON'S NEK (Farquhar's Farm) October 29–30, 1899**
This is fought between the main Boer army under Commander Piet Joubert (1834–1900), and the British garrison of Ladysmith under Sir George White (1835–1912). A British attempt to break out ends in disaster with 317 casualties and 1068 prisoners.

- **MODDER RIVER November 28, 1899**
Piet Cronje (1835–1911), with 9000 Boers, holds a strong position straddling the river when they come under attack by the 1st British Division under Lord Methuen (1845–1942). The British drive the Boers from their trenches for the loss 485 casualties, the Boers suffer 500.

- **STORMBERG December 10, 1899**
Guides mislead General William Gatacre (1843–1906) and his 3000 men when they attempt a night attack on a Boer position. They are ambushed and are forced to withdraw, losing 89 casualties and 633 prisoners.

- **MAGERSFONTEIN December 10–11, 1899**
A division under Methuen attacks 9000 Boers under Cronje. The Highland Brigade in a flank night attack loses 757 men and the British withdraw after losing a total of 1079 men; the Boers lose 320.

- **COLENSO December 15, 1899**
A rash frontal attack by Sir Redvers Buller (1839–1908) on a strong Boer position leads to the loss of 1126 soldiers and ten guns. The attack is an attempt to relieve the siege at Ladysmith.

Right: *Boer and British troops fight fiercely at Magersfontein.*

19TH CENTURY US PRESIDENTS AND VICE-PRESIDENTS

Thomas Jefferson

James Monroe

Andrew Jackson

Abraham Lincoln

PRESIDENT	SERVED	VICE-PRESIDENT	SERVED
John Adams	1797–1801	Thomas Jefferson	1797–1801
Thomas Jefferson	1801–1809	(1) Aaron Burr	1801–1805
		(2) George Clinton	1805–1809
James Madison	1809–1817	(1) George Clinton	1809–1812
		(2) Elbridge Gerry	1813–1814
James Monroe	1817–1825	Daniel T Tomkins	1817–1825
John Quincy Adams	1825–1829	John C Calhoun	1825–1829
Andrew Jackson	1829–1837	(1) John C Calhoun	1829–1832
		(2) Martin Van Buren	1833–1837
Martin Van Buren	1837–1841	Richard M Johnson	1837–1841
William H Harrison	1841	John Tyler	1841
John Tyler	1841–1845	*No vice-president*	
James K Polk	1845–1849	George M Dallas	1845–1849
Zachary Taylor	1849–1850	Millard Fillmore	1849–1850
Millard Fillmore	1850–1853	*No vice-president*	
Franklin Pierce	1853–1857	William R King	1853
James Buchanan	1857–1861	John C Breckenridge	1857–1861
Abraham Lincoln	1861–1865	(1) Hannibal Hamlin	1861–1865
		(2) Andrew Johnson	1865
Andrew Johnson	1865–1869	*No vice-president*	
Ulysses S Grant	1869–1877	(1) Schuyler Colfax	1869–1873
		(2) Henry Wilson	1873–1875
Rutherford B Hayes	1877–1881	William A Wheeler	1877–1881
James A Garfield	1881	Chester A Arthur	1881
Chester A Arthur	1881–1885	*No vice-president*	
Grover Cleveland	1885–1889	Thomas A Hendricks	1885
Benjamin Harrison	1889–1893	Levi P Morton	1889–1893
Grover Cleveland	1893–1897	Adlai E Stevenson	1893–1897
William McKinley	1897–1901	Garret A Hobart	1897–1899

19th Century States of the Union

Sixteen states had been admitted to the union before the 19th century; five joined after.

Number	State	Year
17	Ohio	1803
18	Louisiana	1812
19	Indiana	1816
20	Mississippi	1817
21	Illinois	1818
22	Alabama	1819
23	Maine	1820
24	Missouri	1821
25	Arkansas	1836
26	Michigan	1837
27	Florida	1845
28	Texas	1845
29	Iowa	1846
30	Wisconsin	1848
31	California	1850
32	Minnesota	1858
33	Oregon	1859
34	Kansas	1861
35	West Virginia	1863
36	Nevada	1864
37	Nebraska	1867
38	Colorado	1876
39	North Dakota	1889
40	South Dakota	1889
41	Montana	1889
42	Washington	1889
43	Idaho	1890
44	Wyoming	1890
45	Utah	1896

The Spread of Postage Stamps in the 19th Century

Country	Date of First Issue
Great Britain [UK]	1840
Brazil	1843
United States	1847
France	1849
Belgium	1849
Bavaria (Germany)	1849
Spain	1850
Austria	1850
Victoria (Australia)	1850
Denmark	1851
Canada	1851
The Netherlands	1852
Portugal	1853
Norway	1855
Sweden	1855
New Zealand	1855
Mexico	1856
Russia	1858
Japan	1871
German Empire	1872

Note: Sample countries only; Britain was the first country to introduce stamps and also the only one that did not have its name on its issues. The Universal Postal Union, which regulates the free flow of mail among 170 countries, was founded in 1875. Since 1947 it has been an agency of the United Nations.

19th Century Iron Production

A typical early nineteenth century metal foundry.

Year	Thousand Tons
1820	1000
1830	1800
1840	2700
1850	4700
1860	7220
1870	11 840
1880	18 160
1890	26 750
1900	39 810

Note: The huge increase in the production of iron in the 1870s was due to the new processes of making steel economically. Up to 1890 Britain topped the world in iron production; in that year the United States became the world leader.

19th Century Inventions

YEAR	INVENTION AND COUNTRY
1803	Steam locomotive (England)
1807	Gas street lighting (England)
1826	Corn-reaper (Scotland)
1827	Photography (France)
1827	Matches (England)
1830	Sewing machine (France)
1832	Electric dynamo (France)
1838	Single-wire electric telegraph and Morse code (USA)
1845	Pneumatic tires (Scotland)
1849	Safety pin (USA)
1853	Hypodermic syringe (France)
1856	Internal combustion engine (Italy)
1856	Bessemer process of steel-making (England)
1857	Passenger elevator (USA)
1866	First practical typewriter (USA)
1867	Dynamite (Sweden)
1867	Dry battery (France)
1868	Steam-powered motorcycle
1873	Barbed wire (USA)
1876	Telephone (USA)
1877	Phonograph (USA)
1878–79	Incandescent light (England/USA)
1883	Gasoline engine (Germany)
1884	Fountain pen (USA)
1884	Steam turbine (England)
1885	Automobile (Germany)
1886	Coca-Cola (USA)
1888	Disc record player (USA)
1889	Celluloid roll-film (USA)
1891	Hang-glider (Germany)
1892	Diesel engine (Germany)
1893	Zip-fastener (USA)
1894	Escalator (USA)
1895	Radio (Italy)

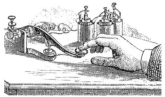

1838 Morse code (USA).

SCRAMBLE FOR AFRICA

Spain, Portugal, The Netherlands, Britain and France all had sizeable empires before the start of the 19th century. Africa was largely untouched, but was carved up during the 1800s.

YEAR	COLONY
1806	Britain occupies the Cape of Good Hope [now part of South Africa]
1822	The USA sets up a colony for freed slaves in Liberia
1822	Egypt conquers Sudan
1830	France begins the occupation of Algeria
1843	Gambia becomes a British Crown colony
1849	France sets up the protectorate of French Guinea
1851	Britain occupies Lagos [now part of Nigeria]
1868	Britain makes Basutoland [Lesotho] a protectorate
1874	Britain occupies the Gold Coast [now southern Ghana]
1879	Belgians begin the occupation of what is now the Democratic Republic of Congo (also called Congo [Kinshasa])
1880	Congo (Brazzaville) comes under French protection
1881	France proclaims a protectorate over Tunisia (then technically part of the Ottoman Turkish empire)
1884	Germany occupies South-West Africa [Namibia]
1884	German protectorate of Kamerun [Cameroon] set up
1884–89	Germany occupies Togoland
1885	Germany occupies German East Africa [later Tanganyika]
1885	Spain sets up protectorates of Río de Oro [Western Sahara] and Spanish Guinea [now Equatorial Guinea]
1885	Mozambique becomes a Portuguese colony
1886	Britain sets up the British Somaliland protectorate
1888	French Somaliland boundaries are agreed
1889	Italian Somaliland colony is established
1889–96	Italy occupies Eritrea
1891	France begins the occupation of Niger
1893	France establishes colonies of French Guinea and Côte d'Ivoire [Ivory coast]
1894	Dahomey becomes a French colony
1894	South African (Boer) Republic takes over Swaziland
1894	Britain establishes protectorate over Uganda
1895	Britain establishes protectorate over East Africa [Kenya]
1895	British South Africa Company occupies Rhodesia [now Zambia and Zimbabwe]
1896	France proclaims Madagascar a colony
1898	Egypt and Britain share control of Sudan

Explorers Stanley and Livingstone meet in Africa.

A FAMILY AFFAIR

During the reign of Britain's Queen Victoria (1837–1901) it seemed as though all the royal heads of state in Europe were related. Her father's younger brother was king of Hanover in Germany from 1837; her mother's brother was King Leopold I of the Belgians from 1831. And her descendants married European royalty.

The marriage of Victoria and Albert, 1840.

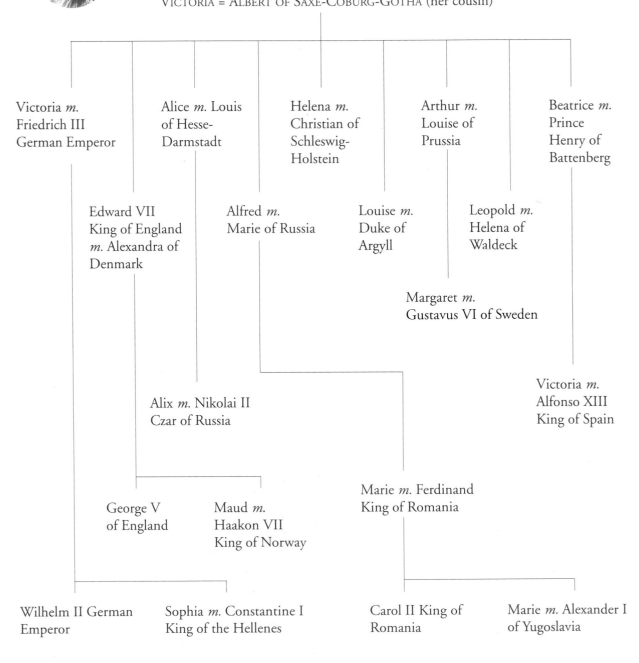

VICTORIA = ALBERT OF SAXE-COBURG-GOTHA (her cousin)

Victoria *m.* Friedrich III German Emperor

Alice *m.* Louis of Hesse-Darmstadt

Helena *m.* Christian of Schleswig-Holstein

Arthur *m.* Louise of Prussia

Beatrice *m.* Prince Henry of Battenberg

Edward VII King of England *m.* Alexandra of Denmark

Alfred *m.* Marie of Russia

Louise *m.* Duke of Argyll

Leopold *m.* Helena of Waldeck

Margaret *m.* Gustavus VI of Sweden

Alix *m.* Nikolai II Czar of Russia

Victoria *m.* Alfonso XIII King of Spain

George V of England

Maud *m.* Haakon VII King of Norway

Marie *m.* Ferdinand King of Romania

Wilhelm II German Emperor

Sophia *m.* Constantine I King of the Hellenes

Carol II King of Romania

Marie *m.* Alexander I of Yugoslavia

RULERS OF THE NETHERLANDS

The Batavian Republic 1798–1805
Ruled as part of France
The Batavian Commonwealth 1805–1806
Rutger Jan Schimmelpennick, Council Pensionary
The Kingdom of Holland 1806–1810
Lodewijk I (Louis Bonaparte) 1806–1810
Lodewijk II (Napoléon-Louis Bonaparte) 1810
The Kingdom of Holland was annexed to France in 1810

United Provinces of The Netherlands 1813–1815
Willem VI, Prince of Orange, as Stadhouder and Prince of the Netherlands
Kingdom of the Netherlands 1815 to date
Willem I 1815–1840
Willem II 1840–1849
Willem III 1849–1890
Wilhelmina 1890–1948

RAILROAD FIRSTS

Stephenson's Rocket, 1929.

1825	Public steam railroad (England)
1828	Railroads in Austria, France and the USA
1830	Passenger railroad service (England)
1835	Belgian and German railroads

1836	Sleeping cars in the USA
1836	Canadian railroad
1838	Russian railroad
1839	Railroads in Italy and The Netherlands
1842	Polish railroad
1844	Swiss railroad
1846	Hungary and Balkans railroads
1847	Danish railroad
1850	Mexican railroad
1853	Railroads in the Indian sub-continent
1854	Railroads open in Australia, Brazil, Egypt, Norway
1856	Railroads in Portugal, Sweden, Turkey
1869	Transcontinental rail link in the USA

From this time on railroads proliferated all over the world.

Railways spread westwards from Europe as far east as Japan.

INDEX